Fostering Industry–Academia Partnerships for Innovation–Driven Trade

Nishant Joshi
Prestige Institute of Management and Research, India

Firdous Ahmad Malik
University of the People, USA

Chanda Gulati
Prestige Institute of Management and Research, India

Abhay Dubey
Prestige Institute of Management and Research, India

A volume in the Advances in Human Resources Management and Organizational Development (AHRMOD) Book Series

Published in the United States of America by
   IGI Global
   Business Science Reference (an imprint of IGI Global)
   701 E. Chocolate Avenue
   Hershey PA, USA 17033
   Tel: 717-533-8845
   Fax: 717-533-8661
   E-mail: cust@igi-global.com
   Web site: http://www.igi-global.com

Library of Congress Cataloging-in-Publication Data

Names: Joshi, Nishant, 1980- editor. | Malik, Firdous Ahmad, 1988- editor.
  | Gulati, Chanda, 1984- editor.
Title: Fostering industry-academia partnerships for innovation-driven trade
  / edited by Nishant Joshi, Firdous Malik, Chanda Gulati, Abhay Dubey.
Description: Hershey, PA : Business Science Reference, [2024] | Includes
  bibliographical references and index. | Summary: "This book investigates
  the profound and transformational terrain that is cultivating
  partnerships between academia and industry"-- Provided by publisher.
Identifiers: LCCN 2024009410 (print) | LCCN 2024009411 (ebook) | ISBN
  9798369330968 (hardcover) | ISBN 9798369330975 (ebook)
Subjects: LCSH: Technological innovations--Economic aspects. | Industrial
  management. | Business and education.
Classification: LCC HC79.T4 F685 2024 (print) | LCC HC79.T4 (ebook) | DDC
  338/.064--dc23/eng/20240405
LC record available at https://lccn.loc.gov/2024009410
LC ebook record available at https://lccn.loc.gov/2024009411

British Cataloguing in Publication Data
A Cataloguing in Publication record for this book is available from the British Library.

The views expressed in this book are those of the authors, but not necessarily of the publisher.

For electronic access to this publication, please contact: eresources@igi-global.com.

Advances in Human Resources Management and Organizational Development (AHRMOD) Book Series

Patricia Ordóñez de Pablos
Universidad de Oviedo, Spain

ISSN:2327-3372
EISSN:2327-3380

Mission

A solid foundation is essential to the development and success of any organization and can be accomplished through the effective and careful management of an organization's human capital. Research in human resources management and organizational development is necessary in providing business leaders with the tools and methodologies which will assist in the development and maintenance of their organizational structure.

The **Advances in Human Resources Management and Organizational Development (AHRMOD) Book Series** aims to publish the latest research on all aspects of human resources as well as the latest methodologies, tools, and theories regarding organizational development and sustainability. The **AHRMOD Book Series** intends to provide business professionals, managers, researchers, and students with the necessary resources to effectively develop and implement organizational strategies.

Coverage

- Organizational Development
- Workplace Culture
- Coaching and Mentoring
- Employee Communications
- Entrepreneurialism
- Talent Identification and Management
- Employment and Labor Laws
- Worker Behavior and Engagement
- Executive Compensation
- Collaborative Method

IGI Global is currently accepting manuscripts for publication within this series. To submit a proposal for a volume in this series, please contact our Acquisition Editors at Acquisitions@igi-global.com or visit: http://www.igi-global.com/publish/.

Enhancing Employee Motivation Through Training and Development
Tricia Mazurowski (Adler University, USA)
Business Science Reference • copyright 2024 • 309pp • H/C (ISBN: 9798369316740) • US $205.00 (our price)

Global Practices on Effective Talent Acquisition and Retention

Titles in this Series

For a list of additional titles in this series, please visit: www.igi-global.com/book-series

Bryan Christiansen (Southern New Hampshire University, USA) Muhammad Abdul Aziz (University of Greenwich, UK) and Elle Lily O'Keeffe (Rasmussen University, USA)
Business Science Reference • copyright 2024 • 531pp • H/C (ISBN: 9798369319383) • US $295.00 (our price)

Convergence of Human Resources Technologies and Industry 5.0
Pawan Kumar (Lovely Professional University, India) Sunil Kumar (Shoolini University, India) Rajesh Verma (Lovely Professional University, India) and Sumesh Dadwal (London South Bank University, UK)
Business Science Reference • copyright 2024 • 363pp • H/C (ISBN: 9798369313435) • US $290.00 (our price)

Building Sustainable Human Resources Management Practices for Businesses
Cristina Raluca Gh. Popescu (University of Bucharest, Romania & The Bucharest University of Economic Studies, Romania) Javier Martínez-Falcó (University of Alicante, Spain & University of Stellenbosch, South Africa) Bartolomé Marco-Lajara (University of Alicante, Spain) Eduardo Sánchez-García (University of Alicante, Spain) and Luis A. Millán-Tudela (University of Alicante, Spain)
Business Science Reference • copyright 2024 • 364pp • H/C (ISBN: 9798369319949) • US $275.00 (our price)

Demystifying the Dark Side of AI in Business
Sumesh Dadwal (Northumbria University, UK) Shikha Goyal (Lovely Professional University, India) Pawan Kumar (Lovely Professional University, India) and Rajesh Verma (Lovely Professional University, India)
Business Science Reference • copyright 2024 • 268pp • H/C (ISBN: 9798369307243) • US $275.00 (our price)

Organizational Management Sustainability in VUCA Contexts
Rafael Perez-Uribe (Universidad de la Salle, Colombia) David Ocampo-Guzman (Santo Tomas University, Colombia & EAN University, Colombia) Carlos Salcedo-Perez (Politecnico Grancolombiano, Colombia) and Andrés Carvajal-Contreras (EAN University, Colombia)
Business Science Reference • copyright 2024 • 435pp • H/C (ISBN: 9798369307205) • US $275.00 (our price)

701 East Chocolate Avenue, Hershey, PA 17033, USA
Tel: 717-533-8845 x100 • Fax: 717-533-8661
E-Mail: cust@igi-global.com • www.igi-global.com

Table of Contents

Foreword

In *Fostering Industry-Academia Partnerships for Innovation-Driven Trade*, the enlightening and foresightful examination of the intersection of industrial innovation and academic rigor is presented. Exhaustive in scope and curated with great care by the renowned editors, this seminal publication explores the complexities and transformative capacity of partnerships between industry and academia.

The chapters comprising this volume provide a comprehensive examination of the ever-changing intersection of academia and industry, interweaving a narrative that reveals the challenges and prospects that characterize this vibrant partnership. This collection deconstructs pivotal themes that are at the heart of contemporary commerce, examining the mutually beneficial relationship between academic research and its practical implementation.

The contributor authors' scrupulous craftsmanship and scholarly acumen are evident in every chapter, which addresses crucial topics such as the necessity for universities to adopt the demands of Industry 4.0 and the transformative impact of AI on human resource management. This compendium provides insights into the successes and obstacles encountered in collaborations between industry and academia. Additionally, it outlines a forward-thinking strategy that seeks to promote sustainable development and economic growth.

Upon conducting an in-depth analysis of cutting-edge pedagogies, the consequences of AI influencers on ethical consumer conduct, and the psychological factors that contribute to stress among students, readers will discover themselves positioned at the precipice of a thought-provoking conversation that surpasses disciplinary boundaries.

This volume transcends the boundaries of conventional academia by providing a beacon of insight and knowledge to a wide range of stakeholders, including policymakers, students, educational and research institutions. This resource is considered indispensable due to its cross-disciplinary appeal and global repercussions; it serves as a foundation for scholarly inquiry and a catalyst for transformative progress.

The collaborative effort of the distinguished authors embodies the spirit of partnerships between industry and academia, showcasing the potential and promise that arises from integrating academic rigor and industrial practicality. The combined knowledge and skills of these individuals emphasize the significance and pertinence of this compilation in influencing a future in which trade driven by innovation is not merely a goal, but an indisputable fact.

As you commence this intellectual journey, it is our sincere desire that the profound intersection of academia and industry will serve as a source of inspiration and courage for you. Collectively, let us respond to the imperative to participate, cooperate, and organize a future characterized by the formidable synergy between academic and industrial endeavors.

Hebatallah Adam
Jindal School of International Affairs, India

Preface

The combination of academic quality and industrial prowess is emerging as a vital driver of innovation and sustainable economic success in the continuously changing global trade scene. *Fostering Industry-Academia Partnerships for Innovation-Driven Trade* explores the complex and transformative space where academia and industry meet, delving into this dynamic interplay.

As editors, we have painstakingly selected a range of ground-breaking and inventive pieces that illuminate several opportunities and challenges that come with industry-academia partnerships. Our mission is to shed light on the way towards a future characterised by cooperative partnerships, where the combined advantages of scholarly study and practical application open the door to novel discoveries and solutions.

This book's chapters look at a variety of topics that are essential to the interaction between academia and business. We provide a thorough examination of the elements that propel innovation-driven trade, from current market trends and the search for sustainable practices to organisational expansion and general efficacy. By engaging with these topics, we aim to provide a robust framework for understanding the potential of collaborative ventures in fostering economic development and sustainable progress.

Chapter 1 discusses the critical need for universities to align their curricula with Industry 4.0 demands. It emphasizes the importance of digital competence, technical proficiency, adaptability, and collaborative skills for modern graduates, advocating for stronger industry-academia collaboration.

Chapter 2 investigates how AI and machine learning can revolutionize human resource management in the gig economy. It highlights AI's role in recruitment, performance management, and personalized training, addressing current challenges faced by gig workers.

Chapter 3 examines successful industry-academic partnerships, identifying key factors that ensure quality and durability in these collaborations. It argues that such partnerships enhance employability and bridge the gap between academic preparation and industry expectations.

Focusing on the Indian education sector, Chapter 4 explores the integration of innovative pedagogies and technology in teaching. It underscores the importance of government and private support for research and invention to foster dynamic educational methods.

The research in Chapter 5 research explores how online reviews influence job seekers' perceptions and decisions. Analyzing data from Indian academics, it sheds light on the interplay between employer branding, online feedback, and talent acquisition strategies.

Chapter 6 investigates the effect of AI influencers on ethical consumer behavior using CASA and TPB theories. It identifies key attributes like authenticity and credibility, which influence consumers' ethical purchasing decisions.

Chapter 7 identifies psychological determinants of stress among students pursuing professional degrees. It highlights the need for addressing factors like depression, feeling loved, and personal life to improve students' mental health and readiness for industry challenges.

Chapter 8 discusses the role of University Business Incubators (UBIs) in fostering entrepreneurship and innovation. It introduces the Technology Readiness Level (TRL) as a measure of startup success and examines the impact of academia-industry partnerships on employment generation.

Chapter 9 examines how ergonomic workplace design affects stress levels among female employees. It evaluates various workspace elements and their contribution to stress, offering insights for better workplace design to enhance employee well-being.

Chapter 10 explores the relationship between sustainable leadership, compassion, and employee well-being. It emphasizes the role of long-term leadership strategies in creating a positive work environment and improving overall employee health.

Chapter 11 assesses the implementation of Work-Based Learning (WBL) in Malaysia's higher education sector. It identifies challenges and provides recommendations to enhance industry participation and better prepare students for the workforce.

Chapter 12 examines the negative impacts of presenteeism and workaholism on employee productivity. It offers insights into addressing these issues to improve workplace health and efficiency.

Chapter 13 explores the effectiveness of AI tutoring in improving essay writing and managing anxiety among university students. It highlights the benefits and challenges of integrating AI in education.

The study in Chapter 14 investigates the impact of Corporate Social Responsibility (CSR) initiatives on employee behavior in the academic sector. It finds that CSR can significantly influence employee engagement and perceptions, enhancing institutional performance.

Chapter 15 discusses the unique challenges faced by financial managers in innovative businesses. It highlights the importance of financial expertise in supporting innovation and ensuring long-term sustainability.

Chapter 16 examines various approaches to developing smart cities in India, focusing on sustainability and technological integration. It discusses different development methods and the challenges faced in implementing smart city projects.

Chapter 17 identifies trends in urban development and sustainability. Analyzing academic research from 2013 to 2023, It highlights the increasing interest in sustainable and intelligent urban solutions, with significant contributions from countries like Italy, Brazil, China, and the UK.

Our intended audience spans a diverse range of stakeholders, including educational and research institutions, central and state government libraries, and policymakers. This book is also designed to serve as a valuable resource for specific courses within BA, B.COM., BBA, MA, M.COM., MBA, and M.Sc. programs in Economics and Finance. Beyond its academic utility, we believe that this book holds global significance, offering insights and strategies that resonate across borders and industries.

Primarily conceived as a research monograph, this volume is a testament to the collaborative spirit that drives innovation. We extend our gratitude to the contributing authors whose work exemplifies the pioneering spirit of industry-academia partnerships. Their contributions underscore the importance of harnessing the collective intelligence and resources of both sectors to address the complex challenges of our time.

In closing, we invite you, our readers, to join us in this exploration of the potent intersection between academia and industry. Through collaboration and shared vision, we can unlock the key to sustainable progress and economic development. Together, let us forge a future where innovation-driven trade is not just a concept, but a reality shaped by the formidable synergy of academic and industrial forces.

Nishant Joshi

Prestige Institute of Management and Research, India

Firdous Ahmad Malik
University of the People, USA

Chanda Gulati
Prestige Institute of Management and Research, India

Abhay Dubey
Prestige Institute of Management and Research, India

Acknowledgment

We are writing to express my sincere appreciation for the instrumental support provided by the Prestige Institute of Management & Research (PIMR) in the creation and success of the book *Fostering Industry-Academia Partnerships for Innovation-Driven Trade* by IGI Global Publications.

The commitment of PIMR in organizing the 15th PIMRG International Conference on "Fostering Industry-Academia Partnership for Driving Innovation and Strategizing Trade and Industry" has been a testament to their dedication to promoting scholarly and innovative endeavors. Their active involvement in conceptualizing the book and the meticulous selection of excellent research papers have undeniably contributed to the success and impact of the publication.

Furthermore, PIMR's collaboration with renowned authors and thinkers has significantly enhanced the academic discourse within the book, elevating its value and relevance within the industry-academia community.

We would like to extend our deepest gratitude to PIMR for their unwavering support and commitment to fostering industry-academia partnerships for driving innovation and strategizing trade and industry. The collaborative efforts have undoubtedly enriched the academic landscape and contributed to the advancement of knowledge in this domain.

Once again, thank you for PIMR's invaluable contributions and support. We look forward to the possibility of future collaborations and endeavors that will continue to drive innovation and excellence in our shared academic pursuits.

Chapter 1
Enhancing Industry–Academic Collaboration for Innovation in the Era of Industry 4.0

Daisy Mui Hung Kee
https://orcid.org/0000-0002-7748-8230
Universiti Sains Malaysia, Malaysia

ABSTRACT

The widening skills gap between industry expectations and academic preparations is a pressing global concern in the era of Industry 4.0. Universities face the challenge of equipping students for the 21st-century workforce, characterized by advanced automation and rapid technological advancements. This requires innovative approaches to enhance students' competencies aligned with Industry 4.0 requirements. Digital competence is now essential for employability, with digital natives needing to navigate technological disruptions effectively. As Industry 4.0 technologies reshape work environments, universities play a crucial role in ensuring graduates are technically proficient and possess adaptive and collaborative skills for success. Bridging the skills gap between academia and industry is important in the context of Industry 4.0's demand for skilled professionals. This chapter's insights will benefit researchers, educators, employers, and policymakers aiming to prepare students. Fostering industry-academia collaboration is key to empowering graduates to thrive in evolving industries.

1. INTRODUCTION

The future of work won't be about college degrees; it will be about job skills. --Stephane Kasriel; Upwork CEO (2018)

Universities play a role in preparing graduates for diverse career paths and meeting the evolving demands of Industry 4.0, necessitating enhanced collaboration between academia and industry to bridge the skills gap (Yoong, Don, & Foroutan, 2017). This collaboration is necessary for developing the specialized knowledge and 21st-century skills needed in today's rapidly transforming job market. In response to the digital disruption shaping industries, digital competence has emerged as a critical employability

DOI: 10.4018/979-8-3693-3096-8.ch001

requirement, particularly for digital natives (Kee et al., 2023). Digital competency, encompassing information management and technology proficiency, is essential for youth employability in the digital age (Kee et al., 2023). Employers prioritize digital skills for problem-solving, creativity, and effective communication across industries (Kee et al., 2023).

The United Kingdom National Committee of Enquiry into Higher Education reveals the alignment of learning with employment needs and the development of general skills valued by employers (Bridges, 2000). Likewise, the Confederation of British Industry (CBI) and Pearson highlights the global demand for graduates equipped with work-relevant attitudes and employability skills (CBI & Pearson, 2016). Employers now seek graduates proficient in both technical competencies and essential soft skills, emphasizing the importance of well-rounded education (Matsouka & Mihail, 2016; Hamid et al., 2014; Ghazali & Bennett, 2017). Figure 1 presents the skills demanded by employers, distinguishing between technical competencies and soft skills crucial for success in the modern workforce. For example, technical skills encompass abilities like data analysis, proficiency in programming languages, engineering expertise, digital marketing proficiency, and cybersecurity knowledge. Alongside these technical competencies, soft skills play a crucial role, including effective communication, collaboration, problem-solving, leadership capabilities, and adaptability.

Figure 1. Skills Required by Employers Today

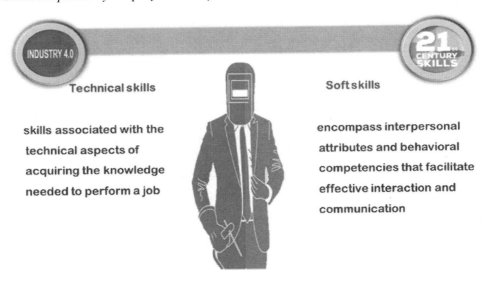

In the context of Industry 4.0, characterized by advanced technologies like IoT, AI, and robotics, traditional education's relevance to evolving job requirements is being reevaluated (Chamorro-Premuzic & Frankiewicz, 2019). Employers increasingly value candidates with unique skills that machines cannot easily replicate, underscoring the importance of interpersonal and adaptability skills (Chamorro-Premuzic & Frankiewicz, 2019). Graduates need to be trained in acquiring skills that align with employers' demands (Harvey, 2001). Developing these skills relies on implementing higher education activities that integrate classroom learning with practical work experiences, such as experiential, project-based, and interactive internships and workshops (Alpaydın & Kültür, 2022). These activities create learning environments that closely simulate real-world workplace scenarios, enhancing graduates' preparedness for employment.

Marr (2023) raised the question of whether traditional degrees retain value for employers amid significant shifts in job requirements emphasizing specialized skills and on-the-job experience. Similarly, Chamorro-Premuzic and Frankiewicz (2019) questioned the alignment between higher education and employers' needs. In their *Harvard Business Review* article titled *"Does Higher Education Still Prepare People for Jobs?"*, They argue that evolving employer demands call for a paradigm shift in higher education. Ismail (2018), the first female Vice-Chancellor of Universiti Sains Malaysia (USM), argues that despite acknowledging the need for knowledge to navigate the Fourth Industrial Revolution, people are now questioning the value of pursuing a degree and whether universities deserve public support. She also highlighted new challenges in higher education, expressing concerns that universities are not adapting quickly enough to current trends. The teachings offered are often perceived as irrelevant and do not align with industry needs. Furthermore, there is dissatisfaction among the public regarding the impact universities have made on industry, community, and society through research innovations.

The future of work emphasizes job skills over credentials, necessitating closer collaboration between academia and industry to meet evolving workforce demands (Chamorro-Premuzic & Frankiewicz, 2019; Kasriel, 2018). Studies in Malaysia highlight the skills gap between graduates and industry expectations, posing challenges to national productivity (Mohd Salleh, Mapjabil, & Legino, 2019; Verma et al., 2018). To foster innovation in the era of Industry 4.0, universities and industries must strengthen collaboration to equip graduates with industry-relevant skills and knowledge (Malaysia Education Blueprint, 2015-2025). By leveraging technologies and innovations, universities can personalize learning experiences and prepare students for success in dynamic work environments.

In summary, industry-academia collaboration is essential for cultivating innovation and ensuring graduates are well-prepared for the demands of Industry 4.0. Universities play a vital role in adopting research-based, innovative approaches to bridge the skills gap and empower graduates to thrive in evolving industries.

2. GLOBAL RECOGNITION OF THE SKILLS GAP

There is a need to "New, non-traditional education options" as no one school even Harvard can ever insulate us from the unpredictability of technological progression and disruption. --Stephane Kasriel; Upwork CEO (2018)

The skills gap between industry expectations and academic preparation is recognized as a widespread global phenomenon, transcending national boundaries and extending beyond the context of Malaysia (Aziz, 2018). Extensive global studies have revealed the existence of this gap, emphasizing its prevalence and impact (CBI & Pearson, 2016; Kasriel, 2018; Chamorro-Premuzic & Frankiewicz, 2019; Okolie, Nwosu, & Mlanga, 2019).

In the Malaysian context, employers have highlighted the skills deficit among graduates, pointing to a significant mismatch between university education and market demands (Aziz, 2018). Employers have expressed concerns over universities' limited capacity to provide students with essential market-relevant skills (Aziz, 2018). Moreover, reports from the Malaysia Education Blueprint (Higher Education)

2015-2025 have echoed these sentiments, citing discrepancies in the supply and demand of graduates, particularly in terms of skills, knowledge, and attitudes. To address this, enhancing university students' competency skills has been recognized as essential. Key skills such as English proficiency, technical expertise, interpersonal skills, and problem-solving abilities are consistently identified as crucial by employers (Malaysian Productivity Corporation, 2017).

The survey, conducted by Economist Impact, supported by Google (Bhandari, 2023), which encompassed 1,375 employees across the Asia-Pacific (APAC) region, including 100 employees from Malaysia, highlighted three key findings:

[1] **Digital Skills Focus:** In Malaysia, 65% of employees prioritize digital skills, with a significant emphasis on basic digital competencies (83.1%). Advanced digital skills such as artificial intelligence (AI), machine learning (ML), cloud computing, and cybersecurity are also gaining prominence. Employers in Malaysia are increasingly prioritizing tech talent, with forecasts indicating a 7.6% growth in demand over the next three years (Malaysian Digital Economy Corporation). Basic digital skills are considered essential by a majority of employees, aligning with national initiatives to cultivate expertise in data analytics, AI, and cybersecurity. The rising demand for cybersecurity professionals reflects Malaysia's heightened digital risks, as evidenced by its position among the top countries for data breaches. Karen Yap, managing director at Connect Gateway Executive Search, highlights AI's potential to boost Malaysia's GDP.

[2] **Soft Skills Emphasis:** 54% of Malaysian employees prioritize soft skills, surpassing the regional average (41.2%). Interpersonal and intercultural communication skills are particularly valued (81.5%).

[3] **Upskilling Responsibility:** The majority of employees in Malaysia believe that employers bear the primary responsibility for upskilling. However, they also perceive a role for the government in providing financial support and addressing information gaps on required skills.

Eusof (2024) highlights the challenges faced by Malaysian employers due to skill shortages, as revealed in the Hays Asia Salary Guide (2017). The survey, drawn from over 3,000 employers across Japan, China, Hong Kong, Malaysia, and Singapore, represents approximately six million employees. It found that key trends of skills shortages and a reliance on temporary staffing from last year are set to continue this year. The report indicates that 97% of employers in Malaysia believe skill shortages will impact their operations in the current year.

Studies have emphasized the need for university students to actively engage in developing their soft skills beyond traditional classroom learning to enhance employability (Becker, 2009; Yoong et al., 2017). Addressing the skills gap requires universities to implement diverse initiatives aimed at equipping graduates with in-demand skills, fostering employability, and contributing to national economic growth. The urgency to address the skills gap is further emphasized by the findings of Ibrahim and Mahyuddin (2017), indicating that a significant percentage of companies believe university graduates require more training, particularly in communication skills. The deficiency in curriculum-aligned skills contributes to graduates' skill gaps (Verma et al., 2018; Mohd Salleh et al., 2019).

Recent reports underscore the urgent need to address the skills gap in Malaysia by prioritizing the development of university students' skills (Kee et al., 2023b; Mohd Salleh et al., 2019). The persistent skills gap locally necessitates innovative, research-based solutions to narrow this divide and enhance graduates' readiness for the job market. Employers have expressed concern over the disparity between what students learn in college and the practical knowledge they need to be job-ready (Chamorro-Premuzic

& Frankiewicz, 2019). This disconnect highlights the importance for universities to adapt and ensure their graduates possess the skills required by employers in today's evolving workforce.

3. DIGITAL TRANSFORMATION: ADDRESSING THE LACK OF OVERALL DIGITALIZATION STRATEGY

Recent global phenomena such as the COVID-19 outbreak, and the accelerating pace of digitalization have sparked discussions about universities' roles in facilitating societal and industrial transitions towards a sustainable future (Sadeghinejad, 2022). Crises throughout history have reshaped societies, and the education sector's digital transformation has become a focal point of interest in recent years. Despite ongoing innovations, this transformation has been slow, failing to meet sector expectations and demands. However, the COVID-19 pandemic, often characterized as a double-edged sword (Kee et al., 2021), despite its challenges, has acted as a catalyst for digital transformation within education. Academics, students, policymakers, and other stakeholders are actively driving digital transformation efforts in this sector (Kang, 2021). The adoption of e-learning models in response to the pandemic has led educational institutions worldwide to develop solutions for continued teaching and learning through digital or self-learning methods. This marks a positive shift towards business model innovation transformation for the entire education industry. Universities must seize this momentum to redefine their value proposition and establish a sustainable education model that aligns with the needs of digital native societies and the dynamics of the modern economy.

In today's competitive and dynamic business environment, nearly all industries have undergone profound "digital transformation" of their business models. For example, Salesforce, Uber, Netflix, and Amazon exemplify the success achieved through digitalization (Trkman, 2019). However, universities have generally not experienced a similar business model transformation. Education has been relatively insulated from disruptive revolutions (Terry & Rory, 2012). The internet has upended traditional businesses (Harden, 2012), allowing for the digitalization of lectures, books, presentations, and other teaching materials at minimal additional cost per student (Trkman, 2019). Despite these developments, universities remain committed to a high-cost business model that has served them well for decades (Kimberly & Bouchikhi, 2016). The Internet and online platforms have further disrupted the landscape (Christensen & Raynor, 2011; DaSilva & Trkman, 2014). It is widely acknowledged that the rapid and unpredictable pace of innovation in the digital world is challenging universities to keep up with demand (Mukerjee, 2014), necessitating speed and agility to seize new opportunities. The inevitability of change in education is widely recognized (Kolb, Fröhlich, & Schmidpeter, 2017).

4. TRANSFORM CHALLENGES INTO VALUE PROPOSITION ENHANCEMENT OPPORTUNITIES

The COVID-19 global health crisis has exposed the shortcomings of the current higher education system and highlighted the urgent need to train educators in digital technology to adapt to the rapidly changing global education landscape (Rashid & Yadav, 2020). The recent pandemic phenomena and the rapid growth of digital technologies have placed unprecedented pressures on universities to remain relevant. Therefore, it is inevitable to establish a resilient and sustainable educational ecosystem that prioritizes research strategies and ensures the post-pandemic education system continues to deliver high-quality learning outcomes and educational experiences to students and educators (Bozkurt, 2022; Pokhrel & Chhetri, 2021; Rashid & Yadav, 2020). Below are discussions on how universities can transform challenges posed by developments like COVID-19 and disruptive digital technologies into valuable opportunities.

Foster Principles of Responsible Management Education (PRME)

The COVID-19 pandemic has marked a pivotal moment in our lives, particularly in education (Bozkurt, 2022). The path to recovery demands extraordinary collaboration among authorities, industries, and societies. Therefore, fostering the Principles of Responsible Management Education (PRME) is crucial for universities to forge partnerships with industries and enhance preparedness for future pandemics (Sadeghinejad, 2022). PRME, a United Nations-supported initiative established in 2007, serves as a platform to promote sustainability in schools, equipping students with the knowledge and capabilities to drive change for a sustainable future. Anchored on six principles—purpose, value, method, research, partnership, and dialogue—PRME fosters connections among universities to ensure they nurture future leaders equipped to balance economic and sustainability goals (Morsing, 2021; UN, 2007). Universities should prioritize training students who possess the intellectual and psychological capacity to make effective decisions during crises. This entails understanding collaboration with affected social groups, managing supply-chain disruptions, optimizing resource allocation, analyzing COVID-19 vaccine distribution successes and failures, innovating business models in uncertainty, co-creating value with communities, employing intuitive decision-making, and implementing other best practices in crisis management (Sadeghinejad, 2022). These real-life crisis management experiences serve as excellent case studies for incorporation into university curricula and research, outlining innovative strategies for managing such crises.

Make Universities Research More Relevant

Universities could enhance their value by enabling academics to assist practitioners in improving business management. Therefore, academics must ensure that their research is widely accessible to managers and incorporate input from managers and employees into study design. To achieve this, universities must evolve their methods for evaluating and promoting educators. Currently, many universities prioritize academics based solely on the number of peer-reviewed publications in prestigious journals with high impact or citation counts. However, this approach may deter socially responsible research, resulting in fewer publications in outlets commonly read by managers, diminished interest among academics conducting research that addresses social problems, reliance on expedited research methods, and unethical research practices (Shapiro & Kirkman, 2018; Tsui, 2013). Therefore, it is crucial for universities to adopt a broader approach to assessing scholarly impact. Shapiro and Kirman (2018) advocate the following changes:

[1] Taking a pluralistic approach to measuring the scholarly impact not just within academia but outside it too. Instead of counting the frequency of a professor's articles cited by peers, there is a need to look at how often the work is recognized or used by students, practicing managers, policymakers, and publication of articles via channels that are mass-distributed to these stakeholders.

[2] Focus on responsible research that positively impacts business and society. It is a research strategy that balances the shareholders' interest with the social-economic outcomes of companies by using rigorous research methods to understand local phenomena and seek truth ethically.

[3] All stakeholders (scholarly researchers, universities administrators, funding agencies, government, practicing managers, and journal editors) work together to encourage and reward responsible research and move beyond the existing limited approaches currently used.

Moving to the New Dynamics of the Online Education Model

The shift to online learning systems during the pandemic has accelerated the adoption of e-learning tools and platforms in higher education, offering a valuable alternative for student engagement. This crisis has highlighted longstanding shortcomings in the current higher education system, revealing the urgent need for innovation through digital technology to adapt to the rapidly changing educational landscape worldwide. The new dynamics in online education present both opportunities and challenges, including increased competition and broader market reach (Sadeghinejad, 2022). Even before the COVID-19 outbreak, education was experiencing significant changes driven by globalization, economic volatility, demographic shifts, and technological advancements. Speed and agility have become critical success factors in today's digital era, garnering considerable attention across academia (Morrissey, 2019).

Online programs are now the fastest-growing segment in education, emphasizing the importance of leveraging digital technology to deliver high-quality knowledge conveniently to students (Morrissey, 2019). Initially aimed at maintaining enrollments in a competitive market, the online delivery model has evolved into a means of boosting enrollment and enhancing the value proposition, particularly during the pandemic when geographical boundaries became less relevant. To align with the goals of PRME, institutions must focus on cultivating tech-savvy students capable of using new technologies to create sustainable value for business and society (Sadeghinejad, 2022). The digital revolution is paving the way for a new generation of technology-driven and responsible universities to thrive with graduates who possess strong technological literacy and responsibility (Sadeghinejad, 2022). By redefining digital learning practices for students and faculty, improving infrastructure readiness, and optimizing workforce deployment models, universities can enhance their value proposition and better prepare students for the demands of today's job market (PWC, 2022).

Leveraging the Global Trend to Unlock Value

The criticisms from multiple perspectives on universities indicate that the culture of the education sector will need to change in line with the wider commercial and organizational environment. New teaching ideas, moving out from the comfort of the existing management model, risks taking, and partnerships with industries are some actions needed by universities to prepare students to face future adventures (Zahir, 2022). Thus, the need for innovation and reform is imperative for the business management education segment. In sum, universities must change their game and transform by leveraging global trends to stay relevant (PWC, 2020). For this, PricewaterhouseCoopers Malaysia recommended the following initiatives for the private higher learning institutions (PWC, 2020):

[1] Establish partnerships with renowned institutions for a competitive edge, research, and student mobility.

[2] Integrate and collaborate with the industry players to build students' employability readiness.

[3] Drive education model reinvention through digital learning.

[4] Diversification of student market, internationalization via partnerships with foreign public universities.

[5] Operational model optimization for cost-effectiveness through program redesign, shared courses, timetable, and resource management.

5. EMPOWERING THE FUTURE WORKFORCE: REAL-LIFE CASE STUDIES

Charting a Path to Industry 4.0: ViTrox's V-ONE Digital Learning Program

ViTrox Technologies is a prominent Malaysian company specializing in the design, development, and manufacturing of automated vision inspection systems for the semiconductor and electronics packaging industries. Founded in 2000 and headquartered in Penang, Malaysia, ViTrox has gained global recognition as a leader in advanced inspection technology. ViTrox's core expertise lies in machine vision technology, AI, and data analytics applied to quality control and inspection processes in manufacturing.

In collaboration with Universiti Sains Malaysia (USM), a leading public research university in Malaysia, ViTrox has initiated a significant program aimed at preparing undergraduate students for Industry 4.0 through digital learning modules. Under this partnership, students participated in ViTrox's V-ONE Digital Learning Towards Industry 4.0 program. This collaboration, marked by a signed Memorandum of Understanding (MOU), signifies an important synergy between academia and industry to enhance students' practical skills for future employment. Students were provided with free access to V-ONE Cloud accounts, enabling them to enroll in modules covering Charting Fundamentals, E-ticketing, and Workflow. Through this immersive experience, students acquired hands-on skills in chart creation, e-ticketing template customization, and workflow management using ViTrox's Industrial 4.0 Big Data Analytics platform. Students received a digital certificate from ViTrox as a token of accomplishment. Below are the testimonials from the participating students.

"Digital learning is a new era for the young generation. By taking ViTrox Digital Learning, I can learn further about the Industry 4.0 Smart Solution V-one. ViTrox platform is user-friendly. The tutorial helps me understand how to handle data analysis, status monitoring, alert plan features, and maintenance ticketing. By taking this learning, I improved my skills and knowledge about IR 4.0 from zero to hero. This experience will be helpful for me in the future." --Amirul Raziq Bin Mohammad Mokhtar

"In my opinion, ViTrox Digital Learning provided an excellent opportunity for us to learn and explore the 4.0 Digital World in our future workplace. Honestly, I think this is a priceless platform that taught us new knowledge about the latest data analysis efficiently. I did enjoy and have fun throughout those videos and quizzes provided, given that the explanation is easy to understand. The assignment provided in the Module was helpful for a beginner like me who learned some basic knowledge of it with the practice opportunity. I am impressed with the overall experiences of ViTrox Digital Learning." --Chan Da Wei

"In my opinion, ViTrox Digital Learning gives us a brand new knowledge we did not approach before. As I know what V-Trox taught us, we can manage the data received to make them into a form that we can easily view, a dashboard with charts. Even better, the chart can get into more detailed data analysis with just a click. This technology will improve the industries' efficiency in operation. To tell the truth, this ViTrox technology makes me feel similar to the digital board we have always seen in future high-tech movies in which they can view data by only using a finger to tap the hologram dashboard. I am really amazed at knowing that such technology exists." --Chew Wei Ping

This initiative exemplifies ViTrox's proactive approach to bridging the skills gap and equipping university graduates with industry-relevant competencies essential for success in the digital era. The collaboration between ViTrox and USM reveals the importance of partnerships between academia and industry in preparing students for the demands of the modern workforce.

Empowering Industry-Ready Graduates: ViTrox College's Work-Based Learning Approach

ViTrox College, founded by ViTrox Technologies and located in Penang, Malaysia, embodies a commitment to bridging theory with practice through innovative educational approaches. The college is designed to prepare students for the demands of Industry 4.0 by implementing Work-Based Learning (WBL), which integrates industry participation to deliver practical knowledge directly to students. Under the WBL framework at ViTrox College, students benefit from a unique learning experience where theoretical knowledge gained in classrooms is complemented by hands-on training within the industry. This WBL approach helps students engage in real-world applications of their education, gaining insights and skills directly applicable to industry needs.

ViTrox College's implementation of WBL represents a new learning culture in Malaysia, aligning with the college's mission to produce industry-ready graduates equipped with both theoretical expertise and practical capabilities essential for success in the evolving job market of Industry 4.0. This innovative educational model exemplifies ViTrox College proactive approach to bridging the skills gap and preparing students for meaningful careers in the technology sector.

Launch Your Career With Develop With Dell

Dell Technologies, a multinational technology company headquartered in Texas, USA, was founded in 1984 by Michael Dell. Over the years, Dell has grown into one of the largest technology infrastructure companies globally, providing a diverse range of products and services. Dell is committed to addressing the skill gap in the technology industry through initiatives like "Develop with Dell," aimed at preparing students for successful careers in technology.

Dell's mission is to empower students with the knowledge, skills, and confidence to excel in the technology industry and foster inclusivity. The "*Develop with Dell*" program, supported by college and university partners, offers participants a transformative learning experience. This program, consisting of on-demand and virtual sessions spanning 10-12 weeks, focuses on two courses: sales and technical support, representing the most sought-after entry-level careers in the technology sector. The "*Develop with Dell*" program plays a role in bridging the skill gap and developing a competent workforce for the digital age.

University Students Engage Globally: Enhancing Research and Collaboration Skills

The Nusantara Worldwide Project, facilitated by the International Business and Professional Management Association (AIBPM), is a collaborative initiative that engages students from various international higher learning institutions in a virtual team setting. This project aims to foster global collaboration and research among students by providing them with the opportunity to work together on case studies and research papers.

Following the MOU between USM and AIBPM, undergraduate students embarked on a transformative journey by participating in global virtual teams and collaborating with peers from international institutions to develop impactful case studies and research papers that bridge academia and industry. This experience marked a significant milestone for the students, showcasing their debut on the international stage with papers slated for publication in esteemed international journals—a true testament to their scholarly contributions. Engaging in this project provides undergraduates with a competitive advantage, equipping them for the job market compared to their peers. Upon successful completion of the project, students received digital certificates of participation, showcasing the value of hands-on experience in consultancy, research, and teamwork. Students benefited from complimentary participation at international conferences facilitated by AIBPM, further refining their presentation and networking abilities. This holistic approach to experiential learning ensures that students are well-prepared for the challenges and opportunities of the global workforce. Below are the testimonials from USM students after completing the project.

"*After participating in the Nusantara Project, it has been an honor and privilege to collaborate with students from other universities to complete this case study. The Nusantara Project has significantly enhanced our ability to apply classroom theory into practice and acquire real-world skills essential in today's business environment. Overall, participating in the Nusantara Project organized by the Association of International Business and Professional Management (AIBPM) has been a fabulous experience and a great achievement for me.*" --Yo Pei Woon

"The main challenge our team faced was the time difference between 2 different countries. Our team consists of 4 Malaysian students and 1 Nigerian student. The time difference between Malaysia and Nigeria is 7 hours. Therefore, we had a communication problem at the beginning of the project. However, we had a great understanding of one another and managed to overcome this problem. Each member was supportive and gave full participation to complete the task regardless of the time differences." --Vinosha Rai

"My team has students from Malaysia and India. I believe that my team and I learned a lot during the project's completion journey, such as the right format to write a research paper and citations, the right way to export the data into SPSS and what data should be presented in the research paper. Honestly, SPSS is not easy for a first-timer like me. Even though we have faced some challenges in communication and timing, it is a tremendous experience that I will never forget. I'm glad to get this opportunity to collaborate with my international counterpart." --Norarnitasha

Through initiatives such as the Nusantara Worldwide Project and participation in international conferences, USM students gain exposure to global collaboration, research publication, and professional networking—essential components of their development as future leaders and consultants in the global workforce.

Preparing Students for Digital Competence and Job Readiness: Penang Young Digital Talent Programme

The Penang Youth Development Corporation (PYDC), a dedicated Penang state government agency focused on youth development, has launched the "Penang Young Digital Talent Programme" to respond to the pervasive role of digital technologies in everyday life. This initiative aims to nurture holistic development among youth, equipping them with essential digital capabilities to thrive in an increasingly technology-driven world. In collaboration with USM, PYDC has signed an MOU.

The Penang Young Digital Talent Programme offers four free digital courses designed to equip students with foundational skills essential for success in the digital economy. These courses cover a range of topics tailored to develop proficiency in key areas of digital expertise. Students engage in modules such as Key Opinion Leader (KOL) development, e-commerce strategies including poster design and copywriting, digital marketing fundamentals, and web design techniques encompassing social media marketing and basic web development. Each course integrates hands-on apprenticeships to provide practical experience and reinforce learning outcomes, preparing participants for the real-world application of their digital competencies. Through the Penang Young Digital Talent Programme, students gain practical skills and competencies that enhance their digital literacy and job readiness. This initiative aligns with the evolving demands of digital technologies, equipping students to contribute to the workforce and drive economic growth through their digital expertise.

Empowering Through Education: Google's Generative AI Learning Courses

Google, founded in 1998 by Larry Page and Sergey Brin, has emerged as a global leader in technology, specializing in Internet-related services and products. Over the years, Google has played a significant role in shaping the digital field, pioneering advancements in search technology, cloud computing, and AI. In its latest initiative, Google has launched ten new generative AI learning courses to address the growing demand for skills in emerging technologies (Google Cloud, 2024). These courses are tailored to equip individuals with a deep understanding of AI and machine learning concepts, preparing them for future job opportunities amidst increasing automation. Recognizing the transformative potential of AI, Google's commitment to education reveals its vision of empowering individuals to thrive in a technology-driven era. This initiative exemplifies Google's dedication to innovation and education, reinforcing its role as a catalyst for technological advancement.

6. CONCLUSION AND NEXT STEPS

In conclusion, this chapter has revealed the proactive measures taken by employers to bridge skill gaps and enhance graduates' readiness for employment. Real-life examples emphasize the importance of broader employer engagement in addressing skills mismatches. Concurrently, universities are critical in this process, adapting curricula to align with advanced technologies and the demands of the digital revolution.

The evolving education, driven by advanced technologies and digital transformation, necessitates a reimagining of education models. There is an increasing demand for graduates proficient in both technical and soft skills to navigate the complexities of Industry 4.0. Higher education institutions globally must innovate and transform to meet these demands, offering refined value propositions and focusing on digital innovation to remain pertinent and impactful.

Looking ahead, the next steps involve universities continuing to evolve and prepare students for the evolving workforce and digital economy. Ongoing innovation, educational reform, and relevance are essential. Academic-industry collaboration, research initiatives, accelerated digital transformation, and global engagement will be crucial in ensuring high-quality learning outcomes and educational experiences that equip graduates to thrive in today's economy. By embracing these strategies and fostering greater employer involvement, higher education institutions can contribute to shaping a workforce that is agile, adaptable, and well-prepared for the challenges and opportunities of Industry 4.0. Employers' active collaboration with universities will further strengthen efforts to curb skills mismatches and ensure graduates are job-ready in the modern economy.

REFERENCES

Alpaydın, Y., & Kültür, K. (2022). Improving the Transition from Higher Education to Employment: A Review of Current Policies. In Akgün, B., & Alpaydın, Y. (Eds.), *Education Policies in the 21st Century*. Maarif Global Education Series. 10.1007/978-981-19-1604-5_5

Aziz, H. (2018, October 3). Graduate skills gap. *New Straits Times*. Retrieved from https://www.nst.com.my/education/2018/10/417327/graduate-skills-gap

Bhandari, R. (2023). Bridging the skills gap: Fuelling careers and the economy in Malaysia. *Economist Impact*. Retrieved from https://impact.economist.com/perspectives/talent-education/bridging-skills-gap-fuelling-careers-and-economy-malaysia

Bozkurt, A. (2022). Resilience, Adaptability, and Sustainability of Higher Education: A Systematic Mapping Study on the Impact of the Coronavirus (COVID-19) Pandemic and the Transition to the New Normal. *Journal of Learning for Development*, 9(1), 1–16. 10.56059/jl4d.v9i1.590

Bridges, D. (2000). Back to the Future : The higher education curriculum in the 21st century. *Cambridge Journal of Education*, 30(1), 37–55. 10.1080/03057640050005762

CBI & Pearson. (2016). *The right combination: CBI/Pearson education and skills survey*. Retrieved from www.cbi.org.uk/cbi-prod/assets/File/pdf/cbi-education-and-skills- survey2016.pdf

Chamorro-premuzic, T., & Frankiewicz, B. (2019, January 14). Does Higher Education Still Prepare People for Jobs? *Harvard Business Review*. https://hbr.org/2019/01/does-higher-education-still-prepare-people-for-jobs

Christensen, C. M., & Raynor, M. E. (2011). The innovator's solution. *Journal of the American College of Radiology, 8*(6), 382. 10.1016/j.jacr.2011.03.004

DaSilva, C. M., & Trkman, P. (2014). Business Model: What It Is and What It Is Not. *Long Range Planning*, 47(6), 379–389. 10.1016/j.lrp.2013.08.004

Eusof, N. S. (2024). Hays: Skill shortages a burden to Malaysian employers. *The Edge Malaysia*. Retrieved from https://theedgemalaysia.com/article/hays-skill-shortages-burden-malaysian-employers

Ghazali, G., & Bennett, D. (2017). Employability for music graduates : Malaysian educational reform and the focus on generic skills. *International Journal of Music Education*, 35(4), 588–600. 10.1177/0255761416689844

Hamid, M. S. A., Islam, R., & Hazilah, A. M. N. (2014). Malaysian graduates' employability skills enhancement : An application of the importance performance analysis. *Journal for Global Business Advancement*, 7(3), 181–197. 10.1504/JGBA.2014.064078

Harden, N. (2012). The End of the University as We Know It - The American Interest. In *The American Interest* (Volume 8, pp. 54–62). https://www.the-american-interest.com/2012/12/11/the-end-of-the-university-as-we-know-it/

Harvey, L. (2001). Defining and measuring employability. *Quality in Higher Education*, 7(2), 97–109. 10.1080/13538320120059990

Ibrahim, D. H. M., & Mahyuddin, M. Z. (2017). *Youth Unemployment in Malaysia : Developments and Policy Considerations.* Retrieved from https://www.bnm.gov.my/files/publication/ar/en/2016/cp04 _003_box.pdf

Ismail, A. (2018). *HEBATising FUTURE TALENTS USM style* [Powerpoint slides]. Retrieved from https://cdae.usm.my/index.php/programmes/academic-excellence/competition

Kang, B. (2021). *How the COVID-19 Pandemic Is Reshaping the Education Service* (Lee, J., & Han, S. H., Eds.)., 10.1007/978-981-33-4126-5_2

Kasriel, S. (2018, October 31). The future of work won't be about college degrees, it will be about job skills. *CNBC.* Retrieved from https://www.cnbc.com/2018/10/31/the-future-of-work-wont-be-about -degrees-it-will-be-about-skills.html

Kee, D. M. H., Al-anesi, M., Chandran, S., Elanggovan, H., Nagendran, B., & Mariappan, S. (2021). COVID-19 as a double-edged sword: The perfect opportunity for GrabFood to optimize its performance. *Journal of the Community Development in Asia*, 4(1), 53–65. 10.32535/jcda.v4i1.998

Kee, D. M. H., Anwar, A., Shern, L. Y., & Gwee, S. L. (2023). Course quality and perceived employability of Malaysian youth: The mediating role of course effectiveness and satisfaction. *Education and Information Technologies*, 28(10), 1–8. 10.1007/s10639-023-11737-1

Kimberly, J. R., & Bouchikhi, H. (2016). Disruption on Steroids: Sea Change in the Worlds of Higher Education in General and Business Education in Particular. *Journal of Leadership & Organizational Studies*, 23(1), 5–12. 10.1177/1548051815606434

Kolb, M., Fröhlich, L., & Schmidpeter, R. (2017). Implementing sustainability as the new normal: Responsible management education – From a private business school's perspective. *International Journal of Management Education*, 15(2), 280–292. 10.1016/j.ijme.2017.03.009

Malaysian Productivity Corporation. (2017). *Productivity report 2016/2017.* Retrieved from https://www .mpc.gov.my/wp-content/uploads/2017/05/Productivity-Report-2017.pdf

Marr, B. (2023, February 9). The future of work: Are traditional degrees still worthwhile? *Forbes.* https://www.forbes.com/sites/bernardmarr/2023/02/09/the-future-of-work-are-traditional-degrees-still -worthwhile/?sh=440803591bfe

Matsouka, K., & Mihail, D. M. (2016). Graduates' employability : What do graduates and employers think? *Industry and Higher Education*, 30(5), 321–326. 10.1177/0950422216663719

Mohd Salleh, N., Mapjabil, J., & Legino, R. (2019). Graduate Work-Readiness in Malaysia: Challenges, Skills and Opportunities. In Dhakal, S., Prikshat, V., Nankervis, A., & Burgess, J. (Eds.), *The Transition from Graduation to Work: Challenges and Strategies in the Twenty-First Century Asia Pacific and Beyond* (pp. 125–142). Springer Singapore. 10.1007/978-981-13-0974-8_8

Morrissey, C. A. (2019). The Digital Transformation of Management Education - A Peer-Reviewed Academic Articles. *Graziadio Business Review, 22*(1). https://gbr.pepperdine.edu/2019/03/the-digital -transformation-of-management-education/

Morsing, M. (2021). PRME – principles for responsible management education. *Responsible Management Education*, 3–12. 10.4324/9781003186311-2

Mukerjee, S. (2014). Agility: A crucial capability for universities in times of disruptive change and innovation. *Australian Universities Review*, 56(1), 56–60.

Okolie, U. C., Nwosu, H. E., & Mlanga, S. (2019). Graduate employability: How the higher education institutions can meet the demand of the labour market. *Higher Education, Skills and Work-Based Learning*, 2042–3896. 10.1108/HESWBL-09-2018-0089

Pokhrel, S., & Chhetri, R. (2021). A Literature Review on Impact of COVID-19 Pandemic on Teaching and Learning. *Higher Education for the Future*, 8(1), 133–141. 10.1177/2347631120983481

PWC. (2020). *Harnessing Education in the New Economy: Private Higher Education Investments in Malaysia*. PricewaterhouseCoopers. https://www.pwc.com/my/en/assets/publications/2020/pwc-harnessing-education-in-the-new-economy.pdf

PWC. (2022). *Impact on the Higher Education Sector*. https://www.pwc.com/sg/en/publications/a-resilient-tomorrow-COVID-19-response-and-transformation/higher-education.html

Rashid, S., & Yadav, S. S. (2020). Impact of COVID-19 Pandemic on Higher Education and Research. *Indian Journal of Human Development*, 14(2), 340–343. 10.1177/0973703020946700

Sadeghinehijad, Z. (2022, April 22). *COVID-19, the digital revolution, and the value proposition of future business schools: Insights from UNPRME*. UBSS Publication. https://www.ubss.edu.au/articles/2022/april/COVID-19-the-digital-revolution-and-the-value-proposition-of-future-business-schools-insights-from-unprme/

Shanmugam, M. (2017, March 25). Unemployment among graduates needs to be sorted out fast. *The Star Online*. Retrieved from https://www.thestar.com.my/business/business-news/2017/03/25/unemployment-among-graduates-needs-to-sorted-out-fast/

Shapiro, D. L., & Kirkman, B. (2018). *It's Time to Make Business School Research More Relevant*. Harvard Business Review. https://hbr.org/2018/07/its-time-to-make-business-school-research-more-relevant

Tan, A. Y. T., Chew, E., & Kalavally, V. (2017). The expectations gap for engineering field in Malaysia in the 21st century. *On the Horizon*, 25(2), 131–138. 10.1108/OTH-12-2015-0071

Tan, S. (2019, April 18). Malaysian Fresh Graduates Can't Secure High-Paying Jobs as They Lack Digital Skills. *World of Buzz*. Retrieved from https://www.worldofbuzz.com/msian-fresh-graduates-cant-secure-high-paying-jobs-as-they-lack-digital-skills/

Terry, A., & Rory, M. (2012). Disruptive pedagogies and technologies in universities. *Journal of Educational Technology & Society*, 15(4), 380–389.

Trkman, P. (2019). Value proposition of business schools: More than meets the eye. In *International Journal of Management Education* (Vol. 17, Issue 3). 10.1016/j.ijme.2019.100310

Tsui, A. S. (2013). The Spirit of Science and Socially Responsible Scholarship. *Management and Organization Review*, 9(3), 375–394. 10.1111/more.12035

UN. (2007). *The principles for responsible management education.* United Nations. https://www.unprme.org/resource-docs/PRME.pdf

Verma, P., Nankervis, A., Priyono, S., Mohd Salleh, N., Connell, J., & Burgess, J. (2018). Graduate work-readiness challenges in the Asia-Pacific region and the role of HRM. *Equality, Diversity and Inclusion*, 37(2), 121–137. 10.1108/EDI-01-2017-0015

Yoong, D., Don, Z. M., & Foroutan, M. (2017). Prescribing roles in the employability of Malaysian graduates. *Journal of Education and Work*, 30(4), 432–444. 10.1080/13639080.2016.1191626

Zahir, I. (2022). *What the Post-COVID-19 world could look like for business schools.* Chartered Association of Business Schools. https://charteredabs.org/what-the-post-COVID-19-world-could-look-like-for-business-schools/

Chapter 2
Managing Gig Economy Workers Through Artificial Intelligence:
Applications and Challenges

Akansha Mer
Banasthali Vidyapith, India

Joshy Mathew
https://orcid.org/0000-0002-0572-1259
University of Technology and Applied Sciences, Al Musanna, Oman

Shweta Arora
Graphic Era Hill University, India

ABSTRACT

Artificial intelligence (AI) has the potential to completely transform the way the gig economy is managed. The study explores the potential of artificial intelligence (AI) to reshape the management of gig economy workers with special reference to human resource management and the challenges faced by such workers. The study has employed an extensive literature review approach. The findings of the study reveal that AI and ML in the hiring and recruiting supports HR by expanding access to opportunities, enhancing personalisation, and mitigating bias and discrimination. AI brings changes in gig workers' performance management by monitoring performance indicators, examination of client input, skill gap identification, performance benchmarking. Furthermore, training platforms driven by AI can assist gig workers in determining the skills they need to acquire and in creating individualized learning plans. The novelty of the study stems from exploring the role of AI training and performance management, which is yet unexplored.

INTRODUCTION

The gig economy operates on the principles of a free market system, wherein temporary roles prevail, and organizations engage independent workers on a contractual basis for short periods. According to McDonnell et al. (2021), the gig economy represents a free and global market in which self-employed

DOI: 10.4018/979-8-3693-3096-8.ch002

workers and customers establish temporary and professional connections that provide extensive adaptability for all involved parties. It represents a labor market where all forms of employment are transitory and accomplished by autonomous workers or freelancers. Consequently, "gig" originates in the music industry, where jobs are ephemeral and clearly defined. A recently published McKinsey report (What Is the Gig Economy? 2023) describes the importance of the gig economy in modern times. The most attractive part of this independent work is freedom and flexibility. According to McKinsey, workers who do "side hustles" and their regular jobs are also considered independent workers. Although these workers have a wide range of ages, incomes, and educational attainment, younger workers and those with lower salaries tend to be overrepresented. The gig workers include professionals such as attorneys, accountants, performers, social media influencers, travelling nurses, and other experts. Technological advancement in digital platforms and remote collaboration tools is the primary reason for the growth of gig workers.

The rise of the gig economy has profoundly transformed the operations of individuals and institutions within the dynamic realm of contemporary labour markets. Technological advancements and evolving perceptions of traditional job structures have resulted in an unparalleled expansion of the gig economy, characterized by transient and adaptable labour arrangements. Artificial intelligence (AI), a prominent technological breakthrough, is gaining momentum as a valuable ally for businesses seeking to optimize labour management within the gig economy. At the confluence of AI and the gig economy, numerous prospects exist for augmenting operational efficiency, streamlining workflows, and facilitating seamless communication between regular and contingent workforces.

The study explores the potential of artificial intelligence to reshape the management of gig economy workers. This study aims to showcase how organizations can utilize intelligent systems to surmount obstacles and take advantage of the possibilities offered by the changing employment environment. Artificial Intelligence has the potential to completely transform the way the gig economy is managed, ushering in a fresh era of efficiency, adaptability, and responsiveness for companies operating across different sectors.

HR Tech to Manage Gig Workers

The study (McDonnell et al., 2021) discusses how HRM activities such as attraction, recruitment and selection, job quality, motivation, and control are deployed by digital platform organisations to manage gig workers. The gig economy, facilitated by digital platforms, is a distinctive and extreme form of work that will reshape the future of work. It involves quickly exchanging data and technological innovations (Hanaysha et al., 2022), offering flexibility for workers, businesses, and consumers. Despite the transactional nature of gig work, there is a growing recognition of the role of technologically mediated HRM practices in the gig economy, where HR activities traditionally associated with organisations are enacted and enabled by algorithms. Various HRM activities deployed by digital platform organisations that gig workers are subject to, including attraction, recruitment and selection, job quality, motivation and control, provide insight into how technology mediates labour management in gig work.

The study conducted by Norlander et al. (2021) examines the perceptions of gig workers, notably uber, taxi, and limousine drivers, regarding technology supervision and its impact on their sense of control and motivation. AI-enabled technological monitoring has the potential to amplify the motivation of gig workers and empower them to monitor their progress and enhance their professional endeavours. Technological monitoring will mitigate biases and favouritism, provide impartial criteria for evaluating employees' performance, and improve transparency and equity within the gig economy. Additionally, incorporating features such as GPS tracking and emergency assistance in technological supervision can instil a sense of security and well-being among gig workers, subsequently enhancing their overall job satisfaction. However, it is essential to note that this increased level of supervision may also entail a reduction in the workers' perceived autonomy and sense of control.

According to Liu et al. (2023), incorporating AI into gig economy platforms for connecting workers with job tasks can positively and negatively affect platform revenue. While AI can improve matching quality and income by better assigning tasks to workers, it can also reveal information about uncertain labour demand to workers, resulting in adverse participation decisions and revenue loss for the platform. The researchers apply their methodology to scenarios involving revenue sharing and work task competition and frequently discover comparable results. They also propose two strategies for mitigating the potential detrimental consequences of AI-powered matching. Under specific scenarios, the AI-adopting platform may benefit by directly disclosing labour demand or competitive information to employees.

The study conducted by Muldoon & Rækstad (2022) examines the impact of digital platforms and application software on the gig economy, with a particular emphasis on the new systems of algorithmic management that have arisen and how they change the structural conditions of employment. The study contends that some algorithms can promote new dominance relationships in which the owners and management of a corporation dominate workers, thereby building a socio-technical system that maintains this domination. The study of algorithmic dominance in the gig economy has broader implications for the labour market, as the increasing usage of algorithms throughout the gig economy may lead to corporate owners' and managers' dominance over workers.

RESEARCH METHODOLOGY

The study has employed extensive literature review approach. The authors have sourced the content from renowned journals, forbes magazine, Harvard Business Review and Mckinsey and Deloitte's report. Articles on Managing Gig Economy Workers through Artificial Intelligence with special reference to human resource management were part of the study. The three main domains of the study in context of human resource management covered for the study are: recruitment and selection, performance management and training and development.

Several keywords were used to source the articles. Keywords used for search of articles are:

Artificial intelligence and gig economy workers, AI and human resource management, recruitment and selection, performance management, training and development, applications, challenges.

All the articles published till 25 November 2023 were part of the study.

Application of Artificial Intelligence in Managing Gig Workers

Recruitment and Selection

According to the report by (Mukherjee, n.d.), the utilisation of AI and ML in the hiring and recruiting of gig workers is expected to enhance efficiency in company processes. Given the immense potential of the gig economy, recruiters are innovating new strategies to assess candidates' abilities and skill levels. The utilisation of AI can heighten the effectiveness of these endeavours. For example, AI can aggregate data using various criteria to generate lists of eligible applicants and recommend superior recruits based on predetermined standards for screening gig talent. Furthermore, AI can facilitate communication with individuals on these lists and assist recruiters in focusing their search for capable prospects. Programs can aid HR managers in evaluating a candidate's suitability, narrowing down the pool of prospects most suited for a specific project. By swiftly analysing candidate data with the assistance of appropriate AI applications, employers can gain insight into each prospect's abilities and career objectives. AI-driven human-machine interfaces can also be directly employed to streamline interviews and automatically schedule follow-up interviews with the most suitable candidates. It enhances businesses' ability to identify top talent and reduces reliance solely on job portals, social media, databases, and similar resources to assess a candidate's potential contribution to a project.

A study by Mariani & Lozada (2023) examines how AI and algorithms are increasingly used in HRM systems, particularly in recruiting processes. It emphasizes how these technologies can improve productivity and cut costs, but they also carry the risk of prejudice and discrimination in choosing candidates. To provide better-regulated activities and ensure workers' rights, the study highlights the necessity for regulations to protect minority and privacy rights. It also recommends the identification and acceptance of national and international legislation.

Defining project specifics and objectives is vital to optimize personnel management when involving gig workers. It is essential to evaluate their profiles for alignment with project requirements. Employing AI platforms to assist in creating exact contracts that define project scopes and expectations can help organizations streamline this process (Mallick, 2023).

Freelancers may encounter challenges when identifying appropriate employment opportunities that align with their expertise and skill repertoire within the rapidly evolving gig economy. Nevertheless, the landscape of job matching has undergone a significant transformation after integrating artificial intelligence AI into the gig economy (Bashar, 2023). The advent of AI-powered platforms, which leverage intricate algorithms and data analysis, has fundamentally altered the dynamics of interactions between independent contractors and their clientele. The study further discusses how AI supports HR in recruiting gig workers.

1. Expanding Access to Opportunities: Artificial intelligence systems analyse a substantial volume of information, encompassing the skills, professional background, and previous projects of self-employed workers, thereby facilitating their alignment with a broader range of relevant job vacancies. Consequently, the pool of potential clients accessible to self-employed workers has broadened, augmenting the probability of securing gratifying employment.
2. Enhanced Efficiency in the Talent Search Process: Platforms driven by artificial intelligence employ intricate algorithms to swiftly sift through vast databases of freelance professionals and employment advertisements. It enables clients to benefit from a streamlined talent search process, simplifying the identification of exceptional individuals who meet their specific criteria and requirements.
3. Enhanced Personalisation: Machine learning techniques are employed by AI-driven job matching services to offer personalised suggestions for clients and freelancers, utilising past preferences, project outcomes, and performance indicators. This ensures that freelancers are paired with employment opportunities that align with their distinct abilities and interests.
4. Mitigating Bias and Discrimination: Through the focus on objective factors such as experience and talents, AI algorithms can assist in mitigating bias and discrimination in job matching. AI-powered platforms facilitate a fair chance for freelancers by eliminating human biases, thereby fostering a more diverse and inclusive gig economy.

5. Real-time Market Insights: AI-powered systems continuously monitor and assess employment inquiries, freelancers' availability, and market trends. By leveraging this up-to-date information, freelancers can adapt their expertise to stay competitive and meet evolving market needs by acquiring valuable insights into emerging employment patterns.
6. Improved Quality Control: Based on the outcomes, assessments, and appraisals of the project, artificial intelligence algorithms possess the capability to assess the efficiency and excellence of self-employed individuals. Guaranteeing that reliable autonomous workers are paired with reliable organisations elevates the level and expertise of the freelance market as a complete entity.

Companies engage gig workers based on the required expertise for a given undertaking, spurred by the swift advancement of technology. The article (Behl et al., 2021) highlights how the surge of AI-based crowdsourcing platforms is a primary catalyst behind the exponential expansion of gig workers. Utilising these platforms, gigs and hiring companies establish a connection. In addition, the surge of gig workers can be attributed to economic labour costs, the absence of job commitment, and the ability to hire personnel according to demand. Crowdsourcing platforms abide by the fundamental principle that numerous individuals should collaborate towards achieving a sole objective. Crowdsourcing platforms equipped with artificial intelligence (AI) simplify the process for gig workers to discover and accept job assignments that employers advertise, granting them access to various micro-jobs.

AI is exerting a substantial influence on the gig economy through various means, foremost among them being the development of intelligent algorithms capable of effectively matching workers with pertinent employment opportunities, surpassing the efficacy of traditional recruitment methodologies (Frąckiewicz, 2023a). These algorithms scrutinise copious amounts of data, encompassing comprehensive information (Khan & Mer, 2023) concerning an individual's inclinations, proficiencies, and professional background, in addition to the distinctive prerequisites of each job. Through this analysis, they ascertain the most suitable job vacancies for workers, ensuring the utmost satisfaction for all parties involved. Consequently, a novel surge of AI-driven job portals has emerged, endowing gig workers with augmented accessibility to hitherto inaccessible prospects.

Recruiters and companies have derived various advantages from using artificial intelligence in the recruitment process (Mer & Virdi, 2022; Mer & Srivastava, 2023). Integrating AI-powered solutions can enhance the efficiency of candidate selection, streamline laborious tasks, and accelerate the screening procedure. By leveraging social media platforms and online channels, recruiters can access a wider pool of potential candidates, expanding the talent pool and increasing the probability of identifying the most suitable candidate for a position (Paramita, 2020). Digitisation facilitates data-informed decision-making in the hiring process, enabling recruiters to assess and utilise extensive amounts of candidate data to make more informed hiring choices.

The article (Williams et al., 2021) focuses on recruitment techniques in the gig economy, focusing on digital platforms that connect self-employed workers with clients for short-term engagements. The study emphasizes the relevance of digital platform labour, in which workers take on temporary gigs mediated by platform businesses via smartphone apps. It underlines the need to understand the attraction and selection processes of hiring people for gig economy jobs on digital platforms. According to the study, digital platforms utilize various techniques to attract workers, including flexible working hours, competitive pay, and excellent ratings from prior customers. The article also examines the selection process, which comprises platforms matching workers with relevant gigs using algorithms and ratings.

Technology has made the gig economy in recruiting possible by introducing online platforms for talent engagement, AI-driven applicant matching, video interviews, and virtual assessments. These technologies help recruiters and candidates communicate remotely and expedite the hiring process (Harris, 2023). Schmidt et al., (2022) suggest modifying the conventional Attraction-Selection-Attrition (ASA) paradigm to incorporate an "organizing" phase in between for gig workers, who frequently use websites owned by third parties to self-organize to strengthen their sense of identity and community. The authors draw attention to the fact that gig workers may join, depart, and be hired by gig employers throughout this organizational stage. The suggested modification to the ASA framework offers a fresh viewpoint on the employment of gig workers. It emphasizes the value of fit on many levels with one's profession, organization, and surroundings.

Performance Management

The article by Tountopoulou et al. (2021) introduces an indirect skill assessment methodology, which utilises artificial intelligence (AI) technology to quantify and identify workers' competencies beyond the conventional selection processes. This methodology encompasses evaluating an individual's performance in playing two content-agnostic serious games (namely, Tetris and 2048), followed by utilising the resultant data to train neural models capable of estimating a player's skill set. The assessment of an individual's gaming performance, outside the context of a situational judgement test (SJT), is employed to gauge their skill set, thereby establishing a correlation between their action sequences and various skills. The application of AI technology permits the creation of innovative datasets encompassing game sessions and corresponding skill evaluations obtained through validated psychometric questionnaires.

An article published in People Matters (Mukerjee, n.d.) describes how enterprises employ AI to allocate tasks to gig workers and oversee their progress. The utilisation of AI empowers employers to assign specific tasks to gig workers and offer constructive feedback to ensure sustained efficacy, as numerous organisations prefer engaging gig workers on a project-oriented basis. Enterprises that excel in talent acquisition can reap the benefits of harnessing Artificial Intelligence (AI) for team coordination. Many AI applications currently available are actively aiding organisations in extracting more excellent value from the gig economy. The coordination of employees, the management of workloads for internal and external teams, and the effective handling of project management represent some of the most common challenges human resource experts face. These challenges can be resolved by utilising AI algorithms within an appropriate setting. AI serves to extend the reach of the gig economy and possesses the potential to assist in the advancement of the gig-based labour paradigm. The repetitive tasks in project management can be automated, providing businesses with clearly defined procedures for effectively managing teams of specialists within and outside the confines of the organisation.

A study by Pletcher (2023) addresses the application of AI algorithms to the performance evaluation of employees, emphasizing the possible advantages of automation in terms of reduced bias, uniformity, and efficiency. Applying AI algorithms to employee performance reviews can improve the process's objectivity, efficiency, and accuracy, which could result in better organizational outcomes and more informed decision-making. Considering the ethical ramifications of these AI models will ensure accountability and justice and guarantee their transparency and explainability. The article by Jarrahi & Sutherland (2019) addresses how gig workers on the Upwork platform acquire the technical literacy necessary to comprehend and manipulate algorithms, allowing them to maintain professional independence while using the site. Gig workers can traverse the site and manipulate or work around algorithmic management to retain some control over their jobs by knowing algorithms.

Enhancing performance is essential for career advancement in the fast-paced world of freelancing. With the help of artificial intelligence (AI), the gig economy has access to many data-driven insights that let independent workers assess their performance and make wise decisions. Algorithms and analytics powered by AI have entirely changed how independent workers monitor their development (Bashar, 2023). This study discusses how AI brings changes in gig workers' performance management.

1. Monitoring performance indicators: Freelancers can oversee performance indicators such as project completion rates, ratings provided by clients, and comments by using AI-driven analytical tools. Freelancers can monitor their progress over time, identify areas that require enhancement, and strive for continuous professional growth by closely observing these metrics.
2. Examination of client input: AI systems analyse client input to extract valuable information about strengths and areas for improvement. Freelancers can enhance their performance, establish lasting connections with clients, and tailor their approach based on a thorough understanding of client expectations, preferences, and satisfaction levels.
3. Market Demand and Trends: Examining market data and trends by AI-driven platforms facilitates the provision of valuable information to independent contractors regarding novel job requirements and industry fluctuations. Freelancers can identify lucrative opportunities within expanding sectors, maintain a competitive edge, and enhance their skill sets by remaining updated with market demands.
4. Pricing and Financial Optimisation: AI algorithms analyse financial data, market rates, and project complexity. It enables freelancers to secure profitable employment opportunities and achieve financial success by establishing competitive fees that accurately reflect their value.
5. Skill Gap Identification: Skill gaps identification is important in the originations (Mer & Virdi, 2024). The identification of skill gaps can be facilitated through the utilisation of AI-powered systems, which evaluate the skill sets of freelancers based on market demand and competitiveness. To maintain competitiveness and effectively address evolving customer requirements, freelancers may invest in targeted learning opportunities by recognising specific areas that necessitate further training or skill enhancement.
6. Performance Benchmarking: Performance benchmarking can be achieved using AI-driven analytics solutions, which compare the work of independent contractors with industry standards. By employing this approach, freelancers are provided with valuable insights and perspectives. Consequently, freelancers can establish goals, evaluate their progress, and strive for excellence in their professional endeavours by understanding how their performance compares to that of their peers.

The study (Meijerink, 2021) emphasizes the significance of customer reviews in identifying talent in the gig economy and online labour platforms. AI impacts talent management in the gig economy by allowing for identifying and evaluating gig workers' talent via customer evaluations and online ratings. Technology is critical to online labour platforms, which are at the heart of the gig economy. AI algorithms can evaluate gig workers' talent and service quality by analyzing customer evaluations and performance data. This data is helpful for talent management in the gig economy since it aids in identifying and selecting talented gig workers for certain activities or projects. Furthermore, AI can help match gig workers with suitable job prospects based on their talents and expertise, improving talent acquisition and development in the gig economy. AI can improve talent management practices in the gig economy by facilitating efficient talent discovery and allocation processes and offering data-driven insights.

Using the job demand resources (JD-R) model as a framework, the study (Hanim Mohsin et al., 2022) investigates the impact of job autonomy and work engagement on the performance of gig workers. The JD-R model's motivational processes are reflected in the links between job autonomy, work engagement, and gig workers' performance. The degree to which people are independent and in charge of their work activities and decision-making processes is called their job autonomy. Workplace autonomy may enhance work engagement and thereby improve performance, according to research (Mer & Vijay, 2021). People are more likely to feel motivated and involved, which raises performance levels (Goswami et al., 2024; Johnson, 2020) when they can make decisions and control their jobs. Work autonomy gives people the freedom to apply their knowledge and abilities, which fosters a sense of accountability and ownership for their work and improves output. Additionally, having autonomy helps people prioritize their work, use their time wisely, and adjust to changing conditions—all of which can lead to better performance results. Gig workers' performance is positively correlated with their work engagement, defined as their enthusiasm, commitment, and focus on their work. Gig workers are more likely to be driven, devoted, and focused when deeply involved, which translates into better performance. Hence, encouraging work engagement among gig workers can positively affect their performance outcomes. Engaged gig workers typically put in extra effort, go above and beyond their job requirements, and exhibit higher levels of productivity and quality in their work. Work engagement also contributes to gig workers' satisfaction and well-being, which can further enhance their performance.

To improve the effectiveness and retention of gig workers on online staffing platforms, the article (Bäker & Natter, 2022) suggests three factors that these platforms might implement into their matching algorithms. Gig worker performance can be significantly enhanced by adding three metrics to the matching algorithms of online employment platforms. Employee performance increased by 55.6 percentage points due to these initiatives being evaluated on a significant European staffing platform.

Training Gig Economy Workers

There is a lot discussion going around whether gig workers should be trained and "how" to train them. It is frequently unclear whether they are regarded as "external people" or as "employees," so their employment status may remain unclear. Because of this, businesses frequently decide to ignore the development needs of contract workers. An Ernst and Young study found that 52% of contingent workers do not receive training from their employer.

Needs for AI-based learning Gig workers may already have specialized skills, so learning and development may be wondering what training topics to assign them. Learning systems powered by artificial intelligence and machine learning will be able to recommend the appropriate courses to freelancers and contingent workers, enabling them to assume responsibility for their own education and make meaningful contributions (Kulkarni, 2019).

Artificial intelligence is going to be a big part of the future of the gig economy as it develops further. AI has the potential to significantly impact skill development and training as well as other areas (Mer & Virdi, 2023; Mer, 2023). The need for workers to acquire new skills and adjust to shifting job requirements will only grow as the gig economy expands. Training platforms driven by AI can assist gig workers in determining the skills they need to acquire and in creating individualized learning plans to help them reach their objectives. This will help businesses access a more skilled and flexible workforce in addition to enabling workers to remain competitive in the gig economy (Frackiewicz, 2023).

Artificial Intelligence (AI) presents a plethora of opportunities to establish a more efficient, effective, and equitable gig economy for all, ranging from enhancing trust and streamlining administrative tasks to improving matching algorithms and skill development. For example, it has been reported that certain app workers are looking for opportunities for professional growth from their employers (Graham, Hjorth, & Lehdonvirta, 2017), as well as social interaction and support from managers and peers, as well as mentoring from more experienced colleagues (Ashford et al., 2018).

For example, Uber argues that it gives employees a voice by organizing quality improvement courses where employees can participate and be heard (Rosenblat, 2018). Duggan et al. (2020) indicated that Uber occasionally provides a training session to enable improvement for drivers who face the possibility of having their account deleted from the platform owing to low customer ratings. There is a charge to attend, though. In essence, having a low driving rating means that you must pay for your own training. Initiatives like this are seen by the organization as the best way to handle the special requirements of app-work and take the place of established HR procedures like training or evaluations (Kuhn & Maleki, 2017).

Challenges of Integrating Artificial Intelligence in Gig Economy

The integration of AI in the gig economy gives rise to a multitude of additional challenges. The challenges stem from the potential for bias in AI systems. These algorithms are designed to match gig workers with suitable opportunities based on various criteria, including location, experience, and skill set. However, if these algorithms are not adequately developed and trained, they may inadvertently perpetuate biases, leading to disparities in employment prospects. To cultivate and maintain the trust of gig workers, artificial intelligence (AI) systems must diligently conform to prevailing data protection legislation, ensuring the safeguarding, security, and confidentiality of the personal data of gig labourers.

According to Frąckiewicz (2023b), securing one's work is the primary challenge. There is a growing apprehension that as AI progresses, it may ultimately supplant human labour in certain occupations. Take, for instance, the ride-sharing industry, where autonomous vehicles may eventually displace human drivers. Consequently, workers may find themselves unemployed, while corporations stand to benefit from cost savings and heightened efficiency.

The use of AI in the gig economy raises doubts regarding the rights and protections afforded to workers. Given that gig workers are often classified as independent contractors rather than employees, they may be ineligible for workers' compensation, paid time off, or health insurance. Policies must address these concerns and ensure that workers' rights are safeguarded as AI continues to blur the boundaries between conventional employment and gig labour.

Li et al. (2022) raises concerns about the growing inequality in gig work brought about by the divide in technology and data, which results in unjust working conditions and a mistrust of platforms. To address these issues, the authors suggest a bottom-up strategy utilizing end-user intelligent assistants to empower gig workers.

Tripathi et al.'s research from 2022 illustrates the difficulties in managing gig workers in an AI-focused workplace. These workplaces do not handle moral, legal, or ethical issues in managing gig workers. Another issue involves eliminating regulatory loopholes and enacting required modifications to address moral and legal issues related to AI-led workplaces. While dealing with AI-based freelancer management solutions, HR professionals also face the issue of acquiring new skills and abilities. Another issue is balancing the presence of humans and machines in the workplace; it can be challenging to determine how much individual freedom should be allowed while creating AI solutions. AI's capability to address the workplace's cultural shifts due to the gig workforce's dynamic nature is also a serious concern.

Artificial intelligence (AI) technology is displacing gig workers by effectively handling jobs that people were doing previously, especially routine task jobs. Gig workers are becoming obsolete as AI technology performs data analysis and copywriting more effectively. The effectiveness and speed with which AI can do jobs are decreasing the need for human freelancers in various capacities. The gig economy is growing more competitive, which benefits individuals with advanced training and expertise (Brown, 2023).

The report (Brandao, 2023) discusses how Artificial Intelligence and automation have a significant influence on jobs and workloads. Employers will have to assist employees in adjusting to working with AI and moving into new positions. Human abilities like creativity, emotional intelligence, and sophisticated problem-solving will also become increasingly important at the same time. Skills gaps are growing as a result of how swiftly technology is developing. Businesses need to invest significantly in retraining and upskilling initiatives for their employees. While new skills in fields like data analysis, digital marketing, and cybersecurity will be highly sought after, specific existing abilities may need to be updated. The growing prevalence of remote and flexible work arrangements will require a shift towards managing hybrid teams. While this can enhance productivity and work-life balance, it also presents challenges related to accountability, organizational culture, and teamwork. It leads to establishing clear policies for a dispersed workforce and finding the right balance between face-to-face and virtual communication.

According to (Jacobsen, 2023), the possibility of job displacement is one of the main worries freelancers have with the development of AI. Some of the jobs and responsibilities that independent contractors have historically filled could be automated as AI systems advance, decreasing the need for their services.

Second, the ease of access to freelance platforms and the attractiveness of remote employment have raised competitiveness. As the market is crowded with freelancers worldwide, standing out and landing high-quality tasks can become more complex.

Finally, freelancers frequently rely on AI-powered platforms for project acquisition and communication. However, this reliance might need fixing if the platforms' algorithms, policies, or price structures change, hurting freelancers' livelihoods.

CONCLUSION

The management of gig economy workers through artificial intelligence has immense potential to enhance productivity, optimize resource allocation, and adapt to the dynamic nature of gig employment. However, particular challenges are associated with using AI in this context. Achieving successful implementation requires navigating a complex path that includes addressing workforce availability, ensuring fair evaluations, overcoming algorithmic bias, and navigating regulatory barriers. Managing gig economy workers with the assistance of AI necessitates a comprehensive strategy that considers the unique aspects of gig labour, promotes efficient communication, and upholds moral principles. Integrating AI technology and a commitment to confronting obstacles directly will open the door for a more efficient, equitable, and sustainable gig economy ecosystem as businesses navigate this intricate terrain.

REFERENCES

Bäker, A., & Natter, M. (2022). Improving gig worker performance and retention on staffing platforms. *Proceedings - Academy of Management, 2022*(1). 10.5465/AMBPP.2022.227

Bansal, P. (2023). AI design of Ride-hailing Platforms : A feminist analysis of workers' precarity. In *Amsterdam University Press eBooks*. 10.5117/9789463728386_ch01

Bashar, S. (2023, July 17). The Gig Economy and AI: How Artificial Intelligence is Changing Freelancing. *Medium*. https://medium.com/@saikat.ipe92/the-gig-economy-and-ai-how-artificial-intelligence-is -changing-freelancing-1039ed9d2533

Behl, A., Sampat, B., & Raj, S. (2021). Productivity of gig workers on crowdsourcing platforms through artificial intelligence and gamification: A multi-theoretical approach. *The TQM Journal*. Advance online publication. 10.1108/TQM-07-2021-0201

Brandao, T. (2023, November 9). *The future of work: Navigating benefits and challenges ahead*. Sesame HR. https://www.sesamehr.com/blog/future-work/

Brown, M. (2023, June 2). *How AI programs are threatening the future of the gig industry - Jarvee*. Jarvee. https://jarvee.com/how-ai-programs-are-threatening-the-future-of-the-gig-industry/

Duggan, J., Sherman, U., Carbery, R., & McDonnell, A. (2021). Boundaryless careers and algorithmic constraints in the gig economy. *International Journal of Human Resource Management, 33*(22), 4468–4498. 10.1080/09585192.2021.1953565

Elayan, M. B. (2022). Transformation of Human Resources Management Solutions as a strategic tool for GIG workers contracting. In *IGI Global eBooks* (pp. 711–734). 10.4018/978-1-6684-3873-2.ch038

Frackiewicz, M. (2023). *Transforming the Gig Economy with AI: Top Opportunities*. Retrieved from https://ts2.space/en/transforming-the-gig-economy-with-ai-top-opportunities/#gsc.tab=00

Frąckiewicz, M. (2023a, May 19). *How AI is Shaping the Future of Work: Profitable Gig Economy Opportunities*. TS2 SPACE. https://ts2.space/en/how-ai-is-shaping-the-future-of-work-profitable-gig -economy-opportunities/#gsc.tab=0

Frąckiewicz, M. (2023b, July 27). *AI in the Gig Economy: Opportunities and Challenges for Workers and Businesses*. TS2 SPACE. https://ts2.space/en/ai-in-the-gig-economy-opportunities-and-challenges -for-workers-and-businesses/#gsc.tab=0

Goswami, I., Mittal, A., Kumar, V., Verma, P., & Mer, A. (2024). Analysing the role of total rewards and compensation in increasing employee motivation. *Int. J. Business Excellence*.

Hanaysha, J. R., Al-Shaikh, M. E., Joghee, S., & Alzoubi, H. M. (2022). Impact of innovation capabilities on business sustainability in small and medium enterprises. *FIIB Business Review, 11*(1), 67–78. 10.1177/23197145211042232

Harris, M. (2023, August 18). *The rise of Flexibility: Navigating the gig economy in recruitment - Hirebee*. Hirebee. https://hirebee.ai/blog/what-is-employer-branding-what-to-pay-attention-to/the-rise-of -flexibility-navigating-the-gig-economy-in-recruitment/

Jacobsen, C. (2023, August 25). *Article*. Mexico Business. https://mexicobusiness.news/entrepreneurs/news/navigating-challenges-and-opportunities-ai-freelancing

Jarrahi, M. H., & Sutherland, W. (2019). Algorithmic Management and Algorithmic Competencies: Understanding and appropriating algorithms in gig work. In *Lecture Notes in Computer Science* (pp. 578–589). 10.1007/978-3-030-15742-5_55

Johnson, D. S. (2020). Public versus private employees: A perspective on the characteristics and implications. *FIIB Business Review*, 9(1), 9–14. 10.1177/2319714519901081

Khan, F., & Mer, A. (2023). Embracing artificial intelligence technology: Legal implications with special reference to european union initiatives of data protection. In *Digital Transformation, Strategic Resilience, Cyber Security and Risk Management* (pp. 119-141). Emerald Publishing Limited.

Knight, B., Mitrofanov, D., & Netessine, S. (2023). The impact of AI technology on the productivity of gig economy workers. *Social Science Research Network*. 10.2139/ssrn.4372368

Kulkarni, R. (2019). https://www.peoplematters.in/article/training-development/training-for-the-gig-economy-the-ld-way-23904

Lang, J., Li, Y., Cheng, C., Cheng, X. Y., & Chen, F. Y. (2023). Are algorithmically controlled gig workers deeply burned out? An empirical study on employee work engagement. *BMC Psychology*, 11(1), 354. Advance online publication. 10.1186/s40359-023-01402-037876010

Li, T. J., Lu, Y., Clark, J., Chen, M., Cox, V. S., Meng, J., Yang, Y., Kay, T., Wood, D., & Brockman, J. B. (2022). A Bottom-Up End-User Intelligent Assistant Approach to Empower Gig Workers against AI Inequality. *arXiv (Cornell University)*. /arxiv.2204.1384210.1145/3533406.3533418

Liu, Y., Lou, B., Zhao, X., & Li, X. (2023). Unintended consequences of advances in matching technologies: Information revelation and strategic participation on GIG-Economy platforms. *Management Science*. Advance online publication. 10.1287/mnsc.2023.4770

Malik, A., Budhwar, P., & Srikanth, N. R. (2020). Gig Economy, 4IR and Artificial Intelligence: Rethinking Strategic HRM. In *Emerald Publishing Limited eBooks* (pp. 75–88). 10.1108/978-1-83867-223-220201005

Mallick, S. (2023, December 14). *People matters - Interstitial site — People matters*. People Matters. https://www.peoplematters.in/article/hr-technology/mastering-gig-economy-recruitment-retention-39779

Mariani, K., & Lozada, F. V. (2023). The use of AI and algorithms for decision-making in workplace recruitment practices. *Journal of Student Research*, 12(1). Advance online publication. 10.47611/jsr.v12i1.1855

McDonnell, A., Carbery, R., Burgess, J., & Sherman, U. (2021). Technologically mediated human resource management in the gig economy. *International Journal of Human Resource Management*, 32(19), 3995–4015. 10.1080/09585192.2021.1986109

Meijerink, J. G. (2021). Talent management in the gig economy. In *Routledge eBooks* (pp. 98–121). 10.4324/9780429265440-6-6

Mer, A. (2023). Artificial Intelligence in Human Resource Management: Recent Trends and Research Agenda. *Digital Transformation, Strategic Resilience. Cyber Security and Risk Management*, 111, 31–56.

Mer, A., & Srivastava, A. (2023). Employee Engagement in the New Normal: Artificial Intelligence as a Buzzword or a Game Changer? In *The Adoption and Effect of Artificial Intelligence on Human Resources Management, Part A* (pp. 15-46). Emerald Publishing Limited

Mer, A., & Vijay, P. (2021). Towards enhancing work engagement in the service sector in India: A conceptual model. In *Doing business in emerging markets* (pp. 118–135). Routledge India. 10.4324/9781003199168-7

Mer, A., & Virdi, A. S. (2022). Artificial intelligence disruption on the brink of revolutionizing HR and marketing functions. *Impact of artificial intelligence on organizational transformation*, 1-19.

Mer, A., & Virdi, A. S. (2023). Navigating the paradigm shift in HRM practices through the lens of artificial intelligence: A post-pandemic perspective. *The Adoption and Effect of Artificial Intelligence on Human Resources Management, Part A*, 123-154.

Mer, A., & Virdi, A. S. (2024). Fostering Creativity, Innovative Service Behaviour, and Performance Among Entrepreneurs in the VUCA World Through Employee Engagement Practices. In *VUCA and Other Analytics in Business Resilience, Part A* (pp. 59-76). Emerald Publishing Limited.

Mer, A., & Virdi, A. S. (2024). Decoding the Challenges and Skill Gaps in Small-and Medium-Sized Enterprises in Emerging Economies: A Review and Research Agenda. *Contemporary Challenges in Social Science Management: Skills Gaps and Shortages in the Labour Market*, 112, 115–134. 10.1108/S1569-37592024000112B007

Mohsin, F., Md Isa, N., Awee, A., & Purhanudin, N. (2022). Growing Gigs: A Conceptual Report on Job Autonomy and Work Engagement on Gig Workers' Performance. *International Journal Of Advanced Research In Economics And Finance*, 4(1), 144–156.

Mukerjee, D. (n.d.). *How AI is fuelling the rise of gig economy*. People Matters. Retrieved December 7, 2023, from https://www.peoplematters.in/article/hr-technology/how-leena-ai-is-helping-employees-become-more-productive-23737

Muldoon, J., & Rækstad, P. (2022). Algorithmic domination in the gig economy. *European Journal of Political Theory*, 22(4), 587–607. 10.1177/14748851221082078

Norlander, P., Jukić, N., Varma, A., & Nestorov, S. (2021). The effects of technological supervision on gig workers: Organizational control and motivation of Uber, taxi, and limousine drivers. *International Journal of Human Resource Management*, 32(19), 4053–4077. 10.1080/09585192.2020.1867614

Paramita, D. (2020). Digitalization in Talent acquisition : A Case study of AI in Recruitment. *SciSpace - Paper*. https://typeset.io/papers/digitalization-in-talent-acquisition-a-case-study-of-ai-in-2cde0gvcal

Pletcher, S. N. (2023). Practical and Ethical Perspectives on AI-Based Employee Performance Evaluation. *OSF Preprints*. 10.31219/osf.io/29yej

Pradhan, D. (2022, September 14). *Gig economy and AI's role in making the gig model thrive | Fuse-Machines Insights*. Fusemachines. https://insights.fusemachines.com/a-new-era-of-gig-workers-and-ais-role-in-making-the-gig-model-thrive/

Schmidt, G. B., Philip, J., Van Dellen, S. A., & Islam, S. (2022). Gig worker organizing: Toward an adapted Attraction-Selection-Attrition framework. *Journal of Managerial Psychology*, 38(1), 47–59. 10.1108/JMP-09-2021-0531

Subbiah, R. (2023). Gig economy. *International Journal for Multidisciplinary Research*, 5(1), 1638. Advance online publication. 10.36948/ijfmr.2023.v05i01.1638

Tountopoulou, M., Vlachaki, F., Daras, P., Vretos, N., & Christoforidis, A. (2021). Indirect skill assessment using AI technology. *Advances in Social Sciences Research Journal*, 8(4), 723–737. 10.14738/assrj.84.10077

Tripathi, M. A., Tripathi, R., Yadav, U. S., & Shastri, R. K. (2022). Gig Economy: Reshaping strategic HRM in the era of industry 4.0 and Artificial intelligence. *ResearchGate*. https://www.researchgate.net/publication/360258253_Gig_Economy_Reshaping_Strategic_HRM_In_The_Era_of_Industry_40_and_Artificial_Intelligence/comments

What is the gig economy? (2023, August 2). McKinsey & Company. https://www.mckinsey.com/featured-insights/mckinsey-explainers/what-is-the-gig-economy

Williams, P., McDonald, P., & Mayes, R. (2021). Recruitment in the gig economy: Attraction and selection on digital platforms. *International Journal of Human Resource Management*, 32(19), 4136–4162. 10.1080/09585192.2020.1867613

Wood, A. J., Graham, M., Lehdonvirta, V., & Hjorth, I. (2018). Good gig, Bad gig: Autonomy and algorithmic control in the global gig economy. *Work, Employment and Society*, 33(1), 56–75. 10.1177/0950017018785616630886460

Zhang, A., Boltz, A., Lynn, J., Wang, C., & Lee, M. K. (2023). Stakeholder-Centered AI Design: Co-Designing Worker Tools with Gig Workers through Data Probes. *CHI '23: Proceedings of the 2023 CHI Conference on Human Factors in Computing Systems*. 10.1145/3544548.3581354

Chapter 3
Examining Successful Models and Collaboration of Industry–Academia

Shilpa Sankpal
https://orcid.org/0000-0003-0916-0345
SVKM's Narsee Monjee Institute of Management Studies, Indore, India

ABSTRACT

The case refers to the mechanics that oil a successful industry academic partnership and collaboration. Different models that exist in this domain have been touched upon with information about what needs to cement this relationship. Research into the factors that have been found to have the most impact on quality and durability of the collaboration has been cited in the case. Even though different fields have different expectations from a student coming out from the academic world, adequate attention to such collaborations can improve employability and reduce the disconnect between industry and academics. There are several benefits of this handholding between these interdependent stakeholders, and an exploration of the benefits that can accrue from the same have been presented through the extant literature on the same.

INTRODUCTION

There has been a standing debate for a very long time in the world of academics – its disconnect with the practical world, the challenges of employability and for classroom ideas to jump out into the real world.

And this debate has never been solved. While this article refers to academia as in the instances of formal education at undergraduate and post graduate level, the truth is that interventions can exist much before the student is done with their twelfth class too. Stories of start-up and entrepreneurship contests are now heard lounder than ever, but the long term stratagem of the same is yet to be tested out.

To be honest if ever the confusion lay in what and why of this bridge, the bottomline would be that students are basically being prepped for the real world, and hence interventions before they pass out would make the shock of the chasm much lower for them. A common strategy that is adopted by most management institutes is to hold extra mural lectures inviting industry resource persons and internships for six to eight weeks with industry.

DOI: 10.4018/979-8-3693-3096-8.ch003

But a common grouse is that not all students approach these lectures and internships with lot of seriousness and industry people also often have too much of their routine jobs to focus on these people who are not going to be looking at the organization more than the blink of the eye hat four weeks is. Yes, pre-placement offers can be a sweetener for students, but for industries that would take a lot of evaluation and processes in place for this to work out.

Objectives of This Case

The current case attempts to outline the frameworks in practice that have been used to structure industry academic partnerships. The case also attempts to collate best practices and recommendations to structure the said partnerships. Ever the division and gap between the academics and industry has existed, it has become more and more pertinent to identify measures that make students real world ready. The benefits and deterrents to industry academic collaborations have been discussed in the case.

METHODOLOGY

The current study is based on chiefly looking at the studies published between 2010 to 2024 and crystallizing the main themes emergent from the same. Nuanced observations emerge from the study of the same.

The Mechanics of Successful Industry Academic Collaboration

A very successful industry academic collaboration would be one, where most students learn from their exposure to the industry or the industry is blessed with opportunity of early evaluation before recruitment, or fruitful outcomes that have commercial viabilities.

Industry Academic collaboration can bring in many innovations such as Coca Cola being able to develop an alternative to plastic bottle due to bottle created by IIT Delhi.

One good practice that can be emulated on a larger scale in IIT Delhi's Industry Day (Press Release, December 2022). Collaborations with industry and research has yielded products that are working solutions to many real life problems. Industries can adopt and commercialize the inventions, and bring credence and commercial value for all stakeholders involved.

However, as academia knows in apt, there are also frameworks around the world that have been tested and implemented to concretize the collaboration. One of the biggest issues is the metrics to measure the ideation process of such collaboration, and the metrics to collate outcomes. Despite the general positive evaluation of the said collaboration there are many barriers to such collaborations between the industry and academia. As Perkmann et al (2013) indicate that the individuals on both side of the collaboration spectrum are being evaluated in their own areas on diverse parameters. In universities, academic careers are built upon publication and reputation of the research outputs and their prestige. The industry person is however, more minted on whether the knowledge generated can give a competitive advantage to the firm that sponsored the research, and whether the knowledge has any transformative quality.

Though such deterrents can be described in several ways, Bruneel, d'Este and Salter (2010), have categorized such deterrents as falling into two core groups – transaction barriers and orientation barriers. According to them, the latter emerge because industry and academia work with different visions and expectations, and the former look at the breadth and gap between industry and academia that leads to additional costs for them to convene together. After all, there will be trade-offs, and business may not be convinced in its view and long termism of the research collaboration, while the academic may be looking for longer range investment and collaboration.

The challenges and barriers have an impact on the balance of adoption of collaboration practices, but the benefits are several. Collaborations between Industry and Academia have been craved for many reasons. Some of the major reasons why the collaborations have been craved for include –

Companies exist to absorb trained and qualified candidates that the universities are entrusted in training and prepping. People who are qualified and trained for certain industries are a boon to the industry (Myoken 2013). Companies get the opportunity to access the knowledge and the technology that is available in the universities and research centres (Barnes et al, 2002).

Companies also get to tap into expensive research settings and infrastructure that may not be accessible elsewhere (Ankrah and AL-Tabbaa 2015). Studies such as those by Bekkers and Bodas Freitas (2008) convey that almost ten percent of innovative products and services have genesis in academic researches. But this win-win situation applies to universities too.

OECD (2015) posits that industry collaborations are an important contributor to university funding. Research and development activities and partnerships with international organization, commercial enterprises have significant upticks for universities. Universities can use these funds for multitude of reasons, and they also gain access to industry machinery. They also benefit from licensing arrangement and income from patents (Barnes et al. 2002).

Di Maria et al (2019) conducted a study on the benefits accrual for universities and industries collaborating in the field of environmental sustainability, and they found that the benefits were more for industries than academicians involved in the research. A very interesting research reported by Alpaydin and Fitjar (2024) was conduced on 232 Norwegian firms. The researchers found that the one of the most significant benefits of successful collaborations is the aspect that it opens the doors for further collaborations. They also felt that the benefits are both direct as well as indirect from the side of the firm. They also felt that while more merit was placed on research based collaborations, there is merit in other types of collaborations as well. They found that both universities and firms can gain traction with informal and education based initiatives.

Universities are often thought to be offering solution based consultancy services (Leten et al., 2014; Serbanica et al., 2015; Steinmo & Rasmussen, 2016; Thomas et al., 2021), but the collaboration can be breaking far more ice than just numbers.

Hewitt-Dundas et al., (2019) posit that collaboration petri dishes both managerial capabilities as well as cognitive capabilities of firms and universities. Leszczyńska & Khachlouf (2018) indicate that when these two parties who otherwise tend to be isolated from each other interact, they develop a deeper understanding of each other.

There is a strong linkage creation that that fosters social bonds and often structures are create that govern the relationship between the firm and the university. Universities can be hand held in upping their methodology to be more of a challenge based learning methodology through collaborations with industries. The relevance of such challenge based assignments can lead firms to identify suitable graduates early, and aids universities in being more relevant to the industry (Gallagher & Savage, 2023).

Universities and academia are entrusted with three core missions at their heart, even if they are worded in a multitude of ways. These three missions are teaching, research and entrepreneurship. These three need alignment within the context of the university's immediate environment and the broader canvas

(Guerrero, Cunningham and Urbano, 2015). This alignment and growth becomes possible, especially in the reference of research and innovation ecosystem, when the universities form a closer patter with industry. Even teaching improves when the universities combine technology transfer/knowledge transfer ideas that bring market knowledge to classroom situations (Rajalo and Vadi, 2017)

There were several frameworks that were found that aimed at understanding this collaboration.

The Imperial College London Framework

Philibin (2010) described the framework that has been used by Imperial College, London. The framework in question had on its plate the task of fulfilling several objectives. Putting the university in perspective, the framework administered emphasis on upping the contracts received from industry, improving the research base and diversification in the research conducted.

The framework opted to organize its framework around the dimensions critical for effective collaboration such as leadership, operational management, organizational structure, social capital, transparency and communication. The rigours of the framework are a function of the formal mechanisms that are put in place to monitor the implementation of the framework. The framework is a composite of both sector and process platform.

Rybnicek and Konigsgruber Model

Another model is one developed by Rybnicek and Konigsgruber (2019) through their investigation of successful university – industry collaborations. They divided their framework into three parts – one that outlined generic collaborations, the other identified factors that are the umbrellas for this model and the moderators in the model.

Figure 1. Rybnicek and Konigsgruber: Model for Industry Academic Collaboration

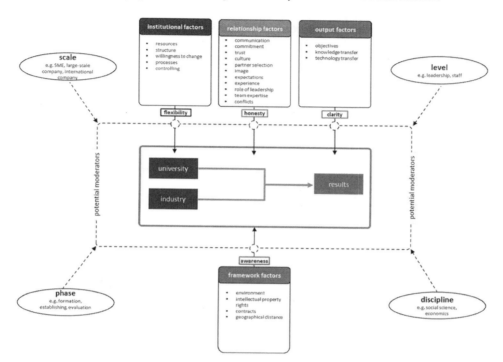

Studies in the Triple Helix System of Innovation (Leydesdorff & Etzkowitz, 2001)

No discussion on collaboration would be complete without referencing the holy trinity of university, industry and government partnerships.

Acuña et al (2024) studied four Latin American countries namely Brazil, Mexico, Chile and Argentina in the perspective of the triple helix system for STEM (Science, Technology, Engineering, and Mathematics). Their study highlighted that while universities primarily shoulder the innovation responsibility and their efforts are often isolated. Only Chile appeared to be relatively more successful in pushing bureaucratic hurdles and roping industry partners well into the ecosystem. Jackson et al (2018) conducted a study in the Australian context and found that it is mutuality that powers the success of the triple helix collaborations.

Making Collaborations Work

A lot of interest has been elicited in terms of factors, outcomes and conceptual clarity on what makes these collaborations stick. The major wheels for successful collaborations include clarity (Hemmert et al. 2014; Franco and Haase 2015; Bruneel et al. 2010), flexibility (Muscio and Vallanti 2014; Hong and Su 2013; Poston and Richardson 2011), honesty (Bstieler et al. 2015; Hemmert et al. 2014; Sellenthin

2011), awareness of the environment (Berbegal-Mirabent et al. 2015; Piva and Rossi-Lamastra 2013; Myoken 2013) among other elements.

Recommendations

Analyzing the recommendations and reviewing the stated ideas, it appears prudent to first have a policy ready to even germinate these type of collaborations. A policy supported by a vision works best for the innovations to happen. Another aspect to keep an eye on is to have a dedicated cell or group working on these collaborations. Best practices from around the world could be studied and incorporated.

Looking at the collaborations only from the perspective of rankings would be incorrect because they dilute the bridge's foundations. But the rankings can definitely be a fillip for the academia to be looking at the collaborations as a way to improve their standing on the lists of different agencies that ascribe value to the same.

Governments can intervene at various levels to help bridge the gap between industry and academia and can open incubators for such projects. Their interest in this intellectual pursuit can bring out socially relevant innovations that have community applications.

While Industry can learn a lot from academia in terms of refreshing the basics, and that they need not re-invent the wheel. But most importantly, academia can learn a lot from industry, because that is where the real life lies. Academics that is not rooted in application and reality, will create candidates who are distanced from the real world.

Individual Candidates who excel in industry projects are more industry ready, Employability continues to be an area of concern overall.

CONCLUSION

Educational Institutes are conditioned and rightfully so to be available to all citizens. Certain academic institutions have the benefit of industry proximity. However, for successful collaborations it is fundamental to not be looking at proximity, but on ability and aptitude.

In conclusion, it is perseverance, priority and perspiration from academia, and intention and innovation from industry that will cement the bond sufficiently.

REFERENCES

Acuña, M. A. O., de Almeida Filho, A. T., & Ramos, F. S. (2024). Modelling the triple helix system innovation of the main economies from Latin America: A coalitional game theory approach. *Scientometrics*. Advance online publication. 10.1007/s11192-024-05020-4

Alpaydın, U. A. R., & Fitjar, R. D. (2024). How do university-industry collaborations benefit innovation? Direct and indirect outcomes of different collaboration types. *Growth and Change*, 12721(2). Advance online publication. 10.1111/grow.12721

Ankrah, S., & AL-Tabbaa, O. (2015). Universities–industry collaboration: A systematic review. *Scandinavian Journal of Management*, 31(3), 387–408. 10.1016/j.scaman.2015.02.003

Barnes, T., Pashby, I., & Gibbons, A. (2002). Effective university–industry interaction: A multi-case evaluation of collaborative R&D projects. *European Management Journal*, 20(3), 272–285. 10.1016/S0263-2373(02)00044-0

Bekkers, R., & Bodas Freitas, I. M. (2008). Analysing knowledge transfer channels between universities and industry: To what degree do sectors also matter? *Research Policy*, 37(10), 1837–1853. 10.1016/j.respol.2008.07.007

Berbegal-Mirabent, J., Sánchez García, J. L., & Ribeiro-Soriano, D. E. (2015). University–industry partnerships for the provision of R&D services. *Journal of Business Research*, 68(7), 1407–1413. 10.1016/j.jbusres.2015.01.023

Bruneel, J., D'Este, P., & Salter, A. (2010). Investigating the factors that diminish the barriers to university–industry collaboration. *Research Policy*, 39(7), 858–868. 10.1016/j.respol.2010.03.006

Bstieler, L., Hemmert, M., & Barczak, G. (2015). Trust formation in university-industry collaborations in the US biotechnology industry: IP policies, shared governance, and champions. *Journal of Product Innovation Management*, 32(1), 111–121. 10.1111/jpim.12242

Delhi Showcases Over, I. I. T. (n.d.). *80 Technologies Developed by its Researchers at 4th Industry Day*. https://home.iitd.ac.in/show.php?id=149&in_sections=Press

Di Maria, E., De Marchi, V., & Spraul, K. (2019). Who benefits from university–industry collaboration for environmental sustainability? *International Journal of Sustainability in Higher Education*, 20(6), 1022–1041. 10.1108/IJSHE-10-2018-0172

Etzkowitz, H., & Leydesdorff, L. (2000). The dynamics of innovation: From National Systems and "Mode 2" to a Triple Helix of university-industry-government relations. *Research Policy*, 29(2), 109–123. 10.1016/S0048-7333(99)00055-4

Franco, M., & Haase, H. (2015). University–industry cooperation: Researchers' motivations and interaction channels. *Journal of Engineering and Technology Management*, 36, 41–51. 10.1016/j.jengtecman.2015.05.002

Gallagher, S. E., & Savage, T. (2023). Challenge-based learning in higher education: An exploratory literature review. *Teaching in Higher Education*, 28(6), 1135–1157. 10.1080/13562517.2020.1863354

Guerrero, M., Cunningham, J. A., & Urbano, D. (2015). Economic impact of entrepreneurial universities' activities: An exploratory study of the United Kingdom. *Research Policy*, 44(3), 748–764. 10.1016/j.respol.2014.10.008

Hemmert, M., Bstieler, L., & Okamuro, H. (2014). Bridging the cultural divide: Trust formation in university–industry research collaborations in the US, Japan, and South Korea. *Technovation*, 34(10), 605–616. 10.1016/j.technovation.2014.04.006

Hewitt-Dundas, N., Gkypali, A., & Roper, S. (2019). Does learning from prior collaboration help firms to overcome the 'two-worlds' paradox in university-business collaboration? *Research Policy*, 48(5), 1310–1322. 10.1016/j.respol.2019.01.016

Hong, W., & Su, Y.-S. (2013) The effect of institutional proximity in non-local university–industry collaborations: an analysis based on Chinese patent data. *Res Policy, 42*, 454–464. 10.1016/j.respol.2012.05.012

Jackson, P., Mavi, R. K., Suseno, Y., & Standing, C. (2018, February). University–industry collaboration within the triple helix of innovation: The importance of mutuality. *Science & Public Policy*, 45(1), 142. 10.1093/scipol/scx093

Leszczyńska, D., & Khachlouf, N. (2018). How proximity matters in interactive learning and innovation: A study of the Venetian glass industry. *Industry and Innovation*, 25(9), 874–896. 10.1080/13662716.2018.1431524

Leten, B., Landoni, P., & Van Looy, B. (2014). Science or graduates: How do firms benefit from the proximity of universities? *Research Policy*, 43(8), 1398–1412. 10.1016/j.respol.2014.03.005

Muscio, A., & Vallanti, G. (2014). Perceived obstacles to university–industry collaboration: Results from a qualitative survey of Italian academic departments. *Industry and Innovation*, 21(5), 410–429. 10.1080/13662716.2014.969935

Myoken, Y. (2013). The role of geographical proximity in university and industry collaboration: Case study of Japanese companies in the UK. *International Journal of Technology Transfer and Commercialisation*, 12(1/2/3), 43–61. 10.1504/IJTTC.2013.064170

OECD. (2015). *OECD science, technology and industry scoreboard 2015: innovation for growth and society*. OECD.

Perkmann, M., Tartari, V., McKelvey, M., Autio, E., Broström, A., D'Este, P., Fini, R., Geuna, A., Grimaldi, R., Hughes, A., Krabel, S., Kitson, M., Llerena, P., Lissoni, F., Salter, A., & Sobrero, M. (2013). Academic engagement and commercialisation: A review of the literature on university– industry relations. *Research Policy*, 42(2), 423–442. 10.1016/j.respol.2012.09.007

Philbin, S. P. (2010). Developing and Managing University-Industry Research Collaborations through a Process Methodology/Industrial Sector Approach. *The Journal of Research Administration*, 41(3), 51–68.

Piva, E., & Rossi-Lamastra, C. (2013). Systems of indicators to evaluate the performance of university–industry alliances: A review of the literature and directions for future research. *Measuring Business Excellence*, 17(3), 40–54. 10.1108/MBE-01-2013-0004

Poston, R. S., & Richardson, S. M. (2011). Designing an academic project management program: A collaboration between a university and a PMI chapter. *Journal of Information Systems Education*, 22, 55–72.

Rajalo, S., & Vadi, M. (2017). University-industry innovation collaboration: Reconceptualization. *Technovation*, 62–63(April), 42–54. 10.1016/j.technovation.2017.04.003

Rybnicek, R., & Königsgruber, R. (2019). What makes industry—University collaboration succeed? A systematic review of the literature. *Journal of Business Economics*, 89(2), 221–250. 10.1007/s11573-018-0916-6

Sellenthin, M. O. (2011). Factors that impact on university–industry collaboration: Empirical evidence from Sweden and Germany. *Business and Economic Review*, 54, 81–100.

Serbanica, C. M., Constantin, D. L., & Dragan, G. (2015). University–industry knowledge transfer and network patterns in Romania: Does knowledge supply fit SMEs' regional profiles? *European Planning Studies*, 23(2), 292–310. 10.1080/09654313.2013.862215

Steinmo, M., & Rasmussen, E. (2016). How firms collaborate with public research organizations: The evolution of proximity dimensions in successful innovation projects. *Journal of Business Research*, 69(3), 1250–1259. 10.1016/j.jbusres.2015.09.006

Thomas, E., Faccin, K., & Asheim, B. T. (2021). Universities as orchestrators of the development of regional innovation ecosystems in emerging economies. *Growth and Change*, 52(2), 770–789. 10.1111/grow.12442

Chapter 4
Collaborating Academia, Industry, and Government:
Enhancing Business Practices Through Innovative Pedagogies

Raino Bhatia

Eternal University, India

Jagneet Kaur
https://orcid.org/0009-0003-0341-3636
Eternal University, India

ABSTRACT

The educational industry is changing due to social needs, technology integration in every field, socio-economic dynamics, and most significantly, educational methods. The groundbreaking adventure uses an integrated method to challenge educational hypotheses, encourage student participation, and equip students for an extensive and interconnected world. India should prioritize inventions and research in academia and industry with the absolute support from government and private agencies. Innovative technology fosters dynamic pedagogy that has replaced the traditionally so-called lecture method with innovative pedagogies to thrive and flourish in the industry-driven society. In the economic climate of today, it is crucial to build a productive partnership among business and academia. The study uses exploratory research. Secondary data were analyzed using content analysis. The final outcome of this chapter is to develop the value of sharing, caring, and giving back to the society by connecting education, industry, and society.

INTRODUCTION

You can't build a great building on a weak foundation,
You must have a solid foundation if you are going to have a strong superstructure

DOI: 10.4018/979-8-3693-3096-8.ch004

- Gordon B, Hinckley

Quality Education is an essential aspect and driving force for transforming the entire nation into empowered society through understanding the needs of the current hour. In this 21st century and coming years we as educationist have to prepare the mind-set of our coming generations to adopt the flexibility and dynamics of this changing world in every aspect of our life. The present landscape of educational sector is experiencing significant upheavals due to societal needs, integration of technology in every sector, socioeconomic dynamics and most importantly the pedagogical approaches (Akhtar & Malik, 2023).The integration of ethical principles and ecologically sustainable practices into everyday activities of educational institutions is increasingly imperative due to the on-going transformation of the educational landscape and the growing emphasis on holistic development. The radical adventure comprises an integrated strategy that seeks to revolutionize conventional educational paradigms, cultivate student participation, and provide learners with the necessary skills like soft skills along with technical skills(Ahmad & Abd Rashid, 2011) for thriving in an emerging complexity and linked global landscape. India ought to dedicate foremost importance to inventions and research. Technological innovation serves as the fundamental basis for fostering creative teaching methods. The swift implementation of using technology into various fields and especially in education system adopting novel methods and techniques of pedagogical practices have led to notable advantages yielding productivity, efficiency (Yankson, 2024) and meaningful learning connected to business world. The robust usage of online resources and platforms have contributed to an equitable allocation of knowledge through the provision of personalized learning experiences that are conducive to the individual requirements of each student. This requires allocating resources towards research and development, creating a favourable climate for innovation, and providing support for entrepreneurship. The impact on business has been noteworthy, compelling the sector to seek cooperation from academics. However, government agencies, lawmakers, and educationists are acknowledging the concerning and unquestionable reality of a continuously growing number of unprepared and jobless young generations. This is primarily caused by the prevailing educational system. Therefore, it is crucial to implement thoughtful steps to enhance the effectiveness of education in fostering skill development. This will enable educated youth to become independent by improving their skills for employment. In the economic climate of today, it is crucial to build a productive partnership among business and academia. In today's contextual environment, collaborative innovation is the key requirement to thrive in this challenging world. Everyone is maximizing efficiency in innovative ideas, processes and output in their respective fields to obtain an edge in the cutthroat scenarios and also to foster enduring growth to have sustainability of their own firms (Hou, et al., 2019). There should be a smart move for business enterprises to team up academia, universities and research sectors in this realm of innovative world that is moving swiftly to the great heights of development of the society.

Over the last forty years, India has made systematic attempts to foster collaboration between academia and industry. According to (Perkmann, Neely, & Walsh, 2011), an increasing number of corporations are engaging in collaborations with academic institutions as an opportunity of achieving their objectives of gaining expertise and development. There is now a heightened level of enthusiasm among academics and policymakers on the impact of higher education on innovation in business. The renaissance of industry has been revolutionized since ages and profoundly impacted every sector of our lives in education, medical, interpersonal and even economic sectors. The transformation in industrial sector has been seen from steam engines to Artificial intelligence highlighting the weighted of adopting technology into our live style. The quality of living and boom of opportunities have emerged with significant benefits of efficiency in working conditions and bringing novel pedagogical practices focusing on personality including cognitive, affective and emotional domains. In the 21st century era, it is observable in the coming years that there is a skill deficit among graduates from reputed universities, hoping to serve the society to the fullest fails to fulfil the actual alignment outcomes with the real-world business sectors and entrepreneurship skills. The scientific and technological oriented world is demanding innovative strategies and pedagogic in our educational setup in order to generate productive outcomes for mapping the skills of academia and industry-based outcomes. The traditional practices in education process were limited to providing knowledge and teaching and ignored the actual mapping of outcomes with intended objectives which is a great concern for academia-industry sector. The outcome- based education has taken a shape in teaching-learning process in which active participation of learners is more focused than teachers delivering their knowledge and information with lecture based method. Teacher role has to be shifted from lecturer to facilitator and giving an autonomy to students with their own pace of their learning and even recognizing their skills, abilities, potentials and ultimate purpose by self-reflections and decision making. Alshare and Sewailem (2018) reveals that there is an imbalance of skills acquiring in the academia sector and professional competencies required in business world. Then even further stated that there is a huge discrepancy of skills in employers and educators. In this competitive world everyone is questing the academia and industry union for identifying and resolving the hands on issues (Zeidan & Bishnoi,2020). Fostering strategic coalition with academia, business enterprises and government sector needs to be strong enough to take position of propelling new heights of innovations and comprehensive development of the nation(Gandhi,2014). Bridging the gaps between academia and business world everyone is trying to ponder upon the innovative strategies to overcome the ground level problem(Nyemba, Mbohwa,Carter, 2021). Larkin(2014) suggested in adopting collaborative projects of academia and industry to connect the pieces and effective outcomes of internship programme. The acquiring knowledge in tertiary sectors in academia and applying skills in industries have to come on same wavelength in implementing quality- based education. The philosophy of The comprehensive document NEP-2020, having a great vision to revolutionize India not in the forms of developing industries and modernizing ourselves like other countries rather producing dynamic, vibrant and enlightened human minds developed holistically to face any challenges coming in his way in the near future. It has also emphasized on quality and sustainable education by improving the way of living and adjusting into the unpredictable circumstances. And the merely and ultimately hope of beacon is focusing on innovations and sustainable development goals as it is providing the glimpses of future oriented thinking and revamping our education system to enhance the job opportunities and even quality living of every person. SDG 4 discusses about quality and inclusivity in education because as well said quality education is the fundamental base of producing quality-oriented humans to sustain in their business life. And SDG 17 talks about international partnership and collaborations so it's important to understand collaborating internal domains as education, industry and government sectors in running the entire nation have to join hands to work together and flourish as a united family. Even NEP-2020 has suggested foreign industries and universities to collaborate with Indian world to develop the nation at large. UNESCO Report states "LEARNING TO BE" in 1997 which emphasized on the collaboration of education and society with cooperative minds to overcome the challenges of academia and industry and work for the betterment of the society.

Research Questions

1. Does the Triple Helix concept encourage innovation and entrepreneurship, which increases job prospects in developing industries?

2. How can the Triple Helix paradigm incorporate problem-based learning, flipped classrooms, and collaborative online learning to improve student learning, skill development, and potential?
3. How can Government support encourage academia-industry collaboration to improve gaps in our system.

Figure 1. Conceptual Framework of the Study

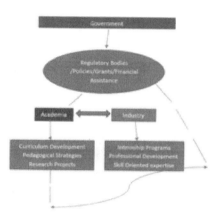

In the figure 1, the conceptual framework describes the role, contribution and goals of academia, industry and government as academia as information source contributing to curriculum framework and implementation of innovative strategies in teaching-learning process with enhanced outcomes. Industry is the joint venture for internship programs and skill-oriented hub in developing and applying knowledge and skills to meet the criteria of educational goals. And the government sector has the major role in regulating and facilitating policy framework in bringing innovations and modifications in education and industry sectors and even providing grants and funds for effective run of the innovative practices to ensure quality education, promote equitable access and foster economic development of the nation. The joint research projects of academia and industry mapping of educational outcomes with industry requirement and focusing on internship programs and skill-oriented courses. Government partnership with academia supports in funding and quality assurance with national bodies And collaborative efforts with industry addressing the skill gaps and working to address these hurdles and implement updated curricula and practical experiences. There is a continuous improvement and scalability of enhanced outcomes in education and business life.

Significance of the Study

A successful partnership between academics and business has plenty of room to positively impact the national economy and revolutionize the future of our nation, and even bringing prosperity in our nation. Higher education institutions and business are going to discover a way to work in collaboration to establish a collaborative relationship to accommodate each other's requirements and provide a significant and long-lasting positive and healthy scenario for everyone(Lee et al.,2020). In modern educational frameworks, the collaborative effort between educational institutions, industry, and society has evolved into in promoting innovative business approaches and cultivating an equitable staff through innovative and dynamic model-Triple Helix Model which can bring support best advantage to everyone in the nation by developing individual in holistic approach.

Research question 1: Does the Triple Helix concept encourage innovation and entrepreneurship, which increases job prospects in developing industries?

Figure 2. Triple Helix Model

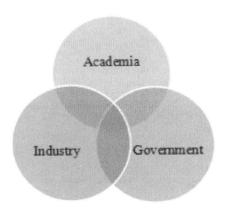

Triple Helix Model is expounded by (Etzkowitz & Leydesdorff, 2000)Henry Etzkowitz and Loet Leydesdorf in 1990. According to the Triple Helix model, innovative thinking is seen as the outcome of collaboration across three key domains: higher education, business, and government. This perspective of amalgamating three domains empowers an ecosystem of knowledge-based learners wherein innovation springs up from the ongoing interaction and synthesis of professional expertise spanning each of those spheres (Carayannis & Campbell, 2018) to give an overall picture of this model. The interdependent relationship and shared goals strengthening of these realms are evident, as each sphere contributes diverse resources, knowledge, and competence to the process of development. An increasing number of universities worldwide have implemented diverse entrepreneurship education programs with the aim of assisting students in developing an entrepreneurial outlook, acquiring both the theory and practice of business development, fostering novel methodologies for learning, and developing a sense of ownership that serves as an extremely helpful tool in professional pursuits (Sharma, 2023). It empowers the young minds to become vision oriented and nurture entrepreneurship skills with their conceptual background of the subjective knowledge which will make the academic resilient and divergent thinkers to face any setbacks of their lives and also transform their knocking threats into great opportunities. The model is absolutely focused on encouraging innovative practices and shaping them to productive members of the dynamic society. The research conducted by (Supriadi, 2024) found the substantial positive contribution of university, industry and government ratio as approximately 30%,40% and 30% respectively towards disseminating quality-based knowledge, fostering economic enlistment and supportive financial aids and policy framework through collaborating academics, business sector and government support with nation and international level. These leads to develop skills among graduating students required for the present business sector and improves job prospects specially in developing nations to resolve the standstill issues of university and industry.

Research question 2 How can the Triple Helix paradigm incorporate problem-based learning, flipped classrooms, and collaborative online learning to improve student learning, skill development, and potential?

Triple Helix model is an innovative model incorporating academics environment, business sector and government support is demanding a paradigm shift in educational pedagogies which will imbibe creativity, entrepreneurship skills, team work, communicative skills, risk enthusiastic, solution-finder and great leader. This can only be possible by changing the academic scenarios by bringing an innovative way of teaching -learning process.

A. Academia Based Innovations

The significance of implementing inventive pedagogical approaches, fostering robust collaborations between business and academics, and consistently adjusting to evolving labour requirements in the market is demonstrated through these outstanding approaches and case investigations. By assimilating knowledge from these illustrations, institutions may strengthen the magnitude, sensitivity, and potency of their programmes, equipping students for achievement in the contemporary job field of the 21st generation (Kamath & Kumar, 2023).

1. **Constructivist Approach:** It is a theoretical framework that believes students generate knowledge by actively engaging with, consuming literature, experiencing, or exchanging ideas with previous understanding. According to constructivist theory, the mission of educators is to figure out how their students would define knowledge, then help them sharpen their understanding and clarify things so that they can amend any oversights that occur at the beginning and improve the worth of the information they possess.

Figure 3. 5Es of Constructivism

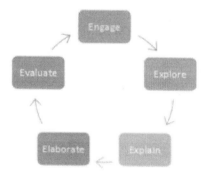

2. **Problem-Posing Model:** Problem-based learning (PBL) is an educational method that focuses on students and involves providing them with delicate, real-life problems (Varma & Malik, 2023). The goal is to encourage students to work together in an interactive way to find solutions. It helps in developing their critical thinking skills, developing divergent thinking and solving their own everyday problems and challenges with comprehensive approach which makes them independent.

Figure 4. Problem-Posing Model

3. **Blended Learning:** Blended learning is an approach to education that integrates virtual and traditional classroom settings to provide students with an additional adaptable, individualised, and productive educational experience. This methodology enables the provision of a wide range of educational opportunities, including online lectures, virtual classrooms, and multi-sensory interaction content, which serve as extra assistance components to conventional classroom instruction (Wu, Lee,, Li,, Huang,, & Huang,, 2023).

Figure 5. Blended Learning

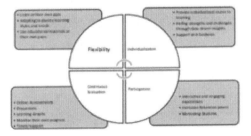

4. **Flipped Classroom Approach:** In the context of a flipped classroom, students acquire fundamental knowledge by engaging with prerecorded lectures or materials at their personalized speed beyond the classroom setting. Classroom time is subsequently dedicated for engaging interactions, training sessions and the practical implementation of ideas.

Figure 6. Flipped Classroom

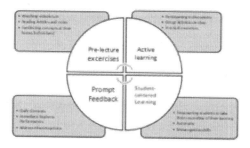

5. **Competency-based Learning:** The completion of predetermined time-based courses is not the primary goal of CBE; rather, it is the mastery of certain skills or competences by students. Students advance when they demonstrate that they have mastered the material, which enables a more individualized learning route.

Figure 7. Competency Based Model

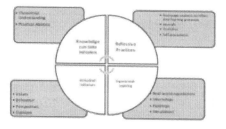

B. Industry Based Innovation

1. **Tech-enabled connectivity and advancement** The Role of Digital Resources in Facilitating Collaboration: A Broadening of Knowledge Horizons. Digital portals, conferences, and virtual conferences enable former students and corporate networking beyond physical boundaries (Ahmed, 2021).

2. **Sustainable Innovations** Sustainable innovations prioritize the development of alternatives that effectively meet present requirements while ensuring that generations yet to come may fulfill their own personal requirements without any compromise. The primary objective of these technologies is to mitigate environmental consequences, foster social accountability, and guarantee a sustainable economy.

3. **Learning Analytic and Large-scale Data:** Organizations monitor student habits, interests, and choices through the application of large-scale analytic of data. The use of learning analytic allows for the improvement of pedagogical plans, recognizing of children at risk, and adaptability of actions (Aithal & Maiya, 2023).

4. **Industry stakeholders** can enhance their collaborations, promote sharing of information, and spur entrepreneurship through the dissemination of industry-specific tools, research findings, and standards of excellence. The provision of resources for learning, heritage sites, and society-driven projects within the community as a whole assist in empowering individuals and cultivate a society which is more equitable and educated.

5. **Gateway to the World:** Envision a global classroom. Intercultural trading platforms, overseas educational programs, and worldwide partnerships offer learners worldwide perspectives and exposure to cultures.

6. **International Citizens, Local Effects:** These programs educate pupils for a rewarding career as well as accountable global citizenship through promoting international understanding and overcoming prejudices.
   - Incorporating these digital channels enables institutions to efficiently:
   - Promote the dissemination of knowledge and expertise to a broader demographic.
   - Facilitate collaboration and integration among academia, industry, and the community. Advocate for the cultivation of lifelong learning and foster intellectual involvement.
   - Develop a cooperative environment that promotes creativity and mutual exchange

Research question 3. How can Government support encourage academia-industry collaboration to improve gaps in our system?

C. Government-Based Innovations

1. National Education Policy-2020 has promoted **multidisciplinary approach** in our education system collaborating research institutes and internship programs in various industries to develop human capabilities in diverse nature. It aims to bridge the gap of compartmentalization of theoretical and practical aspects.

2. The government emphasizes the establishment of **Public-Private Partnerships** (PPPs) as a means to foster working relationships between public institutions and private businesses in the context of initiatives related to research and development. These collaborations harness the knowledge and skills of both industries to spark innovation.

3. The establishment of **entrepreneurial green spaces,** which serve as joint hubs for research institutes, universities, and business entities, is endorsed by the government. This promotes the exchange of knowledge and encourages collaborative research endeavours.

4. The process of **collaborative policymaking** entails engaging with several stakeholders, including individuals, corporations, non-governmental organizations (NGOs), and other relevant parties. This secures the inclusion of a wide range of viewpoints, resulting in regulations that are more thorough and efficient. The emergence of collaboration among agencies arises when multiple governments possess authorities that intersect with one another. Partnership facilitates improved interaction, mitigates redundant work, and results in the development of a more extensive strategy.

Findings and Discussions of the Study

Triple Helix model is useful in developed markets and emerging markets for academicians, business people, government and curriculum frame workers because its innovations and working collaborating rather than standalone spheres fosters flexibility and spirit of learning novel things. USA, Finland, South Korea and many other developed and developing countries have adopted this model (Supriadi et al., 2024) to develop their nation to the fullest and strengthen their nations to compete any odds in their way. The transitional experience occurred in Finland using this model was valuable and how its contribution was effective at global level becoming technology oriented and providing economic value towards its people and fostering innovations and conclusively developing the society and nation at large(Carayannis et al., 2012;Supriadi et al., 2024).

The Advantages of Collaboration and partnership are manifold:

The collaboration between partners facilitates the sharing of resources and expertise, hence enhancing the generation of innovative and efficient solutions.

1. Education Collaboration and Partnership:

Including the expertise of experts from the industry into the learning environment facilitates the embedding of practical skills and knowledge within the educational framework.

Multidisciplinary classroom practices have the potential to produce higher-quality and productive learning environments. Collaborative alliances with different institutions have the potential to enhance exchange between students programs and expand scholastic horizons.

The collaborative effort between educational institutions and research laboratories has the potential to expedite scientific advancement and yield revolutionary findings in the realm of research and innovation.

2. Corporate Teamwork & Partnership:

Working alongside with other organisations can enhance inventions simply utilising their experience, resources, and customer base. The onset of this phenomenon has the potential to quicken creativity and enhance the efficacy of new products new arrivals.

The process of associating with firms that compliment one's own operations serves to broaden one's customer reach and enhance avenues for promotion. Integrated marketing and shared branding can yield significant results. Collaboration with suppliers in supply chain management guarantees a dependable movement of materials and minimises expenses. In addition, partnerships have the potential to foster the adoption of ethical and environmentally conscious sourcing techniques.

3. Government Collaboration:

Enhanced Efficiency and Cost-Effectiveness: Collaboration prevents redundant work and enables more optimal use of resources.

Improved Service Delivery: Through collaborative efforts, governmental entities may offer citizens more extensive and adaptable services.

Enhanced invention: The act of collaborating cultivates an environment that promotes invention, hence resulting in superior resolutions for intricate problems.

Collaborative governance facilitates the cultivation of inclusive and transparency, hence engendering heightened levels of public confidence.

Enhanced Sustainability: Collaboration fosters enduring solutions by taking into account varied viewpoints and ensuring the participation of all stakeholders.

METHODOLOGY

The study uses exploratory research in the methodology. The data is accumulated through search terms as Academic Collaborations, industry-oriented skills and government schemes and practices, innovative pedagogies, Triple Helix Model, from Google, Google Scholar, ERIC, Scopus, Web of Sciences and reputed Journals and Semantic Scholar and reviewed using various research structures to discover, looked into, and interpreted innovations in the educational sector. We gathered material from secondary sources such as publications, books, government reports, journals, and working papers. We analyzed secondary data using content analysis. The exclusion and inclusion criteria were employed to just take keywords and research publication related to education fields. The related literature surveyed the huge impact of integrated model and multidisciplinary approaches rather than watertight compartments in education and business world for 21st century learners and teachers.

Future Directions and Limitations of the Study

As we all have faced unprecedented COVID-19 pandemic affected our lives horribly but only technology was the boon which made our lives on the optimal track and we lived virtually and connected with one another. Virtual collaboration was observable in academia and industry focusing on new ways of teaching and learning synchronous and asynchronous which we all adapted it to slowly and still it is in usage because of major advantages students received through online learning.

Collaborative learning is beneficial mot merely in their learning knowledge construction but even in their interpersonal skills covering affective domain. It will serve the person in the industry lives where team works and collaborative working requirement is top most skills needed to run the vision of the business world.

The Triple Helix model is the interconnection model of academia, industry and government which are considered independent bodies have to follow interdisciplinary approach and work collaboratively to draw out the best in each and every student graduating and hoping for the best opportunities in the business sector with the complete support from government sectors. And if any of the sphere doesn't work judiciously and function properly then we cannot hope for the best and there will be wastage of introducing innovative pedagogic and strategies.

To implement this collaboration partnership and innovative way of thinking and implementing a paradigm shift in academia-industry sector, availability of funds has to be taken a great concern because without financial assistance it couldn't be possible.

Bridging the gaps between academia and industry certain regulatory bodies under government area have to be very much supportive to transform the optimal and accurate curriculum and adequate facilities, opportunities to develop their entire personality holistically.

The 21st century in academia and higher universities is looking for fast- forward thinking including problem thinking, critical analyzing, self-assessing and reflecting and emotional intelligence and adapting to new challenges of our lives. The education domain is adopting interdisciplinary and multidisciplinary approaches as stated in NEP-2020 to bring flexibility, academic excellence, autonomy and quality in academia and industry.

Connecting the knowledge divide between the two sectors has become essential for preparing for the fourth century of manufacturing and the forthcoming fifth era of industrialization, which is projected to occur by 2030. Important considerations include technology, classroom instruction, and legislation (Garbie,2017).

Various skills development programs as Continuing Professional Developmental (CPD), Skills Development and Training(SDT),Professional Development Program(PDP) to hone their skills.

The research-oriented approach has been emphasized in National education Policy-2020 in India to tackle the challenging issues and update innovative ways as educationist and industrialist to bring sustainability and foster development of the nation.

There are many possible ways of dealing and bridging the discrepancy of academia and industry, so all three bodies have to look for positive outcomes and optimistic outlook to deal the unprecedented challenges.

To bridge the gaps of academia and industry is very vast but is not impossible if everyone puts their trivial contribution to implement the current needs of the hour.

The Digital ecosystem and fourth industrial revolution have supported people in getting various jobs placements and learning accessible ways of living their quality lives.

Commercialization is a key factor in strengthening the sector of knowledge by producing prosperity through collaboration between industry and academia. precisely a result, higher education institutions have evolved into entrepreneurial organizations which encourage the industrialization of research outcomes and expertise for financial development and sustainability(Jamail et al., 2015).

CONCLUSION

As long as organizations and stakeholders keep innovating and adapting to meet the ever-evolving needs of learners and employment opportunities, vocational education and training has bright future possibilities in the twenty-first century. Further education and training institutions can play an instrumental part in producing the forthcoming workforce and advancing equitable social and economic growth by adopting novel educational approaches, encouraging resilient industry-academia collaborations, establishing essential abilities, and focusing on issues with technological advances, competencies inequalities, equity, and continuous educational opportunities.

REFERENCES

Ahmad, M. F. B., & Abd Rashid, K. A. (2011). Lecturers' Industrial Attachment Programme to increase Lecturers' Soft Skill and Technological Competencies for Global Stability and Security. *Journal of Sustainable Development*, 4(1), 281.

Ahmed, M. M. (2021). ICT-enhanced instruction in COVID-19 lockdown: A conceptual paper. *International Journal of Case Studies in BusinessIT and Education*, 5(2), 386–398.

Aithal, P., & Maiya, A. K. (2023). Innovations in Higher Education Industry—Shaping the Future. *International Journal of Case Studies in Business, IT, and Education*, 7(4), 283–311. 10.47992/IJCS-BE.2581.6942.0321

Akhtar, F., & Malik, A. (2023). Education and Skills Development: Empowering Youth for Pakistan's Future Workforce. *Pakistan Research Letter, 1*(3), 151-159.

Alshare, K., & Sewailem, M. F. (2018). A gap analysis of business students' skills in the 21st century: A case study of Qatar. *Academy of Educational Leadership Journal*, 22(1), 1–22.

Carayannis, E. G., & Campbell, D. F. (2018). *Smart quintuple helix innovation systems: How social ecology and environmental protection are driving innovation, sustainable development and economic growth*. Springer.

Etzkowitz, H., & Leydesdorff, L. (2000). Leydesdorff, L. The triple helix: An evolutionary model of innovations. *Research Policy*, 29(2), 243–255. 10.1016/S0048-7333(99)00063-3

Gandhi, M. M. (2014). Industry-academia collaboration in India: Recent initiatives, issues, challenges, opportunities and strategies. *The Business & Management Review*, 5(2), 45.

Garbie, I. (2017). Identifying challenges facing manufacturing enterprises toward implementing sustainability in newly industrialized countries. *Journal of Manufacturing Technology Management*, 28(7), 928–960. 10.1108/JMTM-02-2017-0025

Hou, B., Hong, J., Wang, H., & Zhou, C. (2019). Academia-industry collaboration, government funding and innovation efficiency in Chinese industrial enterprises. *Technology Analysis and Strategic Management*, 31(6), 692–706. 10.1080/09537325.2018.1543868

Jamil, F., Ismail, K., & Mahmood, N. (2015). A review of commercialization tools: University incubators and technology parks. *International Journal of Economics and Financial Issues*, 5(Special Issue), 223–228.

Kamath, M., & Kumar, A. (2023). 7 E's of Constructivism in E-learning Skills of University Faculty. (n.d.). International Journal of Case Studies in Business. *IT and Education*, 7(1), 62–73.

Larkin, M. (2014). *Building successful partnerships between academia and industry*. Elsevierconnect.

Lee, C., Lee, D., & Sho, M. (2020). Effect of efficient triple-helix collaboration on organizations based on their stage of growth. *Journal of Engineering and Technology Management*, 58, 101604. 10.1016/j.jengtecman.2020.101604

Nyemba, W. R., Mbohwa, C., & Carter, K. F. (2021). *Bridging the Academia Industry Divide: Innovation and Industrialisation Perspective Using Systems Thinking Research in Sub-Saharan Africa.* Springer. 10.1007/978-3-030-70493-3

Perkmann, M., Neely, A., & Walsh, K. (2011). How should firms evaluate success in university–industry alliances? A performance measurement system. *R & D Management*, 41(2), 202–216. 10.1111/j.1467 -9310.2011.00637.x

Sharma, P. (2023). Industry-Academia Collaboration in India: Recent Initiatives, Issues, Challenges, Opportunities and Strategies. *Vidhyayana-An International Multidisciplinary Peer-Reviewed E-Journal*, 8(s16), 888–909.

Supriadi, A., Permana, I., Afandi, D. R., Arisondha, E., & Kusumaningsih, A. (2024). The Triple Helix Model: University-Industry-Government Collaboration and Its Role in Smes Innovation and Development. *International Journal of Economic Literature*, 2(1), 75–90.

Varma, C., & Malik, S. (2023). *TVET in the 21st Century: A Focus on Innovative Teaching and Competency Indicators.* IntechOpen.

Wu, T.-T., Lee, H.-Y., Li, P.-H., Huang, C.-N., & Huang, Y.-M. (2023). Promoting Self-Regulation Progress and Knowledge Construction in Blended Learning via ChatGPT-Based Learning Aid. *Journal of Educational Computing Research*, 61(8), 3–31. 10.1177/07356331231191125

Yankson, B., Berkoh, E., Hussein, M., & Dadson, Y. (2024). The Role of Industry-Academia Partnerships Can Play in Cybersecurity: Exploring Collaborative Approaches to Address Cybercrime. In *International Conference on Cyber Warfare and Security* (Vol. 19, No. 1, pp. 26-33). 10.34190/iccws.19.1.2169

Zeidan, S., & Bishnoi, M. M. (2020). An effective framework for bridging the gap between industry and academia. *International Journal on Emerging Technologies*, 11(3), 454–461. https://www.education .gov.in/nep/about-nep

Chapter 5
The Whispers in the Halls:
Unveiling the Moderating Effect of Employee Reviews on Organization Selection

Ruturaj Baber
Christ University, Bengaluru, India

Prerna Baber
Jiwaji University, Gwalior, India

Chanda Gulati
Prestige Institute of Management and Research, Gwalior, India

Francesca Di Virgilio
https://orcid.org/0000-0001-6017-9506
University of Molise, Italy

ABSTRACT

Online employee reviews, a hallmark of the digital age, significantly shape organizational image and influence job seeker choices. This research explores how the sentiment (positive or negative) of information in these reviews moderates how job seekers perceive organizations and make decisions during the selection process. By analyzing data from 213 Indian academics, the study aims to understand how job seekers utilize review information and uncover how the reviews' presence and sentiment affect the relationship between organizational image and candidate choices. This research contributes valuable insights into the complex interplay between employer brand, online feedback, and talent acquisition in the digital age, informing strategic recruitment practices and enhancing understanding of contemporary talent acquisition strategies.

DOI: 10.4018/979-8-3693-3096-8.ch005

1. INTRODUCTION

In the contemporary digital age, the transparency and interconnectedness facilitated by the internet have given rise to a phenomenon that profoundly influences the employer-employee relationship—the expression of employees' perceptions through online reviews. With the use of the internet, employees are far more inclined to share their thoughts, feelings, and workplace experiences on their jobs on a several online forums (El said, 2020; Mudambi & Schuff). Along with providing a platform for employees to voice their opinions, ratings like these also have significant impact on companies, adding threads to the complex web of perceptions around employers (Ozcan & Elci, 2020). The impression that a company has in the minds of both present and prospective workers is reflected in its employer brand image. It is a complex concept that is shaped by multiple elements, such as workplace culture, leadership, benefits, and career growth chances. The perspective of employees is a vital factor in shaping the employer brand image in this complex interaction.

The objective of this research is to explore the complex relationship between employees' perceptions, employer brand image, and the significant influence of online review valence as a moderator. Organizations trying to manage their reputations in a world that is becoming more transparent and linked must take great care to understand how employees' voices appear in the digital sphere and how it affects employer brand image (Martin et al., 2011). The presence of online review valence brings an interesting aspect to this study, that framed as the moderator. Favourable evaluations can enhance the positive elements of the employer's brand image, serving as a catalyst for attracting highly skilled individuals and cultivating a positive organizational culture (Sparks & Browning, 2011; Su et al., 2021). In contrast, unfavourable reviews have the ability to damage the reputation of the brand, resulting in difficulties in attracting and retaining employees, as well as hindering overall organizational achievements (Ahmad et al., 2019; Hoppe, 2018).

Our goal is to provide valuable insights that can help organizations navigate the changing landscape of employer-employee relationships in the digital age. This research study will focus on understanding the relationship between employees' perception, employer brand image, and the moderating influence of review valence. Organizations may proactively manage their online presence, strengthen their employer brand, and create good workplaces for current and potential employees by comprehending the complicated nature of these conversations.

2. LITERATURE REVIEW AND DEVELOPMENT OF HYPOTHESES

2.1 Employer Brand Image and Employee Perception

When people think about the employer brand, they probably picture all the financial, practical, and psychological advantages that come with working for that company. According to Backhaus and Tikoo (2004), the concept of brand image, as "what makes one business different from another". Furthermore, it represents the values associated with the workplace by employees, resulting in a high-quality employment experience where individuals feel secure and establish a close bond with their employer (Martin et al., 2011). Organizations that build an effective employer brand image observe greater levels of employee commitment and retention, which ultimately results in enhanced job performance (Hoppe, 2018). The association between the employer's brand image and the perceptions of employees plays an essential role in determining the ability of an organization to attract and retain highly skilled individuals. A positive employer brand image, that encompasses workplace culture, leadership style, and organizational principles and values, may significantly enhance the overall attractiveness of an organization to potential employees (Nguyen & Nguyen, 2022). An employer brand image that is appealing effectively conveys a sincere and authentic impression, establishing a strong bond with individuals who share the same values and vision as the organization (Ek Styvén et al., 2022; Baber et al., 2017). Furthermore, a favourable employer brand image promotes work satisfaction, employee engagement, and loyalty, which influences directly retention rates. Ahmad et al., (2019), explained that employees that have a positive perception of their organization are more likely to retained, resulting in a stable and motivated employee. In contrast, an adverse or inconsistent employer brand image may dissuade potential candidates and raise turnover rates, as unsatisfied employees seek alternative options. In summary, the relationship between employer brand image and employee perceptions is crucial in attracting and retaining a bright and devoted team, eventually determining an organization's long-term performance (Ahmad et al., 2019; Baber et al., 2023a; Nguyen & Nguyen, 2022; Sparks & Browning, 2011). On the basis of above discussion following hypothesis is proposed:

H$_1$: *There is a significant relationship between employer brand image and employee perception.*

2.2 Employees' Online Review Valence as a Moderator

Online reviews are defined by Mudambi and Schuff (2010) as evaluations that are generated by peers and posted on different websites affiliated with third parties or organizations. Users are provided with the opportunity to express their consumption experiences in two formats: self-authored reflections and comparative evaluations that may incorporate visual aids such as emoticons or numerical star ratings. Sparks and Browning (2011) postulate that favourable feedback generally signifies a gratifying user experience, while unfavourable reviews communicate an unsatisfactory user journey. The significance of review valence emerges as a significant aspect in moderating the complex relationship between employer brand image and employee perception. Connelly & McAbee (2024), described review valence, encompassing the positivity or negativity of online feedback, serves as a lens through which employees interpret the employer brand. Favourable reviews amplify the beneficial elements of the employer's brand, strengthening a positive perception among employees. In contrast, unfavourable reviews have the ability to magnify perceived weaknesses, which could diminish employee impressions (Piercy & Carr, 2020; Su et al., 2021). El-Said (2020), elaborated the valence of online reviews serves as a moderator, impacting the intensity and orientation of the association between employer brand image and employee impression. Comprehending this moderation impact is crucial for firms seeking to strategically manage their online reputation and foster a favourable perception among their workforce (El-Said, 2020; Mudambi & Schuff, 2010; Su et al., 2021). On the basis of above discussion following hypothesis is proposed:

H$_2$: *Online reviews moderate relationship between employer brand image and employee perception.*

Figure 1. Proposed Research Model:

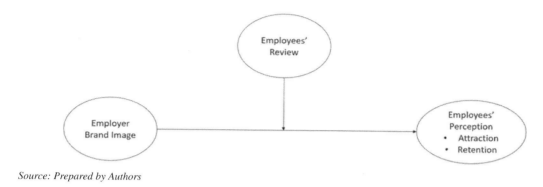

Source: Prepared by Authors

3. RESEARCH METHODOLOGY

3.1 Source of instrument

The responses from the respondent were collected adopting a standardized questionnaire developed previously. The three variables were examined (refer table one). Firstly, employer brand image was measured using scale developed by Ozcan & Elci (2020). The second variable, review valance was measured using scale developed by El-Said (2020). Finally, employees' perception was measured using instrument developed by Ahmad et al. (2020).

Table 1. Source of Instrument

Construct	Source	Items
Employer Brand Image	Adapted Ozcan & Elci (2020)	EB1. I'm in a good relationship with my superiors in the institution where I'm working.
		EB2. In the institution where I'm working, the managers care about the employees.
		EB3. In the institution where I'm working, the managers are sincere with the employees.
		EB4. Competent employees are selected for this institution
Review Valence	Adapted El-Said (2020)	PRV1. I pay more attentions to positive reviews
		PRV2. Positive reviews are of more values
		PRV3. I pay more attentions to those organisations which have larger volume of positive reviews
		NRV1. An abundance of positive reviews will make you dislike an organisation
		NRV2. Negative reviews will terminate your joining intentions
		NRV3. The volume of negative reviews is important

continued on following page

Table 1. Continued

Construct	Source	Items
Employees' Perception (Employee Attention Employee Retention)	Ahmad et al. (2020)	EA1. The organization provides good service conditions to their employees.
		EA2. I find the organization a means of career development.
		EA3. Guiding principles of the organization are satisfactory
		EA4. Organization offers good rewards and opportunities
		EA5. Behavior of the organization toward employees is ethical
		EA6. The organizations offers quality services
		EA7. The information provided by us to the organization is kept confidential
		EA8. Organization also carries out activities for the benefit of society at large
		ER1. There are lot of opportunities for my career growth in this organization
		ER2. The organization provides us with job security
		ER3. The image of the organization is satisfactory
		ER4. The organization recognizes our performances
		ER5. The organization has good quality management practices
		ER6. The organization provides equal opportunities to all employees

Compiled by authors

3.2 Data Collection

A non-probability purposive sampling method was employed to recruit 213 employees from IT firms. Data collection occurred during December 2023 using a standardized online survey. The sample of the study were academicians belonging to higher education in India. The data were collected from three major cities in India, namely, Jaipur, New Delhi, and Nagpur. This approach allowed for the targeted recruitment of relevant participants while acknowledging the inherent limitations of non-probability sampling in generalizability. The collected data was analyzed using CB-SEM to answer the research questions outlined in this study.

4. DATA ANALYSIS

Table 2 presents the demographic data of the 213 participants in our study. The majority of respondents were male (61.5%) and younger than 25 years old (49.8%). Nearly equal proportions held graduate (39%), postgraduate (30.5%), and doctoral (30.5%) degrees. In terms of experience, almost half (47.4%) had less than 5 years, while the remaining participants were split between 6-10 years (24.9%) and 11 or more years (27.7%).

Table 2. Demographic Profile of respondent

Measures		Frequency	Percentage
Gender	**Male**	**131**	**61.5**
	Female	82	38.5
Age	Less than 25 years	106	49.8
	26 years – 45 years	48	22.5
	46 years and above	59	27.7
Level of Education	Graduate	83	39.0
	Post Graduate	65	30.5
	Doctorate	65	30.5
Experience	Less than 5 years	101	47.4
	6 to 10 years	53	24.9
	11 years and above	59	27.7

n =213
Source: Calculated using IBM SPSS 28.0

Table 3 summarizes the average scores and variability of the three key variables in our study. The average employer brand image score was 16.48, with a standard deviation of 3.12. Employee review valance had an average score of 31.94 and a standard deviation of 4.64. Finally, employees' perception received an average score of 70.68, with a standard deviation of 10.88. However, it is crucial to note that interpreting the exact meaning of these values requires understanding the specific scales used to measure each variable.

Table 3. Mean and Standard Deviation

	$\bar{x}$	σ
Employer Brand Image	16.4789	3.12413
Employee Review Valance	31.9437	4.64460
Employees' Perception	70.6761	10.88374

Source: Calculated using IBM SPSS 28.0

Table 4. Measurement of Variables

Construct	Items	Cronbach Alpha	EFA	CFA
EBI	EBI1		0.798	0.82
	EBI2	0.756	0.798	0.82
	EBI3		0.713	0.735

continued on following page

Table 4. Continued

Construct	Items	Cronbach Alpha	EFA	CFA
RV	PRV1	0.866	.853	0.875
	PRV2		.852	0.874
	PRV3		.822	0.844
	NRV1		.891	0.913
	NRV2		.864	0.886
	NRV3		.744	0.766
EP	EA1	0.810	.850	0.872
	EA2		.816	0.838
	EA3		.758	0.78
	EA4		.756	0.778
	EA5		.723	0.745
	EA6		.665	0.687
	EA7		.852	0.874
	EA8		.660	0.682
	ER1		.903	0.925
	ER2		.901	0.923
	ER3		0.900	0.922
	ER4		0.887	0.909
	ER5		0.713	0.735
	ER6		0.738	0.716

Source: Calculated using IBM SPSS 28.0

Table 4 details the measurement of our key constructs: Employer Brand Image (EBI), Review Valance (RV), and Employee Perception (EP). Each construct is measured by several items, and their reliability and validity were assessed using Cronbach's Alpha, Exploratory Factor Analysis (EFA), and Confirmatory Factor Analysis (CFA). The results indicate good internal consistency (Cronbach's Alpha above 0.7) and construct validity (good EFA/CFA scores) for most items within EBI (EBI1: Alpha = 0.756, EFA = 0.798, CFA = 0.82) and RV (PRV1: Alpha = 0.866, EFA = 0.853, CFA = 0.875). However, some items in EP, particularly EA5 (Alpha = 0.723, EFA = 0.745, CFA = 0.745), EA6 (Alpha = 0.665, EFA = 0.687, CFA = 0.687), EA8 (Alpha = 0.660, EFA = 0.682, CFA = 0.682), ER5 (Alpha = 0.713, EFA = 0.735, CFA = 0.735), and ER6 (Alpha = 0.738, EFA = 0.716, CFA = 0.716).

Table 5. Construct and Discriminant Validity

	CR	AVE	EBI	RV	EP
EBI	0.777	0.818			
RV	0.789	0.863	0.698		
EP	0.799	0.838	0.611	0.702	

Source: Calculated by Authors

Table 5 assesses the validity of our constructs. Composite Reliability (CR) values for all constructs (EBI = 0.777, RV = 0.789, EP = 0.799) exceed 0.7, indicating good internal consistency. Additionally, Average Variance Extracted (AVE) values (EBI = 0.818, RV = 0.863, EP = 0.838) are all above 0.5, demonstrating that the measures capture a substantial amount of variance in their respective constructs. Furthermore, the off-diagonal elements, representing correlations between the constructs, are all lower than the square root of the AVE of their corresponding constructs (e.g., EBI-RV = 0.698, square root of EBI's AVE = 0.905), suggesting good discriminant validity and supporting the conclusion that the measures capture distinct concepts.

Table 6. Hetrotrait and MonoTrait (HTMT) RATIO

	EBI	RV	EP
EBI			
RV	0.846		
EP	0.816	0.849	

Source: Calculated by Authors

The HTMT (Heterotrait-Monotrait) ratio table further strengthens the evidence for distinct constructs in our study. All HTMT values (EBI-RV = 0.846, EBI-EP = 0.816, RV-EP = 0.849) fall below the recommended threshold of 0.85, indicating good discriminant validity (refer table 6). This suggests that Employer Brand Image, Review Valance, and Employee Perception are captured by their respective measures as distinct concepts, not simply different facets of the same underlying construct. This bolsters the confidence in our findings and their interpretation regarding the relationships between these constructs.

Table 7. Hypotheses Testing

Hypothesis	Path			Estimate	P-Value	Status
H$_1$	**EBI**	**<-**	**EP**	**0.295**	**0.004**	**Supported**
H$_2$	EBI*RV	<-	EP	0.299	0.000	Supported

r^2 (EP = 0.198)
r^2(EP=0.220)

Source: Calculated using IBM AMOS 28.0

The results support H$_1$. There is a positive and statistically significant relationship between Employer Brand Image (EBI) and Employee Perception (EP). This means that employees tend to have more positive perceptions of their workplace when they have a stronger positive perception of their employer's brand image. The estimate of 0.295 suggests a moderate-strength relationship. The results indicate support for H$_2$. There is a statistically significant interaction effect between Employer Brand Image (EBI) and Review Valance (RV) on Employee Perception (EP). This suggests that the relationship between EBI and EP is moderated by RV. The table 7 reports the R-squared (r^2) values for the model predicting EP. These values (0.198 and 0.220) indicate that the model explains approximately 19.8% to 22% of the variance in EP directly and with moderating influence of review valance.

6. DISCUSSION AND IMPLICATIONS

The acceptance of the H_1 positing a direct relationship between employer brand image and employee perception, specifically in terms of attraction and retention, underlines the significance of a positive employer brand image in shaping employees' views. This finding aligns with the existing literature that emphasizes the impact of a favourable employer brand image on attracting high-quality talent and retaining valuable employees (Ahmad et al., 2019; Martin et al., 2011; Nguyen & Nguyen, 2022). A positive employer brand image, encapsulating aspects such as workplace culture, values, and benefits, evidently contributes to an enhanced perception among employees (Hoppe, 2018). This positive perception, in turn, influences the organization's ability to attract new talent by presenting a compelling image and fosters retention by creating a sense of belonging and job satisfaction (Piercy & Carr, 2020). The acceptance of this hypothesis highlights the pivotal role of employer branding strategies in not only shaping the perceptions but also in nurturing a positive internal environment conducive to attracting and retaining a skilled and committed workforce (Venkat et al., 2023). These findings have practical implications for organizations aiming to optimize their employer branding efforts to create a positive impact on employee perception, attraction, and retention.

This research study's results strongly support H2 by demonstrating a significant moderating impact of online reviews on the association between employer brand image and employee perception. The findings of this research aligned with the previous studies (El-Said, 2020; Mudambi & Schuff, 2010; Su et al., 2021) highlight the significance of considering the online review context as a dynamic element that affects how employees perceive and react to their organization's employer brand. Based on the findings of our research, it appears that organizations that possess a favourable employer brand image and positive online reviews may experience even more substantial advantages (Stockman et al., 2020). Oliveira & Ferreira (2021), examined that the positive reviews can serve as a reinforcement mechanism, validating the positive aspects of the employer brand and contributing to a more favourable employee perception. On the other hand, the study results indicate that unfavourable online reviews may negatively impact on the relationship between strong employer brand image and employee perception (Piercy & Carr 2020; Sparks & Browing, 2011). Negative comments may cause employees to question the credibility of the company's positive reputation (Kashive et al., 2020). Organizations must address negative feedback online to protect their internet reputation and maintain a positive image among employees.

7. MANAGERIAL IMPLICATIONS

For effective strategic brand management, it is crucial to proactively oversee a company's online presence on review platforms. Responding quickly to employee reviews shows that you care about their feedback and show that your company is attentive to their needs. A pleasant impression is helped by strategic employer branding efforts that are in line with the intended image. To prevent problems from becoming public knowledge online, it is helpful to set up official channels for internal feedback. Culture of open discourse can be fostered through training employees on effective feedback and communication (Baber et al., 2023b). Consistently replying to evaluations on the internet, whether favourable or unfavourable, shows professionalism and shows that you're dedicated to getting better. Organizations may successfully navigate the ever-changing world of online employee reviews by utilizing these tactics. This will help shape a favourable picture of the employer brand and encourage a supportive culture in the workplace.

8. THEORETICAL IMPLICATIONS

This study adds to our theoretical knowledge of the intricate connection between valence of review, employer brand image, and employees' online evaluations of their work experience. The study contributes to the fields of organizational behaviour, human resource management, and online reputation management by delving into these multifaceted interactions. The results can enrich existing theories and help to enhance hypotheses on employee views, company reputation, and digital platforms' impact on employer-employee relationships. This theoretical investigation contributes to a more complete comprehension of how organizations can make effective use of internet platforms to manage their reputations and foster favorable perceptions of their employer brand. The research adds to the growing body of organizational theory by providing theoretical insights into the relationship between employees' online expressions, the formation of employer brand images, and the moderating influence of review valence. It highlights the importance of taking a comprehensive approach to understanding this complex interaction.

9. FUTURE RESEARCH AND LIMITATIONS

Although this work has provided helpful insights, it is important to acknowledge its limits. The conclusions may be contingent on the setting, as industry and cultural factors could impact the dynamics under investigation. Extrapolating the findings to other contexts should be done carefully. Furthermore, the rapid evolution of online platforms and communication patterns presents a problem in terms of the temporal dynamics of the digital landscape. A snapshot of the study may not capture the ongoing changes in their entirety. Lastly, the interpretation of review valence may be subject to bias due to the subjective nature of sentiment analysis. The outcomes might be influenced by varying interpretations provided by individuals or sentiment analysis tools. Finally, although the study recognizes the moderating influence of review valence, it did not thoroughly investigate other potential moderators, therefore providing an opportunity for future research to go deeper into this area. These constraints present prospects for further enhancement and expansion in future research endeavours.

10. CONCLUSION

The complex interplay between employees' online reviews, employer brand perception, and the moderating effect of review valence is explored in this study. Offering a detailed grasp of how digital expressions impact employer-employee interactions. Recognizing the significance of online review valence as a moderator, the research expands existing models, providing a deeper insight into the contingencies influencing the impact of employee sentiments on organizational reputation. This study provides useful insights that can help scholars and practitioners navigate the intricacies of the modern employer-employee relationship, eventually promoting favourable organizational reputations and strong employer brand images in this digital era.

REFERENCES

Ahmad, A., Khan, M. N., & Haque, M. A. (2019). Employer branding aids in enhancing employee attraction and retention. *Journal of Asia-Pacific Business*, 21(1), 27–38. 10.1080/10599231.2020.1708231

Baber, P., Baber, R., & Di Virgilio, F. (2023a). Exploring the relationship between workplace spirituality, spiritual survival and innovative work behavior among healthcare professionals. *International Journal of Healthcare Management*, 1–12. 10.1080/20479700.2023.2199555

Baber, R., Baber, P., & Sanyal, A. (2023b). Power and Politics: A Case of Hotel Amada. *FIIB Business Review*, 12(3), 238–242. 10.1177/23197145221139687

Baber, R., Upadhyay, Y., & Kaurav, R. P. S. (2017). Individuals' Motivation for Joining a Social Group: Examining Their Homogeneity. *Asia-Pacific Journal of Management Research and Innovation*, 13(1-2), 43–51. 10.1177/2319510X18760616

Backhaus, K., & Tikoo, S. (2004). Conceptualizing and researching employer branding. *Career Development International*, 9(5), 501–517. 10.1108/13620430410550754

Connelly, B. S., & McAbee, S. T. (2024). Reputations at work: Origins and outcomes of shared person perceptions. *Annual Review of Organizational Psychology and Organizational Behavior*, 11(1), 251–278. 10.1146/annurev-orgpsych-110721-022320

Ek Styvén, M., Näppä, A., Mariani, M., & Nataraajan, R. (2022). Employee perceptions of employers' creativity and innovation: Implications for employer attractiveness and branding in tourism and hospitality. *Journal of Business Research*, 141, 290–298. 10.1016/j.jbusres.2021.12.038

El-Said, O. A. (2020). Impact of online reviews on hotel booking intention: The moderating role of brand image, star category, and price. *Tourism Management Perspectives*, 33, 100604. 10.1016/j.tmp.2019.100604

Hoppe, D. (2018). Linking employer branding and internal branding: Establishing perceived employer brand image as an antecedent of favourable employee brand attitudes and behaviours. *Journal of Product &amp. Journal of Product and Brand Management*, 27(4), 452–467. 10.1108/JPBM-12-2016-1374

Kashive, N., Khanna, V. T., & Bharthi, M. N. (2020). Employer branding through crowdsourcing: Understanding the sentiments of employees. *Journal of Indian Business Research*, 12(1), 93–111. 10.1108/JIBR-09-2019-0276

Martin, G., Gollan, P. J., & Grigg, K. (2011). Is there a bigger and better future for employer branding? Facing up to innovation, corporate reputations and wicked problems in SHRM. *International Journal of Human Resource Management*, 22(17), 3618–3637. 10.1080/09585192.2011.560880

Mudambi & Schuff. (2010). Research note: What makes a helpful online review? A study of customer reviews on amazon.com. *MIS Quarterly, 34*(1), 185. 10.2307/20721420

Nguyen, H. M., & Nguyen, L. V. (2022). Employer attractiveness, employee engagement and employee performance. *International Journal of Productivity and Performance Management*, 72(10), 2859–2881. 10.1108/IJPPM-04-2021-0232

Oliveira, M., Proença, T., & Ferreira, M. R. (2021). Do corporate volunteering programs and perceptions of corporate morality impact perceived employer attractiveness? *Social Responsibility Journal*, 18(7), 1229–1250. 10.1108/SRJ-03-2021-0109

Özcan, F., & Elçi, M. (2020). Employees' perception of CSR affecting employer brand, brand image, and corporate reputation. *SAGE Open*, 10(4). 10.1177/2158244020972372

Piercy, C. W., & Carr, C. T. (2020). Employer reviews may say as much about the employee as they do the employer: Online disclosures, organizational attachments, and unethical behavior. *Journal of Applied Communication Research*, 48(5), 577–597. 10.1080/00909882.2020.1812692

Sparks, B. A., & Browning, V. (2011). The impact of online reviews on hotel booking intentions and perception of trust. *Tourism Management*, 32(6), 1310–1323. 10.1016/j.tourman.2010.12.011

Stockman, S., Van Hoye, G., & da Motta Veiga, S. (2020). Negative word-of-mouth and applicant attraction: The role of employer brand equity. *Journal of Vocational Behavior*, 118, 103368. 10.1016/j.jvb.2019.103368

Su, L., Yang, Q., Swanson, S. R., & Chen, N. C. (2021). The impact of online reviews on destination trust and travel intention: The moderating role of online review trustworthiness. *Journal of Vacation Marketing*, 28(4), 406–423. 10.1177/13567667211063207

Venkat, M. V. V., Khan, S. R. K., Gorkhe, M. D., Reddy, M. K. S., & Rao, S. P. (2023). Fostering Talent Stability: A Study on Evaluating the Influence of Competency Management on Employee Retention in the Automotive Industry. *Remittances Review, 8*(4).

Chapter 6
Unveiling the Future:
AI Influencers and Ethical Consumerism – A Casa Theory and Theory of Planned Behaviour Exploration

Amarjit Kaur Passi
Sri Aurobindo College of Commerce and Management, India

Pooja Mehta
Sri Aurobindo College of Commerce and Management, India

Rajinder Kaur
Chandigarh University, Mohali, India

Sandeep Singh
Punjabi University, Patiala, India

ABSTRACT

This study explores how AI influencers affect ethical consumerism through CASA theory and the theory of planned behavior. It examines attributes like parasocial interaction, perceived authenticity, and credibility, with ethical buying attitudes mediating ethical buying intentions. A quantitative analysis of 547 North Indian social media users aware of AI influencers, using SmartPLS 4.0, revealed these attributes significantly impact ethical consumerism. Despite its cross-sectional nature and focus on North Indian users, the study suggests other influential AI attributes might exist. Integrating TPB and CASA theory offers insights for tech entrepreneurs to enhance AI trustworthiness and for marketers to improve virtual influencer strategies, promoting ethical consumerism by encouraging environmentally friendly choices and individual responsibility. This study uniquely combines AI influencer attributes, ethical consumerism, CASA theory, and TPB, emphasizing the mediating role of ethical buying attitudes.

DOI: 10.4018/979-8-3693-3096-8.ch006

1. INTRODUCTION

Consumers increasingly prioritize ethics in purchasing, emphasizing environmental considerations and ethical company practices. This shift from conventional to Ethical Consumerism reflects changing values. Various factors, including economic, social, and environmental aspects, influence consumer choices. Ethical Consumerism, defined through these criteria, highlights a transformation in how goods and services are perceived and used, underscoring the broader impact of consumption on society and the environment throughout history. During the twentieth century, economic theory operated on the assumption that the majority of individuals act rationally to optimize their utility and satisfaction (Roach et al., 2019). Ecological consumerism is developing from an environmental perspective, prompting researchers to explore the motivations behind consumers' intentions to buy environmentally friendly products (Chen et al., 2022). The evolution of Ethical Consumerism is notably influenced by technological advancements, particularly in marketing and influencer strategies. Over the past two decades, the internet's transformative impact, coupled with the rise of Artificial Intelligence (AI), has reshaped customer decision-making. From sluggish desktop connections to the emergence of AI, technology has played a pivotal role in enhancing customer engagement and reshaping branding and purchasing dynamics. The proliferation of social media, with over 700 million active users in India alone, has sparked a digital marketing revolution. Influencer marketing, valued at over $12 billion in India in 2022, has become a prominent tool for promoting sustainable products and driving ethical consumerism.

The integration of AI into influencer marketing has given rise to a unique phenomenon – AI Influencers. These digital creations, characterized by personality-driven marketing and AI technology, have gained significant traction (Influencer Marketing Hub, 2021). Virtual influencers like Miquela Souza and Shudu Gramm have amassed millions of followers, challenging traditional influencer relationships. Despite being artificial, AI influencers surpass human influencers in average engagement rates, showcasing their effectiveness in delivering compelling content and fostering interaction. This trend is not limited to the United States but has a global presence, indicating the widespread appeal of AI influencers. The concept of AI influencers dates back to the early 2010s, originating from virtual avatars used in gaming and entertainment. Marketing professionals, according to research, have increasingly collaborated with AI influencers, with a majority expressing satisfaction. However, challenges such as cost, senior management's tech aptitude, hardware requirements, and privacy concerns hinder the mainstream adoption of AI influencers in marketing.

The growth of AI adoption faces obstacles from multiple concerns raised by marketing managers, society, and consumers. These include factors like cost implications, limited technological proficiency among senior management, availability issues, hardware requirements, and privacy concerns (Pitt, 2020). Despite the growing influence of AI influencers in shaping consumer ethical decision-making, comprehensive studies on their impact on promoting Ethical Consumerism are scarce. This research aims to fill this gap by identifying factors driving consumer engagement towards ethical choices and providing insights for effectively leveraging AI influencers in promoting ethical buying. While AI influencers are gaining popularity, there is still a considerable distance to cover before their widespread acceptance in mainstream marketing practices.

Within the vast literature on Artificial Intelligence and Influencer Marketing, numerous studies explore Ethical Consumer Behavior. However, existing research predominantly centers on AI influencers within the marketing landscape and their influence on buying intentions. Notably, studies, such as those by Jhang (2022) and Sands et al. (2022), extensively delve into AI influencer attributes and their impact on marketing dynamics. Yet, gaps persist, motivating the current study to make a distinctive contribution to the available literature. While prior research primarily scrutinized buying intentions in ethical decision-making scenarios (Ren et al., 2020), this study diverges by focusing on the broader spectrum of AI influencers' roles throughout the customer's decision-making journey. This study delves into the intricate realm of AI influencer marketing, exploring its increasing impact on Ethical Consumerism through the application of theoretical frameworks like the Computers Are Social Actors (CASA) Theory and the Theory of Planned Behavior. By identifying the traits of AI influencers that shape individual decisions towards ethical consumption, the research sheds light on the nuanced relationship between technology and ethical choices. Emphasizing the role of Attitude towards Ethical Buying as a mediator, the study elucidates the psychological processes influencing Ethical Buying Intention. Through the lens of theoretical frameworks such as the CASA Theory and the Theory of Planned Behaviour, the research discerns various properties of AI influencers that sway individual decisions towards ethical purchases. Recognizing Attitude Towards Ethical Buying as a pivotal mediator enhances our comprehension of the psychological factors guiding Ethical Buying Intention. This investigation not only contributes to the expanding field of consumer behavior but also underscores the potential of AI influencers to act as catalysts for fostering ethical purchasing behaviors in today's digitally interconnected society. The study adds to this investigation by providing vital insights into the changing environment of consumer behavior in the age of AI influencers, providing a comprehensive knowledge of how digital entities impact ethical decision-making. This research presents a detailed examination of the changing dynamics between technology and ethical decisions by investigating the function of AI influencers in promoting ethical consumption. By exploring these uncharted territories, the research seeks to deepen our understanding of how AI influencers specifically contribute to and shape ethical consumer behavior beyond mere purchase intentions. This broader perspective aims to enhance the holistic comprehension of the intricate dynamics between AI influencers and consumers in the context of ethical decision-making.

2. THEORETICAL UNDERPINNINGS AND HYPOTHESIS FORMULATION

2.1 Theoretical Underpinnings

2.1.1. Theory of Planned Behaviour

Numerous studies in the realm of ethical consumption have underscored the efficacy of both the Theory of Reasoned Action (TRA) and the Theory of Planned Behavior (TPB) in elucidating factors influencing individual behavioral intentions. The TPB, as articulated by Ajzen (1991), stands out as one of the most influential models in numerous investigations, as evidenced by research conducted by Chen and Tung (2014) and Yadav and Pathak (2016). The Theory of Planned Behavior (TPB) is a psychological framework to describe and predict human behavior. It is a development of the older Theory of Reasoned Action (TRA). According to the TPB, individual behavior is essentially driven by one's intentions, which are impacted by three important factors: attitude toward the attitude, subjective norms, and perceived behavioral control. This research aligns with the TPB, integrating it as a crucial component of our conceptual framework. However, our study diverges in its exclusion of subjective norms and Perceived Behavioral Control (PBC) in explicating ethical conduct.

Our research endeavors to utilize the TPB to comprehend how AI influencers contribute to shaping intentions for ethically motivated purchases following immersive customer engagement. Addressing a gap in existing literature, previous studies have primarily focused on individual intentions towards ethical buying. Yet, the current research seeks to go beyond by examining how AI influencers play a transformative role in shaping and altering attitudes towards the intention of ethical purchasing. This nuanced exploration aims to provide a comprehensive understanding of the intricate dynamics between AI influencers and consumers in the context of ethical decision-making.

2.1.2 Computers Are Social Actors (CASA) Theory

The Computers Are Social Actors (CASA) Theory is a psychological theory that investigates how humans attach social characteristics to computers and interact with them as if they were social beings. The CASA Theory, which was developed in the context of human-computer interaction, proposes that when engaging with computers, people tend to apply social norms, expectations, and behaviors, treating them as if they have human-like features Reeves and Nass, 1996); Broadbent et al., 2013). This anthropomorphism of technology entails imbuing computers with social characteristics such as intentionality and emotions, impacting user perceptions and behaviors. The idea emphasizes the influence of users' social cognitive processes on their interactions with technology, offering light on the intricate interplay between people and computers in modern society. CASA has practical consequences for user interface design. As per the CASA Theory, individuals instinctively incorporate social cues when interacting with computers, treating them akin to human entities (Reeves & Nass, 1996). The CASA paradigm (Nass and Moon, 2000; Reeves & Nass, 1996) has emerged as a significant conceptual framework elucidating people's interactions and behavioral responses to evolving new media technologies. The inclination of internet users to express interpersonal responses to computers reflects a broader tendency for humans to anthropomorphize both nonhuman and inanimate entities (Wang et al., 2015). The current study delves into varied societal responses to AI-powered virtual influencers, exploring the ways in which individuals engage with and react to these technologically driven entities.

2.2 Hypothesis Formulation

2.2.1 Attitude Towards Ethical Buying and Ethical Buying Intention

The Theory of Planned Behaviour, introduced by Ajzen (1991), posits that individuals' behavioural intentions are influenced by their attitudes, subjective norms, and perceived behavioural control, ultimately shaping their actual behaviour. An individual's stance is shaped by the level of significance attributed to a specific behaviour, as elucidated by Paetzold and Busch (2014). The analysis reveals that the positivity or negativity of a person's attitude plays a pivotal role in determining their inclination to partake in a particular behaviour, as indicated by Singh et al. (2021). The factors influencing the strength of the correlation between attitude and behavioural intention have long captivated researchers' attention, as evidenced by the work of Costarelli and Colloca (2007). In the context of ethical consumption, a positive attitude toward ethical buying is expected to foster a stronger inclination to engage in ethical consumer practices. Moreover, research indicates that individuals who harbour a sense of moral obligation regarding ethical considerations are more prone to cultivate favorable attitudes and intentions toward ethical purchasing, as demonstrated in studies conducted by Shaw and Shiu in 2002.

Thus, following hypothesis is proposed:

H1: Attitude towards Ethical Buying is positively related to Ethical Buying Intention.

2.2.2 Mediating Role of Attitude Towards Ethical Buying Between Parasocial Interaction (AI Influencers Attributes) and Ethical Buying Intention

The Theory of Planned Behaviour, formulated by Ajzen in 1991, emphasizes the pivotal role of attitudes in shaping behavioural intentions, subsequently exerting an impact on actual behaviour. Therefore, a favourable attitude towards ethical purchasing is expected to be associated with an elevated predisposition to engage in ethical consumption, as elucidated by Carrington et al. (2010). In a recent study conducted by Magano et al. (2022), the focus was on testing the mediating role of the attitude toward influencers in the relationship between influencer attributes and purchase intention. This research delves into the intricate dynamics of how individuals' attitudes towards influencers serve as a mediator, influencing the connection between the attributes of influencers and their intentions to make a purchase. Furthermore, the influence of interacting parasocially with a virtual influencer on consumers' perceptions of AI influencers is explored in research by Um (2023). The findings suggest that such parasocial interaction fosters positive perceptions, subsequently impacting consumers' decision-making processes. In alignment with this, our current investigation aims to comprehend how the attributes of AI influencers, experienced through parasocial interaction, shape individuals' attitudes towards ethical buying.

Thus, following hypothesis is proposed:

H2: Attitude towards Ethical Buying positively mediates the relation between Parasocial Interaction (AI Influencers Attributes) and Ethical Buying Intention.

2.2.3 Mediating Role of Attitude Towards Ethical Buying Between Perceived Authenticity (AI Influencers Attributes) and Ethical Buying Intention

AI influencers' attributes encompass elements such as Parasocial Interaction, perceived authenticity, and credibility. An affirmative attitude towards ethical purchasing is anticipated to be connected with an enhanced proclivity for engaging in ethical consumption, as emphasized by Carrington et al. in 2010. In an effort to delve deeper into this relationship, Abid et al. (2023) conducted a study aiming to scrutinize the mediating role of attitudes toward influencers in the correlation between influencer attributes and purchase intention. This research seeks to unravel the intricate mechanisms through which individuals' attitudes towards influencers act as mediators, shaping the link between various attributes of influencers and their intentions to make a purchase. The significance of authenticity in advertising is highlighted by both Miller (2015) and Um (2023), who found that the authenticity of advertising positively influences customer attitudes. Additionally, the perceived authenticity of a celebrity has been demonstrated to be intricately connected to consumer attitudes and purchasing intentions, as elucidated by Tripp et al. (1994). Building upon this knowledge, our current investigation endeavors to comprehend how the attributes of AI influencers, particularly experienced through perceived authenticity, contribute to shaping individuals' attitudes towards ethical buying.

Thus, following hypothesis is proposed:

H3: Attitude towards Ethical Buying positively mediates the relation between Perceived Authenticity (AI Influencers Attributes) and Ethical Buying Intention.

2.2.4 Mediating Role of Attitude Towards Ethical Buying between Credibility (AI Influencers Attributes) and Ethical Buying Intention

Information characterized by credibility is widely acknowledged to wield an affirmative influence on customer attitudes and purchase intentions, as asserted by Kusumasondjaja et al. (2012). This underscores the pivotal role that the perception of credibility plays in shaping consumers' perceptions and subsequent actions. In alignment with this, Singh and Banerjee's (2018) study not only reaffirmed the importance of credibility but also elucidated the mediating function of attitude in the credibility-intention relationship. Moreover, Magano et al. (2022) undertook a comprehensive study aimed at unraveling the intricate dynamics of the relationship between influencer attributes, specifically credibility, and the intention to make a purchase. The focal point of their investigation was the mediating role of attitude towards influencers. By exploring how consumers' attitudes function as intermediaries in the link between influencer credibility and purchase intention, the current study contributes valuable insights into the nuanced aspects of consumer decision-making processes. This body of research collectively emphasizes the interconnected nature of credibility, attitudes, and purchase intentions, shedding light on the intricate pathways through which these factors influence consumer behavior.

Thus, following hypothesis is proposed:

H4: Attitude towards Ethical Buying positively mediates the relation between credibility (AI Influencers Attributes) and Ethical Buying Intention.

3. RESEARCH METHODOLOGY

Figure 1 illustrates the model integrating **Computers Are Social Actors (CASA) Theory** and the Theory of Planned Behaviour (TPB). Attitude towards Ethical Buying, Ethical Buying Intention, and AI Influencer Attributes, which encompassed Parasocial Interaction, Perceived Authenticity, and Credibility.

Figure 1. Conceptual Model

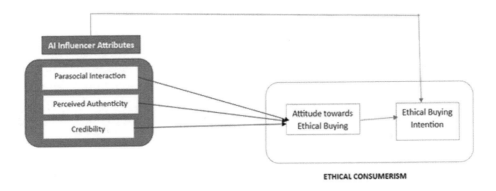

4.1 Research Method

Due to the causal investigative nature of this study, a quantitative analysis method was employed using a survey research technique (Creswell, 2003). Self-administered questionnaires were utilized for collecting quantitative data.

4.2 Population and Sampling

The population for this study consisted of social media users from the North Indian region, including Delhi and the National Capital Region, Haryana, Punjab, and Chandigarh. Past research suggests that non-probability snowball sampling is most suitable in cases where the population is difficult to access (Wagner et al., 2014), a specific type of population is required (Nardi, 2006), and there is an interconnected network of people or organizations. Consequently, a non-probability snowball sampling technique was employed to collect data, as the target population was specific (i.e., social media users familiar with AI influencers) and formed an interconnected network of such users. The chain referral method was used, where existing respondents referred future respondents from among their acquaintances. The study utilized an A-priori Sample Size Calculator for Structural Equation Models from https://www.danielsoper.com/statcalc/calculator.aspx?id=89. Parameters included an effect size of 0.3, a statistical power level of 0.8, 5 latent variables, 19 observed variables, and a probability level of 0.05. Results (see Figure 2) suggest a minimum sample size of 150 to detect the effect, 112 for the model structure, and a recommended minimum of 150. Therefore, the study's sample size is deemed sufficient.

Anticipated effect size: 0.3

Desired statistical power level: 0.8

Number of latent variables: 5

Number of observed variables: 19

Probability level: 0.05

Calculate!

Minimum sample size to detect effect: **150**

Minimum sample size for model structure: **112**

Recommended minimum sample size: **150**

4.3 Research Instrument

The survey instrument was divided into two sections. Section I assessed demographic information, while Section II gathered responses related to various constructs of the study. Section II included items organized into the following sub-sections: Attitude towards Ethical Buying, Ethical Buying Intention, and AI Influencer Attributes, which encompassed Parasocial Interaction, Perceived Authenticity, and Credibility. These latent constructs were measured using adapted statements from existing literature, incorporating revisions as recommended by Netemeyer et al. (2003). Pre-testing methods, including semi-structured interviews, were conducted to ensure the measurement items were correctly worded and understandable. After finalizing the items, an exploratory factor analysis (EFA) was performed to assess the appropriateness of each item within its construct. The EFA results showed that items related to the study's constructs loaded onto their respective constructs. A complete list of our items with their individual sources is shown in Table 1.

Table 1. Measurement items - Mean, Standard Deviation and Factor Loadings

Construct		Items	Adapted from	Mean	SD	Factor Loading
Parasocial Interaction	**PS1**	I think I understand AI Influencer quite well.	Um, N. (2023)	3.02	1.26	0.856
	PS2	I would like to have a friendly chat with AI Influencer.		2.88	1.34	0.816
	PS3	AI Influencer makes me feel comfortable, as if I were with a good friend.		3.08	1.39	0.787

continued on following page

Table 1. Continued

Construct		Items	Adapted from	Mean	SD	Factor Loading
Perceived Authenticity	AUTH1	AI Influencer posts authentic photos and videos.	Khuat, H. (2023)	2.99	1.38	0.846
	AUTH2	AI Influencer has a unique personality.		3.00	1.35	0.820
	AUTH3	AI Influencer shares random thoughts and moments about their life.		2.98	1.39	0.815
Credibility	CRED1	AI Influencer is sincere.	Khuat, H. (2023)	2.92	1.44	0.854
	CRED2	AI Influencer is trustworthy.		3.12	1.23	0.848
	CRED3	I would trust the AI Influencer's product review.		3.11	1.22	0.835
	CRED4	AI Influencer is knowledgeable.		3.03	1.19	0.815
	CRED5	AI Influencer demonstrated expertise in her field.		3.04	1.16	0.808
	CRED6	AI Influencer is experienced in her field.		3.07	1.37	0.782
Attitude towards ethical buying	ATT1	I would prefer to buy products that use biodegradable material in packaging.	Han and Yoon (2015)	2.71	1.32	0.772
	ATT2	I would wish to buy those products that are picked up and recycled for other use.		2.57	1.35	0.803
	ATT3	I would buy biodegradable products even if they belong to a less well-known company.		2.63	1.35	0.836
Ethical Buying Intention	INT1	I consider purchasing sustainable clothes.	Brandão, A., & da Costa, A. G. (2021)	2.51	1.230	0.826
	INT2	I intend to buy sustainable clothes instead of conventional clothes in the future.		2.49	1.34	0.827
	INT3	I might buy sustainable clothes in the future.		2.43	1.27	0.819
	INT4	I would consider buying sustainable clothes if I happen to see them in an online store.		2.32	1.21	0.844

4.4 Pilot Study

Before the final data collection, pilot testing was conducted to assess the internal consistency and reliability of the scale. A limited sample size, typically 30 to 50 respondents, is recommended as a rule of thumb to measure Cronbach's alpha and understand the degree of homogeneity for a given scale in different contexts (De Von et al., 2007; Saunders et al., 2012; Howell, 2013). Therefore, the pilot study involved 50 respondents randomly selected from the population. The results from the pilot study indicated that the values of Cronbach's alpha exceeded the minimum acceptable level of 0.70. Consequently, the study proceeded with the final data collection without making any further modifications to the questionnaire.

4.5 Data Collection

The study utilized both primary and secondary data. Primary quantitative data were gathered through online and offline modes. Out of 750 distributed questionnaires, 615 were returned, with 547 fully completed by social media users familiar with AI influencers. These 547 responses were used for further analysis, resulting in a response rate of 73%. Secondary data were sourced from books, journals, online and offline publications, and reports from various governmental and non-governmental organizations to construct the study's conceptual framework.

4.6 Common Method Bias

Self-reported data can be susceptible to common method bias (Podsakoff et al., 2003). To address this issue, the study implemented techniques from Lin et al. (2019) and Farooq et al. (2018). Respondents were assured of their anonymity and were not informed about the study's objective. Additionally, Harman's one-factor test (1976) was used to check for common method variance (Podsakoff et al., 2003). All items were entered into a factor analysis to extract a single factor, which accounted for 30.45% of the total variance, well below the 50% threshold. Therefore, common method bias was not a concern in this study.

4.7 Descriptive Statistics

Most participants were male (291; 53.19%), with the largest age group being 31 to 40 years old (254; 46.4%). A notable portion of respondents (356; 65.08%) reported monthly incomes between 25,000 to 50,000.

4.8 Data Analysis Tool

The study utilized SmartPLS 4.0 software, adhering to the approach outlined by Hair et al. (2021) for assessing reliability, validity, theory, and hypotheses. The Partial Least Squares (PLS) method, a variance-based structural equation modelling (SEM) technique, was employed. This method, consisting of measurement model and structural model stages, was chosen due to its suitability for theory development, handling complex linear models, and accommodating non-normal samples.

4. DATA ANALYSIS

4.1. Reliability and Validity

Following the steps outlined by Hair et al. (2019), the initial analysis of the PLS-SEM results focused on the measurement model. This involved assessing internal consistency reliability, convergent validity, and discriminant validity. Reliability of the questionnaire was evaluated using Cronbach's alpha coefficient and composite reliability coefficient. As shown in Table 2, the Cronbach's alpha values for each dimension exceeded the minimum acceptable level of 0.70, indicating satisfactory reliability. Additionally, the composite reliability (CR) values for all constructs ranged between 0.70 and 0.95, confirming internal consistency (Hair et al., 2019). Convergent validity was assessed using the average variance extracted

(AVE), with all AVE values in Table 2 exceeding 0.50, demonstrating that the latent variables explained more than 50% of their indicators' variance. Further evidence of convergent validity was provided by the outer loadings in Table 2, all of which were greater than 0.7. Therefore, the measurement model's convergent validity is robust.

Table 2. Outer Loadings, Cronbach's Alpha, Composite reliability and AVE

Name of latent Variable	Indicators	Outer Loadings	Cronabach's Alpha	Composite reliability	AVE
Parasocial Interaction	PS1	0.874	0.800	0.882	0.713
	PS2	0.805			
	PS3	0.852			
Perceived Authenticity	AUTH1	0.881	0.843	0.846	0.760
	AUTH2	0.872			
	AUTH3	0.863			
Credibility	CRED1	0.844	0.840	0.887	0.593
	CRED2	0.799			
	CRED3	0.817			
	CRED4	0.851			
	CRED5	0.861			
	CRED6	0.720			
Attitude towards Ethical buying	ATT1	0.826	0.793	0.794	0.707
	ATT2	0.849			
	ATT3	0.847			
Ethical buying intention	INT1	0.866	0.880	0.882	0.736
	INT2	0.844			
	INT3	0.864			
	INT4	0.857			

Three methods have been proposed for assessing discriminant validity: the cross-loading test, the Fornell-Larcker criterion, and the heterotrait-monotrait ratio (HTMT) (Hair et al., 2021). Among these, the HTMT ratio is recommended as the preferred method for confirming discriminant validity (Hair et al., 2021). In this study, all three methods were used to confirm discriminant validity. The cross-loading results are presented in Table 3. According to the Fornell-Larcker criterion, "the square root of the AVE of each construct should be higher than the construct's highest correlation with any other construct in the model." Table 4 shows that the square root of the AVE for each construct is indeed higher than the construct's highest correlation with any other construct (with diagonal values in bold). According to the HTMT criterion, the HTMT values for constructs should not exceed 0.85 (Hair et al., 2021). Table 5 shows that all values are well below 0.85, confirming the discriminant validity (Henseler et al., 2015).

Table 3. Cross Loadings

	ATT	AUTH	CRED	INT	PS
ATT1	**0.826**	0.23	0.213	0.34	0.229
ATT2	**0.849**	0.226	0.181	0.378	0.199
ATT3	**0.847**	0.252	0.172	0.322	0.197
AUTH1	0.235	**0.881**	0.191	0.337	0.367
AUTH2	0.267	**0.872**	0.166	0.312	0.348
AUTH3	0.229	**0.863**	0.191	0.277	0.321
CRED1	0.206	0.168	**0.844**	0.093	0.136
CRED2	0.164	0.177	**0.799**	0.102	0.121
CRED3	0.178	0.168	**0.817**	0.114	0.1
CRED4	0.168	0.169	**0.851**	0.132	0.081
CRED5	0.212	0.171	**0.861**	0.107	0.071
CRED6	0.07	0.102	**0.720**	0.064	0.059
INT1	0.385	0.301	0.107	**0.866**	0.213
INT2	0.326	0.299	0.1	**0.844**	0.23
INT3	0.368	0.33	0.107	**0.864**	0.202
INT4	0.336	0.289	0.147	**0.857**	0.207
PS1	0.238	0.351	0.126	0.177	**0.874**
PS2	0.178	0.308	0.084	0.186	**0.805**
PS3	0.209	0.345	0.101	0.258	**0.852**

Table 4. Fornell Larcker Criterion

	ATT	AUTH	CRED	INT	PS
ATT	0.841				
AUTH	0.28	0.872			
CRED	0.225	0.209	0.77		
INT	0.413	0.356	0.134	0.858	
PS	0.248	0.397	0.124	0.248	0.844

Note: The values on diagonal represent the square of AVE for the corresponding construct.

Table 5. HTMT Ratios

	ATT	AUTH	CRED	INT
AUTH	0.343			
CRED	0.273	0.254		
INT	0.492	0.411	0.16	
PS	0.309	0.481	0.154	0.292

5.3 Assessment of Structural Model

After evaluating the measurement model, the structural model was examined following the guidelines provided by Hair et al. (2019) and Wong (2016). This assessment included examining collinearity, the significance of path coefficients, and the R^2 value. The study employed the bootstrapping procedure to generate t-statistics for testing the significance of β values (Preacher and Hayes, 2008), using a total of 5,000 bootstrapped samples (Shrout and Bolger, 2002). The analysis was conducted at a significance level (α) of 0.05, with a t-table statistic of 1.96. Collinearity diagnostics were performed using the variance inflation factor (VIF) values calculated from the latent variable scores of the exogenous constructs. All VIF values were below 3, indicating no collinearity issues in the model. Results indicated that ATT has a significant direct impact (β = 0.329, t-value = 8.027) on INT, explaining a significant portion of the variance (R^2 = 0.238, p-value = 0.000). Therefore, H1 is supported (Table 6).

Table 6. Results of Path Analysis

Hypothesised Path		ß	t Statistics	p Value	Decision
H1	ATT → INT	0.329	8.027	0.000	Supported
H2	PS → ATT → INT	0.051	3.111	0.002	Supported
H3	AUTH → ATT → INT	0.061	3.759	0.000	Supported
H4	CRED → ATT → INT	0.055	3.573	0.000	Supported

5.4 Mediation Analysis

ATT was found to have a significant partial mediating effect (β = 0.051, p-value = 0.002, t-value = 3.111) on the relationship between PS and INT, thus supporting H2. H3 was also supported by the results (β = 0.061, p-value = 0.000, t-value = 3.759), revealing the partial mediation effect of ATT on the relationship between AUTH and INT. Furthermore, H4 was tested for the mediation effect, which was significant with β = 0.055 (p-value = 0.000, t-value = 43.573). The results are presented in Table 6 and Figure 3.

Figure 3. Path Analysis

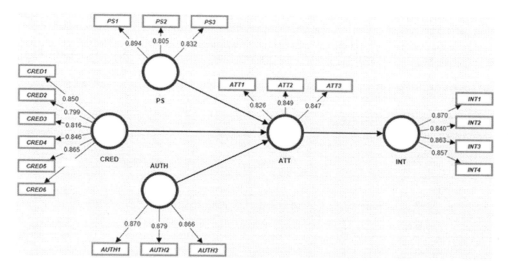

5. FINDINGS AND DISCUSSION

Examining Hypothesis 1, which posits that attitude towards ethical buying is positively related to ethical buying intention. The findings support this hypothesis, revealing a significant positive relationship between attitude towards ethical buying and ethical buying intention. This suggests that individuals with favourable attitudes towards ethical buying are more inclined to express intentions to engage in ethical consumer behaviour, aligning with prior research emphasizing the influential role of attitudes in shaping consumer intentions and behaviours (Ajzen, 1991). Moving to Hypothesis 2, which suggests that attitude towards ethical buying mediates the relationship between parasocial interaction with AI influencers and ethical buying intention, our results corroborate this assertion. It is found that the positive influence of parasocial interaction on ethical buying intention is partially mediated by individuals' attitudes towards ethical buying. This underscores the pivotal role of attitude as a mechanism through which interactions with AI influencers impact consumer behaviour (Magano et al., 2022). Consistent with Hypothesis 3, the findings demonstrate that attitude towards ethical buying mediates the relationship between perceived authenticity of AI influencers and ethical buying intention. This suggests that consumers' perceptions of authenticity positively influence their attitudes towards ethical buying, subsequently affecting their intention to engage in ethical consumer behaviour, a finding in line with previous research highlighting the importance of authenticity in shaping consumer attitudes and intentions (Abid et al., 2023). Similarly, our results support Hypothesis 4, indicating that attitude towards ethical buying mediates the relationship between credibility of AI influencers and ethical buying intention. This implies that consumers' perceptions of AI influencers' credibility positively influence their attitudes towards ethical buying, consequently impacting their intention to engage in ethical consumer behavior, consistent with the notion that credibility is a key determinant of consumer attitudes and intentions (Singh and Banerjee, 2018).

In summarizing our findings, we underscore the importance of fostering positive attitudes towards ethical consumption, as attitude towards ethical buying emerged as a significant predictor of ethical buying intention. Additionally, the mediation analyses highlight the central role of attitude in translating perceptions of AI influencers into intentions to engage in ethical consumer behavior. These findings underscore the significance of ethical considerations in consumer decision-making processes, particularly in the context of influencer marketing with AI influencers. Practically, the findings suggest that marketers should prioritize building trust, authenticity, and credibility in AI influencers to positively influence consumers' attitudes towards ethical buying and, ultimately, their ethical buying intentions. By considering these implications, stakeholders can effectively navigate the influence of AI influencers on ethical consumer behavior, contributing to both academic understanding and real-world marketing practices.

6. IMPLICATIONS

6.1 Theoretical Implications

This study contributes to the field of virtual AI influencers and ethical consumerism by expanding traditional persuasion theories, like the CASA and TPB, to include virtual AI influencers. It shows that AI influencers can impact consumer attitudes and behaviours similarly to human influencers, validating and extending these theories in digital and AI-mediated communication. Additionally, the research identifies new dimensions specific to virtual entities, emphasizing the need to update existing credibility frameworks. Furthermore, it integrates AI influencers into ethical consumerism frameworks, revealing how AI-driven recommendations influence ethical buying intentions. The study also highlights the applicability of parasocial interaction theory to virtual AI influencers, indicating that consumers form connections with AI influencers, which can drive ethical consumption behaviours. Moreover, it emphasizes the interconnected nature of social media networks and the role of AI influencers within them, calling for further exploration of their influence on ethical consumerism. Lastly, the inclusion of AI influencers complicates consumer behaviour models, suggesting the need for future models to consider AI and algorithm-driven interactions in shaping consumer decisions and ethical behaviour.

6.2 Practical Implications

Understanding the impact of virtual AI influencers on consumer behaviour, especially in ethical consumerism, is crucial for marketers. Knowing how these influencers affect perceptions of ethical brands can help shape marketing strategies to reach ethically conscious consumers. Authenticity and Transparency are important when using virtual AI influencers. Being transparent about their AI nature can build trust and prevent negative reactions. It's essential for the messaging promoted by virtual AI influencers to align with the brand's ethical values. Education and Awareness Campaigns can help consumers understand virtual AI influencers and evaluate their messages critically. Compliance with regulations ensures transparency and consumer protection in influencer marketing. Collaboration with AI Developers can improve the credibility of virtual AI influencers and their promotion of ethical consumerism. Continuously monitoring consumer responses helps gauge the effectiveness of influencer campaigns. Long-term ethical commitments are necessary to maintain trust and loyalty among ethically conscious consumers. Considering these factors helps stakeholders navigate the impact of virtual AI influencers on ethical consumerism, benefiting both academia and real-world applications.

7. LIMITATIONS AND FUTURE RESEARCH DIRECTIONS

While the research has yielded insightful findings, it is critical to realize its limits. The use of a cross-sectional technique that focuses just on north Indian users suggests that establishing relationship between variables should be addressed with caution. The study provides a snapshot in time, and establishing the temporal evolution of the factors revealed may need a more detailed longitudinal approach. Furthermore, the scope of AI influencer attributes explored in this study may not cover the entire range of variables impacting Ethical Consumerism. Because consumer behaviour is dynamic, and emerging AI influencer traits may play a role in moulding ethical decisions. Future study should attempt to perform a more in-depth examination of these characteristics, assuring a thorough grasp of the multiple mechanisms at work.

Future research might use a longitudinal approach to gain a more dynamic picture of the phenomena under the study. This method would allow researchers to study changes and advancements in ethical consumer behaviour across time, offering insights into the long-term viability of identified trends as well as the potential formation of new patterns. Extending the geographic reach beyond North Indian users is critical for improving the findings' generalizability. Cultural, economic, and societal issues can all have an impact on ethical consumer behaviour. Researchers can capture contextual differences in AI influencer impact on ethical decisions by adding participants from multiple geographical places, contributing to a more robust and globally relevant body of information. This acknowledgement of the research's limitations highlights the ever-changing nature of AI influencer dynamics and stresses the importance of broad and ongoing research. It urges researchers to keep an eye out for new trends and to perform in-depth examinations into the plethora of elements impacting ethical judgments in various consumer marketplaces. While the study is a good starting point, it also highlights the need for continued research to keep up with the rapidly evolving world of AI influencers and their impact on ethical consumer behaviour.

REFERENCES

Abid, M. A., Shafique, F., Zahid, M., Mehmood, S., & Asim, N. (2023). *Impact of Social Media Influencers on Consumers Purchase Intentions to Buy Pakistani Food: Investigating The Mediating Role Of Consumer Attitude*. Academic Press.

Ajzen, I. (1991). The theory of planned behavior. *Organizational Behavior and Human Decision Processes*, 50(2), 179–211. 10.1016/0749-5978(91)90020-T

Broadbent, E., Kumar, V., Li, X., Sollers, J.III, Stafford, R. Q., MacDonald, B. A., & Wegner, D. M. (2013). Robots with display screens: A robot with a more humanlike face display is perceived to have more mind and a better personality. *PLoS One*, 8(8), e72589. 10.1371/journal.pone.007258924015263

Carrington, M. J., Neville, B. A., & Whitwell, G. J. (2010). Why ethical consumers don't walk their talk: Towards a framework for understanding the gap between the ethical purchase intentions and actual buying behaviour of ethically minded consumers. *Journal of Business Ethics*, 97(1), 139–158. 10.1007/s10551-010-0501-6

Chen, L., Wu, Q., & Jiang, L. (2022). Impact of environmental concern on ecological purchasing behavior: The moderating effect of Prosociality. *Sustainability (Basel)*, 14(5), 3004. 10.3390/su14053004

Chen, M. F., & Tung, P. J. (2014). Developing an extended theory of planned behavior model to predict consumers' intention to visit green hotels. *International Journal of Hospitality Management*, 36, 221–230. 10.1016/j.ijhm.2013.09.006

Costarelli, S., & Colloca, P. (2007). The moderation of ambivalence on attitude–intention relations as mediated by attitude importance. *European Journal of Social Psychology*, 37(5), 923–933. 10.1002/ejsp.403

Creswell, J. (2003). *Research Design: Qualitative, Quantitative and Mixed Methods* (2nd ed.). Sage Publications.

De Von, H. A., Block, M. E., Moyle-Wright, P., Ernst, D. M., Hayden, S. J., Lazzara, D. J., Savoy, S. M., & Kostas-Polston, E. (2007). A psychometric toolbox for testing validity and reliability. *Journal of Nursing Scholarship*, 39(2), 155–164. 10.1111/j.1547-5069.2007.00161.x17535316

Farooq, M. S., Salam, M., Fayolle, A., Jaafar, N., & Ayupp, K. (2018). Impact of service quality on customer satisfaction in Malaysia airlines: A PLS-SEM approach. *Journal of Air Transport Management*, 67, 169–180. 10.1016/j.jairtraman.2017.12.008

Farooq, M. S., Salam, M., Jaafar, N., Fayolle, A., Ayupp, K., Radovic-Markovic, M., & Sajid, A. (2017). Acceptance and use of lecture capture system (LCS) in executive business studies: Extending UTAUT2. *Interactive Technology and Smart Education*, 14(4), 329–348. 10.1108/ITSE-06-2016-0015

Hair, J. F.Jr, Hult, G. T. M., Ringle, C., & Sarstedt, M. (2016). *A Primer on Partial Least Squares Structural Equation Modeling (PLS-SEM)*. Sage Publications.

Hair, J. F., Risher, J. J., Sarstedt, M., & Ringle, C. M. (2019). When to use and how to report the results of PLS-SEM. *European Business Review*, 31(1), 2–24. 10.1108/EBR-11-2018-0203

Henseler, J., & Fassott, G. (2010). Testing moderating effects in PLS path models: an illustration of available procedures. In *Handbook of Partial Least Squares* (pp. 713–735). Springer. 10.1007/978-3-540-32827-8_31

Henseler, J., Ringle, C. M., & Sarstedt, M. (2015). A new criterion for assessing discriminant validity in variance-based structural equation modeling. *Journal of the Academy of Marketing Science*, 43(1), 115–135. 10.1007/s11747-014-0403-8

Howell, K. (2013). *An Introduction to the Philosophy of Methodology*. SAGE Publications. 10.4135/9781473957633

Kusumasondjaja, S., Shanka, T., & Marchegiani, C. (2012). Credibility of online reviews and initial trust: The roles of reviewer's identity and review valence. *Journal of Vacation Marketing*, 18(3), 185–195. 10.1177/1356766712449365

Lin, H., Zhang, M., Gursoy, D., & Fu, X. (2019). Impact of tourist-to-tourist interaction on tourism experience: The mediating role of cohesion and intimacy. *Annals of Tourism Research*, 76, 153–167. 10.1016/j.annals.2019.03.009

Miller, F. M. (2015). Ad authenticity: An alternative explanation of advertising's effect on established brand attitudes. *Journal of Current Issues and Research in Advertising*, 36(2), 177–194. 10.1080/10641734.2015.1023871

Nardi, P. (2006). *Doing Survey Research. A Guide to Quantitative Methods*. Pearson Education.

Nass, C., & Moon, Y. (2000). Machines and mindlessness: Social responses to computers. *The Journal of Social Issues*, 56(1), 81–103. 10.1111/0022-4537.00153

Netemeyer, R., Bearden, W., & Sharma, S. (2003). *Scaling Procedures: Issues and Applications*. Sage Publications. 10.4135/9781412985772

Paetzold, F., & Busch, T. (2014). Unleashing the powerful few: Sustainable investing behaviour of wealthy private investors. *Organization & Environment*, 27(4), 347–367. 10.1177/1086026614555991

Pitt, B. (2020). *The study of how XR technologies impact the retail industry, now and in the future*. Academic Press.

Podsakoff, P. M., MacKenzie, S. B., Lee, J. Y., & Podsakoff, N. P. (2003). Common method biases in behavioral research: A critical review of the literature and recommended remedies. *The Journal of Applied Psychology*, 88(5), 879–903. 10.1037/0021-9010.88.5.87914516251

Preacher, K. J., & Hayes, A. F. (2008). Asymptotic and resampling strategies for assessing and comparing indirect effects in multiple mediator models. *Behavior Research Methods*, 40(3), 879–891. 10.3758/BRM.40.3.87918697684

Reeves, B., & Nass, C. (1996). *The media equation: How people treat computers, television, and new media like real people*. Academic Press.

Ren, X., Wang, X., & Sun, H. (2020). Key person ethical decision-making and substandard drugs rejection intentions. *PLoS One*, 15(3), e0229412. 10.1371/journal.pone.022941232191721

Roach, B., Goodwin, N., & Nelson, J. (2019). *Consumption and the consumer society*. Global Development and Environment Institute, Tufts University.

Saunders, M., Lewis, P., & Thornhill, A. (2012). *Research Methods for Business Students* (6th ed.). Pearson Education.

Shaw, D., & Shiu, E. (2002). An assessment of ethical obligation and self-identity in ethical consumer decision-making: A structural equation modelling approach. *International Journal of Consumer Studies*, 26(4), 286–293. 10.1046/j.1470-6431.2002.00255.x

Shrout, P. E., & Bolger, N. (2002). Mediation in experimental and non-experimental studies: New procedures and recommendations. *Psychological Methods*, 7(4), 422–445. 10.1037/1082-989X.7.4.4221 2530702

Singh, M., Mittal, M., Mehta, P., & Singla, H. (2021). Personal values as drivers of socially responsible investments: A moderation analysis. *Review of Behavioral Finance*, 13(5), 543–565. 10.1108/RBF-04-2020-0066

Singh, R. P., & Banerjee, N. (2018). Exploring the influence of celebrity credibility on brand attitude, advertisement attitude and purchase intention. *Global Business Review*, 19(6), 1622–1639. 10.1177/0972150918794974

Tripp, C., Jensen, T. D., & Carlson, L. (1994). The effects of multiple product endorsements by celebrities on consumers' attitudes and intentions. *The Journal of Consumer Research*, 20(4), 535–547. 10.1086/209368

Um, N. (2023). Predictors affecting effects of virtual influencer advertising among college students. *Sustainability (Basel)*, 15(8), 6388. 10.3390/su15086388

Wagner, D., Vollmar, G., & Wagner, H. T. (2014). The impact of information technology on knowledge creation: An affordance approach to social media. *Journal of Enterprise Information Management*, 27(1), 31–44. 10.1108/JEIM-09-2012-0063

Wang, S., Lilienfeld, S. O., & Rochat, P. (2015). The uncanny valley: Existence and explanations. *Review of General Psychology*, 19(4), 393–407. 10.1037/gpr0000056

Wong, K. K. K. (2016). Mediation analysis, categorical moderation analysis, and higher-order constructs modeling in partial least squares structural equation modeling (PLS-SEM): A B2B example using Smart-PLS. *Marketing Bulletin*, 26(1), 1–22.

Yadav, R., & Pathak, G. S. (2016). Young consumers' intention towards buying green products in a developing nation: Extending the theory of planned behavior. *Journal of Cleaner Production*, 135, 732–739. 10.1016/j.jclepro.2016.06.120

Chapter 7
Dealing With Stress and Making Students Industry Ready:
Role of Spirituality

Tarika Singh Sikarwar
https://orcid.org/0000-0002-9778-0589
Prestige Institute of Management and Research, Gwalior, India

Anivesh Singh Goyal
Prestige Institute of Management and Research, Gwalior, India

Monika Gupta
IPS College, India

Nidhi Jain
Prestige Institute of Management and Research, Gwalior, India

Harshita S. Mathur
Prestige Institute of Management and Research, Gwalior, India

ABSTRACT

The purpose of this study is to find the psychological determinants of the mental stress of students while they are pursuing a professional degree. Using a sample of college-going students, an effort is made to peep into such students' mental stress-determining factors. Three major determinants came into focus, namely depression and tearfulness, feeling loved, and personal life, which was confirmed using confirmatory factor analysis. Such mental stress determinants, if addressed, could lead to progress in the mental health of our students and the happiness of the society of which they are part. Spiritual and educational strategies can be used to understand better symptoms related to mental stress and treatments thereof making them industry-ready.

DOI: 10.4018/979-8-3693-3096-8.ch007

I. INTRODUCTION TO MENTAL HEALTH AS A PREREQUISITE IN PROFESSIONALS

To establish the foundation for comprehending the critical role that mental health plays in the life of students in professional courses, a growing recognition of the correlation between mental health and overall performance, has been delved into. It has been established that there is a vital role that mental health plays as a necessary precondition for persons seeking professional jobs.

The World Health Organization has well-defined mental health as "mental health is a state of well-being in which an individual realizes his or her abilities, can cope with the normal stresses of life, can work productively, and can make a contribution to his or her community (Mokhtar et al., 2013)". Mental health is a broad term beyond the healthy mental condition and includes many factors affecting the health of the mind including stress a factor. Education, parenting, gender, socioeconomic aspects, culture, physical appearance, family culture, health literacy, and many similar factors affect a healthy mental state (O'Donnell, 2017). A good and happy life is a reflection of a healthy mind. Maintaining sound and happy mental health is one of the precedents of quality life. It is pretty shocking to know that more than 50% of the world's population suffers from any kind of mental disorder. The most common mental illnesses are anxiety and depression (Storrie, Ahern, and Tuckett, 2010).

Mental health problems can be at any stage of life (Erevik et al., 2020). Young people are hardly aware, and if conscious, they hardly admit that they have any mental disorder, are stressed, and need help to cope (Hardjom, Haryono, Bashori, 2021). Talking about mental health and stress, also accepting it is still considered taboo, especially in Indian Society. One of the reasons can be the fear of rejection from friends and Society. But the reality is anxiety, depression, and eating disorders are much more common among young students. Students feel stressed from exams, feel pressure from family, colleagues, and friends to do good in the exams, they feel pressured to social presence, go outside, have fun, etc(Yavuz & Dilmaç, 2020). The typical sign of mental stress like feeling irritation, constant feeling tired, mood swings, headaches, and insomnia is considered expected in the young generation and is often ignored(Squires et.al, 2020). The present study is an effort to understand the determinants of mental stress in young students in professional courses coming from different social and cultural backgrounds.

II. DEFINING DETERMINANTS OF MENTAL STRESS AMONGST STUDENTS IN PROFESSIONAL COURSES

A thorough investigation, removing layers to reveal the critical elements that influence mental stress in students enrolled in professional programs. An effort is made to examine and comprehend the complex network of factors that contribute to the mental stress that students encounter during their educational journey, ranging from academic expectations to external influences.

The determinants of mental stress among students in professional courses are complex and multifaceted. They interact with various factors, including individual characteristics, social context, and coping strategies. Additionally, the concept of spiritual well-being can also play a significant role in how students navigate and cope with stress during challenging times.

As we learn more about how environmental influences affect mental stress, both inside and outside of educational institutions come under examination. This clarifies the external factors that contribute to the stress experiences of the students by encompassing the institutional culture, peer dynamics, and societal expectations.

A thorough examination is conducted of personal determinants, such as resilience, individual coping strategies, and expectation management skills. Our goal is to discover critical areas for intervention and assistance that can have a positive impact on student's mental health by comprehending the interactions between personal characteristics and external stressors. Furthermore, we have tried to delves into how social media, technology, and the digital environment shape students' emotional stress. Through analyzing how the virtual world affects students' mental health, we reveal how these contemporary influences add to the story of stress in general.

Academic demands: The main sources of stress for students are frequently the demanding curriculum, long study plans, and high expectations that come with professional courses. The stress levels in students might be increased by things like a full course load, difficult homework, and impending exams.

Performance Pressure: Students' mental health can be severely impacted by the pressure to do well academically, obtain internships or placements, and fulfill career objectives. The students' stress levels are elevated by performance-related stressors, such as peer competition, fear of failing, and the need for perfection.

Time Restraints: Juggling personal obligations, extracurricular activities, and part-time employment with academic obligations can lead to time limits that increase stress. The difficulties managing time and conflicting priorities can cause extreme tension and worry.

Financial Stress: Students enrolled in professional courses experience additional stress due to financial obligations such as living expenses, student loans, and tuition fees. There are potential effects on students' mental health due to financial instability and the pressure to control spending while seeking an education.

Social and Peer Pressure: Stress among students can be caused by social dynamics in academic settings, such as peer pressure, social comparison, and feelings of inferiority or loneliness. There are many ways in which students' stress levels are influenced by interpersonal connections, societal expectations, and the demand for social approval.

Work-Life Balance: For students enrolled in professional courses, finding a balance between their personal and academic obligations might be difficult. The stress levels might rise as a result of challenges in keeping a healthy work-life balance, such as little free time, lack of sleep, and disregard for self-care.

Perceived Future Uncertainty: Students may experience stress as a result of perceived future uncertainty, which includes concerns about professional performance, labor market conditions, and future career opportunities. Anxiety and nervousness are exacerbated by worries about post-graduation plans, job stability, and meeting career expectations.

The uncertainty surrounding the student's life, along with fears about personal health and the health of loved ones, can contribute to heightened stress levels and can lead to difficulties in maintaining focus, motivation, and academic performance and placements.

III. SPIRITUAL WELL-BEING AS KEY SKILLS FOR PROFESSIONAL STUDENTS

The exploration of the often-overlooked aspect of spiritual well-being and its significant influence on professional students' skill set in this insightful part. spiritual well-being has a transforming potential to create resilient, empathic, and morally grounded professionals, going beyond technical proficiency and academic prowess.

The concept of well-being revolves around the idea of feeling connected to something, other than ourselves and finding purpose and meaning in life. It can have an impact on reducing stress and improving our ability to cope with challenges. Believing in something other than ourselves gives us a sense of direction and helps us navigate situations. Engaging in practices like meditation, prayer or mindfulness can be a way to manage emotions and reduce stress. Being part of communities provides a sense of belonging and social support, which can counteract feelings of loneliness or isolation. People who are inclined often develop resilience that allows them to adapt better when faced with tough circumstances. Having beliefs also enables students to see challenges as opportunities for growth (Bahuguna., Bangwal, & Kumar, 2023).

It's important to note that the impact of these factors varies from student to student depending on their characteristics, background, socioeconomic status, and existing mental health conditions. Institutions, teachers, and mental health professionals play a role in providing support and resources that help students manage stress effectively and enhance their well-being during and after challenging times, like the pandemic.

IV. CHALLENGING FACTORS IN STUDENTS LIFE: DELVING INTO PREVIOUS STUDIES

We have to address the different obstacles that students in professional courses may run into while trying to keep their mental health in excellent condition. Understanding that mental health is a continuous process rather than a static state, there are various obstacles, students in professional courses encounter and these may affect their mental health as a necessary precondition for achieving professional success.

Mental stress has its expression in anxiety, depression, and somatic symptoms, which have severe and long-term repercussions. Students face significant lifespan changes (Thurber and Walton, 2012), some of which are very stressful (Herrera et al., 2017; Divaris et al., 2013). Joining college is an important transition for students from late puberty to adulthood (Arnett, 2000). The adulthood transitional changes from adolescence may be in financial, housing, social, and emotional aspects. This phase of transition may lead to interactive encounters, which may be stressful for some adults and have been proven by researchers (Bruffaerts et al., 2018 quoted for Blanco et al., 2008; Hunt & Eisenberg, 2010; Verger et al. 2010).

Several determinants relate to mental stress in college-going students like demographic (for example, gender, family organization, income; Graner et al., 2018), culture, religion, and social characteristics (like societal backing, problems making friends: Agarwal, & Mehrotra, 2023), and facets of academic Life (academic performance, feelings of leaving the course; Lima, Domingues, Ramos-Cerqueira, 2006; Amaral et al., 2008; Eisenberg and Hunt, 2013; Elani et al., 2014; Silva and Cerqueira, 2014; Costa et al., 2014). It is proven through research that the fraction of students who feel mental stress during their student is increasing (Nedregård and Olsen, 2014) as the phase becomes more demanding and causes mental illness (Nerdrum, Rustøen, and Rønnestad, 2009). At a worldwide level, mental health as expressed in terms of mental stress is stressed as a foremost civic health encounter (Stallmann, 2008; Storrie, Ahren, and Tuckett, 2010).

Universities and colleges cover a large part of young people. Taking admission to a college or university brings along many changes in social relations. It hence is an empathetic aspect (Kumar M & Balaiya J 2017) as students feel the incidence of many psychological problems (Lau Y & Yin L 2011). The severe element of mental stress is gender (AlKandari, 2017). There are gender dissimilarities mainly in disorders like depression, anxiety, stress, and somatic complaints. In India, girls students, since childhood, start fulfilling multiple roles and hence are at greater risk of undergoing mental disorders as compared to boys (Gomel, 1997; Kulkarni, 2008; Leigh J et al 2005). Academic stress and poor mental health are observed more in girl students (Subramani C et al 2017). More academic anxiety is seen in girls compared to boys (Kumari, 2018). One of the research works done in Australia has found that female students aged between 25–and 34 years had the utmost degrees of mental health complications (Said, Kypri, and Bowman, 2013). Similar results are quoted in work done by Eisenberg D et al. (2012), Steel et al. (2014), and Eisenberg, Hunt &Speer (2012).

Parenting touches different facets of children's psychological health (Casuso H et al., 2019), together with self-esteem (DeHart, Pelham, Tennen, 2006), expressive regulation (Mullen P et al 2017), socio-emotional adjustment, and well-being (Fletcher et. al, 2008). Family aspects like the quality of care provided by parents to their children during the early days make a significant difference in leading pathways for a child's life. Behavior problems have serious, long-lasting effects (Angold and Costello, 2001; Moffitt and Scott, 2008). If such issues are identified early, adverse outcomes can be reduced (Caspi, Begg, and Dickson, 1997; Shaw, Gilliom, and Ingoldsby, 2003). Researchers have identified that the child-parent relationship is a precursor to this problem. Family trouble, a poor couple working, parenting agony, motherly psychopathology, and lack of social support are some of the antecedents of the problem(Mathiesen and Sanson, 2000; Skovgaard et al.,2007; Briggs-Gowan et al., 2006 in Nomaguchi K et al 2020; Lindholdt L et al., 2022; Skovgaard, 2008; Jun WH et al 2017 Inadequate levels of sensitive parenting and harsher discipline (Mathiesen KS and Sanson, 2000) are associated with the aggravation of these problems in the later part of Life (Keys et al.,2021).

Parenting style has a profound positive or negative impact on children's mental health not only at the childhood stage but also at the adolescent stage (Dwairy & Menshar, 2006; Kerr, Stattin, and Ozdemir, 2012). Work done in Europe and America has demonstrated the relationship between honest child-rearing type and positive youngster results, bringing about developed confidence and improved psychological well-being (Möller et. al, 2016; García et al., 2018; Steinberg L, 2001; Gupta M et al 2015; Haghighi M et al 2019; Piko and Balazs, 2012; Tian et al., 2012). Minor degrees of delicate child nurture and more severe order lead to conduct issues in youngsters (Miner, Clarke-Stewart, 2008). Opposite young people with dictator guardians show the most minimal confidence levels when contrasted with other child-rearing styles (Martinez and Garcia (2007).

The children's perception of parenting sturdily affected kids psychological wellness alongside the connection between guardians and kids' (Ching Yu et al., 2019). Parenting is additionally influenced by social and social convictions (Bornstein, Cote, and Venuti, 2001; Smetana, 2017; Robinson et al., 2002), geographic area financial status (Rural and Appalachian Youth and Families Consortium, 1996), culture (Boyd Franklin N, 2003), and race/nationality (Morrissette, 1994).

Research has proved that directing behaviors by parents is also related to childhood anxiety (Wood et al., 2003). Even Parents have a substantial influence on future adolescent optimism Kerpelman JL et al (2008). The studies have also concluded that academic stress is more felt in the Indian context (Deb, Strodl, and Sun, 2015).

City life has benefits as well as risks (Dye C, 2008). The thing that is universal in all the research related to mental stress is that Urban Life creates more mental disorders (Krabbendam L et al 2005; Peen et al., 2010; Nick Manning, 2019; Frissen et al., 2017). Urban Life includes both rich and poor and is a multiplier of inequality (Amin 2007; Scambler and Scambler, 2015; Nick Manning, 2019). Metropolitan Life represents facets related to disparities of income, status, and power (Nick Manning, 2019) apparent in various ways. Socioeconomic status is one reason for mental stress (Link and Phelan, 1995).

The natural environment is associated with better psychological well-being (Rachel Kaplan et al 2011), and fewer physical ailments. Children's relationships to the natural environment have been much studied (Kazemi M et al 2004), and a direct impact on children's working or well-being explored (Taylor A F et al 2001, 2002; Taylor, Wiley AF, 1998; Grahn et al., 1997)

Mental well-being has a basic essential function at various times of Life, checking young age (Hamideh M et al. 2016; El Ansari et al 2010). Some emotional well-being develops before the age of 18 with a period from 18 to 25 (Kessler et al., 2007). It is visible that there is more incidence of mental stress issues among students in higher education and this is now a growing concern(Castillo and Schwartz, 2013; Psychiatrists TRCo, 2011). Pre-existing health problems even get aggravated when students enter universities (Zivin et al., 2009; Mortier et al., 1981Auerbach et al., 2016; O'Donnell et al., 2017).

There are indications that the importance of different relationships varies with age (Kazemi et al., 2004). In a study conducted by Prabu (2015), it has been proved that the level of stress is higher in higher secondary students in private schools than in government schools (Sharkar N et al., 2016; McNall et al, 2016).

The utmost palpable element of loneliness is the individual's genuine social relationships (Segrin, 2017). Solitary people have fewer social contacts. Alone, students go for minor dating, indulge in fewer social activities, and have a smaller number of friends (Rubin A et al 1982); Su, 2022). The less favorable the students are on the quality of their connections to such extents as positive regard, empathy, and authenticity, the lonelier students, reported being. Children of divorced parents (Wallerstein J 1980) are more likely to become lonely.

Siblings are an installation in the family lives of kids and young people. A group of workers reports their function in each other's ordinary encounters as buddies, compatriots, warriors, and as the focal point of social examinations (Susan M et al 2012).

Connections between siblings can be Life's most powerful and longest-enduring connections (Burbidge, 2013; Baber, Baber, & Sanyal, 2023). There are significant experiences (Cicirelli, 1989), both in social and conflictual aspects, produced due to relationships between siblings (Brody, GH et al., 1997). Such relationships nurture children's social, cognitive, and psychosocial development. It has been reported that siblings have both long-term and short-term advantages (Blanco et al 2008; Cicirelli, 1989; Sherman A. et al., 2006). Sibling relationships contribute to the development of children (Lobato D et al., 1988) by acting as teachers, negotiators of parental attention and control, and peers to socialize and provide experience. The role of a sibling is more critical during early, and middle adulthood, wherein siblings provide' friendship and support, which is generally mature (Keys J et al 2021). Studies have shown that having a sibling has been found to augment positive feelings such as competence and self-worth. Family psychiatry history also affects the mental health of students in institutes. A prevalence of children (71%)

detailed either a parent or a kid with a mental issue (Behere A et al 2017). Even though there are numerous positive results of growing up with kin having a mental or conduct problem, commonplace kin can encounter unsafe impacts of overseeing and adapting to the special requests and worries of having kin with these sorts of troubles (Kim & Tummala-Narra, 2022).

Furthermore, there are other studies done by Williams P et al., (2003) who found that siblings are negatively affected by their siblings with some disorders. In this regard, the level of responsibilities and privileges compared to ordinary families is more on the child without disease. The other aspect of sibling relationships is that the process of leaving home (far from parents, siblings, and friends) is another cause of stress (Mohd H et al., 2018). A kid may experience depression due to a loss of a meaningful relationship, or a change in the family (an older sibling leaves the house, a new sibling joins the family, parents separate, a grandparent dies). The sibling relationship is considered to have an extraordinary impact on youthfulness and may influence positive emotional wellness (Liu et al., 2015).

Parental employment status can be employed, unemployed, disabled, or housewife; among mothers only (Maynard D et al 2015). Employment status affects the physical health of children and adolescents (Anderson P et al 2003; Bacikova M et al 2014) and has long-term magnitudes on their children's development. In specific, fathers' and mothers' hire affect both the family's income and the time devoted to children's development. Research has also looked at parental unemployment and the severe effects that it can have on adolescents' psychological well-being (Bacikova M et al 2014) and personality development.

If parents are over-involved in work psychologically, whether or not they work long hours(Stewart D Friedman, 2018), it hurts the child's mental health. Some research results like that of Tajeri (2010) also suggested a negative correlation between mothers' occupations and students' educational performance (Belwal, Al Maqbali, & Belwal, 2023).

Household income has a more substantial impact on mental health and leads to stress problems in children and adolescents (Reiss F et al., 2013; Glasscock et al., 2013). Several lifetime mental disorders are associated with low household income levels (Sareen et al., 2011). There is a significant relationship between financial hardship and mental health concerns (Ibrahim A et al 2011; Eisenberg et al., 2012). Students with a low income had the maximum rates of mental health problems (Said D et al 2013). Indeed, researchers have discovered that money shortage has much adverse bearing on mental health in students. Paces of psychopathology and different kinds of mental problems (e.g., despondency, uneasiness) are higher among low-pay families than among people from center and high-pay families (Santiago et al., 2012; Wadsworth M et al 2005). Moreover, kids from low-pay families are bound to participate in deceptive conduct, for example, violent conduct and substance misuse (Thoits, 1982).

Poverty affects personal satisfaction and social alteration (Wilkins et al., 2004). As cited in (Carol D et al., 2009), as youths, when they know about monetary challenges in their families, their fulfillment with their family and climate gets influenced. Poverty has accumulative effects, and the long-lasting experience of poverty increases teenagers' danger of mental problems, for example, sadness, social hazards, and substance use (Fergusson D et al 2013).

V. CASE STUDY: STORIES OF PROFESSIONAL STUDENTS

This section weaves real-life student tales about obstacles during professional studies to humanize the statistical narrative. Through the quantitative data, the goal is to provide a comprehensive and compassionate view of the inspirational journey.

The stories are collected through a method of a cross-section questionnaire survey for full-time students under the age of 25 years, who were pursuing any professional degree, was conducted. Students taking full-time professional courses were part of the survey. Even International students were excluded as heterogeneous groups (Barlett S et al; Nedregård P et al., 2014). An email was sent to the students with a link to the online Questionnaire for all the students in the sample. It was mentioned in the communication that participation is entirely voluntary. The survey consisted of forty questions on a Likert-type scale and thirteen questions related to their personal information related to age, family income, education, family occupation, siblings, etc. The Questionnaire for assessing mental stress was adopted from the PMH scale (Lukat et al., 2016) and the PGI Health Questionnaire (Wig N, 2012) based on the Cornell Medical Index Health Questionnaire. Out of more than 500 questionnaires sent through emails and WhatsApp, only 259 questionnaires were found complete in all details and were further used for analysis purposes. This section provides a reflective perspective on the process of collecting and analyzing primary questionnaire data.

The summary of the research project is presented in Figure I.

Figure 1. Research Process

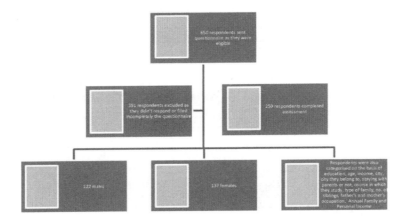

Figure 2a. Demographic Breakup

Demographic Breakup and Descriptive Analysis

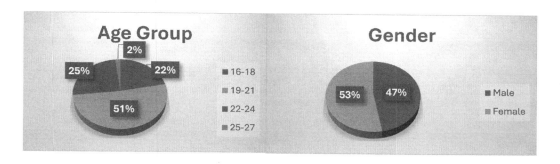

Graph I   Graph II

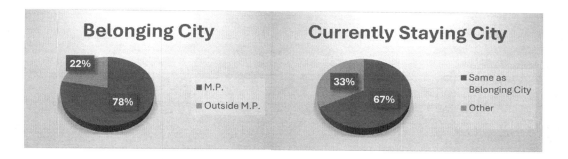

Graph III   Graph IV

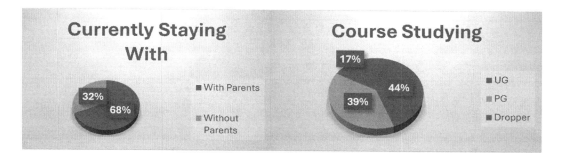

Graph V   Graph VI

Figure 2b. Descriptive Analysis

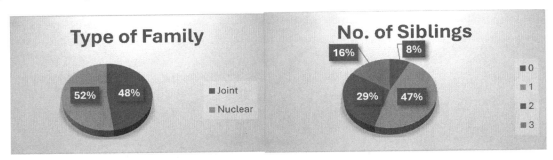

Graph VII   Graph VIII

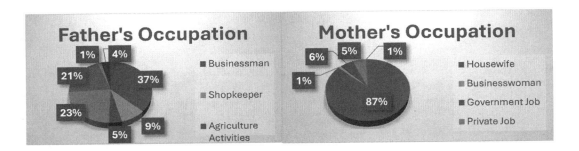

Graph IX   Graph X

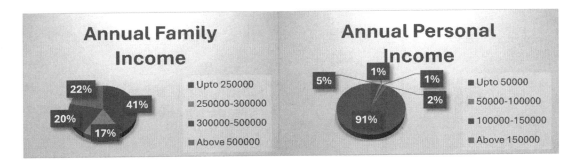

Graph XI   Graph XII

Discussion for graphs I to XII: There were a total of 259 respondents. Major student respondents (133) were from the age group 19-21. More than ¾ of the total respondents are from just two age groups i.e. 19-21 and 22-24 (graph I). The number of male and female respondents is about equal i.e. 122 and 137 respectively (graph II). 202 respondents i.e. 78% belong to Madhya Pradesh and others belong outside

Madhya Pradesh in India (graph III). It is observed that 67% of total respondents are currently living in the same city they belong to (graph IV) and 68% of total respondents living with their parents, while around 32% moved to another city and living without parents (graph V). 115 respondents (44%) were studying in various undergraduate professional programs while 100 respondents (39%) were studying in various postgraduate professional programs (graph VI). Also, 44 (17%) respondents had taken a break from studies for the preparation of various exams. Respondents equally belong to the joint family and nuclear family (graph VII). About half of the respondents have one sibling and 30% of respondents (76) have two siblings followed by 16% and 8% having three siblings and no siblings respectively (graph VIII). The top 3 occupations of the father of respondents are businessman, government job, and private job with a share of 37%, 23%, and 21% respectively, followed by shop owners (9%) and agricultural activities (5%) (Graph IX). Mothers of respondents are mostly housewives (87%), followed by government jobs (6%), private jobs (5%), and businesswomen (1%) graph 10). 41% of respondents (107) have an annual family income of up to 2.5 lahks. Also, a good share of respondents (22%) found having an annual family income above 5 lakhs (graph XI). It is also observed that 91% of the respondents don't have any income while only 5 students have an annual income above 1.5 lahks (graph XII).

Therefore, a large number of college-going students of Madhya Pradesh living with their parents have responded. Most of these have one sibling and no personal income. The major share of respondents has an annual family income ranging from 2.5 lakhs – to 3 lakhs with their father's occupation being business and job and their mother being a housewife.

VI. LEARNING FROM THE INSPIRATIONAL JOURNEY OF STUDENTS

The summary of the main conclusion drawn from survey of students emphasizes the importance of statistical knowledge in enabling educational institutions to develop settings that prioritize students' mental health while fostering academic performance. The goal is to issue a call to action for all sections of society, especially educators to use statistical insights to improve the professional studies environment. PASW 18 software was used to carry out statistical analysis. Using the same, the instrument's reliability was found to be .868. The sample was found adequate (with a value of more than .8) to undermine further factors as the KMO value for sampling adequacy was .887. Using the Principal axis factoring method, the major ten psychological determinants of mental stress were extracted (Refer to Table I).

Table 1. Summary results of EFA

Factor Name	Eigen Value	
	Total	% of Variance
Depression and Tearfulness (Factor 1)	10.751	26.878
Not Feeling Loved (Factor 2)	4.635	11.587
Disturbed Personal Life (Factor 3)	1.974	4.935

Determinants of Mental Stress: Real Life Stressors in Professional Stress

1. Depression and Tearfulness

Depression and Tearfulness emerged as the most crucial factor with 10.7512 as the Eigenvalue and explaining the 26.878% variance. Twenty-four questions were clubbed together in this factor. Depression is a state of mind or an issue that causes an industrious sentiment of misery and loss of intrigue. It influences how you feel, think, and act and prompts a range of emotional and physical issues. One may experience difficulty doing ordinary everyday exercises. Some of the time, one may feel as though Life does not merit living or an episode of the blues, sentiments of trouble, mournfulness, vacancy or sadness, outrage outbursts, loss of interest, anxiety, rest unsettling influence, and so on are a piece of it (Yang H et al 2020)

2. Not Feeling Loved

Not Feeling Loved emerged as the second most crucial factor with 4.635 as Eigenvalue and explained the 11.587% variance. Eleven questions clubbed together in this factor. Students lack the feeling of love post-second wave of COVID-19. Making them feel loved and wanted can help them mentally. They need to be adored, trusted, comprehended, esteemed, and safe(Mental Health Organization U.K.).

Making them feel adored and bolstered (and having the option to offer love and backing consequently) is a magnificent method to begin expanding confidence (Gold A, 2016). Dorsey S et al. (2015) found the effect of not feeling adored as dominatingly showing in emotional troubles and some behavior issues (e.g., meandering, taking, joining awful companion gatherings, utilizing liquor, savagery, getting away from home) in the children of Tanzania.

3. Disturbed Personal Life

Disturbed Personal Life emerged as the third most crucial factor with 1.975 as the Eigenvalue and explaining the 4.935% variance. Two questions relating to happiness and satisfaction in Disturbed Personal Life were clubbed together in this factor. Connell J et al. (2012) recognized six primary dominants of quality of life important for an individual viz., "well-being-being; control, autonomy, and choice; self-perception; belonging; activity; and hope and hopelessness." The Disturbed Personal Life of students' is disturbed and changed in present times, making it a reason for increased stress.

3 Confirmatory Factor Analysis

The Constructs derived with the help of Exploratory Factor Analysis (EFA) have been confirmed with the help of CFA which is a multivariate statistical procedure that is used to test how well the measured variables represent the number of constructs. The Summarized table for model fit has been presented in Table II.

Table 2. Summary results of CFA

Measure	Chi-Square	*P* Value	CFI	GFI	AGFI	SRMR	RMSEA	PCLOSE
Threshold	<3	>0.05	>0.95	>0.95	>0.80	<0.09	<0.05	>0.05
Output Value	2.552	0.000	0.740	0.731	0.700	0.131	0.078	0.000

As the validity measures are near the optimum range, the model is considered an acceptable one. Hence, The Hypothesized Structural Model was found to be the best model to fit the data (Table II).

The Confirmatory Factor Analysis (CFA) analysis was conducted using AMOS 18 to confirm the factors extracted by Exploratory Factor Analysis (EFA) test the formulated hypotheses and evaluate the hypothesized structural model. The emerged structural model (Figure 1) fits well with the data. Chi Square or cmin / df (X2)= 2.552, p value = 0.000; CFI= 0.740, GFI= 0.731; AGFI= 0.700; SRMR= 0.131; RMSEA= 0.131; PCLOSE= 0.000.

Figure II demonstrates the modification indices adjustment done to achieve the corresponding best model fit with the data. All the modification indices adjusted were found to be justified as per the assumptions of Confirmatory Factor Analysis (CFA). The correlation (r) between Factors named Depression and Tearfulness and Factor two named Not Feeling Loved is -0.16, Correlation (r) between Factor two named Self Satisfaction and Factor three named Disturbed Personal Life is -0.23. The correlation between Factor One and Factor Three is 0.19 (Figure II).

Figure 3. CFA Model for Mental Stress

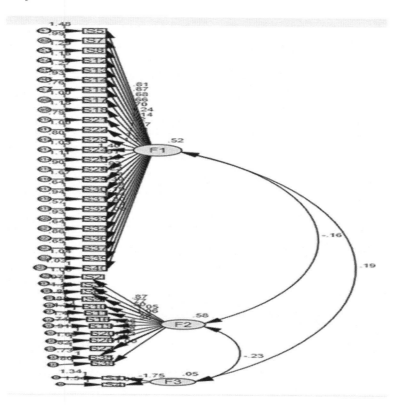

VII. ADDRESSING CHALLENGES FACED BY STUDENTS IN PROFESSIONAL COURSES

We examine the complex issues that students in professional courses face in their particular domains and how these issues may affect mental health. Given that every professional course has its own set of demands, dynamics, and stresses, this subheading aims to highlight the distinctive elements that influence mental health considerations across a range of professional fields.

One way to conceptualize good mental health is as an emotional state of well-being that enables one to thrive and fully enjoy life. Everyone experiences difficult times in their daily lives. The ability to adjust to negative experiences varies greatly, first for one person and then for the next, and plays a major role in determining whether or not people live fulfilling lives.

Students in Professional courses may use these suggestions as the tools they need to overcome obstacles and become resilient, career-ready people by examining workable and efficient ways to deal with stress barriers. Here, the emphasis is on doable tactics that not only reduce stress but also encourage the growth of critical abilities necessary for success in the workplace (Baber, Baber, & Di Virgilio, 2023).

Students are the base of society. The determinants of the mental stress of students pursuing any professional degree, as found through cases studied, give insight into the mental stress of the students. These are the students who are in the process of getting industry-ready. These stressors, if addressed, could lead to progress in the mental health of our students and further in the society of which they are part. A social determinant of mental well-being requires activity over various divisions and levels. Industry readiness encompasses not just technical proficiency but also the ability to overcome obstacles mentally. Offering resources, mentorship, and support systems to students while they pursue their academic goals can aid in their development of the mental toughness required for a smooth transition into the workforce.

Many students do not ask for professional help for mental health problems. Students can be encouraged to seek professional health or early detection and delay the progression of such issues. The frequency of psychological and mental disorders in students is much these days. Hence there should be counseling services available at colleges, and universities to avoid any tragic outcomes and help students cope with the mental crisis. Qualified counselors may be able to assess, diagnose, intervene, and further counsel the students and should be available on a flexi-time basis or telephonically when needed.

Adding to it, educational strategies can be used for a better understanding of symptoms related to mental stress and treatments thereof (KuokA et al., 2019). Parents can be guided on handling the negative perception of their parenting concerning the mental stress of the children.

VIII. RECOMMENDATIONS FOR IMPROVING PROFESSIONAL SKILL DEVELOPMENT

It is needed to comprehend how mental health and professional abilities intersect to offering concrete suggestions. This recognises the mutually beneficial relationship that exists between professional achievement and mental health, and it attempts to provide useful advice on developing mental health as a means of developing and refining critical professional abilities.

The importance of self-awareness is emphasised at the outset of the chapter. Professionals can better understand their strengths, shortcomings, and triggers by engaging in introspective exercises and mindfulness techniques. People can customize their skill development path to fit their own strengths and growth areas by cultivating self-awareness.

Educational institutions can incorporate spiritual components into their support systems by providing mindfulness courses, meditation sessions, or areas set apart for introspection and self-exploration (Khatri, & Gupta, 2022). Students' general development and preparedness for the working world can also be enhanced by fostering conversations on ethics, values, and personal development. It is imperative to guarantee that these practices are inclusive and show respect for a range of viewpoints and views.

REFERENCES

Agarwal, R., & Mehrotra, A. (2023). Work-stress content analysis using social media data. *FIIB Business Review*.

Ahmed, G. K., Khedr, E. M., Hamad, D. A., Meshref, T. S., Hashem, M. M., & Aly, M. M. (2021). Long-term impact of COVID-19 infection on sleep and mental health: A cross-sectional study. *Psychiatry Research*, 114243. Advance online publication. 10.1016/j.psychres.2021.11424334673325

AlKandari, N. Y. (2020). Students anxiety experiences in higher education institutions. In *Anxiety The new achievements*. IntechOpen.

Amaral, G. F., Gomide, L. M., Batista, M. D., Píccolo, P. D., Teles, T. B., Oliveira, P. M., & Pereira, M. A. (2008). SintomasdepressivosEmacadêmicos de medicina Da Universidade federal de Goiás: Um estudo de prevalência. *Revista de Psiquiatria do Rio Grande do Sul, 30*(2), 124-130. doi:10.1590/s0101-81082008000300008

Amin, A. (2007). Re-thinking the Urban Social. *City (London, England)*, 11(1), 100–114. 10.1080/13604810701200961

Anderson, P. M., Butcher, K. F., & Levine, P. B. (2003). Maternal employment and overweight children. *Journal of Health Economics*, 22(3), 477–504. 10.1016/S0167-6296(03)00022-512683963

Angold, A., & Costello, E. J. (2001). The epidemiology of depression in children and adolescents. *The Depressed Child and Adolescent, 2*, 143-178.

Arnett, J. J. (2000). Emerging adulthood: A theory of development from the late teens through the twenties. *The American Psychologist*, 55(5), 469–480. 10.1037/0003-066X.55.5.46910842426

Auerbach, R. P., Alonso, J., Axinn, W. G., Cuijpers, P., Ebert, D. D., Green, J. G., Hwang, I., Kessler, R. C., Liu, H., Mortier, P., Nock, M. K., Pinder-Amaker, S., Sampson, N. A., Aguilar-Gaxiola, S., Al-Hamzawi, A., Andrade, L. H., Benjet, C., Caldas-de-Almeida, J. M., Demyttenaere, K., & Bruffaerts, R. (2016). Mental disorders among college students in the World Health Organization World Mental Health Surveys. *Psychological Medicine*, 46(14), 2955–2970. 10.1017/S0033291716001665527484622

Baber, P., Baber, R., & Di Virgilio, F. (2023). Exploring the relationship between workplace spirituality, spiritual survival and innovative work behavior among healthcare professionals. *International Journal of Healthcare Management*, 1–12. 10.1080/20479700.2023.2199555

Baber, R., Baber, P., & Sanyal, A. (2023). Power and Politics: A Case of Hotel Amada. *FIIB Business Review*, 12(3), 238–242. 10.1177/23197145221139687

Bacikova-Sleskova, M., Benka, J., & Orosova, O. (2014). Parental employment status and adolescents' health: The role of financial situation, parent-adolescent relationship and adolescents' resilience. *Psychology & Health*, 30(4), 400–422. 10.1080/08870446.2014.97664525322966

Bahuguna, P. C., Bangwal, D., & Kumar, R. (2023). Talent management and its impact on organizational commitment: An empirical investigation of Indian hospitality industry. *FIIB Business Review*, 12(2), 176–192. 10.1177/23197145221101436

Bartlett, S., & Ross, J. (2022). Mental health and wellbeing of tertiary learners: What do we need to know? *Contemporary Research Topics, 66.*

Behere, A. P., Basnet, P., & Campbell, P. (2017). Effects of family structure on mental health of children: A preliminary study. *Indian Journal of Psychological Medicine*, 39(4), 457–463. 10.4103/0253-7176.21176728852240

Belwal, S., Al Maqbali, A. A. H., & Belwal, R. (2023). Understanding the Impact of Occupational Stress on the Home Environment: Evidence from Oman. *FIIB Business Review*, 12(3), 263–278. 10.1177/23197145221132064

Blanco, C., Okuda, M., Wright, C., Hasin, D. S., Grant, B. F., Liu, S., & Olfson, M. (2008). The mental health of college students and their non-college-attending peers: Results from the National Epidemiologic Study on Alcohol and Related Conditions. *Archives of General Psychiatry*, 65(12), 1429–1437. 10.1001/archpsyc.65.12.142919047530

Bornstein, M. H., Cote, L. R., & Venuti, P. (2001). Parenting beliefs and behaviors in northern and southern groups of Italian mothers of young infants. *Journal of Family Psychology*, 15(4), 663–675. 10.1037/0893-3200.15.4.66311770473

Boyd-Franklin, N. (2003). *Black families in therapy*. Guildford Press.

Bratman, G. N., & Alvarez, H. O. (2021). Psychological impacts from COVID-19 among university students: Risk factors across seven states in the United States. *PLoS One*, 16(1), e0245327. 10.1371/journal.pone.024532733411812

Briggs-Gowan, M. J., Carter, A. S., Bosson-Heenan, J., Guyer, A. E., & Horwitz, S. M. (2006). Are infant-toddler social-emotional and behavioral problems transient? *Journal of the American Academy of Child and Adolescent Psychiatry*, 45(7), 849–858. 10.1097/01.chi.0000220849.48650.5916832322

Brody, G. H., Stoneman, Z., & Burke, M. (1987). Child temperaments, maternal differential behavior, and sibling relationships. *Developmental Psychology*, 23(3), 354–362. 10.1037/0012-1649.23.3.354

Bruffaerts, R., Mortier, P., Kiekens, G., Auerbach, R. P., Cuijpers, P., Demyttenaere, K., & Kessler, R. C. (2018). Mental health problems in college freshmen: Prevalence and academic functioning. *Journal of Affective Disorders*, 225, 97–103. 10.1016/j.jad.2017.07.04428802728

Burbidge, J. G. (2013). *Effect of sibling relationships on well-being and depression in adults with and without developmental disabilities*. Queen's University.

Caspi, A., Begg, D., Dickson, N., Harrington, H., Langley, J., Moffitt, T. E., & Silva, P. A. (1997). Personality differences predict health-risk behaviors in young adulthood: Evidence from a longitudinal study. *Journal of Personality and Social Psychology*, 73(5), 1052–1063. 10.1037/0022-3514.73.5.10529364760

Castillo, L. G., & Schwartz, S. J. (2013). Introduction to the Special Issue on College Student Mental Health. *Journal of Clinical Psychology*, 69(4), 291–297. 10.1002/jclp.2197223381839

Casuso-Holgado, M. J., Moreno-Morales, N., Labajos-Manzanares, M. T., & Montero-Bancalero, F. J. (2019). The association between perceived health symptoms and academic stress in Spanish higher education students. *European Journal of Education and Psychology*, 12(2), 109–123. 10.30552/ejep. v12i2.277

Cicirelli, V. G. (1989). Feelings of attachment to siblings and well-being in later life. *Psychology and Aging*, 4(2), 211–216. 10.1037/0882-7974.4.2.2112789748

Connell, J., Brazier, J., O'Cathain, A., Lloyd-Jones, M., & Paisley, S. (2012). Quality of Life of people with mental health problems: A synthesis of qualitative research. *Health and Quality of Life Outcomes*, 10(1), 138. 10.1186/1477-7525-10-13823173689

Costa, E. F., Rocha, M. M., Santos, A. T., Melo, E. V., Martins, L. A., & Andrade, T. M. (2014). Common mental disorders and associated factors among final-year healthcare students. *Revista da Associação Médica Brasileira*, 60(6), 525–530. 10.1590/1806-9282.60.06.00925650851

Dashiff, C., DiMicco, W., Myers, B., & Sheppard, K. (2009). Poverty and Adolescent Mental Health. *Journal of Child and Adolescent Psychiatric Nursing*, 22(1), 23–32. 10.1111/j.1744-6171.2008.00166. x19200289

Deb, S., Strodl, E., & Sun, J. (2015). Academic Stress, Parental Pressure, Anxiety and Mental Health among Indian High School Students. *International Journal of Psychology and Behavioral Sciences*, 5(1), 26–34.

DeHart, T., Pelham, B. W., & Tennen, H. (2006). What lies beneath: Parenting style and implicit self-esteem. *Journal of Experimental Social Psychology*, 42(1), 1–17. 10.1016/j.jesp.2004.12.005

Divaris, K., Mafla, A. C., Villa-Torres, L., Sánchez-Molina, M., Gallego-Gómez, C. L., Vélez-Jaramillo, L. F., & Polychronopoulou, A. (2013). Psychological distress and its correlates among dental students: A survey of 17 Colombian dental schools. *BMC Medical Education*, 13(1), 91. Advance online publication. 10.1186/1472-6920-13-9123802917

Dorsey, S., Lucid, L., Murray, L., Bolton, P., Itemba, D., Manongi, R., & Whetten, K. (2015). A qualitative study of mental health problems among orphaned children and adolescents in Tanzania. *The Journal of Nervous and Mental Disease*, 203(11), 864–870. 10.1097/NMD.00000000000038826488916

Dwairy, M., & Menshar, K. E. (2006). Parenting style, individuation, and mental health of Egyptian adolescents. *Journal of Adolescence*, 29(1), 103–117. 10.1016/j.adolescence.2005.03.00216338432

Dye, C. (2008). Health and urban living. *Science*, 319(5864), 766–769. 10.1126/science.115019818258905

Eisenberg, D., Hunt, J., & Speer, N. (2012). Help-seeking for mental health on college campuses: Review of evidence and next steps for research and practice. *Harvard Review of Psychiatry*, 20(4), 222–232. 10 .3109/10673229.2012.71283922894731

El Ansari, W., & Stock, C. (2010). Is the health and wellbeing of university students associated with their academic performance? Cross sectional findings from the United Kingdom. *International Journal of Environmental Research and Public Health*, 7(2), 509–527. 10.3390/ijerph702050920616988

Elani, H. W., Allison, P. J., Kumar, R. A., Mancini, L., Lambrou, A., & Bedos, C. (2014). A systematic review of stress in dental students. *Journal of Dental Education*, 78(2), 226–242. http://www.jdentaled .org/ content/78/2/226.full.pdf+html. 10.1002/j.0022-0337.2014.78.2.tb05673.x24489030

Erevik, E. K., Pallesen, S., Vedaa, Ø., Andreassen, C. S., Dhir, A., & Torsheim, T. (2020). General and alcohol-related social media use and mental health: A large-sample longitudinal study. *International Journal of Mental Health and Addiction*, 19(6), 1991–2002. 10.1007/s11469-020-00296-y

Fergusson, D. M., Woodward, L. J., & Horwood, L. J. (2013). Risk factors and life processes associated with the onset of suicidal behaviour during adolescence and early adulthood. *Psychological Medicine*, 30(1), 23–39. 10.1017/S003329179900135X10722173

Frissen, A., van Os, J., Lieverse, R., Habets, P., Gronenschild, E., & Marcelis, M. (2017). No evidence of association between childhood urban environment and cortical thinning in psychotic disorder. *PLoS One*, 12(1), e0166651. 10.1371/journal.pone.016665128045900

García, O. F., Serra, E., Zacarés, J. J., & García, F. (2018). Parenting styles and short- and long-term socialization outcomes: A study among Spanish adolescents and older adults. *Psychosocial Intervention*, 27(3), 153–161. 10.5093/pi2018a21

Glasscock, D. J., Andersen, J. H., Labriola, M., Rasmussen, K., & Hansen, C. D. (2013). Can negative life events and coping style help explain socioeconomic differences in perceived stress among adolescents? A cross-sectional study based on the West Jutland cohort study. *BMC Public Health*, 13(1), 532. 10.1186/1471-2458-13-53223724872

Gold, A. (2016, July 12). *Why self-esteem is important for mental health.* Retrieved from https://www .nami.org/Blogs/NAMI-Blog/July-2016/Why-Self-Esteem-Is-Important-for-Mental-Health

Grahn, P., & Stigsdotter, U. A. (2003). Landscape planning and stress. *Urban Forestry & Urban Greening*, 2(1), 1–18. 10.1078/1618-8667-00019

Graner, K. M., Moraes, A. B., Torres, A. R., Lima, M. C., Rolim, G. S., & Ramos-Cerqueira, A. T. (2018). Prevalence and correlates of common mental disorders among dental students in Brazil. *PLoS One*, 13(9), e0204558. 10.1371/journal.pone.020455830261025

Gupta & Mehtani. (2015). Parenting Style and Psychological Well-Being among Adolescents: A Theoretical Perspective. *ZENITH International Journal of Multidisciplinary Research, 5(2),* 74-84.

Haghighi, M., & Gerber, M. (2019). Does mental toughness buffer the relationship between perceived stress, depression, burnout, anxiety, and sleep? *International Journal of Stress Management*, 26(3), 297–305. 10.1037/str0000106

Hardjom, S., & Haryono, S., & Bashor, K. (2021). The Role of Coping Strategies in Achieving Psychological Well Being in Students During the Covid-19 Pandemic with Religiosity as a Moderator Variable. *Psychology and Education*, 58(5), 25–34.

Herrera, R., Berger, U., Genuneit, J., Gerlich, J., Nowak, D., Schlotz, W., & Radon, K. (2017). Chronic stress in young German adults: Who is affected? A prospective cohort study. *International Journal of Environmental Research and Public Health*, 14(11), 1325. 10.3390/ijerph1411132529088088

Huang, C., Hsieh, Y., Shen, A., Wei, H., Feng, J., Hwa, H., & Feng, J. (2019). Relationships between parent-reported parenting, child-perceived parenting, and children's mental health in Taiwanese children. *International Journal of Environmental Research and Public Health*, 16(6), 1049. 10.3390/ijerph1606104930909532

Hunt, J., & Eisenberg, D. (2010). Mental health problems and help-seeking behavior among college students. *The Journal of Adolescent Health*, 46(1), 3–10. 10.1016/j.jadohealth.2009.08.00820123251

Ibrahim, A., Kelly, S., & Glazebrook, C. (2011). Analysis of an Egyptian study on the socioeconomic distribution of depressive symptoms among undergraduates. *Social Psychiatry and Psychiatric Epidemiology*, 47(6), 927–937. 10.1007/s00127-011-0400-x21626055

Jouybari, L., Manchri, H., Sanagoo, A., Sabzi, Z., & Jafari, S. Y. (2017). Hamideh Manchri, Akram Sanagoo, Leila Jouybari, Zahra Sabzi, Seyyed Yaghob Jafari (2016). The relationship between mental health status with academic performance and demographic factors among students of university of medical sciences. *Journal of Nursing and Midwifery Sciences*, 4(1), 8–13. 10.18869/acadpub.jnms.4.1.8

Jun, W. H., & Lee, G. (2017). Comparing anger, anger expression, life stress and social support between Korean female nursing and general university students. *Journal of Advanced Nursing*, 73(12), 2914–2922. 10.1111/jan.1335428556972

Kaplan, R., & Kaplan, S. (2011). Well-being, Reasonableness, and the Natural Environment. *Applied Psychology. Health and Well-Being*, 3(3), 304–321. Advance online publication. 10.1111/j.1758-0854.2011.01055.x

Kazemi, M., Ansari, A., Allah Tavakoli, M., & Karimi, S. (2004). The Effect of the Recitation of Holy Quran on Mental Health in Nursing Students of Rafsanjan University of Medical Sciences. *JRUMS*, 3(1), 52-57. http://journal.rums.ac.ir/article-1-53-en.html

Kerpelman, J. L., Eryigit, S., & Stephens, C. J. (2008). African American adolescents' future education orientation: Associations with self efficacy, ethnic identity, and perceived parental support. *Journal of Youth and Adolescence*, 37(8), 997–1008. 10.1007/s10964-007-9201-7

Kerr, M., Stattin, H., & Ozdemir, M. (2012). Perceived parenting style and adolescent adjustment: Revisiting directions of effects and the role of parental knowledge. *Developmental Psychology*, 48(6), 1540–1553. 10.1037/a002772022448987

Kessler, R. C., Amminger, G. P., Aguilar-Gaxiola, S., Alonso, J., Lee, S., & Ustun, T. B. (2007). Age of onset of mental disorders: A review of recent literature. *Current Opinion in Psychiatry*, 20(4), 359–364. 10.1097/YCO.0b013e32816ebc8c17551351

Keys, J., Dempster, M., Jackson, J., Williams, M., & Coyle, S. (2021). The psychosocial impact of losing an eye through traumatic injury and living with prosthetic restoration: A thematic analysis. *Acta Psychologica*, 219, 103383. 10.1016/j.actpsy.2021.10338334352606

Khatri, P., & Gupta, P. (2022). Impact of Workplace Spirituality on Employee Well-Being: The Mediating Role of Organizational Politics. *FIIB Business Review*.

Kim, J., & Tummala-Narra, P. (2022). Rise of anti-Asian violence and the COVID-19 pandemic for Asian Americans. *Asian American Journal of Psychology*, 13(3), 217–219. 10.1037/aap0000301

Krabbendam, L., & van Os, J. (2005). Schizophrenia and urbanicity: A major environmental influence–conditional on genetic risk. *Schizophrenia Bulletin*, 31(4), 795–799. 10.1093/schbul/sbi06016150958

Kulkarni, J. (2008). Women's Mental Health. *The Australian and New Zealand Journal of Psychiatry*, 42(1), 1–2. 10.1080/00048670701762662180584 37

Kumar, M. H., & Baliya, J. N. (2017). Study on mental health among college students with respect to their cognitive styles. International Journal of Law. *Psychology and Human Life*, 4(2), 8–13.

Kuok, A. C., & Rashidnia, J. (2019). College students' attitudes toward counseling for mental health issues in two developing Asian countries. *Spiritual Psychology and Counseling*, 4(1), 67–84. 10.37898/spc.2019.4.1.0056

Lau, Y., & Yin, L. (2011). Maternal, obstetric variables, perceived stress and health-related quality of life among pregnant women in Macao, China. *Midwifery*, 27(5), 668–673. 10.1016/j.midw.2010.02.00820466467

Leigh, J., Bowen, S., & Marlatt, G. A. (2005). Spirituality, mindfulness and substance abuse. *Addictive Behaviors*, 30(7), 1335–1341. 10.1016/j.addbeh.2005.01.01016022930

Lima, M. C., Domingues, M. D., & Cerqueira, A. T. (2006). Prevalência E fatores de risco para transtornosmentaiscomuns entre estudantes de medicina. *Revista de Saude Publica*, 40(6), 1035–1041. 10.1590/S0034-89102006000700011117173160

Lindhoïdt, L., Labriola, M., Andersen, J. H., Kjeldsen, M. M. Z., Obel, C., & Lund, T. (2022). Perceived stress among adolescents as a marker for future mental disorders: A prospective cohort study. *Scandinavian Journal of Public Health*, 50(3), 412–417. 10.1177/14034948219937193 3641501

Link, B., & Phelan, J. (1995). Social Conditions As Fundamental Causes of Disease. *Journal of Health and Social Behavior*, 35, 80–94. 10.2307/26269587560851

Liu, J., Sekine, M., Tatsuse, T., Fujimura, Y., Hamanishi, S., & Zheng, X. (2015). Association among number, order and type of siblings and adolescent mental health at age 12. *Pediatrics International*, 57(5), 849–855. 10.1111/ped.1262925808043

Lobato, D., Faust, D., & Spirito, A. (1988). Examining the effects of chronic disease and disability on children's sibling relationships. *Journal of Pediatric Psychology*, 13(3), 389–407. 10.1093/jpepsy/13.3.3893058922

Lukat, J., Margraf, J., Lutz, R., van der Veld, W. M., & Becker, E. S. (2016). Psychometric properties of the Positive Mental Health Scale (PMH-scale). *BMC Psychology*, 4(1), 8. 10.1186/s40359-016-0111-x26865173

Manning, N. (2019). Sociology, biology and mechanisms in urban mental health. Social Theory & Health. *Journal of Marriage and Family*, 82(1), 198–223.

Martinez, I., & Garcia, J. F. (2007). Impact of parenting styles on adolescents' self-esteem and internalization of values in Spain. *The Spanish Journal of Psychology*, 10(2), 338–348. 10.1017/S1138741600006600017992960

Mathiesen, K. S., & Sanson, A. (2000). Dimensions of early childhood behavior problems: Stability and predictors of change from 18 to 30 months. *Journal of Abnormal Child Psychology*, 28(1), 15–31. 10.1023/A:100516591690610772347

Maynard, D.-M., & Fayombo, G. (2015). Influence of Parental Employment Status on Caribbean Adolescents' Self-Esteem. *International Journal of School and Cognitive Psychology.*, 2, 1–6. 10.4172/1234-3425.1000123

McHale, S. M., Updegraff, K. A., & Whiteman, S. D. (2012, October 1). Sibling Relationships and Influences in Childhood and. Adolescence. *Journal of Marriage and Family*, 74(5), 913–930. 10.1111/j.1741-3737.2012.01011.x24653527

McNall, L. A., & Michel, J. S. (2016). The relationship between student core self-evaluations, support for school, and the work–school interface. *Community Work & Family*, 20(3), 253–272. 10.1080/13668803.2016.1249827

Miner, J. L., & Clarke-Stewart, K. A. (2008). Trajectories of externalizing behavior from age 2 to age 9: Relations with gender, temperament, ethnicity, parenting, and rater. *Developmental Psychology*, 44(3), 771–786. 10.1037/0012-1649.44.3.77118473643

Moffitt, T. E., & Scott, S. (2008). Conduct disorders of childhood and adolescence. In *Rutter's child and adolescent psychiatry* (5th ed.). Blackwell Publishing Ltd. 10.1002/9781444300895.ch35

Mohamad, M. H., Baidi, N., & Nor, H. N. A. (2018). The relationship between mental health, stress and academic performance among college student. *The European Proceedings of Social & Behavioural Sciences*. 10.15405/epsbs.2018.07.02.60

Mokhtar, M. M., Rosenthal, D. A., Hocking, J. S., & Satar, N. A. (2013). Bridging the gap: Malaysian youths and the pedagogy of school-based sexual health education. *Procedia: Social and Behavioral Sciences*, 85, 236–245. 10.1016/j.sbspro.2013.08.355

Möller, E. L., Nikolić, M., Majdandžić, M., & Bögels, S. M. (2016). Associations between maternal and paternal parenting behaviors, anxiety and its precursors in early childhood: A meta-analysis. *Clinical Psychology Review*, 45, 17–33. 10.1016/j.cpr.2016.03.00226978324

Morrissette, P. J. (1994). The holocaust of first nation people: Residual effects on parenting and treatment implications. *Contemporary Family Therapy*, 16(5), 381–392. 10.1007/BF02197900

Mortier, P., Demyttenaere, K., Auerbach, R. P., Green, J. G., Kessler, R. C., & Kiekens, G.. (1981). The impact of lifetime suicidality on academic performance in college freshmen. *Journal of Affective Disorders*, 2015(186), 254–260.26254617

Mullen, P. R., Morris, C., & Lord, M. (2017). The experience of ethical dilemmas, burnout, and stress among practicing counselors. *Counseling and Values*, 62(1), 37–56. 10.1002/cvj.12048

Munni. (2018). A Study of Academic Anxiety in Relation to Mental Health in Adolescents. *International Journal of Current Research and Review*. DOI: 10.7324/IJCRR.2018.1066

Nedregård, T., & Olsen, R. (2014). *Studentenes Helse- OgTrivselsundersøkelse SHOT 2014*. Available at: http://www.vtbergen.no/wp-content/uploads/2013/10/VT0614_6214_SHoT2014.pdf

Nerdrum, P., Rustoen, T., & Helge Roinstead, M. (2009). Psychological distress among nursing, physiotherapy, and occupational therapy students: A longitudinal and predictive study. *Scandinavian Journal of Educational Research*, 53(4), 363–378. 10.1080/00313830903043133

O'Donnell, M. L., Schaefer, I., Varker, T., Kartal, D., Forbes, D., Bryant, R. A., & Steel, Z. (2017). A systematic review of person-centered approaches to investigating patterns of trauma exposure. *Clinical Psychology Review*, 57, 208–225. 10.1016/j.cpr.2017.08.00928919323

Peen, J., Schoevers, R. A., Beekman, A. T., & Dekker, J. (2010). The current status of urbanrural differences in psychiatric disorders. *Acta Psychiatrica Scandinavica*, 121(2), 84–93. 10.1111/j.1600-0447.2009.01438. x19624573

Piko, B.F., & Balazs, M.A. (2012). Control or involvement? Relationship between authoritative parenting style and adolescent depressive symptomology. *Eur Child Adolesc Psychiatry, 21*, 149–155.

Prabu, S., (2015). A Study on Academic Stress among Higher Secondary Students. *International Journal of Humanities and Social Science Invention*.

Psychiatrists TRCo. (2011). *Mental health of students in higher education*. Author.

Reiss, F. (2013). Socioeconomic inequalities and mental health problems in children and adolescents: A systematic review. *Social Science & Medicine*, 90, 24–31. 10.1016/j.socscimed.2013.04.02623746605

Rubin, A. (1982). *Research and Therapy*. New York: Wiley.

Rural and Appalachian Youth and Families Consortium. (1996). Parenting practices and interventions among marginalized families in Appalachia: building on family strengths. *Fam Relat, 45*, 387–396.

Said, D., Kypri, K., & Bowman, J. (2013). Risk factors for mental disorder among university students in Australia: Findings from a web-based cross-sectional survey. *Social Psychiatry and Psychiatric Epidemiology*, 48(6), 935–944. 10.1007/s00127-012-0574-x22945366

Santiago, C. D., Etter, E. M., Wadsworth, M. E., & Raviv, T. (2012, May). Predictors of responses to stress among families coping with poverty-related stress. *Anxiety, Stress, and Coping*, 25(3), 239–258. 10.1080/10615806.2011.58334721614698

Sareen, J., Afifi, T. O., McMillan, K. A., & Asmundson, G. J. (2011). Relationship between household income and mental disorders: Findings from a population-based longitudinal study. *Archives of General Psychiatry*, 68(4), 419–427. 10.1001/archgenpsychiatry.2011.1521464366

Scambler & Scambler. (2015). Theorizing health inequalities: The untapped potential of dialectical critical realism. *Social Theory & Health 13, 3*(4), 340–354.

Segrin, C. (2017). Indirect effects of social skills on health through stress and loneliness. *Health Communication*, 34(1), 118–124. 10.1080/10410236.2017.138443429053380

Shankar, N. L., & Park, C. L. (2016). Effects of stress on students' physical and mental health and academic success. *International Journal of School & Educational Psychology*, 4(1), 5–9. 10.1080/21683603.2016.1130532

Shaw, D. S., Gilliom, M., Ingoldsby, E. M., & Nagin, D. S. (2003). Trajectories leading to school-age conduct problems. *Developmental Psychology*, 39(2), 189–200. 10.1037/0012-1649.39.2.18912661881

Sherman, A. M., Lansford, J. E., & Volling, B. L. (2006). Sibling relationships and best friendships in young adulthood: Warmth, conflict, and well-being. *Personal Relationships*, 13(2), 151–165. 10.1111/j.1475-6811.2006.00110.x

Silva, A. G., Cerqueira, A. T., & Lima, M. C. (2014). Social support and common mental disorder among medical students. *Revista Brasileira de Epidemiologia*, 17(1), 229–242. 10.1590/1415-790X201400010018E-NG24896795

Skovgaard, A. M., Houmann, T., Christiansen, E., Landorph, S., Jørgensen, T., Olsen, E. M., Heering, K., Kaas-Nielsen, S., Samberg, V., & Lichtenberg, A. (2007). 2008 The prevalence of mental health problems in children 11/2 years of age – the copenhagen child cohort 2000. *Journal of Child Psychology and Psychiatry, and Allied Disciplines*, 48(1), 62–70. 10.1111/j.1469-7610.2006.01659.x17244271

Smetana, J. G. (2017). Current research on parenting styles, dimensions, and beliefs. *Current Opinion in Psychology*, 15, 19–25. 10.1016/j.copsyc.2017.02.01228813261

Squires, L. R., Hollett, K. B., Hesson, J., & Harris, N. (2020). Psychological distress, emotion dysregulation, and coping behaviour: A theoretical perspective of problematic smartphone use. *International Journal of Mental Health and Addiction*, 19(4), 1284–1299. 10.1007/s11469-020-00224-0

Stallmann, H. M. (2008). Prevalence of psychological distress in university students: Implications for service delivery. *Australian Family Physician*, 37, 673–677.18704221

Steel, Z., Marnane, C., Iranpour, C., Chey, T., Jackson, J. W., Patel, V., & Silove, D. (2014). The global prevalence of common mental disorders: A systematic review and meta-analysis 1980–2013. *International Journal of Epidemiology*, 43(2), 476–493. 10.1093/ije/dyu03824648481

Steinberg, L. (2001). We know some things: Parent–adolescent relationships in retrospect and prospect. *Journal of Research on Adolescence*, 11(1), 1–19. 10.1111/1532-7795.00001

Stewart, . (2018). https://hbr.org/2018/11/how-our-careers-affect-our-children

Storrie, K., Ahern, K., & Tuckett, A. (2010). A systematic review: Students with mental health problems-A growing problem. *International Journal of Nursing Practice*, 16(1), 1–6. 10.1111/j.1440-172X.2009.01813.x20158541

Su, T. (2022). Does family cohesion moderate the relationship between acculturative stress and depression among Asian American immigrants? *Asian American Journal of Psychology*, 13(2), 141–148. 10.1037/aap0000227

Subramani, C., & Kadhiravan, S. (2017). Academic stress and mental health among high school students. *Indian Journal of Applied Research*, 7(5), 404–406.

Tajeri, B. (2010). *A survey on the influence of mothers' employment on behavioral and educational performance of children.* Available from http://pooyamoshavereh.persianblog.ir/post/82

Taylor, A. F., Kuo, F. E., & Sullivan, W. C. (2001). Coping with ADD: The surprising connection to green play settings. *Environment and Behavior*, 33(1), 54–77. 10.1177/00139160121972864

Taylor, A. F., Wiley, A., Kuo, F. E., & Sullivan, W. C. (1998). Growing up in the inner city: Green spaces as places to grow. *Environment and Behavior*, 30(1), 3–27. 10.1177/0013916598301001

Thoits, P.A. (1982). Life stress, social support, and psychological vulnerability: epidemiological considerations. *J Community Psychol.*, 10(4), 341–362.

Thurber, C. A., & Walton, E. A. (2012). Homesickness and adjustment in university students. *Journal of American College Health*, 60(5), 415–419. 10.1080/07448481.2012.67352022686364

Tian, L., Chen, G., Wang, S., Liu, H., & Zhang, W. (2012). Effects of parental support and friendship support on loneliness and depression during early and middle adolescence. *Acta Psychologica Sinica*, 44(7), 944–956. 10.3724/SP.J.1041.2012.00944

Verger, P., Guagliardo, V., Gilbert, F., Rouillon, F., & Kovess-Masfety, V. (2010). Psychiatric disorders in students in six French universities: 12-month prevalence, comorbidity, impairment, and help-seeking. *Social Psychiatry and Psychiatric Epidemiology*, 45(2), 189–199. 10.1007/s00127-009-0055-z19381424

Wadsworth, M. E., & Achenbach, T. M. (2005, December). Explaining the link between low socioeconomic status and psychopathology: Testing two mechanisms of the social causation hypothesis. *Journal of Consulting and Clinical Psychology*, 73(6), 1146–1153. 10.1037/0022-006X.73.6.114616392987

Wallerstein, J. S., & Kelly, J. B. (1980). The effects of parental divorce: Experiences of the child in later latency. In Hartog, J. (Ed.), *4s. The Anatomy of Lonelinex.* International Universities Press.

Wig, N. (2012). Chapter-60 a model for rural psychiatric Services Raipur rani experience. *Community Mental Health in India*, 603-616. 10.5005/jp/books/11688_60

Wilkins, A. J., O'Callaghan, M. J., Najman, J. M., Bor, W., Williams, G. M., & Shuttlewood, G. (2004). Early childhood factors influencing health-related quality of life in adolescents at 13 years. *Journal of Paediatrics and Child Health*, 40(3), 102–111. 10.1111/j.1440-1754.2004.00309.x15009573

Williams, P. D., Williams, A. R., Graff, J. C., Hanson, S., Stanton, A., Hafeman, C., Liebergen, A., Leuenberg, K., Setter, R. K., Ridder, L., Curry, H., Barnard, M., & Sanders, S. (2003). A community-based intervention for siblings and parents of children with chronic illness or disability: The ISEE Study. *The Journal of Pediatrics*, 143(3), 386–393. 10.1067/S0022-3476(03)00391-314517525

Wood, J. J., McLeod, B. D., Sigman, M., Hwang, W.-C., & Chu, B. C. (2003). Parenting and childhood anxiety: Theory, empirical findings, and future directions. *Journal of Child Psychology and Psychiatry, and Allied Disciplines*, 44(1), 134–151. 10.1111/1469-7610.0010612553416

Yang, H., Bin, P., & He, A. J. (2020). Opinions from the epicenter: An online survey of university students in Wuhan amidst the COVID-19 outbreak1. *Journal of Chinese Governance*, 5(2), 234–248. 10.1080/23812346.2020.1745411

Yang, L., Zhao, Y., Wang, Y., Liu, L., Zhang, X., Li, B., & Cui, R. (2015). The effects of psychological stress on depression. *Current Neuropharmacology*, 13(4), 494–504. 10.2174/1570159X13041508311 5050726412069

Yavuz, B., & Dilmaç, B. (2020). The relationship between psychological hardiness and mindfulness in University students: The role of spiritual well-being. *Spiritual Psychology and Counseling*, 5(3), 257–271. 10.37898/spc.2020.5.3.090

Zivin, K., Eisenberg, D., Gollust, S. E., & Golberstein, E. (2009). Persistence of mental health problems and needs in a college student population. *Journal of Affective Disorders*, 117(3), 180–185. 10.1016/j.jad.2009.01.00119178949

Chapter 8
Influence of Industry–Academia Collaboration on Technology Maturity and Employment Generation:
A Conceptual Framework

Amanpreet Singh Chopra
https://orcid.org/0009-0009-7181-8794
Chitkara Business School, Chitkara University, Punjab, India

Sridhar Manohar
https://orcid.org/0000-0003-0173-3479
Chitkara Business School, Chitkata University, Punjab, India

Saurabh Agarwala
Engineers India Limited, India

ABSTRACT

The university ecosystem has reached a tipping point where these educational hubs are adopting pathways to achieve 'third mission' of entrepreneurship. These efforts are strengthened by the growth of university business incubators (UBIs) and the evolving nature of their collaboration with industry to support the technological growth of new ventures. Thriving on competitive advantage derived from innovative products or services, these startups under the aegis UBIs follow technological growth pathways through exploratory and/or exploitative innovation. The chapter will introduce the growth in technology readiness level (TRL), the maturity of technology offerings of a startup as determinate of venture success. The chapter, while relying on theoretical frameworks of innovation, TRL, and employment, would develop a conceptual framework of the impact of collaborative partnership between academia and industry on the innovation strategy of entrepreneurial venture and its influence on the technology success of the venture and to understand overall impact on generation on employment opportunities.

DOI: 10.4018/979-8-3693-3096-8.ch008

1. INTRODUCTION

The University ecosystem in India has evolved from just being a standalone medium for imparting quality education to a multidimensional entity to support students' entrepreneurial ventures and take them from ideation to commercial success. These universities, through imparting entrepreneurial education as part of their curriculum and development of technology transfer and incubation centres under their aegis are extending a range of tangible and intangible support services to the incubatee or students' entrepreneurial firms to metamorphosis into a successful business venture. These are being done either by leveraging their internal resource base or through industry collaboration. It is worthwhile to note that while university students possess novel technological or business ideas, their entrepreneurial acumen may not be adequately developed to take this ideation to a successful commercial offering. This may be due to a variety of reasons including lack of support in terms of infrastructure, administration, mentoring, training, networking, intellectual property, business development, commercial & financial knowledge, funding etc. for which they look forward to university-based incubation centres. These centres either leveraging their internal resources or through external industrial support are in the process of developing their capabilities and expanding their capacities to support these nascent entrepreneurial ventures. Thus, triggering a new phase and of Industry-Academia collaboration with a mission to support nascent but innovative ventures towards commercial and technological success. As these startups are mostly based on unique technology offerings, it is critical that at the evolution stage, they receive technological support in various forms to improve the maturity level of their technology offerings.

This chapter will analyse the growth of these university-based incubators in the Indian educational ecosystem and the evolving nature of their collaboration with industry to support the technological growth of these startups. Startups thrive on competitive advantage derived from innovative products or processes. They follow mutually exclusive pathways towards innovation either through exploratory or exploitative innovation. Another enquiry of this chapter would be on the two distinct innovation pathways these startups would take to move towards the venture success i.e. the choice of Exploratory or Exploitative innovation pathways before the startups adopt. Further, the chapter will introduce the growth in Technology Readiness Level (TRL), a framework developed by NASA as one of the determinates of startup success and will propose the conceptual framework of collaborative support structure of University sponsored UBIs and Industry, the technology orientation of Startups and the impact of this Academia-Industry partnership on the Technological Readiness Level.

This chapter will also introduce 4th generation of business model of UBIs with graduation from 1st generation of infrastructure support to 2nd generation of UBIs offering administrative and business offerings to the 3rd generation which includes networking, mentoring, marketing and finance as part of their support system. The 4th generation of UBIs with industry collaboration is envisioned to offer service portfolio which is much broader and deeper than the previous generations. This would be helpful for the universities to develop their collaborative business model along with industry which could lead to better performance of incubatee firms on technological matrices. The chapter would also contribute to the existing literature on university startup ecosystem and entrepreneurship by developing a conceptual framework which could be taken up for further empirical research.

2. RISE OF ENTREPRENEURIAL UNIVERSITIES

The University ecosystem across the globe has seen a radical shift in terms of change of their mission from being the provider of knowledge, and inventor of technology to the provider of support systems for the development of new ventures which is termed as their third mission – Entrepreneurship or terming as Entrepreneurial Universities (Etzkowitz, 2013). In this quest towards their third mission, the role or collaboration with industry is critical. The industry has always developed a strong relationship towards developing entrepreneurial traits. In the panel data of 33 countries, this critical role of industry and its positive relationship with economic and entrepreneurial growth was noted. This 'N-Shaped' relationship leads to more success in opportunity-based entrepreneurship with a positive impact on technology and overall venture growth (Xin and Park, 2024).

With the development of high technology and innovative solutions for the industry at forefront of University mission, the need for collaboration between Universities possessing complementary infrastructure and skill sets was also established for undertaking joint research activities, technology transfer between universities, co-patenting and exchange of students and researchers with the intent of generating technological value for the industry (Pereira et al., 2023). Utilizing the theory of planned behaviour, the empirical analysis of students of eight universities suggests the positive impact of creativity and attitude on the entrepreneurial intention of the students with university support system provided through technology transfer office and incubation centres moderating this relationship and the need was felt for further development of these incubators through microfinancing (Anjum et al., 2020).

Universities as centre of knowledge generation and delivery have moved into their third phase of development as hub for entrepreneurship. This phase which is led by the need for collaborative partnership with industry is graduation over the historical development phases of university growth of education, development and protection of innovation and growth of technology transfer office, thus, closing the circle of knowledge (Etzkowitz, 2013). These multi-facade collaborations are also designated as precursors to the radical innovations and technological breakthroughs in the university technological ecosystem (Block and Keller, 2008) thus supporting their graduation where research was considered as part of the university function to the development of entrepreneurial traits as part of 3rd academic revolution (Etzkowitz, 2013).

Another actor in this ecosystem is the government and the productive interactions between University-Industry-Government are key determinants of introducing, developing and marketing the innovation thus leading to a holistic knowledge-based development with Universities progressing from an educational or research facilitator towards offering complete range of incubation services to promote entrepreneurism in its ecosystem (Etzkowitz, 2004). It is also established that Universities through the incubation of new technology enterprises and industry collaboration would result in positive impact on the development, marketing, and commercialization of these technologies leading to introduction of new products and services in new markets (Zhou and Wang, 2023).

This led to enquiry on the current and prospective structure of Incubation centres through the which these universities provide entrepreneurial support to startups. Traditionally the support structure consists of Infrastructure support, which primarily comprises office & lab space, test facilities, utilities, administrative facilities are the basic amenities that incubatees seek from UBIs. In the majority of the cases, the founders/co-founders of Incubatee firms are first-generation entrepreneurs mostly university undergraduates with no or little experience in managing a new company or business venture. Therefore, they depend upon UBI's experience for guidance in investing, and core sectoral knowledge of how and other entrepreneurial aspects and would like to interact with UBI teams which are experienced, competent and professional with hands-on experience in entrepreneurship. Further, Incubatee firms seek continued access and availability to financial resources, especially during their incubation period. The incubatees expect UBIs to provide them with access to seed funding, to begin with, and later on opportunities for a future round of fundraising with investors. Incubatees also look towards UBIs to provide mentoring support both from internal and external experts in the area of technology and business. This would help reduce their innovation cycle, validate their innovation and develop business acumen. UBIs are also required to provide re-innovation, strategic and marketing advisory support to incubatee firms which is critical for the growth plan of the firm.

Business development is another area which is key to firm success and incubatee wants support in terms of developing their go-to-market strategy, development/refinement/validation of the business model and long-term growth strategy. Leapfrogging the technology curve through early product adoption and development of product portfolio is essential for the swift growth of startups for which incubatee firms wants UBIs to leverage their connections with other universities and R&D centres. Incubatee firms also expects UBIs to be more proactive in arranging business development sessions, hackathon, ideathon, growth camps and pitching sessions and also facilitate by being part of accelerator programs for rapid growth of these firms. During the initial period of incubation, incubatee does not possess adequate business knowledge as compared to investors or venture capitalists, therefore, they want a complete range of knowledge-based programs to develop their business acumen which would be essential for their long-term success. These being the traditional aspects of the UBIs support system, the incubatee firms need more support for other functions like Corporate Governance which led to the development of 4th Generation of University Incubators.

Along with corporate governance, it is noted that new entrepreneurs accept their lack of legal know-how in terms of regulatory filings, listing and requirements of companies act. Further, as most of these firms are technology-based companies, the innovations would result in the development of Intellectual Property (IP) in the form of patents or processes. Therefore, these incubatee firms expect UBIs to offer attorney and intellectual property filing support as part of their service portfolio.

3. INNOVATION ORIENTATION

The foundation of innovation orientation of startups is on two pathways. One, as they ideate their product or services which would offer radical newness or another in which they would build upon the existing innovations. It is established that the Innovation orientation of the entrepreneur is an essential ingredient to track customer needs and development of innovative products and services which would have a positive impact on the firm performance. However, it is also noted that innovation orientation on a standalone basis is not sufficient to accomplish higher firm performance but needs to be supplemented with market orientation (Ergur and Kusecu, 2013) and global integration with identification of positive impact of economic globalisation on the performance of Indian companies in eleven economic sectors (Verma and Srivastava, 2023).

(March, 1991) in seminal paper introduced innovation possibilities related to organizational learning as Exploratory which comprises of Exploration of new possibilities or the Exploitation of existing knowledge by refining and redefining in the current context. It was also noted that in the case of knowledge or learning, the adoption of an exploration strategy is more advantageous as compared to the exploitation strategy in the long run but in the short term, exploitation would be beneficial. Extending this theoretical knowhow from learning to innovation, it was proposed that Exploratory innovation is the strategy of indulging in radical innovation by the startup firm i.e. Exploring the new idea for a product or process on the other hand, exploration of existing novel ideas, technologies or processes for providing new product or services to the customers would result in exploitation strategy adoption by the startup firm (Daradkeh and Mansoor, 2023). These innovation pathways would determine the impediments to the maturity of the technology offerings of these startups. Comparing the performance of exploration vs exploitation orientation, it was established that based on the availability of internal and external resources, the new ventures should explore both strategies in tandem for their survival and growth (Lavie et al, 2010).

On the other hand, there exists contrary arguments on the biases of contemporary research towards positive results of the innovation orientation with respect to market and competitive advantage and argues about the diminishing results of innovation in terms of increased cost, market risk and reduced employee motivation (Simpson et al, 2006; Gu and Su, 2018). Taking resource based view and social network theory, it is also established that innovation orientation in itself is not relevant for improved performance and this calls for external partnerships both in technology and market space in contemporary literature between startups and industry. However, it is noted that while these partnerships result in first mover advantage for the startup the results on the performance are constrained by higher liabilities and low and gradual acceptance of these products and services (Gu and Su, 2018)

4. TECHNOLOGY READINESS LEVEL (TRL)– CORNERSTONE OF ENTREPRENEURIAL GROWTH

For the new startups which are predominantly technology-driven, the growth of their technology offering is the cornerstone of the development of their venture. This growth or maturity in technology from ideation to pilot and finally to commercial scale would lead to growth overall growth of the startup. In the contemporary literature, the utilization of Technology Readiness Level, a framework developed by American space agency NASA to assess the maturity level of the technologies being used in its space missions has started getting prominence as an evaluating factor of startup growth. The TRL level ranges from the lowest level of maturity at Level 1 i.e. of basic research principles to the highest maturity level at 9 i.e. of implementation or deployment of technology and this framework is also used as a comparison tool between different technologies (Mankins, 1995). The maturity levels and the corresponding definitions are presented in Table 1.

Table 1. Technology Readiness Levels

Technology Readiness Level (TRL)	Definitions
Level -1	*Basic principles observed and reported*
Level -2	*Technology concepts and/or applications formulated*
Level -3	*Analytical and experimental critical function and/or characteristic proof-of-concept*
.Level -4	*Component and/or breadboard validation in laboratory Environment*
Level -5	*Component and/or breadboard validation in relevant environment*

continued on following page

Table 1. Continued

Technology Readiness Level (TRL)	Definitions
Level -6	*System/sub-system model or prototype demonstration in relevant environment*
Level -7	*System prototype demonstration in space environment*
Level -8	*Actual system completed and flight qualified through test and demonstration*
Level -9	*Actual system flight proven through successful mission operations*

Source: Menkins, 1995

The framework has been adopted by various regulatory bodies in USA, European Union, Japan and others and has become an International standard for the establishment of maturity level of technologies (Vik et al., 2021). The assessment of technologies using Technology Readiness Level is getting prominence with use in Information and Communication Technologies (Fast-Berglund et al., 2014), Agriculture (Vik et al 2021), Chemicals (Solis and Silveria, 2020), Artificial Intelligence with application in self-driven cars, home cleaning robots and virtual assistants (Martinez-Plumed et al., 2021). This is also being assessed as a tool for startups to overcome Valley of Death (VoD) and government agencies in USA are also undertaking assessment of technologies through consolidation of TRL scales into Basic Research, Applied Research, Development and Implementation scale (USDTT, 2017). Further, European Investment Bank has consolidated these 9 TRL levels into more broad-based levels of Research, Development, Innovation and Product Support (EARTO, 2014).

However, it is also noted that TRL is constrained by limitations concerning cost, challenges, risk mitigation, marketability, benefits and commercialization (USDTT, 2017; Heder, 2017). To overcome these constraints the framework is further modified and expanded with the inclusion of Market Readiness Level (MRL), Regulatory Readiness Level (RRL), Acceptance Readiness Level (ARL) and Organizational Readiness Level (ORL) to develop a comprehensive scale of Balanced Readiness Level Assessment (BRLa) and was applied to 36 emerging technologies in agriculture domain to assess their maturity levels (Vik et al., 2021).

Number of measures of technology and innovation activities are defined in the literature in terms of proportion of number of researchers, number of patents, copyrights, graduation of startup and access to external knowledge source (Colombo and Delmastro, 2002) which also results in increased speed to market of innovation (Grimalde and Grandi, 2005). Considering number of patents as control variable, it was observed that UBIs have positive impact on the R&D alliance between the startups while public incubators were more instrumental in forging the commercial alliances (Grilli and Marzano, 2023). Further, the positive impact of University and UBI support on innovation performance of University Spin-Offs and Incubatees was also established (Corsi and Previcipe, 2016). In the context of India, the positive impact of technology business incubation and incubation process on R&D contribution to the national economy was noted with new product development, number of patent applications, granted patents and contribution of new product to sales as performance parameters (Mungila Hillemane, 2020). On the other hand, it is noted that technology incubators have more positive impact of implementation of technology innovation in terms of the introduction of new products in market and R&D expenditure as compared to UBIs (Goraczkowska, 2020). To achieve this, it is also imperative for these startups that a flexible and holistic approach to address the needs and aspirations of stakeholders should also be adopted (Shalender, 2022).

As the majority of startup firms associated with UBI possess unique technological solutions to existing or new problems, it is imperative that the impact of UBI and Industry support on the maturity or growth in Technology Readiness Level (TRL) of the startup is considered as part of the output of the conceptual model.

5. THE INDUSTRY-ACADEMIA COLLABORATIVE FRAMEWORK

As discussed in the previous sections, Technology Readiness Level (TRL) is the framework developed by the American space agency NASA to assess the maturity level of the technologies being used in its space missions, which while being used as a tool for measurement of technology growth is also utilized a comparison tool between different technologies. The framework has been adopted by various regulatory bodies in the USA, European Union, Japan and others and has become an International standard for the establishment of the maturity level of technologies in various industries. This chapter has deliberated on the effectiveness of Technology Readiness Level as a measure of performance for university-based startups and how the technological support provided by the industry in terms of turning lab scale concept to pilot and later to commercial scale enhances the performance of technology startup and the support provided by the university in terms of protecting Intellectual property complements the industry offerings.

As the majority of incubated firms associated with UBI possess unique technological solutions to existing or new problems, the technology and innovation must be analysed in tandem with the collaborative support provided by the UBIs. This chapter, relying on the theoretical frameworks of Resource based view (Barney, 1991), Innovation orientation (March, 1991) and Technology Readiness Level (Mankins, 1995) propose following conceptual framework of collaborative impact of industrial and university support on the innovation strategy adopted by the students' entrepreneurial venture and its influence on the technology readiness level of the startups as presented in the Industry-Academica collaborative framework for entrepreneurial support as Figure-1 below;

Figure 1. Industry-academica collaborative framework for entrepreneurial support

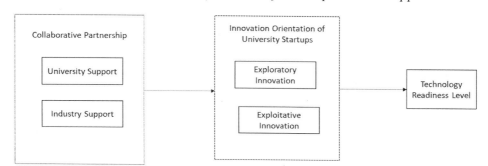

In the context of Indian entrepreneurial ventures, limited research is available which has analysed the impact of the university business Incubation system on the success of startups and further research on the collaborative support of industry with these UBIs is also lacking. While studies have introduced few success parameters for UBIs success, limited attempts have been made in the contemporary research domain to analyse the effect of startup innovation orientation measured through exploration and exploitation innovation strategies on technological growth and technological readiness level of the incubatee firm. The conceptualization of NASA framework of Technology Readiness Level to gauge the technological success or scalability of the university incubatee firms is a novel introduction to the research domain.

6. DISCUSSION

Innovation is the key to success for organisations across all domains especially for the creation, survival and growth of new ventures as the ability to create and implement novel ideas offers a critical competitive edge. This innovation potential can be harnessed through a symbiotic and synergistic model between universities and industrial partners. Universities which have embarked upon their third mission of nurturing and developing entrepreneurship need to develop collaborative partnerships with industry to facilitate new ventures with access to knowledge, resources, ideas, expertise, and mentorship to harness market opportunities.

Universities as knowledge creators and disseminator encourages a culture of research, reasoning, and academic excellence. The flow of fundamental knowledge from academia to the practical approach-seeking industry ensures cutting-edge research offering practical solutions while accelerating the speed of innovation. To this effect, the emergence of benchmarks of Technology Readiness Level provides a structured roadmap for technology development and monitoring for new ventures. It offers University-based startups to align their technology development goals towards different phases of maturity to advance from the ideation stage to implementation. The framework suggested can serve as a valuable mode for synergising theoretical acumen from academia and commercial aspects from the industry. Investment from the industry in new technology startups is contingent upon the existing and growth of TRL status. By clearly mentioning the TRL status, startups can underline progress and attract more capital, catalysing growth and development. It also offers a powerful framework for startups, investors, and the incubation industry as by comprehending and applying the TRL system, startups can strategically plan their development, attract investors, forge collaborations, and increase their chances of success. Embracing TRL levels empowers stakeholders to navigate the complex startup landscape and drive transformative technological advancements towards real-world impact.

The proposed partnership framework between academia and industry significantly amplifies R&D efforts. Universities provide access to facilities such as laboratories, expert faculty, and a talented base of students which is complemented by the market acumen of industry representatives and business insights and these collaborations promise multidisciplinary viewpoints, leading to market defining innovations. These entrepreneurial ventures are also complemented by industry through the development of ecosystem that thrives on groundbreaking ideas and commercial validation of products and services. Further, with the rapidly changing technological scenario, industry demand for skilled professionals increases. Partnerships between academia and industry can jointly develop curricula that meet the industry's needs. Modes such as internships, co-op programs, and joint research projects can be explored to provide students with practical experience. This prepares a talent pipeline that is not only aware of real-world problems but is also equipped with the skills to drive the industry. The collaborative partnerships could lead to the development of technological solutions for future challenges such as environmental degradation, sustainability and inclusive development. Adding intellectual capital of academia to the resources and expertise of industry creates a formidable force that can tackle such challenges and this synergy, can not only develop innovative solutions but can also leverage cutting-edge technologies, driving positive societal impact.

The entrepreneurial spirit mixed with innovation is the basis of technological development and growth. An outside-in innovation or exploration orientation resides in indulging in activities of experimental discovery. This innovation orientation relates its knowledge base with external knowledge increasing innovativeness and on the other hand, the inside-out process pushes ideas to market through licensing intellectual property to the market environment. Coupling the two approaches by working with complementary partners promotes success. An ambidextrous view of innovation entails both exploratory and exploitative innovations. but striking a balance between the two is a tough act because both activities draw resources and thus strain the system. University start-ups struggle to provide resources for both and find it difficult to manage trade-offs between the two approaches. Since exploration and exploitation rest on different organisational routines and capabilities, start-ups can specialise in one of them. In technological innovations, if start-up decides to invest heavily in refining the existing commercialization, it can reduce the possibility of the development of new expertise.

Universities are running incubator programs to identify and support innovative ideas provide a support system across the value chain and create an enabling environment to trigger creative ideas and hand-holding these ventures to enable growth of innovation to an enterprise stage. These university support programs are designed to support innovators through various stages of development from Proof-of-concept (POC) stage where the startup demonstrates a fundamental functioning demonstration of the idea or hypothesis to prototype-stage with development of a viable product. Therefore, university shall anchor all its entrepreneurship-related efforts through incubation facilities for nurturing innovations and startups as without this support for innovation, new enterprises are unlikely to succeed. To this effect, TRL levels serve as a common factor among stakeholders, enabling effective communication and collaboration between start-ups, research institutions, and industry partners. By branding technology projects with TRLs can assist investors in determining the risk and growth potential while the universities/researchers can use TRLs to streamline incubation programs. Moreover, by incorporating TRL levels into evaluation and selection criteria, incubators can ensure a better fit between startups and their programs and this alignment also allows incubators to provide guidance, resources, and connections to help startups progress through the TRL stages, reducing risks and maximizing their chances of success.

7. LIMITATIONS AND FUTURE RESEARCH DIRECTION

Every research is marred by limitations and is never complete by itself. The conceptual framework of Academia-Industry collaboration to support the technological growth of new ventures by stepping up their Technological Readiness Level is at a very nascent stage. This conceptual framework could be further refined, developed and modified by incorporating other constituents of technological growth of new ventures. It is also worth noting that technology is one of the many constituents that define startup success. This chapter has limited itself by solely focusing on the technology aspect of venture growth whereas, numerous other factors like funding growth, growth in partnership, increase in market share, revenue growth etc could have been made part of the success determinants. Being a conceptual model, future research could be on the empirical testing of this model with reference to UBIs and their technological incubatees. Further, as no scale is available for Technological Readiness level, an attempt should be made to develop and validate TRL scale so that it can be made part of future academic research on technology development.

REFERENCES

Anjum, T., Farrukh, M., Heidler, P., & Díaz Tautiva, J. A. (2020). Entrepreneurial intention: Creativity, entrepreneurship, and university support. *Journal of Open Innovation*, 7(1), 11. 10.3390/joitmc7010011

Barney, J. (1991). Firm Resources and Sustained Competitive Advantage. *Journal of Management*, 17(1), 99–120. 10.1177/014920639101700108

Block, F., & Keller, M. R. (1970). Where Do Innovations Come From? Transformations in the US National Innovation System, 1970-2006. *Innovation*.

Colombo, M. G., & Delmastro, M. (2002). How effective are technology incubators? *Research Policy*, 31(7), 1103–1122. 10.1016/S0048-7333(01)00178-0

Corsi, C., & Prencipe, A. (2016). Improving Innovation in University Spin-Offs: The Fostering Role of University and Region. *Journal of Technology Management & Innovation*, 11(2), 13–21. 10.4067/S0718-27242016000200002

Daradkeh, M., & Mansoor, W. (2023). The impact of network orientation and entrepreneurial orientation on startup innovation and performance in emerging economies: The moderating role of strategic flexibility. *Journal of Open Innovation*, 9(1), 100004. 10.1016/j.joitmc.2023.02.001

Ergün, H. S., & Kuşcu, Z. K. (2013). Innovation orientation, market orientation and e-loyalty: Evidence from Turkish e-commerce customers. *Procedia: Social and Behavioral Sciences*, 99, 509–516. 10.1016/j.sbspro.2013.10.520

Etzkowitz, H. (2004). The evolution of the entrepreneurial university. *International Journal of Technology and Globalisation*, 1(1), 64–77. 10.1504/IJTG.2004.004551

Etzkowitz, H. (2013). Anatomy of the entrepreneurial university. *Social Sciences Information. Information Sur les Sciences Sociales*, 52(3), 486–511. 10.1177/0539018413485832

European Association of Research & Technology Organization. (2014). *The TRL Scale as Research & Innovation Policy Tool*. EARTO Recommendations.

Gorączkowska, J. (2020). Enterprise innovation in technology incubators and university business incubators in the context of Polish industry. *Oeconomia Copernicana*, 11(4), 799–817. 10.24136/oc.2020.032

Grilli, L., & Marzano, R. (2023). Bridges over troubled water: Incubators and start-ups' alliances. *Technovation*, 121, 102689. 10.1016/j.technovation.2022.102689

Grimaldi, R., & Grandi, A. (2005). Business incubators and new venture creation: An assessment of incubating models. *Technovation*, 25(2), 111–121. 10.1016/S0166-4972(03)00076-2

Gu, Y., & Su, D. (2018). *Innovation orientations, external partnerships, and start-ups' performance of low-carbon ventures.Journal of Cleaner Production*, 194, 69–77. 10.1016/j.jclepro.2018.05.017

Héder, M. (2017). From NASA to EU: The evolution of the TRL scale in Public Sector Innovation. *The Innovation Journal*, 22(2), 1–23. https://eprints.sztaki.hu/9204/

Lavie, D., Stettner, U., & Tushman, M. L. (2010). Exploration and exploitation within and across organizations. *The Academy of Management Annals*, 4(1), 109–155. 10.5465/19416521003691287

Mankins, J. C. (1995). *Technology readiness levels: A white paper.* http://www. hq. nasa. gov/office/codeq/trl/trl. Pdf

March, J. G. (1991). Exploration and exploitation in organizational learning. *Organization Science*, 2(1), 71–87. 10.1287/orsc.2.1.71

Martínez-Plumed, F., Gómez, E., & Hernández-Orallo, J. (2021). Futures of artificial intelligence through technology readiness levels. *Telematics and Informatics*, 58, 101525. 10.1016/j.tele.2020.101525

Mungila Hillemane, B. S. (2020). Technology business incubators in India: What determines their R&D contributions to the national economy? *International Journal of Innovation Science*, 12(4), 385–408. 10.1108/IJIS-03-2020-0020

Pereira, D., Leitão, J., Oliveira, T., & Peirone, D. (2023). Proposing a holistic research framework for university strategic alliances in sustainable entrepreneurship. *Heliyon*, 9(5), e16087. 10.1016/j.heliyon.2023.e1608737215802

Shalender, K. (2022). *Key Variables in Team Dynamics in Small Businesses and Start-ups* (pp. 141-153). World Scientific Publishing Co. Pte. Ltd. 10.1142/9789811239212_0007

Simpson, P. M., Siguaw, J. A., & Enz, C. A. (2006). Innovation orientation outcomes: The good and the bad. *Journal of Business Research*, 59(10-11), 1133–1141. 10.1016/j.jbusres.2006.08.001

Solis, M., & Silveira, S. (2020). Technologies for chemical recycling of household plastics – A technical review and TRL assessment. *Waste Management (New York, N.Y.)*, 105, 128–138. 10.1016/j.wasman.2020.01.03832058902

US Department of Transport, Federal Highway Administration (2017), *Technology Readiness Level Guidebook*, FHWA-HRT-17-047.

Verma, B., & Srivastava, A. (2023). Impact of different dimensions of globalisation on firms' performance: An unbalanced panel-data study of firms operating in India. *World Review of Entrepreneurship, Management and Sustainable Development*, 19(3-5), 360–378. 10.1504/WREMSD.2023.130618

Vik, J., Melås, A. M., Stræte, E. P., & Søraa, R. A. (2021). Balanced readiness level assessment (BRLa): A tool for exploring new and emerging technologies. *Technological Forecasting and Social Change*, 169, 120854. 10.1016/j.techfore.2021.120854

Xin, S., & Park, T. (2024). The roles of big businesses and institutions in entrepreneurship: A cross-country panel analysis. *Journal of Innovation & Knowledge*, 9(1), 100457. 10.1016/j.jik.2023.100457

Zhou, J., & Wang, M. (2023). The role of government-industry-academia partnership in business incubation: Evidence from new R&D institutions in China. *Technology in Society*, 72, 102194. 10.1016/j.techsoc.2022.102194

Chapter 9
Analysing the Impact of Ergonomic Elements on Stress Among Female Corporate Employees

Nupur Chauhan
Department of Psychology, St. Xavier's College, Jaipur, India

Yash Mathur
Department of Psychology, St. Xavier's College, Jaipur, India

ABSTRACT

As the global workforce diversified, the understanding of physical, cognitive, and organisational ergonomics in the workplace became crucial. This study examined the influence of ergonomic workspace design on stress experienced by female employees. It scrutinised the effects of various elements within the workspace environment, including workstation seating arrangements, lighting, organisation of information, and interpersonal dynamics among colleagues and how these factors contribute to stress levels among women working in both public and private sector settings. The research comprised 40 participants selected from multinational corporations and government agencies through convenience sampling. Stress levels were assessed utilising the stress scale developed by Dr. Vijay Lakshmi and Dr. Shruti Narain, and ergonomic factors were explored through a self-developed questionnaire. The statistical method of analysis of variance (ANOVA) was employed to compute results and derive conclusions regarding the influence of workspace ergonomics on stress levels among female employees.

INTRODUCTION

In an increasingly fast-paced and technology-driven world, the importance of optimising human performance and well-being cannot be overstated. This is where the concept of ergonomics comes into play. Ergonomics revolves around designing and arranging environments, tools, and systems to fit the capabil-

DOI: 10.4018/979-8-3693-3096-8.ch009

ities, limitations, and needs of individuals. The goal is to create an environment that not only enhances efficiency and productivity but also minimises the risk of discomfort, injuries, and stress-related issues.

Stress can be defined as an experience or perceived challenge which exceeds the capabilities of an individual's coping resources and prepared resilience consequently affecting the emotional & physical well being (Monroe,2009).

International Ergonomics Association defines Ergonomics as "The scientific discipline concerned with the understanding of interactions among humans and other elements of a system, and the profession that applies theory, principles, data and methods to design in order to optimise human well-being and overall system performance" (Dul et.al, 2012).

Ergonomics is a scientific principle which combines the collective knowledge of anatomy and physiology, psychology, engineering and statistics to make sure that the practical designs assists the strengths and abilities of people who use it (Bridger, 2008).

According to the International Ergonomics Association ergonomics can be broadly categorised into three types, each focusing on different aspects of human interaction with their surroundings (Burov,2019).

Types of Ergonomics

- **Physical Ergonomics** is concerned with the physical relationship between individuals and their work environment. It involves designing workstations, tools, and equipment to minimise physical strain, fatigue, and discomfort. Proper workstation layout, appropriate seating, and well-designed tools are essential considerations in this aspect of ergonomics.

- **Cognitive Ergonomics** pertains to mental processes such as perception, memory, decision-making, and attention. It aims to optimise the design of tasks, interfaces, and information displays to reduce cognitive load and enhance information processing. This is particularly important in complex work settings, such as control rooms and user interfaces.

- **Organisational Ergonomics**, also known as macro-ergonomics, focuses on the optimization of entire organisational structures and systems. It involves studying the interactions between various components of an organisation, such as its culture, policies, and workflows, to improve overall efficiency, communication, and employee satisfaction. Environmental Ergonomics takes into account the influence of external factors like lighting, temperature, noise, and air quality on human performance and comfort. Designing environments that promote a balance between these factors contributes to creating a conducive and comfortable atmosphere for work and daily activities.

REVIEW OF LITERATURE

According to the World Health Organisation, "Stress can be defined as a state of worry or mental tension caused by a difficult situation." It is a natural human response that prompts us to address challenges and threats in our lives. Everyone experiences stress to some degree (WHO). The American Psychological Association defines stress as a phenomenon which directly or indirectly affects every system of the human body, it influences how people feel and behave (APA). By causing physiological and psychological changes stress contributes to deteriorating mental and physical health, resulting in an overall reduced life quality.

Stressors are specific events, situations, circumstances, or factors that trigger or elicit stress in individuals. There are many different types of stressors in workplaces for women employees such as burn out, too much job pressure, frustration, inadequate staff and working hours etc. All these factors can lead to poor mental and physical health.

Johnston, Jull, Souvlis & Jimmieson (2008) examined in their study that the interaction of physical and psychosocial factors in the workplace has a stronger association with neck pain and disability than the presence of either factor alone. This finding has important implications for strategies aimed at the prevention of musculoskeletal problems in female office workers.

Mork, Falkenberg, Fostervold, & Throud (2018) concluded in their study that exposure to direct glare on computer screens resulted in increased trapezius muscle blood flow, increased blink rate, and forward bending of the head. Psychological stress induced a transient increase in trapezius muscle activity and a more forward-bent posture leading to increased musculoskeletal problems in healthy females with normal binocular vision, and accordingly, both visual and psychological factors must be taken into account when optimising computer workstations which is a part of workplace ergonomics to reduce physiological responses that may cause excessive eyestrain and musculoskeletal load.

Zhou et al. (2018) concluded in their study that there's a significant sequential mediating effect of affect and perceived stress on the mental health of female employees of China.

Migliore, Ricceri, Lazzarato & D'Errico (2021) in their study on impact of different work organisational models on gender differences in exposure to psychosocial and ergonomic hazards at work and in mental and physical health concluded that the employees in workplaces characterised by lower monotony, repetitiveness, and production constraints may contribute to reduce exposure to job strain among working women.

Kote, et al. (2023) conducted a research on prevalence and associated factors of stress and anxiety among female employees of Hawassa industrial park in Sidama regional state, Ethiopia, the major findings of this study were that work related stress and anxiety was prevalent in female employees and there's a statistically significant association between overtime work, poor social support and work anxiety.

All the researches which have been cited so far have a commonality in them that stress related issues in workplaces of a female employee directly or indirectly originates from some kind of ergonomic factor whether it is physical, cognitive, or organisational.

METHODOLOGY

Sample

The sample of this study consisted of 40 women employees working in the corporate industry, 26 of them were from the private sector and 14 of them were from the public sector. The sample was randomly selected from different multinational companies and government offices for the convenience of sampling.

Hypothesis

H_1: Work space ergonomics significantly impact the stress level of female employees.

H_2: Work space ergonomics does not impact the stress level of female employees.

H_3: There will be an significant impact of ergonomics on the stress of female employees from the private sector.

H_4: There will be a significant impact of ergonomics on the stress of female employees from the public sector.

Tools

The following measures were used in this study:

1. **Stress Scale (LVNS)** (Lakshmi & Narain,2014): This scale is composed of a total of 40 questions which are only to be answered as yes or no in the options, the scale measures 4 dimensions of stress namely pressure, physical stress, anxiety and frustration. The test-retest reliability of this scale is 0.82 which is significant at 0.01 level of significance .
2. **Ergonomic elements rating scale**: This is a self developed questionnaire for this study, it consists of 10 questions related to workspace ergonomic elements. Individuals can rate their workspace ergonomics on the basis of its physical, cognitive and organisational characteristics on a 5 point descriptive scale.

Procedure

The study commenced with the selection of a sample from Jaipur city, Rajasthan, India. Subsequently, appropriate research tools were chosen, and the investigation commenced. Individuals were carefully selected and categorised into subgroups based on the organisational background of their workplace, distinguishing between those in the private and public sectors. The responses of the participants were collected via online forms, with full transparency regarding the study's objectives and nature being provided to them beforehand.

Statistical Analysis

To statistically analyse the impact of workspace ergonomics on stress ANOVA (Analysis of Variance) was used. Analysis was done separately for female employees from the private sector and public sector.

RESULTS

Table 1. Mean scores on Stress Scale and Ergonomic elements rating scale for female employees from private sector (N=26)

Measures	Mean	Standard Deviation (SD)
Stress Scale	14.8	7.29
Ergonomic elements rating scale	36.84	5.09

Table 2. Mean scores on Stress Scale and Ergonomic elements rating scale for female employees from public sector (N=14)

Measures	Mean	Standard Deviation (SD)
Stress Scale	38.07	10.31
Ergonomic elements rating scale	12.57	4.81

26 female employees from the private sector were part of this study and as shown in Table 1 the mean of their scores for Stress Scale was 14.8 and for Ergonomic elements rating scale the mean score was 36.84. Standard deviation of their scores for Stress Scale was 7.29 and for Ergonomic elements rating scale the standard deviation was 5.09.

On the other hand 14 female employees from the public sector participated in this study and as shown in Table 2 the mean of their scores for Stress Scale was 38.07 and for Ergonomic elements rating scale the mean score was 12.57. Standard deviation of their scores for Stress Scale was 10.31 and for Ergonomic elements rating scale the standard deviation was 4.81.

Table 3. Results of ANOVA test both of the subgroups of the sample

Subgroup	F-ratio	Significance
Female employees of private sector	159.33042	Significant at 0.01 level of significance
Female employees of public sector	70.26152	Significant at 0.01 level of significance
Female employees (complete sample)	226.38	Significant at 0.01 level of significance

The score sets of Female employees of private sector and public sector for both stress scale and ergonomic elements rating scale were analysed respectively through ANOVA. The resulting F-ratio for the private sector subgroup was 159.33042 which is significant on 0.01 level of significance and for the sub group which consisted of employees from the public sector the F-ratio came out to be 70.26152 which is also significant on 0.01 level of significance. When the same data was analysed collectively without the subgroup distinctions the resulting F-ratio was 226.38 which is significant on 0.01 level of significance. Table 3.

These results firmly indicate that ergonomic elements in a workspace significantly impact the stress of female corporate employees regardless of their organisational background.

Table 4. Results of dimension wise analysis for private sector

Dimension	F-ratio	Significance
Pressure	800.13	Significant at 0.01 level of significance
Physical stress	1159.41	Significant at 0.01 level of significance
Anxiety	682.40	Significant at 0.01 level of significance
Frustration	1072.62	Significant at 0.01 level of significance

The dimensional score sets of Female employees of the private sector for both stress scale and ergonomic elements rating scale were analysed through ANOVA. The F-ratio value for Pressure, Physical stress, Anxiety & Frustration came out to be 800.13, 1159.41, 682.40 & 1072.62 respectively and all of them are Significant at 0.01 level of significance. By this it can be concluded that ergonomics directly impacts Pressure, Physical stress, Anxiety & Frustration in female employees of the private sector. Table 4.

Table 5. Results of dimension wise analysis for public sector

Dimension	F-ratio	Significance
Pressure	481.02	Significant at 0.01 level of significance
Physical stress	733.31	Significant at 0.01 level of significance
Anxiety	353.51	Significant at 0.01 level of significance
Frustration	653.40	Significant at 0.01 level of significance

The dimensional score sets of Female employees of the public sector for both stress scale and ergonomic elements rating scale were analysed through ANOVA. The F-ratio value for Pressure, Physical stress, Anxiety & Frustration came out to be 481.02, 733.31, 353.51 & 653.40 respectively and all of them are Significant at 0.01 level of significance. By this it can be concluded that ergonomics directly impacts Pressure, Physical stress, Anxiety & Frustration in female employees of the public sector. Table 5.

DISCUSSION

Ergonomics plays a pivotal role in both individual well-being and the operational dynamics within corporate settings. Despite its critical relevance, the significance of ergonomic factors often remains overlooked, resulting in potential mental health risks for employees in the corporate sphere. Female employees who already encounters multifactorial stress in their lives whether it be maternal stress, family stress, relationship stress or health stress among all these sources of mental distress ergonomics in their workplaces could be a potential source which went unnoticed in general awareness as well as in the world of academia, this should not become trend before it's too late. While the importance of addressing multifactorial stressors in women's lives is increasingly recognized, the role of ergonomics in the workplace remains an overlooked aspect of this conversation. By raising awareness of the potential impact of ergonomic design on female employees' mental health and well-being, organisations can take proactive steps to create more supportive and inclusive work environments. Moreover, integrating ergonomic principles into academic research and professional training programs can ensure that future generations of workplace leaders are equipped to prioritise the holistic health and wellness of all employees. The intersection of multifactorial stress and workplace ergonomics represents a critical area for further exploration and action. By acknowledging the unique challenges faced by female employees and addressing the role of ergonomics in mitigating workplace stressors, we can work towards creating healthier, more equitable work environments for all. This proactive approach is essential to prevent the escalation of workplace-related mental health issues and ensure the well-being and productivity of female employees both now and in the future.

In particular, female employees encounter heightened vulnerability to stress due to their multifaceted roles in both professional and societal domains. Research by Migliore, Ricceri, Lazzarato & D'Errico (2021) underscores that work environments characterised by reduced monotony and production constraints can notably mitigate the exposure to job strain among working women, highlighting the substantial impact of ergonomic considerations on the mental and physical health of employees.

It's imperative to acknowledge that inadequate ergonomic conditions not only compromise employee health but also impede overall productivity. The comprehensive classification of ergonomics into physical, cognitive, and organisational domains emphasises that it encompasses not just physical structures but also cognitive elements such as work-related instructions, tools, and interpersonal dynamics.

Studies like the one conducted by Kote et al. (2023) on stress and anxiety among female employees at the Hawassa Industrial Park in Ethiopia reveal a notable prevalence of work-related stress and anxiety among women. The research underscores the statistical correlation between factors like overtime work and inadequate social support with increased work anxiety, shedding light on the influential role of cognitive and organisational ergonomics in exacerbating stress among female employees.

The findings of the present study underscore the direct and significant impact of ergonomic factors on the stress levels of female employees across both private and public sectors. This aligns with the research by Shyi et al. (2018), which observed a sequential mediating effect of affect and perceived stress on the mental health of female employees in China, further emphasising the global relevance of ergonomic considerations in mitigating employee stress and fostering well-being.

Additionally, the landmark findings of this study revealed that ergonomics have a direct significant impact on female employees' pressure, physical stress, anxiety and frustration as well, which is consistent for both public and private sector employees.

Considering the concrete results and findings of this study it is suggested that workspace incharges such as HR managers should concentrate their undivided attention on the stress causing ergonomics of their workspace. Creating a conducive workspace that prioritises ergonomics as crucial for the overall well-being and productivity of employees. A thoughtfully designed ergonomic setup will not only significantly reduce the risk of musculoskeletal issues but it will also be an aid to the mental health of the employees, enhancing comfort and promoting a better workspace environment. Incorporating adjustable chairs, ergonomic desks, proper lighting, and positioning computer screens at eye level, proper work instructions, informational organisation, and a healthy interpersonal environment among colleagues can help mitigate strain on the body and mind. By investing in ergonomic solutions, employers not only prioritise the health of their workforce but also pave the way for increased focus, efficiency, and long-term job satisfaction among employees. The fact that there are only few studies which focus on the ergonomic factors of the workplace, and even fewer of them talk about the mental stress apart from musculoskeletal adversities especially among female employees of the Indian subcontinent makes this research important as an initiative. For the future prospects of this study further expansion of the sample to collect more data from a larger sample size essentially from tier 2 & tier 3 cities of the country is important to validate the findings of this study and to direct the much demanded attention towards this domain.

REFERENCES

Bridger, R. (2008). *Introduction to ergonomics*. Crc Press.

Burov, O. (2020). Human Factors/Ergonomics in eWorld: Methodology, Techniques and Applications. In Karwowski, W., Trzcielinski, S., & Mrugalska, B. (Eds.), *Advances in Manufacturing, Production Management and Process Control. AHFE 2019. Advances in Intelligent Systems and Computing* (Vol. 971). Springer. 10.1007/978-3-030-20494-5_43

Dul, J., Bruder, R., Buckle, P., Carayon, P., Falzon, P., Marras, W.S., Wilson, J.R. & van der Doelen, B.A. (2012). Strategy for human factors/ergonomics: developing the discipline and profession. *Ergonomics, 55*(4), 377-95. 10.1080/00140139.2012.661087

Ergonomics—Physiopedia. (n.d.). Retrieved 23 December 2023, from https://www.physio-pedia.com/Ergonomics

Johnston, V., Jull, G., Souvlis, T., & Jimmieson, N. L. (2010). Interactive effects from self-reported physical and psychosocial factors in the workplace on neck pain and disability in female office workers. *Ergonomics, 53*(4), 502–513. 10.1080/00140130903490069220309746

Kefelew, E., Hailu, A., Kote, M., Teshome, A., Dawite, F., & Abebe, M. (2023). Prevalence and associated factors of stress and anxiety among female employees of hawassa industrial park in sidama regional state, Ethiopia. *BMC Psychiatry, 23*(1), 103. 10.1186/s12888-023-04575-536774468

Lakshmi, V., & Narain, S. (2014). *Manual for Stress Scale SS-LVNS*. National Psychological Corporation.

Migliore, M. C., Ricceri, F., Lazzarato, F., & d'Errico, A. (2021). Impact of different work organisational models on gender differences in exposure to psychosocial and ergonomic hazards at work and in mental and physical health. *International Archives of Occupational and Environmental Health, 94*(8), 1889–1904. 10.1007/s00420-021-01720-z34050822

Monroe, S. M., Slavich, G. M., & Georgiades, K. (2009). The social environment and life stress in depression. In Gotlib, I. H., & Hammen, C. L. (Eds.), *Handbook of depression and its treatment* (2nd ed., pp. 340–360). Guilford Press.

Mork, R., Falkenberg, H. K., Fostervold, K. I., & Throud, H. M. S. (2018). Visual and psychological stress during computer work in healthy, young females—Physiological responses. *International Archives of Occupational and Environmental Health, 91*(7), 811–830. 10.1007/s00420-018-1324-529850947

Stress. (n.d.). Retrieved 23 December 2023, from https://www.apa.org/topics/stress

Stress: Signs, Symptoms, Management & Prevention. (n.d.). Retrieved 23 December 2023, from https://my.clevelandclinic.org/health/articles/11874-stress

Zhou, S., Da, S., Guo, H., & Zhang, X. (2018). Work–Family Conflict and Mental Health Among Female Employees: A Sequential Mediation Model via Negative Affect and Perceived Stress. *Frontiers in Psychology, 9*, 544. 10.3389/fpsyg.2018.0054429719522

Chapter 10
Understanding Employee Well-Being in the Education Industry Through the Innovative Approach of Sustainable Leadership

Richa Banerjee
Narsee Monjee Institute of Management Studies, India

Abhijeet Singh Chauhan
Prestige Institute of Management and Research, India

Subeer Banerjee
Shriram Institute of Information Technology, India

Moniruzzaman
Canada Global University, Canada

ABSTRACT

The present work landscape prioritizes employee well-being. This research embarks on a critical exploration of how sustainable leadership and compassion synergize as catalysts for fostering employee well-being. Recognizing the interconnected nature of leadership styles and their impact on organizational culture, this study aims to unveil actionable insights. By unravelling the intricate dynamics between sustainable leadership and compassion, the research seeks to empower organizations with the knowledge to create environments that not only support the holistic health of their employees but also fortify long-term resilience and success. The data for the study was collected from 260 respondents using a standardised, 7-point Likert scale, from teachers of B schools of the Central Indian region using non-purposive probability sampling. The study shows the role that sustainable leadership plays in creating a happy work environment and improving employees' overall well-being. According to the findings, there is a clear link between long-term leadership and employee well-being.

DOI: 10.4018/979-8-3693-3096-8.ch010

1. INTRODUCTION

The academic landscape has undergone a profound transformation, transitioning from a solely service-oriented industry to a profit-driven sector, bringing forth new challenges in talent acquisition and retention. In this era of rapid technological advancements and dynamic market landscapes, the traditional perception of education is evolving (Kaltiainen & Hakanen, 2022; Barnard and Simbhoo, 2014). The paradigm shift towards a profit-oriented industry underscores the critical need for innovative leadership approaches that prioritize employee well-being. As organizations grapple with economic pressures, employee expectations, and societal concerns, a new era demands sustainable leadership infused with compassion, emerging as a potent catalyst for cultivating employee well-being.

The challenges studied in this research are intricately linked to organizations grappling with addressing the well-being of their employees. Traditional leadership, often characterized by a power-centric and profit-driven focus, lacks the ability to foster holistic employee well-being (Vincent-Höper & Stein, 2019). This approach, devoid of thoughtfulness towards employees, leads to serious repercussions, including diminished employee engagement and burnout, ultimately impacting organizational performance (Jaškevičiūtė, 2021). Recognizing the need for a new leadership perspective that aligns with industrial expectations, it becomes imperative to transcend the traditional boundaries of leadership (Zabala, 2021).

The field of study in leadership predominantly concentrates on various leadership styles, employee engagement, and interventions for well-being (Jaškevičiūtė, 2021; Cignitas et al., 2022). However, a substantial gap exists in understanding the close relationship between Sustainable Leadership (SL) and ethical, socially responsible practices. A forward-thinking and compassionate leader, with a nurturing attitude and consideration for Employee Well-Being (EWB), raises questions about the role of SL as a potent tool for improving EWB and organizational performance. This research seeks to bridge this gap by exploring SL and compassion as powerful tools for cultivating EWB.

Examining the interlinkages of these multifaceted concepts, the study aims to uncover novel perceptions and practical approaches, particularly through the lens of Building Collaborative Culture and Encouraging Knowledge Exchange. The focus is on guiding industrial leaders to create environments where employees can flourish both personally and professionally. The ultimate goal is to provide a detailed framework that advances theoretical understanding, offering recommendations for leaders seeking to embrace a compassionate and sustainable approach to enhance employee well-being and organizational success.

Compassion in an organization, viewed as creating an environment with empathy, understanding, and care as core values, acknowledges the human component of the workplace. It promotes a culture that prioritizes employee well-being, fosters meaningful relationships, and cultivates a sense of belonging. Compassionate leaders play a pivotal role in creating a supportive work environment that improves employee well-being, engagement, and productivity. Organizations fostering compassion attract and retain talented employees who share their values and purpose. Ultimately, compassion contributes to creating a more compassionate and sustainable work environment, benefiting both individuals and the organization.

In the present study, the authors delve into the impact of Sustainable Leadership on employee well-being, with compassion serving as a mediator. The research aspires to contribute to reshaping the future of leadership, placing EWB as a priority and recognizing employee well-being as a fundamental backbone of the industry. Through the exploration of Building Collaborative Culture and Encouraging Knowledge Exchange, the study endeavors to guide organizations towards a future where collaboration, knowledge sharing, and compassionate leadership are integral components of fostering employee well-being and organizational success.

1.1 Theoretical Framework

1.1.1 Stewardship Theory

The relationship between SL, employee compassion, and EWB is deeply rooted in the principles of stewardship theory. Stewardship theory provides a robust theoretical foundation for understanding how leaders, acting as stewards of their organizations, can have a profound impact on the well-being of their employees through the cultivation of compassion. Ship theory emphasis the concept of resource custodian (Hernandez, 2012). according to the theory the leaders are considered as a custodian who is responsible for safeguarding and enhancing the resources of the organization (Greyvenstein & Cilliers, 2012).

The theory has perfect alignment with the theories of SLand its practice, which has responsibility of resource management as a priority for a long term next (Sady et al., 2019). Sustainable leaders have ethical principles as guiding principles and they make decision that not only benefit the organization but also contribute to a greater good of the stakeholders and environment. (Hu et al., 2019). The leader has commitment towards tractor says which are sustainable add That create a culture in organization which leads to financial success as well as employee wellbeing (Rahim et al., 2021).

Within the context of stewardship theory, sustainable leaders are more inclined to exhibit compassionate behaviors towards their employees (Greyvenstein & Cilliers, 2012). The emphasis on resource custodianship naturally extends to human capital—the organization's most valuable resource (Basri et al., 2021). Compassionate leaders, acting as stewards of their employees' well-being, foster a work environment characterized by empathy, understanding, and genuine care. They recognize that the EWB is intricately tied to the organization's long-term success and, by extension, their own success as leaders. In this relationship, SLpractices set the stage for the cultivation of employee compassion. Leaders who select sustainability over other principles are more likely to embrace ethical and socially responsible behaviors, which, in turn, create a culture of trust and psychological safety. Employees feel valued and supported, and they, in turn, are more likely to exhibit compassionate behaviors toward their colleagues. Compassion flows organically within the organization, as employees understand that they are being cared about their well-being and the well-being of their peers. Ultimately, the synergy between stewardship theory, sustainable leadership, employee compassion, and employee well-being underscores the profound impact that ethical and responsible leadership practices can have on the holistic health of organizations. Leaders who see themselves as stewards of their organizations' resources and their employees' well-being are not only fostering a culture of compassion but also creating workplaces where individuals thrive, finding purpose and satisfaction in their roles. This interconnected relationship between stewardship, sustainability, compassion, and well-being represents a pathway to creating healthier, more engaged, and more sustainable organizations.

Figure 1. Proposed Research Model

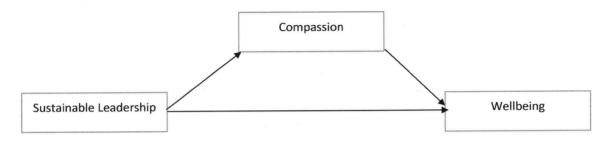

1.2 Review of Literature

1.2.1 Sustainable Leadership and Compassion

Sustainable leadership is a new domain of effective leadership that has recently emerged to address concerns concerning sustainable development (Iqbal and Ahmad, 2021). The cornerstones of SL practises are enduring perspectives, systemic innovation, employees development, and worth. We summarised various studies to demonstrate how SL is still operationalized: On the one hand, Avery and Bergsteiner (2011) outlined a comprehensive range of SL practises from a strategic management viewpoint by embracing the concept of corporate social responsibility (CSR). Furthermore, Lee (2017) integrates internal CSR and supportable HRM elements into sustainable leadership, demonstrating how multiplicity management, member of staff growth, organisational fairness, progress, and work-life balance affect gratification, enthusiasm, and performance. Choi (2021), on the other hand, operationalized SL as specific behavioural practises associated with servant, authentic, and ethical leadership styles. Furthermore, Hallinger and Suriyankietkaew (2018) evaluated the cornerstone for SL in "Rhineland approach capitalism in Germany" emphasising on social care, emphasising employee and societal responsibility. based on findings, the subsequent characteristics are summarised in a theoretical context: SL connects the vision and organisational goals to the wellbeing of people, ethical behaviour, community concern of leaders and organisations, investor engagement in such vision, and innovation ability for a proper system. SL and its associated principles, when paired with knowledge and experience, boost the output of CSR's triple bottom line performance, which includes social, ecological, and economic performance (van Veldhoven and Peccei, 2015; Hallinger and Suriyankietkaew, 2018). There is some evidence that SL has an impact on long-term performance (Iqbal et al., 2020a) and employee satisfaction (mostly impacted by employee valuing, ethical behaviour, and shared vision; Suriyankietkaew and Avery, 2014). Individualised concern "serves as a carrot" to meet the personal demands of employees. Choi (2021) recently demonstrated that managers' SL has a considerable impact on employee welfare, particularly when it is geared towards servant and authentic leadership practises. Similarly, virtuous leadership behaviour, which is associated with SL due to its ethical approach, has been demonstrated to have an impact on work-related wellbeing (affect, job satisfaction, and work engagement), with trust in the leader acting as a mediator (Hendriks et al., 2020). SL aspires to improve the lives of all stakeholders while also benefitting in the present and future. It highlights the critical importance of sustainability at the individual, business, and societal levels..

H1: Sustainable leadership positively influences level of compassion amongst employees

1.2.2 Compassion and Wellbeing

Compassion at work promotes to the development of high-quality connections by strengthening relational resources such as loyalty, trust, and interpersonal closeness, which leads to the healing of people in distress (Dutton et al., 2007). According to Ryan and Deci (2001), there are two major philosophical perspectives on well-being: happiness-oriented (i.e., hedonism), which defines well-being as the subjective experience of happiness; and eudaimonism, which focuses on realising human potential and views well-being as the result of personal success, self-actualization, or self-positioning. Compassion can be viewed as a sign of intrapersonal well-being, a way of relating to oneself and others, and a means of enhancing eudaimonic enjoyment (Neff & Costigan, 2014). According to the eudaimonic perspective, wellbeing and happiness are subjective experiences that are consistent over time and involve life satisfaction and good affect (Howell et al., 2007). There is evidence that compassion improves nurses' well-being. Wahl et al. (2018) discovered that compassion allows nurses to feel joy, satisfaction, and fulfilment in their professional work by connecting with their patients and their suffering, allowing the nurses to fulfil their professional and/or personal commitment to finding meaning in their work. As a result, compassion promotes employee commitment while decreasing turnover and absenteeism (Dutton et al., 2007), and all of these personal and environmental job traits are associated with employees' well-being. Higher levels of self-compassion, according to Bag et al. (2022), are connected with improved wellbeing. Muris et al. (2018) also confirm that students' mental health is substantially predicted by self-compassion. Furthermore, Zessin et al. (2015) found that the self compassion and well being are associated positively in general adult populations.

H2: Compassion positively influences level of well-being amongst employees

1.2.3 Mediating Role of Compassion

A compassionate work environment with access to learning opportunities is an important resource for dealing with stressful job (Gustavsson and Lundqvist, 2021). Compassionate organisations can foster such a work atmosphere. Employees adopt compassionate behaviours in organisations based on how they engage with one another (Banker and Bhal, 2020), knowledge is shared, and employees have open communication with one another (Gustavsson and Lundqvist, 2021). According to Banker and Bhal (2020), managers have an impact on the establishment of compassionate organisations, and SLappears to have the necessary traits. These leaders have a long-term vision, larger societal aims, ethical behaviour, and social responsibility (Hallinger and Suriyankietkaew, 2018). Leaders who are overly focused on short-term goals, put excessive pressure on people, and are untrustworthy encourage organisations with low levels of compassion. Sustainable leadership, on the other hand, promotes organisational learning due to its long-term aims (Sharma and Lenka, 2019) and knowledge-sharing culture (Kantabutra and Avery, 2013). SLfosters a vision that is supported by organisational values such as moderation, mutual respect, and individual value; these values underpin employee satisfaction, commitment, and performance (Hargreaves and Fink, 2007). Sustainable leaders have a long-term vision and foster information dissemination in their organisations through open communication (Park and Kim, 2018), which is framed by ethical behaviours (Kantabutra and Avery, 2013). Leaders' ethical practises cause their followers to become more sensitive to their peers' concerns and more empathetic, enhancing compassion in their organisations, and compassion is a driver of wellbeing (Manriquede-Lara and Viera-Armas, 2019). Thus, compassionate work environments are promoted by sustainable leaders through values such as integrity, empathy, accountability, authenticity, presence, and dignity (Shuck et al., 2019), empathy, ethical/moral values, and supportive organisational culture combined with favourable human resource practises (Banker and Bhal, 2020), all of which result in employee well-being. Empathetic leaders, as long-term leaders, are required to create compassionate organisations with a common moral virtue that fosters social and emotional interactions between employees and between them and their organisations, resulting in virtuous organisations (Karakas et al., 2017). Addressing compassion in healthcare organisations is especially important because care without compassion can be detrimental to patients and potentially unethical (Renzenbrink, 2011). Sadly, not all hospitals are operated with compassion, and despite its importance, there is lack of explanation regarding this . Banker and Bhal (2020) emphasised the importance of identifying elements that encourage compassion in these organisations.

H3: Compassion positively mediates the relationship between sustainable leadership and employee wellbeing.

1.3 Scope and Research Objectives of the Study

1. To check the effect of sustainable leadership on compassion
2. To measure the effect of sustainable leadership on employee wellbeing
3. To measure the effect of compassion on employee well being
4. To check the mediating effect of compassion on linkage of sustainable leadership and employee wellbeing.

The present study is divided into 5 parts. The initial part of the study is introduction and background of the research. The study considered stewardship theory as theoretical background of present research. The review of existing literature helped in developing hypothesis and objectives of the study. The second part of the paper is about the methodology used for data collection and data analysis. Where next part of the paper talks about the results drawn after analysis of the study and discussion of the findings. In the last part of the paper the implications and conclusion of the study are presented.

2. METHODOLOGY

The research was empirical in nature and employed a cross-sectional research design. It involved surveys to measure the role of SLon compassion and employee well-being. The sample of research included teachers of B-schools in central India. For the selection of sample, the study utilized purposive sampling technique. Participation of respondents was voluntary, and informed consent was obtained from all participants.

For the data collection purpose, 300 survey forms were distributed amongst the teachers out of which 260 teachers responded to the survey form having a response rate of 86% which considered as very good. Out of 260 responses, 220 responses were deemed useful for the data analysis. The data was collected using standardized scales on sustainable leadership, compassion and employee well-being.

SL was measured by adopting a 4-item scale developed by Di Fabio and Peiró (2018). Compassion was measured using a 3-item scale adapted by Lilius et al. (2008). Wellbeing was measured using a 5-item scale adopted by Han (2020). Responses on all the items were collected on a seven point Likert type scale (1 = strongly disagree to 7=strongly agree). The research adhered to ethical guidelines, ensuring participants' informed consent, confidentiality, and the right to withdraw from the study at any time.

3. RESULTS AND DISCUSSION

Table 1. Outer loadings

	Compassion	**Sustainable Leadership**	**Well Being**
C1	0.858		
C2	0.836		
C3	0.883		
SL1		0.806	
SL2		0.764	
SL3		0.767	
SL4		0.660	
WB1			0.901
WB2			0.906
WB3			0.898
WB4			0.878
WB5			0.876

Table 1 denotes the outer loadings of items in each constructs. Measurement of outer-loading was conducted, which depicts the input of each variable or item on the overall construct. The threshold limit for the same is above 0.5. Hence, the constructs of the study confirmed outer-loadings criterion (Heir et al., 2017)

Table 2. Reliability Analysis and Convergent Reliability

	Reliability	**rho_A**	**CR**	**AVE**
Compassion	0.825	0.843	0.894	0.738
Sustainable Leadership	0.741	0.749	0.837	0.564
Well Being	0.936	0.940	0.951	0.796

Table 1 discloses the cronbach's - alpha value of constructs Compassion, SLand Wellbeing. The cronbach's - alpha value of mentioned constructs were beyond threshold edge of 0.7. Therefore, cronbach's - alpha reliability was established. Similarly, rho alpha reliability and composite reliability was measured, obtained values for compassion, SLand wellbeing were also greater than 0.7.

Convergent validity assesses the relatedness of individual scale items (Susarla, Barua and Whinston, 2003). It refers to relatedness among measures explaining the measurement of same construct that to what extent the measures are related (Netemeyer, Bearden and Sharma, 2003). In the words of Fornell & Larcker (1981), the convergent validity was analyzed by inspecting factor-loads & AVE. In the study, under table 1, the AVE value for each variable such as Compassion, SLand Wellbeing indicated more than 0.5 values, which is acceptable.

Table 3. Discriminant Validity

	Compassion	Sustainable Leadership	Well Being
Compassion	0.859		
Sustainable Leadership	0.221	0.751	
Well Being	0.326	0.315	0.892

Analysis of Discriminant validity designates the individuality of a variable or we can say it construct, whether the score of the measures are contaminated by the interference of some other construct or are unique (Schwab, 2013). According to this the off diagonal values should be greater than it's inter – item correlation values (Hair et al., 2017). Table 3 elucidates that every variables differentiates with other in terms of off-diagonal scores. Hence criterion was established.

Table 4. VIF values

	VIF
C1	1.646
C2	2.020
C3	2.171
SL1	1.770
SL2	1.671
SL3	1.540
SL4	1.354
WB1	2.641
WB2	1.901
WB3	2.356
WB4	1.834
WB5	1.866

The structural model must be free from multi-collinearity issues. For this motive, VIF values were assessed, and values should below 3.33, i.e. the threshold value suggested by (Diamantopoulos et al. 2008) for all constructs in research. The VIF values were mentioned in the table 4 where the values for each item were less than the threshold limit 3.33. Hence, it can be stated that the model is free from multi – collinearity issues.

3.1 Structural Model Assessment

In structural model assessments, the interdependence of the constructs and predictive relevance has been examined (Hair et al., 2017). Several approaches were used to accomplish the structural model assessment. 5000 bootstraps were used to get the required probability values (Hair et al., 2020). Multi-colinearity should be avoided in the structural model. The coefficient of determination (Adjusted R^2) for all components was calculated, including Compassion (40.9%) and Employee Wellbeing (56.2%). R^2 or Adj. R^2 values more than 20% are deemed high in social science research (Rasoolimanesh et al., 2017). F^2 values reveal the size of the effect of exogenous constructions on endogenous constructs. There are particular rules for determining the effect size of constructs, such as "0.02 (small effect), 0.15 (medium effect), & 0.35 (large effect)" (Cohen, 2013). According to the findings of this study, SL has a substantial effect size on compassion (0.42) and employee well-being (0.58). Compassion has a significant impact on employee well-being (0.37). The predictive relevance of the model was calculated using Stone-Geisser's Q-square. Values greater than 0.02 will help to generalise the prediction usefulness of the research model (Richter et al. 2016). The Q^2 values for compassion (0.036) and employee wellbeing (0.042) indicate that SL is the strongest predictor of employee wellbeing. The SRMR value was found to be 0.062, which is less than the criterion of .08 (Hu & Bentler, 1999), indicating that the model is well-fitting.

Figure 2. The structural relationship between sustainable leadership, compassion, and employee well-being

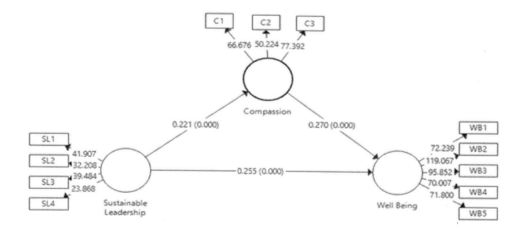

Table 5. Direct Effects

	Original Sample (O)	Sample Mean (M)	Standard Deviation (STDEV)	T Statistics (|O/ STDEV|)	P Values
Compassion -> Well Being	0.270	0.270	0.036	7.577	0.000
SL-> Compassion	0.221	0.222	0.031	7.030	0.000
Sustainable Leadership -> Well Being	0.255	0.257	0.031	8.158	0.000

Table 5 provides the results pertaining to relationship amongst variables (Sustainable leadership, Compassion and Employee wellbeing). There is a positive and significant relationship between compassion and wellbeing (Beta: 0.270, P- Value: 0.000). The results also revealed that SLis positively and significantly related to compassion (Beta: 0.221, P- Value: 0.000) and Well-being (Beta: 0.255, P- Value: 0.000). Therefore, Hypothesis 1, 2 and 3 were supported.

Table 6. Indirect Effects

	Original Sample (O)	Sample Mean (M)	Standard Deviation (STDEV)	T Statistics (IO/ STDEVI)	P Values
Sustainable Leadership -> Compassion -> Well Being	0.059	0.060	0.011	5.339	0.000

Table 6 provides the results pertaining to the mediating effect of compassion on the relationship between sustainable leadership and well-being and it was found that compassion has a positive mediating effect on the relationship between sustainable leadership and Well-being (Beta: 0.059, P-Value: 0.000). Therefore, hypothesis 4 was supported.

4. POLICY IMPLICATIONS

The research carries significant implications for higher education institutions. Firstly, the findings offer valuable guidance for leadership development programs, enabling institutions to enhance the skills of leaders by emphasizing the importance of building collaborative cultures and encouraging knowledge exchange. Additionally, the research shapes organizational policies and practices, advocating for the prioritization of collaborative environments and knowledge-sharing platforms. These insights also inform the design and implementation of targeted employee wellbeing initiatives, tailored to address specific challenges faced by employees in the higher education sector, fostering a positive work environment.

Furthermore, the study influences strategic organizational planning, prompting institutions to integrate principles of sustainable leadership, collaboration, and knowledge exchange into their long-term strategies. This alignment contributes to organizational resilience and success. The research also prompts a revaluation of recruitment and retention strategies, highlighting the appeal of institutions committed to collaborative culture and knowledge exchange in leadership practices. It emphasizes the role of sustainable leadership in attracting and retaining talented faculty and staff, thereby contributing to a stable and positive work environment.

Moreover, the study underscores the need for measurement and evaluation metrics specific to sustainable leadership and employee wellbeing in higher education. Institutions can adapt these metrics to assess the effectiveness of their leadership practices and employee wellbeing initiatives, fostering continuous improvement. Additionally, the research contributes to academic literature by advancing the understanding of the intricate relationship between sustainable leadership, collaborative culture, knowledge exchange, and employee wellbeing in higher education. Finally, the insights pave the way for cultural transformation initiatives, encouraging institutions to intentionally cultivate collaborative and knowledge-sharing cultures, ultimately leading to positive workplace transformations and improved employee morale and satisfaction. In essence, this research provides a comprehensive roadmap for higher education institutions to integrate sustainable leadership practices, collaborative cultures, and knowledge exchange for the benefit of employee wellbeing and overall organizational success.

4.1 Limitations

The study has few limitations as nobody can be perfect. The first limitation that the author's identified in the study was the sample size. The sample was limited, or it may be non-representative of the whole population. Like the study only involves individuals from a single industry hence, the conclusions may not be generalizable to a larger population. Furthermore, because the study did not use a cross-sectional design, it may not capture changes over time. Longitudinal studies are better adapted to analysing the evolution of employee well-being in response to SLand compassion. Another sample limitation is that the data obtained for the study, via self-report questionnaires and interviews, may be prone to social desirability bias, in which participants submit answers they believe are socially acceptable. This could lead to an overestimation of the positive consequences of empathetic leadership.

Another disadvantage is connected to data collection method; when data is acquired using a single method (e.g., surveys), it can result in common method variance, which means that the observed associations between variables are exaggerated due to the method of data collection.

The study's second restriction is related to the analysis of the acquired data. Causation can be difficult to establish in investigations like these. It may be difficult to determine whether SLand compassion directly produce greater employee well-being. The study may not fully account for all relevant contextual elements, such as economic situations, industry-specific issues, or organisational culture, that could influence the association between leadership, compassion, and employee wellbeing.

Another disadvantage is that it can be difficult to account for all potential confounding variables that may influence employee well-being. This might make attributing changes entirely to a long term leadership and compassion challenging. Furthermore, EWBis a subjective construct that can be influenced by individual perception and experiences that vary from person to person and industry to industry.

5. CONCLUSION

In the realm of building collaborative culture and encouraging knowledge exchange, the study sheds light on the pivotal role that sustainable leadership (SL) plays in fostering a positive work environment and enhancing overall employee wellbeing. The findings underscore that sustainable leader, prioritizing long-term organizational success and employee wellbeing, cultivate compassion within the workforce through an empathetic and ethical approach. This approach creates an environment where employees feel valued, supported, and motivated to actively contribute to the organization's success. The research highlights a strong relationship between SL and improved employee wellbeing, as employees under such leaders experience reduced stress levels and enhanced mental and emotional health. Notably, the study emphasizes the importance of nurturing compassion within the organization, as it not only improves relationships among colleagues but also fosters teamwork and collaboration. In embracing sustainable leadership principles, leaders can expect a more cohesive workforce that collaboratively pursues and achieves collective goals. The study's conclusion, drawn from evident results, underscores the direct and indirect impact of SL and compassion on employee wellbeing, contributing to the ongoing discourse on building collaborative cultures and fostering knowledge exchange. However, it acknowledges the need for caution in generalizing findings due to the study's limited sample size and population specificity.

REFERENCES

Avery, G. C., & Bergsteiner, H. (2011). Sustainable leadership practices for enhancing business resilience and performance. *Strategy and Leadership*, 39(3), 5–15. 10.1108/10878571111128766

Bag, S. D., Kilby, C. J., Kent, J. N., Brooker, J., & Sherman, K. A. (2022). Resilience, self-compassion, and indices of psychological wellbeing: A not so simple set of relationships. *Australian Psychologist*, 57(4), 249–257. 10.1080/00050067.2022.2089543

Banker, D. V., & Bhal, K. T. (2020). Understanding compassion from practicing managers' perspective: Vicious and virtuous forces in business organizations. *Global Business Review*, 21(1), 262–278. 10.1177/0972150917749279

Barnard, A., & Simbhoo, N. (2014). South African managers in public service: On being authentic. *International Journal of Qualitative Studies on Health and Well-being*, 9(1), 20630. 10.3402/qhw. v9.2063024434054

Basri, M., Husain, B., & Modayama, W. (2021). University students' perceptions in implementing asynchronous learning during Covid-19 era. *Metathesis: Journal of English Language, Literature, and Teaching*, 4(3), 263–276. 10.31002/metathesis.v4i3.2734

Choi, H. J. (2021). Effect of chief executive officer's sustainable leadership styles on organization members' psychological well-being and organizational citizenship behavior. *Sustainability (Basel)*, 13(24), 13676. 10.3390/su132413676

Cignitas, C. P., Arevalo, J. A. T., & Crusells, J. V. (2022). *The effect of strategy performance management methods on employee wellbeing: A case study analyzing the effects of balanced scorecard.* Academic Press.

Cohen, J. (2013). *Statistical power analysis for the behavioral sciences*. Academic press. 10.4324/9780203771587

Di Fabio, A., & Peiró, J. M. (2018). Human Capital Sustainability Leadership to promote sustainable development and healthy organizations: A new scale. *Sustainability (Basel)*, 10(7), 2413. 10.3390/ su10072413

Diamantopoulos, A., Riefler, P., & Roth, K. P. (2008). Advancing formative measurement models. *Journal of Business Research*, 61(12), 1203–1218. 10.1016/j.jbusres.2008.01.009

Dutton, J. E., Lilius, J. M., & Kanov, J. M. (2007). The transformative potential of compassion at work. *Handbook of transformative cooperation: New designs and dynamics, 1*, 107-126.

Dutton, J. E., Lilius, J. M., & Kanov, J. M. (2007). The transformative potential of compassion at work. In Piderit, S. K., Fry, R. E., & Cooperrider, D. L. (Eds.), *Handbook of transformative cooperation: New designs and dynamics* (pp. 107–124). Stanford University Press. 10.1515/9781503625969-006

Elardo-Zabala. (2021). The Leadership Styles of the Local Universities and Colleges' Administrators. *International Journal of Educational Management and Development Studies, 2*(2), 20-37.

Fornell, C., & Larcker, D. F. (1981). Evaluating structural equation models with unobservable variables and measurement error. *JMR, Journal of Marketing Research*, 18(1), 39–50. 10.1177/002224378101800104

Greyvenstein, H., & Cilliers, F. (2012). Followership's experiences of organisational leadership: A systems psychodynamic perspective. *SA Journal of Industrial Psychology*, 38(2), 1–10. 10.4102/sajip.v38i2.1001

Gustavsson, M., & Lundqvist, D. (2021). Learning conditions supporting the management of stressful work. *Journal of Workplace Learning*, 33(2), 81–94. 10.1108/JWL-09-2019-0116

Hair, J. F.Jr, Howard, M. C., & Nitzl, C. (2020). Assessing measurement model quality in PLS-SEM using confirmatory composite analysis. *Journal of Business Research*, 109, 101–110. 10.1016/j.jbusres.2019.11.069

Hair, J. F.Jr, Matthews, L. M., Matthews, R. L., & Sarstedt, M. (2017). PLS-SEM or CB-SEM: Updated guidelines on which method to use. *International Journal of Multivariate Data Analysis*, 1(2), 107–123. 10.1504/IJMDA.2017.087624

Hallinger, P., & Suriyankietkaew, S. (2018). Science mapping of the knowledge base on sustainable leadership, 1990–2018. *Sustainability (Basel)*, 10(12), 4846. 10.3390/su10124846

Han, J. H. (2020). The effects of personality traits on subjective well-being and behavioral intention associated with serious leisure experiences. *J. Asian Fin. Econ. Bus.*, 7(5), 167–176. 10.13106/jafeb.2020. vol7.no5.167

Hargreaves, A., & Fink, D. (2007). *Sustainable leadership*. John Wiley.

Hendriks, M., Burger, M., Rijsenbilt, A., Pleeging, E., & Commandeur, H. (2020). Virtuous leadership: A source of employee well-being and trust. *Management Research Review*, 43(8), 951–970. 10.1108/MRR-07-2019-0326

Hernandez, M. (2012). Toward an understanding of the psychology of stewardship. *Academy of Management Review*, 37(2), 172–193. 10.5465/amr.2010.0363

Howell, R., Kern, M., & Lyubomirsky, S. (2007). Health benefits: Meta-analytically determining the impact of well-being on objective health outcomes. *Health Psychology Review*, 1(1), 83–136. 10.1080/17437190701492486

Hu, L. T., & Bentler, P. M. (1999). Cutoff criteria for fit indexes in covariance structure analysis: Conventional criteria versus new alternatives. *Structural Equation Modeling*, 6(1), 1–55. 10.1080/10705519909540118

Hu, X., Chong, H. Y., & Wang, X. (2019). Sustainability perceptions of off-site manufacturing stakeholders in Australia. *Journal of Cleaner Production*, 227, 346–354. 10.1016/j.jclepro.2019.03.258

Iqbal, Q., & Ahmad, N. H. (2021). Sustainable development: The colors of sustainable leadership in learning organization. *Sustainable Development (Bradford)*, 29(1), 108–119. 10.1002/sd.2135

Jaškevičiūtė, V. (2021). Trust in organization effect on the relationship between HRM practices and employee well-being. *SHS Web of Conferences*.

Kaltiainen, J., & Hakanen, J. J. (2023). Why increase in telework may have affected employee well-being during the COVID-19 pandemic? The role of work and non-work life domains. *Current Psychology (New Brunswick, N.J.)*, 1–19.36718392

Kantabutra, S., & Avery, G. (2013). Sustainable leadership: Honeybee practices at a leading Asian industrial conglomerate. *Asia-Pacific Journal of Business Administration*, 5(1), 36–56. 10.1108/17574321311304521

Lee, H. W. (2017). Sustainable leadership: An empirical investigation of its effect on organizational effectiveness1. *International Journal of Organization Theory and Behavior*, 20(4), 419–453. 10.1108/IJOTB-20-04-2017-B001

Lilius, J. M., Worline, M. C., Maitlis, S., Kanov, J., Dutton, J. E., & Frost, P. (2008). The contours and consequences of compassion at work. *Journal of Organizational Behavior: The International Journal of Industrial. Journal of Organizational Behavior*, 29(2), 193–218. 10.1002/job.508

Manrique-de-Lara, P., & Viera-Armas, M. (2019). Does ethical leadership motivate followers to participate in delivering compassion? *Journal of Business Ethics*, 154(1), 195–210. 10.1007/s10551-017-3454-1

Muris, P., van den Broek, M., Otgaar, H., Oudenhoven, I., & Lennartz, J. (2018). Good and bad sides of self-compassion: A face validity check of the self-compassion scale and an investigation of its relations to coping and emotional symptoms in non-clinical adolescents. *Journal of Child and Family Studies*, 27(8), 2411–2421. 10.1007/s10826-018-1099-z30100697

Neff, K. D., & Costigan, A. P. (2014). Self-Compassion, Wellbeing, and Happiness: Mitgefühl mit sich selbst. *Wohlbefinden und Glücklichsein. Psychologie in Österreich*, 2, 114–119.

Netemeyer, R. G., Bearden, W. O., & Sharma, S. (2003). *Scaling procedures: Issues and applications.* Sage Publications.

Rahim, H. F., Mooren, T. T., van den Brink, F., Knipscheer, J. W., & Boelen, P. A. (2021). Cultural identity conflict and psychological well-being in bicultural young adults: Do self-concept clarity and self-esteem matter? *The Journal of Nervous and Mental Disease*, 209(7), 525–532. 10.1097/NMD.0000000000001332 34009862

Rasoolimanesh, S. M., Ringle, C. M., Jaafar, M., & Ramayah, T. (2017). Urban vs. rural destinations: Residents' perceptions, community participation and support for tourism development. *Tourism Management*, 60, 147–158. 10.1016/j.tourman.2016.11.019

Renzenbrink, I. (2011). The inhospitable hospital. *Illness, Crises, and Loss*, 19(1), 27–39. 10.2190/IL.19.1.c

Richter, N. F., Cepeda-Carrión, G., Roldán Salgueiro, J. L., & Ringle, C. M. (2016). European management research using partial least squares structural equation modeling (PLS-SEM). *European Management Journal*, 34(6), 589–597. 10.1016/j.emj.2016.08.001

Ryan, R. M., & Deci, E. L. (2001). On happiness and human potentials: A review of research on hedonic and eudaimonic wellbeing. *Annual Review of Psychology*, 52(1), 141–166. 10.1146/annurev.psych.52.1.14111148302

Sady, M., Żak, A., & Rzepka, K. (2019). The role of universities in sustainability-oriented competencies development: Insights from an empirical study on Polish universities. *Administrative Sciences*, 9(3), 62. 10.3390/admsci9030062

Schwab, D. P. (2013). *Research methods for organizational studies.* Psychology Press. 10.4324/9781410611284

Sharma, S., & Lenka, U. (2019). Exploring linkages between unlearning and relearning in organizations. *The Learning Organization*, 26(5), 500–517. 10.1108/TLO-10-2018-0164

Shuck, B., Alagaraja, M., Immekus, J., Cumberland, D., & Honeycutt-Elliott, M. (2019). Does compassion matter in leadership? A two-stage sequential equal status mixed method exploratory study of compassionate leader behavior and connections to performance in human resource development. *Human Resource Development Quarterly*, 30(4), 537–564. 10.1002/hrdq.21369

SuSarla, A., Barua, A., & Whinston, A. (2003). Under-Standing The Service Component of Application Service Provision: An Empirical Analysis of Satisfaction With ASP Services. *MISOudrierty, 27*(1).

Van Veldhoven, M., & Peccei, R. (Eds.). (2014). *Well-being and performance at work: The role of context.* Psychology Press. 10.4324/9781315743325

Vincent-Höper, S., & Stein, M. (2019). The role of leaders in designing employees' work characteristics: Validation of the health-and development-promoting leadership behavior questionnaire. *Frontiers in Psychology*, 10, 1049. 10.3389/fpsyg.2019.0104931156499

Wahl, C., Hultquist, T. B., Struwe, L., & Moore, J. (2018). Implementing a peer support network to promote compassion without fatigue. *The Journal of Nursing Administration*, 48(12), 615–621. 10.1097/NNA.00000000000069130431516

Zessin, U., Dickhäuser, O., & Garbade, S. (2015). The relationship between self-compassion and well-being: A meta-analysis. *Applied Psychology. Health and Well-Being*, 7(3), 340–364. 10.1111/aphw.1205126311196

Chapter 11
Bridging Theory and Practice:
Implementing Work-Based Learning in Malaysian Higher Learning Institutions

Sheue Hui Lim
ViTrox College, Malaysia

Loke Kean Koay
ViTrox College, Malaysia

Kok Ban Teoh
ViTrox College, Malaysia

Daisy Mui Hung Kee
https://orcid.org/0000-0002-7748-8230
Universiti Sains Malaysia, Malaysia

ABSTRACT

In recent years, there has been a growing demand within the industry for a more structured approach to tertiary education aimed at narrowing the knowledge gap among potential talents. Work-based learning (WBL) has emerged as a method wherein the industry actively engages in knowledge delivery. Within WBL frameworks, students are immersed in industry settings, learning directly from seasoned professionals. However, the structure and implementation of WBL in Malaysia's higher education sector still lack clarity. Challenges such as low industry participation rates, student adaptation to this approach, and the role of higher education institutions remain undefined, given that WBL represents a new learning culture in Malaysia. The study recommends the improved implementation of WBL in the Malaysian context to promote its widespread adoption and to foster greater collaboration between industry and academia in WBL initiatives, thereby better preparing tomorrow's workforce for the demands of the modern economy.

1. INTRODUCTION

Now, trends are changing. Employers want "job-ready" graduates. --Ismail (2018)

DOI: 10.4018/979-8-3693-3096-8.ch011

Work-based learning (WBL) has received significant attention in the higher education sector as there is a pressing need to bridge the gap between industry and education. WBL involves direct industry participation in the delivery of knowledge. According to Ismail, Mimi, and Sofurah (2021) and Watisin (2017), WBL students gain theoretical knowledge in the classroom while also learning practical applications directly within the industry. WBL reveals the importance of learning through work experience and collaboration between higher learning institutions and industries. Moreover, Konstantinou and Miller (2021) highlighted that problem-based, experiential learning integrated into work-based modules offers a genuine opportunity for students to bridge the gap between the workplace (industry) and the classroom (higher education institution).

Qian and Kee (2023) looked into the factors influencing creativity, such as individual and team learning orientation, transformational leadership, and creative self-efficacy, further emphasizing the importance of learning-oriented approaches. Adeel et al. (2023) complement this perspective by emphasizing the importance of knowledge sharing ability, autonomous motivation, and task involvement in fostering employee creativity. Furthermore, Adeel, Batool, Kee, and Madni (2023) stress the insufficiency of cognitive absorption alone for individual learning, highlighting the crucial roles of knowledge absorption capacity and technological opportunity.

Ibrahim and Mahyuddin (2017) cite a 2014 survey by the World Bank and TalentCorp (See Figure 1), which found that 90% of companies believe that university graduates should have more training, and 81% of companies rate communication skill as the major skill deficit among graduates. Furthermore, 80% of companies reveal that universities' curricula do not inculcate the demanding skills for the market, and this is leading the graduates to face a deficiency in their skills. This finding is consistent with Verma et al. (2018) and Mohd Salleh et al. (2019) findings. The New Straits Times (3 October 2018), in its article titled "Graduate skills gap," reported that employers in Malaysia mentioned a remarkable skills gap among graduates. Employers emphasized that the low proficiency in the English language and the deficiency of soft skills such as critical thinking, creativity, and communication are among the main reasons for unemployed graduates (Aziz, 2018). Besides, communication skills are considered the No.1 soft skills required to make graduates qualified to be hired (Ward, 2017; Lim, Lee, Yap, & Ling, 2016).

Figure 1. Summary of World Bank and TalentCorp Survey

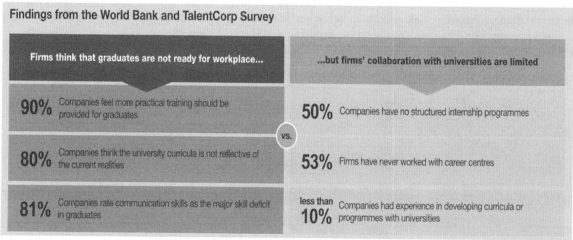

Source: Ibrahim and Mahyuddin (2017)

Indeed, the skills gap between graduates and industry is a global phenomenon transcending national borders (Aziz 2018). Malaysian university students, like their counterparts worldwide, encounter substantial challenges in achieving work readiness. One of the major challenges is the lack of industry training and skills development systems, thus expressing the urgent need to improve the graduates' work-ready skills (Verma et al., 2018). Several studies mentioned that Malaysian graduates lack different skills required in the 21st Century such as English language proficiency, technical skills, positive character, creativity, problem-solving, critical thinking, communication skills, decision-making, analytical skills, teamwork, independence, lifelong learning, appropriate attitudes, and decision-making (Singh et al., 2012; Hanapi & Nordin, 2014; Ibrahim & Mahyuddin, 2017; Tan et al., 2017; Verma et al., 2018; Aziz, 2018). Thus, it is important to help address the graduates' skills gap in Malaysia by focusing more on developing university students' skills (Mohd Salleh et al., 2019). Figure 2 illustrates the phenomenon of the skills gap between industry expectations and academic preparation among graduates worldwide. Universities are increasingly called upon to play a pivotal role in equipping students with the most sought-after skills necessary for navigating the complexities of the 21st century.

Figure 2. Graduate Skills Gap

Graduate Skills Gap

**The mismatch between the skills employers need (demand)
and the skills graduate have (supply)**

The findings from a survey conducted by the Khazanah Research Institute (KRI) reveal a significant trend in Malaysia's labor market (HR Asia, 4 March 2024). While the salaries of degree and diploma holders have improved, the report reveals that more than a third of them are still trapped in mismatched jobs. The report highlights that many local graduates who initially enter mismatched jobs tend to remain in this situation over time.

Recognizing the persistent challenge of the skills gap among graduates in Malaysia, there is an urgent call to propose innovative research-based solutions to mitigate this issue. In response, we recommend the implementation of WBL. Building upon these insights, our objective is to develop a comprehensive reference guideline tailored for WBL stakeholders within higher education institutions. This initiative aims to facilitate greater industry involvement in WBL, thereby effectively addressing the nation's skills gap and enhancing workforce preparedness. The overarching aim of WBL is to bridge the gap between academia and industry by seamlessly integrating theoretical knowledge with practical industry experience. As highlighted by Adan, Douni, and Hisham (2021), WBL fosters holistic learning within authentic, real-world contexts, empowering students to gain invaluable firsthand experience and effectively address the graduate skills gap.

2.0 THE IMPLEMENTATION OF WBL IN MALAYSIA

Graduates are employed based on competency and skills. Where they graduate from does not matter. What CGPA they had received also no longer matters. What they know and what they can do matters. --Ismail (2018)

Polytechnics and community colleges in Malaysia have been pioneers in implementing the WBL approach. The initial WBL initiative in Malaysia was a collaboration between Proton automotive manufacturers and community colleges. At the Proton Training Centre (PTC), the WBL structure involves industry teachers delivering lessons, with a ratio of 25% classroom-based learning and 75% on-the-job training at Proton Edar Service Centres (PESC) (Ismail et al., 2015). This model emphasizes a blend of classroom and industry-based learning, with the majority of the focus on practical training within the industry. Following the success of WBL in the automotive sector, polytechnics in Malaysia incorporated this approach into advanced diploma courses. In February 2007, eleven Kolej Komuniti also implemented the WBL Programme (Shayne Spaulding, Ian Hecker Emily Bramhall, 2020).

Another WBL framework in Malaysia is the "2u2i" system, introduced by the Ministry of Higher Education (MOHE) Malaysia in 2015 as part of the Malaysia Education Blueprint 2015-2025 (Higher Education). In this framework, '2u' represents two years spent at a university, college, polytechnic, or community college, while '2i' denotes one year spent in industry-based learning. Variants such as '3u1i' and '1u3i' also exist, reflecting different ratios of academic and industry-based learning. This innovative degree program format allows students to build networks, gain valuable exposure, and acquire work experience early in their academic journey (Yusof et al., 2020). As of 2017, six public universities in Malaysia have adopted the 2u2i learning model.

2.1 The Challenges Faced in WBL Implementation

Employers lament the gap between what students learn in college and what they are actually expected to know in order to be job-ready.   --Chamorro-premuzic & Frankiewicz (2019)

Implementing WBL requires collaboration among three key stakeholders: the industry, the learning institutions, and the students. However, industry coaches often face challenges in teaching and guiding students due to limited pedagogical exposure and formal education training (Watson et al., 2018). Furthermore, the high level of dedication required from industry coaches often deters the industry from accepting WBL students. Coaches must allocate significant time to each student during WBL sessions to ensure effective exposure and education. Additionally, the industry incurs costs for preparing study materials for WBL sessions, with limited cooperation from higher education institutions (Joshi et al., 2018).

Despite successful implementations of WBL in community colleges and universities, standardizing the structure and efforts among all involved parties remains a challenge. There is a misalignment between the industry, university, and students in the practical implementation of WBL (Watson et al., 2018). Moreover, concerns have been raised that WBL is undervalued as a form of learning, leading to inadequate student engagement in workplace settings (Musset, 2019). This lack of familiarity with the learning model has contributed to low industry participation in WBL in Malaysia.

3.0 RELATIONSHIP BETWEEN INDUSTRY COACH, LECTURER AND STUDENT

We argue that the engagement and collaboration of all three parties in the WBL model are essential. Continuous discussion and feedback mechanisms among these parties are necessary to ensure the effective implementation of WBL. A triangle relationship comprising WBL stakeholders, as illustrated in Figure 3.

Figure 3. WBL Stakeholders Relationship in Triangle

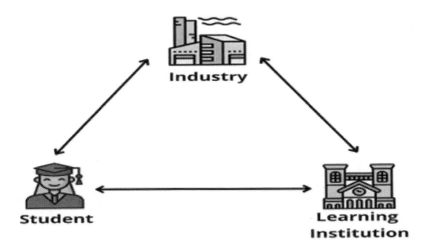

The higher education institution takes the initiative to arrange a discussion involving lecturers, students, and industry coaches at least one month before the WBL placement commences. This discussion ensures that the industry coach comprehends the students' abilities and mentally prepares them for the challenges they will encounter during the WBL. One of the benefits for WBL students is the enhancement of their self-confidence, self-efficacy, and motivation (Morley, 2018).

Additionally, this discussion enables the industry coach to grasp the ongoing WBL requirements, such as marking rubrics, project quantity, type, and duration for both students and lecturers. This is crucial as mentoring academics remains a relatively novel and untested concept (Lindqvist et al., 2023).

When the industry coach proposes projects for students to undertake during WBL, it provides students with time to prepare through self-learning before the commencement of WBL. This collaborative effort among all three parties resonates with the notion posited by Rowley (2005) and Rosenberg (2012) that WBL demands significant effort from individuals and organizations to establish a shared plan.

It is important for the industry coaches to align their expectations with those of the students to ensure a successful WBL and bring the benefit to student learning experience. Furthermore, there is a need for smooth communication between the school, industry partners, and students to ensure the WBL system operates seamlessly, fostering an environment conducive to learning and professional growth.

'Pre-WBL Alignment Discussion' is a proactive approach to synchronize the expectations of industry coaches with those of lecturers and students at the beginning of the process. This approach aims to establish a common understanding among all parties involved, fostering collaboration and mutual support. Additionally, the coach could clarify the learning goals with the lecturer and achieve mutual understanding, ultimately enhancing the potential for a successful WBL experience.

Besides, the communication should persist during WBL. The onus of initiating this communication lies with the lecturer, as they must ensure that guidance from the industry coach to the student is adequate. Otherwise, it could diminish the student's learning efficiency and erode their interest in continuing with this learning model. The discussion during WBL, referred to as 'WBL Check-Ins Discussion,' addresses this issue.

In order to gather feedback from both the student and industry coach for possible improvements, the industry coach should guide how students can improve their performance in projects assigned by the industry coach. Alternatively, they can acknowledge the competencies demonstrated by the students. This exchange will be known as the 'Post-WBL Discussion.' The student suggests that it would be helpful for the coach to review the project together with both the student and the lecturer.

3.1 Role of Higher Education Institutions, Industry, and Students

3.1.1 Higher Education Institutions

Academicians or lecturers serve as the connection between academic learning and real-world application. They are responsible for organizing the syllabus in a way that ensures the achievement of both course learning outcomes (CLOs) and program learning outcomes (PLOs). This alignment is recognized as one of the success factors for WBL partnerships, as identified by various scholars such as Talbot (2017), Khampirat and Bandaranaike (2019), Nottingham (2016), Linehan and Sheridan (2009), Emelo (2011), and White (2012). It underscores the importance of collaborative development between higher learning institutions and industries in designing WBL programs.

Besides, lecturers play a crucial role in preparing students with essential knowledge and skills before they enter the industry. They must ensure that students have a strong foundation and necessary prerequisites. Throughout the implementation of WBL, lecturers should regularly meet with both students and industry coaches, acting as mediators to facilitate smooth collaboration. Simultaneously, lecturers are responsible for ensuring that students receive adequate self-learning support during WBL. This support enhances student autonomy and initiative, as highlighted by Van Alten (2020). Some students have expressed the need for more self-learning opportunities, noting that university teachings primarily cover basic concepts.

From an industrial point of view, there is a concern about the limited scope of subjects covered by lecturers in school, primarily focusing on basic concepts and leaving extensive self-learning tasks for students. This observation indicates a gap between the theoretical knowledge provided in traditional classrooms and the practical skills required in real-world settings, as expressed by students experiencing a significant contrast between their academic learning and the demands of WBL environments. This discrepancy poses a challenge for both students and industry coaches, who struggle to bridge the gap between theory and practical application due to students' lack of foundational knowledge before entering WBL. The issue of insufficient grasp of fundamental concepts was the most significant obstacle encountered during WBL. Recognizing the importance of addressing this issue, there is a necessity for higher education institutes to provide robust self-learning support to students throughout the WBL session. By offering additional resources and guidance, educational institutions can better equip students with the necessary knowledge and skills, facilitating a smoother transition into the practical aspects of their chosen field.

3.1.2 Industry

In the WBL model, an industry coach is an employee of an organization who is appointed by the employer and agreed upon by the learning institution to teach, mentor, guide and assess the students at the workplace. Industry coaches play a pivotal role as they are entrusted with guiding students regarding technical knowledge throughout the WBL process. Unlike traditional teaching roles, the coach's responsibilities lean towards providing advice, mentoring, coaching, and supervision rather than direct instruction, as noted by Lindqvist et al. (2023). Coaches have the authority to assign projects and tasks to students, allowing them to apply and practice the knowledge they have acquired. While lecturers primarily focus on delivering academic content, it falls upon the coach to determine the types of projects to assign to students in the WBL assessment. This underscores the coach's proactive involvement in shaping students' practical experiences and ensuring alignment between theoretical learning and real-world applications within the WBL framework.

Moreover, the industry coaches can conduct regular check-ins with the students to ensure they can handle their assigned tasks effectively. Prior to WBL, the higher learning institution can provide a general briefing to the coach. This briefing outlines expectations, project guidelines, task assignments, and grading criteria. The industry coach also highlighted the importance of attending coach training provided by the institute before beginning to coach the student. Besides, the industry coaches need to ensure that the students follow the safety and health provisions that are being practiced in the workplace as required by legislation. In general, the main role of industry coaches is to guide students and share their workplace knowledge with them.

3.1.3 Student

WBL opens an opportunity for the students to dive into the industry early. They will spend part of the semester working with industry coaches, joining discussions, and taking charge of their learning. Students must show they are eager to learn and adapt, as Toorani and Khorshidi (2011) pointed out in the context of WBL, which aims to provide a real work environment for the students to experience. This experience gives them a taste of real-world work settings and teaches them how each team member contributes to making products.

WBL allows students to engage repeatedly in various real-world situations, hence enhancing their confidence and increasing their self-efficacy (Grosemans et al., 2020). Students are exposed to their industry coaches as their role models and are able to master work-based experiences through "learning by doing." Work-based experience promotes the application of knowledge and skills and helps direct the students toward the right choice of career planning (Jackson & Meek, 2022). Through WBL, students are able to develop and enhance their employability skills and be provided with a range of opportunities relevant to employability and career development.

In Self-Efficacy Theory, Bandura (1986) described that the first source of self-efficacy is through mastery experience. Personal experiences have been found to have the highest impact on self-efficacy beliefs and, thereby, on future behavior. By mastering the experience during WBL, students who possess such skills and abilities would be more competent. Likewise, an individual with greater self-efficacy tries harder and shows more persistence, even when encountering unforeseen obstacles. This learning approach gives the students more self-confidence in their abilities to face challenges and obstacles in their future careers (Drysdale & McBeath, 2018).

In today's ever-expanding global markets, the demand for organizations to stay competitive is more pressing than ever. This means that employers are increasingly relying on their workers to continuously develop their skills. By doing so, not only does productivity improve, but organizations also become better equipped to tackle the challenges posed by their competitors. Creativity skills are incredibly important for graduate students across various fields, and creativity is one of the 21st century skills needed for employability (Morris, 2022).

Furthermore, creativity skills are the keys to success in the evolving global economy and it is also becoming a vital objective in lifelong learning. Thus, students should be equipped creatively to apply the knowledge to the solution of real-world problems and WBL is one of the alternatives (Perusso & Wagenaar, 2023). Through WBL, they are well prepared to solve problem skills and be taught to foster the critical thinking and analysis skills required for identifying real problems or making critical judgments they will have to face in their professional career (Scott, 2020). Besides, the value that creativity offers lies in the individual ability to enable the development of novel and effective solutions to the dynamic problems that result from all forms of change (Cropley, 2015). According to Bandura (1986), highly creative people possess a definite and strong sense of self-efficacy, if not in general, in their expertise. This concurs with the role of WBL in providing dynamic learning opportunities in the formation of students' self-efficacy and creativity.

4. WBL IMPLEMENTATION

WBL takes on formalized structures across different institutional and teaching-learning settings. These can range from short, experiential engagements with an employer to semester-long placements and even extend to year-long immersive experiences. The current study of WBL models in one of the private higher education institutions typically lasts for 14 weeks, equivalent to one semester with a day release approach. During this time, students attend the workplace daily for 14 weeks and are assigned a project. In the final week, they are required to present their project. Students are expected to complete their learning, project work, and presentation within the WBL period.

When students start their WBL in the industry, they require time to grasp the department's operations, adjust to the workplace culture, and establish a good relationship with their industry coach. Feedback from industry coaches, as mentioned in interviews, suggests that it typically takes students about 2 to 4 weeks to adapt to the working environment. Additionally, adaptation involves maintaining a positive attitude, showing curiosity, and having confidence, as noted by Savickas and Porfeli (2012).

Self-learning plays a vital role in WBL. During WBL, students must take the initiative to engage in self-learning. This is because while higher learning institutions provide students with fundamental knowledge, there is often a gap when students apply theories in real-world situations. Self-learning helps bridge this gap and ensures successful project implementation. According to the Organisation for Economic Cooperation and Development (OECD) (2018), students should be given opportunities to explore how topics connect within and across disciplines and relate to real-life situations. The timing for self-learning is not fixed or prescribed by the coach or student, but coaches should anticipate that students will engage in self-learning as needed.

Although students receive fundamental knowledge during lectures, it can be challenging for them to apply it immediately. Both students and industry coaches emphasize the importance of self-dedication and self-learning in WBL. Therefore, self-learning is essential for students to succeed in WBL. Self-learning support is crucial in this model because it keeps students informed and motivated to participate in the learning process (Moos & Bonde, 2016).

In response, higher education institutions offer support by providing self-learning materials. For instance, they may grant students access to online learning resources (Sabeh et al., 2021) for studying and research purposes. Additionally, the month leading up to the WBL placement is a valuable opportunity for students to prepare. Industry coaches can communicate the expected topics for the WBL in advance, allowing students to spend this time familiarizing themselves with the basics. The student emphasized the significance of the online library access provided by the school, stating that it is crucial for WBL as it involves extensive self-learning. Following the "Pre-WBL Discussion," higher education institutions, particularly the lecturer, can guide students in accessing online resources for self-learning. They can also provide notes related to the project assigned by the industry coach to support students' self-learning needs.

Coaching is a vital aspect of WBL, providing students exposure to the industry and enabling them to acquire theoretical knowledge and workplace soft skills simultaneously. However, since coaches are full-time employees, they may mistakenly believe that coaching students will hinder their work progress. It is recommended for the Coaches to dedicate approximately 15% to 20% of their weekly schedule to working with students, translating to 1 to 2 hours per day. This recommendation aligns with the findings of Aini et al. (2016), who suggested that at least one and a half hours per week per person should be allocated for coordination and supervision by a coach in WBL.

4.1 WBL Assessment Criteria

Assessment methods in WBL differ significantly from traditional assessment approaches, mainly focusing on project-based evaluation. This shift in assessment emphasizes student ownership of the assessment process, adopting a learner-centered and problem-centered approach (Gray, 2001). The assessment methods encompass a range of approaches, both formal and informal, that can be formative or summative in nature, as long as they effectively measure Learning Outcomes (LOs) (Ali, 2019). Depending on the approach and structure of WBL, proper assessments must be formulated to assess the LOs. In WBL assessment, the assessment methods should be constructively aligned with the achievement of the LOs. The purpose of assessment is to ensure that effective learning of the course content has taken place.

Students are evaluated by both the institution and industry coach based on projects assigned by the coach. The evaluation weightage is evenly distributed, with 50% from the industry coach and 50% from the lecturer. Generally, the assessment encompasses a project, report, and presentation. It is important to note that the assessment framework may vary depending on the organization's WBL context, as observed in the company.

Scholtz (2020) emphasizes that assessment content should align with the main competencies and objectives achieved during the work placement. Each activity's purpose should be clearly outlined to demonstrate its relevance to achieving desired outcomes, and appropriate evidence of learning in practice should be provided. It is recommended to assign concept-proven projects to students during WBL without involving any private or confidential information of the company.

When assigning a project to a student, the industry coach must take into account the company's private and confidential matters since the student is not an official employee of the company. The study suggests that projects given to students should avoid involving any private or confidential information and the company's core technology.

Another characteristic of WBL projects is that they must focus on improving processes, products, and procedures, ultimately benefiting the company upon completion by the student. As noted by Arani, Alagamandan, and Tourani (2004), WBL projects are directly relevant to the employing organization.

While these projects may pose challenges for students, they aim to simulate real workplace scenarios, fostering skills such as problem-solving, innovation, communication, and teamwork. This aligns with one of the characteristics of WBL highlighted by Aini et al. (2016), where learning programs are tailored to meet workplace needs and participant requirements rather than being solely based on academic curricula.

5. CONCLUSION

WBL is a beneficial module for adoption in Malaysia's Higher Education Institutions. It significantly improves the student learning experience through several key strategies. Firstly, it fosters stronger partnerships with industries, ensuring that the curriculum is designed and delivered in collaboration with real-world professionals. This not only provides students with valuable insights into industry practices but also enhances the relevance and applicability of their learning. WBL enables students to learn directly from industry practitioners and reduces the knowledge transfer period after graduation. Secondly, WBL emphasizes experiential learning in real-world settings, enabling students to develop essential 21st-century skills such as creativity, communication and problem-solving through hands-on experiences. Lastly, WBL promotes independent learning paths. These combined efforts aim to produce graduates who are not only academically skilled but also well-rounded, talented, and equipped to meet the market needs. This study aims to provide an overview to all WBL practitioners, particularly industry coaches and students participating in WBL. It suggests conducting the WBL model based on insights from industry coaches and students who have previously participated in WBL.

In summary, three key discussions are essential: Pre-WBL Alignment Discussion, WBL Check-Ins Discussion, and Post-WBL Discussion. Higher learning institutions must ensure that students receive adequate self-learning support and regularly monitor their progress. Coaches should allocate sufficient time to students, ideally 1-2 hours per day. Projects assigned to students must meet three criteria: no involvement of private or confidential information, significant impact, and no disruption to current work progress. To ensure the quality implementation of WBL in providing opportunities for real-world learning, it is important for all parties involved to be appropriately supported by both higher education institutions and industry.

Overall, WBL is a valuable learning module, but its execution requires careful consideration, particularly regarding industry involvement. Therefore, this study suggests implementing WBL in the Malaysian context to promote WBL in Malaysia and address industry concerns about participation.

REFERENCES

Aan Alten, D. C., Phielix, C., Janssen, J., & Kester, L. (2020). Self-regulated learning support in flipped learning videos enhances learning outcomes. *Computers & Education*, 158, 104000. 10.1016/j.compedu.2020.104000

Adan, N., Douni, R., & Hashim, H. A. (2021). Industry Perception on the Implementation of Work-Based Learning (WBL) in Politeknik Ibrahim Sultan. *Politeknik & Kolej Komuniti.Journal of Social Sciences and Humanities*, 6(1), 87–98.

Adeel, A., Batool, S., & Kee, D. M. H. (2023). Why cognitive absorption is not enough: The role of knowledge absorption capacity and technological opportunity for individual learning. *Asian Academy of Management Journal*, 28(2), 239–274. 10.21315/aamj2023.28.2.9

Adeel, A., Sarminah, S., Jie, L., Kee, D. M. H., Qasim, D. Y., & Alghafes, R. A. (2023). When procrastination pays off: Role of knowledge sharing ability, autonomous motivation, and task involvement for employee creativity. *Heliyon*, 9(10), e19398. 10.1016/j.heliyon.2023.e1939837767479

Aini, W., Kustono, D., Dardiri, A., & Kamdi, W. (2016). Work-based learning for enhancing the capacity of engagement: Lesson from stakeholders perspective literature. In *AIP Conference Proceedings* (Vol. 1778, No. 1, p. 030052). AIP Publishing LLC.

Ali, L. (2019). The Design of Curriculum, Assessment and Evaluation in Higher Education with Constructive Alignment. *Journal of Education and e-learning Research*, 5(1), 72–78. 10.20448/journal.509.2018.51.72.78

Atkinson, G. (2016). *Work-Based Learning and Work-Integrated Learning: Fostering Engagement with Employers*. National Centre for Vocational Education Research Ltd.

Aziz, H. (2018, October 3). Graduate skills gap. *New Straits Times*. Retrieved from https://www.nst.com.my/education/2018/10/417327/graduate-skills-gap

Bandura, A. (1986). *Social foundations of thought and action: A social cognitive theory*. Prentice Hall.

Chamorro-premuzic, T., & Frankiewicz, B. (2019, January 7). Does Higher Education Still Prepare People for Jobs? *Harvard Business Review*.

Chan, Y. F., & Balaraman, S. (2019). Strategies to Close the Knowledge Gap of New Engineers in The Automotive Industry in Malaysia. *International Journal of Academic Research in Business and Social Sciences, 9*(13), 270-283.

Cropley, D. H. (2015). *Creativity in engineering: Novel solutions to complex problems. Explorations in creativity research*. Elsevier Academic Press. 10.1016/B978-0-12-800225-4.00002-1

Drysdale, M. T. B., & McBeath, M. (2018). Motivation, self-efficacy and learning strategies of university students participating in work-integrated learning. *Journal of Education and Work*, 31(5–6), 478–488. 10.1080/13639080.2018.1533240

Grosemans, I., Coertjens, L., & Kyndt, E. (2020). Work-related learning in the transition from higher education to work: The role of the development of self-efficacy and achievement goals. *The British Journal of Educational Psychology*, 90(1), 19–42. 10.1111/bjep.1225830506557

Ibrahim, D. H. M., & Mahyuddin, M. Z. (2017). *Youth Unemployment in Malaysia : Developments and Policy Considerations*. Retrieved from https://www.bnm.gov.my/files/publication/ar/en/2016/cp04_003_box.pdf

Ismail, A. (2018). *HEBATising FUTURE TALENTS USM style* [Powerpoint slides]. Retrieved from https://cdae.usm.my/index.php/programmes/academic-excellence/competition

Ismail, S., Mohamad, M. M., Omar, N., Heong, Y. M., & Kiong, T. T. (2015). A Comparison of The Work-Based Learning Models and Implementation in Training Institutions. *Procedia: Social and Behavioral Sciences*, 204, 282–289. 10.1016/j.sbspro.2015.08.153

Jackson, D., Shan, H., & Meek, S. (2022). Employer development of professional capabilities among early career workers and implications for the design of work-based learning. *International Journal of Management Education*, 20(3), 100692. 10.1016/j.ijme.2022.100692

Jonathan, L. Y., & Laik, M. N. (2019). Using experiential learning theory to improve teaching and learning in higher education. *European Journal of Social Sciences Education and Research*, 6(1), 123. 10.26417/ejser.v6i1.p123-132

Joshi, G., Teferi, M. Y., Miller, R., Jamali, S., Groesbeck, M., Van Tol, J., McLaughlin, R., Vardeny, Z. V., Lupton, J. M., Malissa, H., & Boehme, C. (2018). High-Field magnetoresistance of organic semiconductors. *Physical Review Applied*, 10(2), 024008. Advance online publication. 10.1103/PhysRevApplied.10.024008

Jussila, J., Raitanen, J., Partanen, A., Tuomela, V., Siipola, V., & Kunnari, I. (2020). Rapid product development in university-industry collaboration: Case study of a smart design project. *Technology Innovation Management Review*, 10(3), 49–59. 10.22215/timreview/1336

Khampirat, B., Pop, C., & Bandaranaike, S. (2019). The effectiveness of work-integrated learning in developing student work skills: A case study of Thailand. *International Journal of Work-Integrated Learning*, 20, 126–146.

Konstantinou, I., & Miller, E. (2021). Self-managed and Work-Based Learning: Problematising The Workplace–Classroom Skills Gap. *Journal of Work-Applied Management*.

Lim, Y. M., Lee, T. H., Yap, C. S., & Ling, C. C. (2016). Employability skills, personal qualities, and early employment problems of entry-level auditors: Perspectives from employers, lecturers, auditors, and students. *Journal of Education for Business*, 91(4), 185–192. 10.1080/08832323.2016.1153998

Lindqvist, H., Weurlander, M., Barman, L., Wernerson, A., & Thornberg, R. (2023). Work-based learning partnerships: Mentor-teachers' perceptions of student teachers' challenges. *Educational Research*, 65(3), 392–407. 10.1080/00131881.2023.2234384

Mohamad, M. M., Ismail, S., & Faiz, N. S. M. (2021). A tie between educational institution and industry: A66 case study of benefit from work-based learning. *Journal of Technical Education and Training*, 13(1), 128–138.

Moos, D. C., & Bonde, C. (2016). Flipping the classroom: Embedding self-regulated learning prompts in videos. Technology. *Knowledge and Learning*, 21(2), 1–18. 10.1007/s10758-015-9269-1

Morley, D. A. (2018). *Enhancing Employability in Higher Education through Work Based Learning*. Palgrave Macmillan. 10.1007/978-3-319-75166-5

Morris, T. H. (2022). How Creativity Is Oppressed through Traditional Education. *On the Horizon*, 30(3), 133–140. 10.1108/OTH-09-2022-124

Musset, P. (2019). *Improving work-based learning in schools*. OECD Social, Employment and Migration Working Papers, No. 233, OECD Publishing. 10.1787/1815199X

Nottingham, P. (2016). The use of work-based learning pedagogical perspectives to inform flexible practice within higher education. *Teaching in Higher Education*, 21(7), 790–806. 10.1080/13562517.2016.1183613

Organisation for Economic Cooperation and Development (OECD). (2018). *The future of education and skills: Education 2030*. OECD Education Working Papers.

Perusso, A., & Wagenaar, R. (2023). Electronic work-based learning (eWBL): A framework for trainers in companies and higher education. *Studies in Higher Education*, 1–17. 10.1080/03075079.2023.2280193

Qian, C., & Kee, D. M. H. (2023). Exploring the path to enhance employee creativity in Chinese MSMEs: The influence of individual and team learning orientation, transformational leadership, and creative self-efficacy. *Information (Basel)*, 14(8), 449. 10.3390/info14080449

Sabeh, H. N., Husin, M. H., Kee, D. M. H., Baharudini, A. H., & Abdullah, R. (2021). A systematic review of the DeLone and McLean model of information systems success in an e-learning context (2010-2020). *IEEE Access: Practical Innovations, Open Solutions*, 9, 81210–81235. 10.1109/ACCESS.2021.3084815

Scholtz, D. (2020). Assessing workplace-based learning. *International Journal of Work-Integrated Learning*.

Scott, D. (2020). Creatively expanding research from work-based learning. *Journal of Work-Applied Management*, 12(2), 115–125. 10.1108/JWAM-03-2020-0015

Singh, P., Narasuman, S., & Thambusamy, R. X. (2012). Refining teaching and assessment methods in fulfilling the needs of employment : A Malaysian perspective. *Futures*, 44(2), 136–147. 10.1016/j.futures.2011.09.006

Talbot, J. (2017). Curriculum Design For The Post-Industrial Society: The Facilitation Of Individually Negotiated Higher Education In Work-Based Learning Shell Frameworks In The United Kingdom. *The Journal of Educational Research*, 11(2).

Tan, A. Y. T., Chew, E., & Kalavally, V. (2017). The expectations gap for engineering field in Malaysia in the 21st century. *On the Horizon*, 25(2), 131–138. 10.1108/OTH-12-2015-0071

Toorani, H., & Khorshidi, A. (2012). Introduction to Work-based Learning. *Journal of Educational and Management Studies.*, 2(1), 1–6.

Watisin, W. (2017). *Pelaksanaan program pembelajaran berasaskan kerja politeknik bersama industri* (Doctoral dissertation, Universiti Tun Hussein Onn Malaysia).

Yusof, M. F. M., Wong, A., Ahmad, G., Aziz, R. C., & Hussain, K. (2020). Enhancing Hospitality and Tourism Graduate Employability Through The 2u2i Program. *Worldwide Hospitality and Tourism Themes.*

Chapter 12
Enhancing Workforce Competencies:
Addressing Job Demand and Workaholism During COVID-19

Vandana Shukla
Jiwaji University, Gwalior, India

Umesh Holani
Jiwaji University, Gwalior, India

Garima Mathur
 https://orcid.org/0000-0003-1166-2192
Prestige Institute of Management and Research, Gwalior, India

ABSTRACT

Changes in work environments and conditions have sparked new study areas that can provide understanding for the implementation of organizational interventions targeted at promoting and maintaining healthy and productive workplaces. Presenteeism is a phenomenon that can potentially pose significant problems to businesses. It has been discovered that the negative consequences are far worse than absenteeism. This study looks at the harmful effects of workaholism and job demand on presenteeism in the workplace. The data has been collected from 200 executive employees of manufacturing units in the Gwalior region. This study has crucial implications for researchers and practitioners, and it emphasizes the importance of the attribute in dealing with presenteeism, which could improve employee productivity. This research could help management figure out what steps they can take to overcome executive presenteeism.

INTRODUCTION

In the fast changing world almost all the organizations are facing challenges in terms of skills needed to understand changes to be brought in and then implementing them. The workforce is not prepared yet to get over the unforeseen. Interestingly, the COVID-19 pandemic has highlighted the precariousness and instability of various economic sectors. Workplace conditions have changed considerably, hurting

DOI: 10.4018/979-8-3693-3096-8.ch012

employees' physical and mental health in addition to the health crises. Organizations and employees may make inefficient and inadequate decisions as an outcome of the expected global economic crisis, and occupational health psychology may face new issues.

The pandemic's duration was much more difficult and challenging for manufacturing organizations and their employees. When there was an environment of fear, distrust, and disappointment, the employees of essential goods manufacturing organizations still had to go to work. There was no other option in front of manufacturing employees, and it was very hard to manage the manpower as so many employees were affected by COVID-19 and many were serving the 14-day quarantine period enforced by the government as the medical requirement. Even though there was fear of life of employees and their families, employees had to go due to job insecurity as many of the organizations shut down during the pandemic time.

On the other side, the focus emphasized on Workforce preparedness and collaboration between industry and academics which may promote innovation and technological advancement. This collaboration is needed for developing research work and a qualified workforce. This relationship also contributes to the advancement of society and societal progress. The industry-academia collaborations support the implementation of novel solutions and also provide new career opportunities. Working together between industry and academia is beneficial to both parties. At the same, the current study tried to understand the existing academic research work on variables like presenteeism, job demand, and workaholism simultaneously focusing on how employees face challenges related to these variables practically. This study is an effort to find a gap between the required skills to face issues regarding presenteeism, job demand, and workaholism in the workplace and the actual knowledge and research work done by academicians. The study also tried to bridge this gap by collecting responses from the managerial/ executive employees of manufacturing organizations and applying the theories developed by the academicians. The responses reveal the practical issues of the industry's personnel. The results of the study must benefit the industry, the academicians, and society as a whole.

Following the global economic downturn and financial crisis, a very large number of businesses shut down or re-engineered, aiming to accomplish more with less. Employers prioritize employee productivity in the current competitive, technologically advanced, and fast-moving work environment. An employee's productivity can be thought of as a spectrum ranging from zero to total productive work engagement (for example, if he or she is away from work). Absenteeism is the term used to describe when someone does not show up for work because they are sick. However, a new concept of presenteeism has developed through time, in which, 'people go to work even when they are sick' (Aronsson, Gustafsson, & Dallner, 2000).

Presenteeism, or employees reporting to work while sick, has attracted the interest of practitioners and researchers alike (Hemp, 2004). Presenteeism is a developing trend that contrasts with absenteeism in that it generates far more productivity loss than absenteeism. Because of the demonstrated links between presenteeism and productivity loss, several studies have viewed presenteeism as a negative element in the workplace. The COVID-19 outbreak is the most difficult for the manufacturing organizations as well as the employees. There are very few studies on the phenomenon of presenteeism, especially in the manufacturing organization. It is a less focused area due to the challenges of data collection from the employees of manufacturing studies and because of the perception that they do not get stressed as their tasks do not require direct interaction with the customers. This study could serve as a foundation for future research in this area.

Presenteeism

Although presenteeism can be viewed as an effort on the part of employees, many research studies have focused on that, like absenteeism, as a counterproductive work behaviour with negative implications (Escorpizo, 2008), along with the outcomes of other variables such as role ambiguity and productivity (Zhou, Martinez, Ferreira & Rodrigues, 2016). The main reasons for its occurrence are numerous and can be classified as personal and contextual elements. Suffering from psychiatric disease, having a low educational level, being old, and being a parent are examples of the first category, whereas situational antecedents include leadership, uncertainty about promotion chances, the work environment, and time pressure. All of the causes can stem from negative elements based on the factors stated. However, this is not true, as variables such as work enjoyment, self-confidence, and self-satisfaction could be the reason for showing up sick to work.

As a result of ill health or injury, which are commonly referred to as "occupational disabilities, presenteeism may indicate the companies' productivity losses in terms of job quality and amount managed to be accomplished. This viewpoint is consistent with Hemp's (2004) findings, which revealed that working in poor health had a negative influence on both the amount and quality of work. This is because unwell people work at a slower speed and have less precision due to a lack of focus. Those working in the education, health, and welfare sectors are among those who frequently experience this occurrence. Teachers and nurses are two examples of occupations.

A worsened health condition, lower performance, and work discontent are all common outcomes. As previously said, presenteeism has a detrimental impact not only on the individual but also on the entire business. Presenteeism is more difficult to measure (Zhang, Bansback, and Anis, 2011) which can exacerbate the negative consequences. Once again, it is important to emphasize that the outcomes shown are not always negative (i.e., Somewhere workers report instances where presenteeism was advantageous to their recovery from sickness or their productivity increased in such situations as compared to being absentee).

Workaholism

Aside from workload, recent changes observed in work environments, such as a more work-oriented culture, have been linked to an increase in the number of workaholic employees, defined as "people whose need for work has become so excessive that it causes a noticeable disturbance or interference with their bodily health, personal happiness, and interpersonal relations, as well as their smooth social functioning." Since Oates initially characterized workaholism as a "compulsion or uncontrollable drive to work incessantly," other scholars have focused their attention on the subject. Workaholism is recognized as a legitimate behavioral addiction from a clinical standpoint, and the phrase "work addiction" has been commonly used to describe the disorder. In contrast to Andreassen, Pallesen, Moen, Bjorvatn, Waage, and Schaufeli (2018) shall use workaholism as a synonym for work addiction in this study. Furthermore, it has been established that workaholism is a real and enduring disorder characterized by compulsive overworking. The condition affects up to 10% of people in industrialized countries and is linked to decreased psychosocial functioning, which has therapeutic implications. Some research work results showed that workaholism is linked to obsessive–compulsive personality. As far as career prospects go, workaholism has a positive outcome, but it has also been related to many negative outcomes, such as an increased risk of high stress, high blood pressure, sleeping difficulties, work–life balance conflict, and lower relationship satisfaction, according to organizational studies. In general, research on workaholism has concentrated mostly on the negative effects on employees' health and quality of work life with little attention paid to the relation between workaholism and job performance.

Workaholism is a confusing and complex phenomenon. The definitions differ in scope, focusing solely on cognitive or behavioral components and highlighting explicitly abnormal or normal features of the syndrome. We can infer that researchers investigating workaholism employ a pathogenic approach, emphasizing the origins and consequences of maladaptation and sickness or the causes of excessive engagement and its positive effects on an employee. The existing state of knowledge makes settling on a single definition challenging. It appears crucial and desirable to seek broad and comprehensive definitions that encompass the entire complexity of workaholism without imposing a single point of view. In this regard, it's worth mentioning Ng, Sorensen & Feldman's (2007) more modern definition, which argues that "workaholics are individuals who like the process of working, are preoccupied with working, and spend large hours and personal time to work." Following Smith and Seymour (2004), Ng, Sorensen and Feldman believe that any type of addiction, including workaholism, should be examined using three types of mental processes or dimensions: behavior, cognition, and affect. Ng, Sorensen & Feldman operationalize the aspects of workaholism using a three-part approach:

- "Cognitive dimension: obsession with work manifests as a serious involvement in work that cannot be limited or controlled; constant thoughts about work that arise even when the person is not working"
- "Affective dimension: positive emotions related to work, which is the main source of satisfaction and pleasure, and negative emotions that appear when the person is not working (e.g., fear, sense of guilt, depression)."

Job Demands and Presenteeism

One prominent argument for sick leave is that it is a logical decision toward achieving a goal. Absence is specifically considered as logical conduct, decided by cost-benefit analyses of the alternative behaviour, namely presenteeism, and the potential repercussions of that activity. In addition to the need for individual cost-benefit analyses, Johansson and Lundberg (2004) stress the significance of the workplace as a restriction that may limit individual options. Constraints are situations or demands for attendance that include both favorably valued and negatively valued aspects (e.g., prizes for minimal absenteeism) (e.g., individual financial position). For two reasons, the focus of this study is on employment expectations. First, if we can show that job demands, presenteeism, and burnout are all linked over time, then job demands can be used as a pretext for workplace interventions and hence improvement. Second, presenteeism is found to be positively associated with workplace demands in general, as well as specific needs such as time pressure, conflicting expectations, and work pressure.

Job demands are those aspects of a job that require a consistent amount of physical, mental, emotional, or cognitive effort from the employee. As a result, job demands are associated with physiological and/or psychological costs (e.g., exhaustion). Although job expectations are not always bad, they might become stressful if achieving them necessitates extra effort and the person has not fully recovered from earlier work sequences. In this study, we incorporate a traditional and more general measure of occupational demands, namely workload, as well as specific demands namely work needs and physical demands. We hypothesize that job demands increase presenteeism in employees, which means they are more willing to go to work on days when they are sick. Because job needs must be satisfied for employees to perform adequately, they will be motivated to do everything possible to meet these demands so that their performance remains at the desired level. Demanding work qualities, according to Hobfoll (2001), generate losses since they deplete people's resources. When losses occur, people use resource conservation techniques (based on expected outcomes) to successfully adjust by investing the resources available to them. As a result, we anticipate that the higher the job demands, the greater the effort individuals will put forth to satisfy them and the greater the likelihood that they will work while sick to avoid performance degradation (i.e., resource loss). Job demands, in this context, indicate not just feeling pressured to work harder but also feeling pressured to attend meetings, especially in the Covid era (Xie, Ifie, & Gruber, 2022).

RELATED WORKS

A study by Mokhtar, Daniella & Abdullah, Nurul-Azza and Roshaizad, Najwa (2020), with a sample of 347 diplomatic officials from the National Institute of Public Administration (INTAN) in Johor and Terengganu provides insights into presenteeism that are beneficial for research scholars and interested policymakers. They used demographic characteristics as well as three key variables to make up this data. Each component has a sub-dimension; (1) presenteeism: the ability to accomplish a task while avoiding interruptions; (2) job demand: workload, emotional, and cognitive demands, and (3) job insecurity: the importance and likelihood of an event occurring. The data was obtained using a paper and pencil cross-sectional questionnaire and analyzed using SPSS version 22. In Pearson correlation studies, there was a substantial correlation between avoiding disruption (a sub-dimension of presenteeism) and the likelihood that an incident would occur (a sub-dimension of job insecurity), but no significant correlation between the other variables. It could be a base or starting point for more research to improve workplace productivity and well-being.

The majority of presenteeism research has stressed its prevalence, determinants, and effects on employee and organizational health. Only a few studies (Côté, Karine & Lauzier, Martin & Stinglhamber, Florence, 2020) have looked into the impact of presenteeism on workers' attitudes and motivation. This study examines the mediating effect of workaholism on the link between presenteeism and job demand. Using past research as a foundation, this study proposes that perceived organizational support be considered a modulator of job demand and workaholic' links. The results of bootstrapped regression analysis, presented as a mediated moderation model, reveal three significant findings. For starters, presenteeism is linked to lower levels of job satisfaction and engagement. Second, presenteeism affects job happiness through work involvement. Third, organizational support (perceived) moderates the relationship between work engagement and job happiness, such that feeling supported by the company has an impact on job satisfaction even when work engagement is low. Overall, this study is one of a few that have looked at the interaction between presenteeism and its repercussions in terms of job attitudes.

In the same aspect as Mazzetti, Greta & Vignoli, Michela & Schaufeli, Wilmar & Guglielmi, Dina (2017) looked at the mediating and moderating effects of presenteeism in the relationship between workaholism and work–family conflict. An online survey was completed by 1065 white-collar employees from an Italian corporation, and hypotheses were tested using a bootstrapping approach. According to the findings, presenteeism mediated the link between workaholism and work–family conflict. Furthermore, management support reduced the mediating effect of presenteeism: workaholism was strongly associated to presenteeism for employees reporting lower levels of support than for those reporting higher levels of support. Presenteeism was also linked to higher levels of work-family conflict. The current research examines the protective role of managerial assistance in preventing workaholic employees from forcing themselves to go to work even when they are sick. As a result, early intervention targeted at reducing the negative relationship between workaholism and work–family conflict should focus on developing supportive leadership abilities among managers.

H1: There is a positive relationship between Workaholism and presenteeism.

Using the job demands-resources (JD-R) paradigm, examine how aspects of the psychosocial work environment (particularly, job demands and resources) are connected to presenteeism, and in particular, if they are indirectly connected through burnout and work engagement (McGregor, Magee Caputi and Iverson, 2016). A cross-sectional study of 980 working Australians examined the relationships among employment demands (such as workplace bullying, time constraints, and work-family conflict), resources (such as leadership and social support), burnout, job engagement, and presenteeism. The hypothesized hypotheses were tested using path analysis while controlling for participant variables (i.e., sex, age, work level, duration, and education). Higher job demands (bullying in the workplace, time pressure, and work-family conflict) and poorer job resources (leadership only) were found to be connected to presenteeism indirectly through increased burnout. Increased job resources (leadership and social support) were linked to presenteeism indirectly through increased work engagement. The findings support the JD-R model, implying that presenteeism may be caused by the stress and burnout associated with meeting excessive job demands, as well as the decreased work engagement and increased burnout caused by a lack of resources in the workplace. Intervention programs could concentrate on teaching employees how to better handle job responsibilities and promoting the resources available at work as an innovative approach to address the issue of growing presenteeism. This research is significant since it is one of the first to look at the theoretical basis of presenteeism and its origins.

According to Deery, Stephen & Walsh, Janet & Zatzick, and Christopher (2014), presenteeism, or working while sick, is an increasing problem in the workplace. The relationship between job demands, presenteeism, and absenteeism was investigated in this study. With the primary goal of investigating the mediation effects of presenteeism and the moderating impacts of organizational justice on this connection, we evaluated a moderated mediation model of the effects of job demands on absenteeism. The study found that high job demands were linked to presenteeism, which predicted longer absence spells, based on a sample of 227 emergency services call center workers. Furthermore, presenteeism mediated the association between job demands and absenteeism through employee beliefs of distributive fairness. Points for practitioners Work overload and rigorous attendance control techniques might encourage presenteeism, therefore, companies should be aware of this. Managers must understand that presenteeism can lead to prolonged periods of absence. Employee perceptions of fair outcomes reduce presenteeism's negative impact on absenteeism.

Demerouti, Evangelia & Blanc & Schaufeli, Wilmar & Hox, Joop, (2009), focus on the fact that an employee staying at work when they should be at home due to illness is known as presenteeism, the polar opposite of absenteeism. Presenteeism is a significant issue for businesses since employees who show up for work when they are sick reduce productivity. The study's main goal is to look at the long-term links between job demands, burnout (exhaustion and depersonalization), and presenteeism. Job demands would lead to presenteeism, and presenteeism would lead to both exhaustion and depersonalization over time, they hypothesized. The hypotheses were tested on a group of 258 staff nurses who completed questionnaires at three-time points separated by 1.5 years. The outcomes were mostly in line with expectations. Job demands increased presenteeism, and presenteeism eventually led to depersonalization.

The relationship between exhaustion and presenteeism has been discovered to be reciprocal, implying that when employees are exhausted, they mobilize compensatory measures, which in turn increase their exhaustion.

H2: There is a positive relationship between job demand and presenteeism.

Figure 1. Conceptual Model

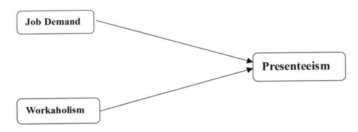

For the conceptual model of the study refer to figure 1. It shows the relationship between job demand and presenteeism and Workaholics and presenteeism.

Research Objectives

The research intends to focus on the effect of job demand and workaholic behavior of managerial/executive employees on presenteeism in the manufacturing industry.

PROPOSED METHODS

Design and Sample

A cross-sectional survey of 200 executives working in the manufacturing sector was used in this study. The data was collected online by sending emails and using WhatsApp. In total, 350 survey invitations were sent among the respondents of different manufacturing units in Gwalior, out of which 226 responded; the response rate was approximately 65%, which can be considered a good response rate (Babbie, 1990). After missing data and outliers were removed, the final usable data was reduced to 200 samples.

Instruments

The instruments utilized were validated scales that had undergone back-to-back translations and were adapted from earlier research. The directions were explained to the respondents, and a method example was demonstrated to help them comprehend.

Presenteeism

The short version of the Standford Presenteeism Scale (SPS-6) created by Koopman was used to assess presenteeism (2002). All of the items were positive, with responses ranging from (1)
Strongly Disagree to (7) Strongly Agree on a 7-Likert scale. The scale's dependability value was relatively high, at $\alpha=.75$.

Job Demand

Five items were adopted from the Job Content Questionnaire (JCQ) developed by Karasek and his colleagues (1985) and 14 items were taken from the Veldhoven Mejimen Experience and Evaluation of Work questionnaire (1994). Workload (5 items), emotional (7 things), and cognitive demands were all included on a seven-point scale. The scale's dependability value was relatively high, at $\alpha=.72$.

Workaholism

DUWAS scale, as adapted by Kravina, Falco, Girardi, and De Carlo in Italian (2010). The scale has ten items and is aimed at detecting the two dimensions of excessive and compulsive working. "I persist in my job even when my colleagues have already gone" for working excessively, and "I believe that there is something inside me that motivates me to work hard" for working compulsively are examples of items for these two dimensions. Because workaholism indicates the propensity to overwork compulsively, we used a composite score of workaholism, which is the average of the two scales of working excessively and obsessively (Schaufeli et al., 2008). The whole scale had an alpha of .77.

The participants were then chosen at random, with the number of managers in each stratum being proportional to the size of the stratum. The survey was completed anonymously on the internet. To access the online questionnaire participants were allotted a login identification code and a personal password. Additionally, they were informed that no personal information would be gathered for the study.

ANALYSIS

The data was put to statistical assessment to understand the relationship between variables.

Demographic Characteristics of the Sample

Table 1. Demographic Characteristics of the respondents

Parameters	Frequency	Percentage
Gender		
Female	30	15.0%
Male	170	85.0%

continued on following page

Table 1. Continued

Parameters	Frequency	Percentage
Age		
Less than 25years	29	14.7%
26-35 years	65	32.9%
36-45 years	64	32%
46-55 years	30	14.7%
Above 55 years	12	5.7%
Education		
Graduation	58	28.6%
Post-Graduation	115	57.5%
Others	27	13.9%

Table 1 indicates the demographic characteristics of the respondents.

Level of Presenteeism, Job Demand, and Workaholism Among Respondents

The frequency of each variable utilized in this study, presenteeism, workaholics & job demand is listed in table 2. Each of the factors was divided into three categories: low, moderate, and high. The outcomes are listed in table 2 below: -

Table 2. Frequency Levels of the Variables

VARIABLE	LEVEL	FREQUENCY	PERCENTAGE (%)
Presenteeism	Low	4	2.0%
	Moderate	130	65.0%
	High	66	33.0%
TOTAL		200	100%
Job Demand	Low	18	9.0%
	Moderate	170	85.0%
	High	12	6.0%
TOTAL		200	100%
Workaholism	Low	10	5.0%
	Moderate	148	74.0%
	High	42	21.0%
TOTAL		200	100%

Figure 2. Graph showing Frequency Levels of the Variables

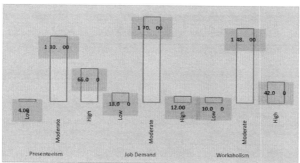

For better understanding, Figure 2 represents the frequency levels of all variables in graphical form in three categories low, moderate, and high.

The frequency levels of the three variables evaluated in this study are shown in Table 2. The majority of respondents indicated moderate to high levels of presenteeism, with 130 respondents (65%) reporting moderate and 66 respondents (33%) reporting high levels of presenteeism, leaving only 4 respondents (2%) reporting low levels of presenteeism. When it came to job demand, the majority of the samples had moderate needs (85 percent). 12 respondents (6.0%) had high job expectations, while 9% of respondents had low job demands. Finally, 148 respondents (74.0%) reported moderate workaholism in their occupations, whereas 42 respondents (21.0%) reported high workaholism and just 10 respondents (5.0%) reported low workaholism.

Further regression was applied between variables. The value of R square ranges between 0 to 1, here it is 0.567 which shows that Job demand and Workaholism together explained a 56.7% variance in presenteeism as the dependent variable.

Through the results, we can ascertain that the antecedent variable job demand was found to positive and significantly affecting the presenteeism (b= 0.265, p>0.05). Likewise, the workaholism factor was also a significant antecedent to presenteeism (b= 0.472, p>0.05). It indicates that job demand and workaholics have a positive and significant relationship with presenteeism in manufacturing industries in Gwalior supporting H1 and H2 both.

CONCLUSION AND DISCUSSION

These findings revealed that presenteeism can be viewed as a high-risk organizational behaviour with strong long-term links to job demands and burnout (Pei, Lin, Li, Zhu & Xi, 2020; Demerouti, Le Blanc, Bakker, Schaufeli & Hox, 2009). According to the findings, workplace presenteeism should be avoided. The manuscript's expected contribution is to not only place presenteeism on the study agenda but also to get both companies and scientists to pay attention to its negative impacts on employee well-being and, as a result, on the organization.

In a large sample of industrial executives with leadership roles and responsibilities, the relationship between presenteeism, workaholism, and job demand was explored. Through workaholism, the proposed model predicted both direct and indirect relationships between self-oriented perfectionism and presenteeism. Job demand, as expected, had a positive correlation with workaholism (Langseth-Eide, 2019). As a result, industrial executives who establish high-performance goals for themselves may dedicate more time to their work and think about it almost obsessively, even when they are detaching and resting (i.e., self-oriented perfectionism may lead to workaholism). This finding supports the findings of recent investigations and, in particular, the theory that workaholism is driven by personal perfectionism.

Workaholism, on the other hand, was linked to presenteeism (Gillet et al, 2021). Workaholics, because of their perfectionistic impulses, tend to work harder, to perform their work alone, to have difficulties delegating work to coworkers, and to feel indispensable to the company, going to work even when unwell. This is consistent with prior research, which found that workaholism encourages people to go to work even when their health is poor and/or disease is present.

These findings can serve as a springboard for more research into employee difficulties in firms. The government as well as the private sector might use it as a guide and implement suitable steps to avoid large cost and productivity losses due to presenteeism. The job's workload should be manageable and not overload the staff. Management should set up a good schedule with ample time for employees to finish tasks, especially when they are sick. Management should enable them to take a break; once the sick employee recovers, productivity may increase significantly. Employees may feel forced to show up for work if there is a job need, but the quality of their labor will be doubtful.

This research has the potential to increase employee knowledge of the consequences of job demand on presenteeism. As a result, to realize the vision and mission, people and the company must collaborate to accomplish unprecedented heights. However, a better-defined conceptual framework would be required, which may be obtained through fast-growing presenteeism research. The findings of presenteeism studies were comparable, however; the extent and strength of the association differed. This is due to the adaptiveness component, which is dependent on individual characteristics and cultures, which were not addressed in this study. As a result, this could be one of the study gaps that could serve as a foundation for future research in this area.

IMPLICATIONS OF THE STUDY

The study tries to recognize the impact of job demand and workaholism on presenteeism in manufacturing units at the executive level for which the study had theoretical and practical implications. The current study must be helpful to understand the concept of presenteeism and its antecedents and provide some intensity for the other variables that have a significant effect on presenteeism. With a better understanding of presenteeism and its antecedents, management can improve the skills of employees and create a better work culture and supporting work environment. If the organizational environment is supportive and employees get good leadership, they are always ready to face any type of contingency. That can help to prevent the negative outcomes of presenteeism and improve the work-life, which ultimately improves the happiness index of the employee and their family.

The study helps academic researchers and students address presenteeism, job demand, and workaholism with practical applications and provides support for developing advanced, appropriate, and desirable skills in this field in the current scenario. With collaboration with industry and academics, organizations easily get skilled, knowledgeable, and specialized candidates who can understand better the term presenteeism and its antecedents theoretically as well as practically. They can easily face challenging issues with the same and quite better to handle them., which can reduce the adverse outcomes of presenteeism such as distress, mental and physical health issues, turnover intention, poor performance, productivity loss, and job insecurity. Organizations can get people who are actually well-trained and quite ready to work in the new practical environment with the knowledge gained during academic years. Organizations also can improve overall performance and productivity by adopting new relevant techniques developed by academicians, which must ensure a competitive advantage for the organizations.

The present study aimed at bridging the gap between theoretical learning and real industry needs about presenteeism, job demand, and workaholism. It can be a crucial driver of economic development, and innovation, and can increase employability. As the sample of the study is managerial/executive level employees of manufacturing units, the problem of presenteeism, job demand, and workaholism, their antecedents, and predictors can be understood in a more practical way that an employee faces in their routine professional and personal life and this helps academicians in prepare the students with the skill required in actual job floor. This may help in the recognition of skill gaps- what industries need and what type of skills we deliver.

REFERENCES

Andreassen, C. S., Pallesen, S., Moen, B. E., Bjorvatn, B., Waage, S., & Schaufeli, W. B. (2018). Workaholism and negative work-related incidents among nurses. *Industrial Health*, 56(5), 2017–0223. 10.2486/indhealth.2017-022329760300

Aronsson, G., Gustafsson, K., & Dallner, M. (2000). Sick but yet at work. An empirical study of sickness presenteeism. *Journal of Epidemiology and Community Health*, 54(7), 502–509. 10.1136/jech.54.7.50210846192

Côté, K., Lauzier, M., & Stinglhamber, F. (2021). The relationship between presenteeism and job satisfaction: A mediated moderation model using work engagement and perceived organizational support. *European Management Journal*, 39(2), 270–278. 10.1016/j.emj.2020.09.001

Deery, S., Walsh, J., & Zatzick, C. D. (2014). A moderated mediation analysis of job demands, presenteeism, and absenteeism. *Journal of Occupational and Organizational Psychology*, 87(2), 352–369. 10.1111/joop.12051

Demerouti, E., Le Blanc, P. M., Bakker, A. B., Schaufeli, W. B., & Hox, J. (2009). Present but sick: A three-wave study on job demands, presenteeism and burnout. *Career Development International*, 14(1), 50–68. 10.1108/13620430910933574

Escorpizo, R. (2008). Understanding work productivity and its application to work-related musculoskeletal disorders. *International Journal of Industrial Ergonomics*, 38(3-4), 291–297. 10.1016/j.ergon.2007.10.018

Gillet, N., Austin, S., Fernet, C., Sandrin, E., Lorho, F., Brault, S., Becker, M., & Aubouin Bonnaventure, J. (2021). Workaholism, presenteeism, work–family conflicts and personal and work outcomes: Testing a moderated mediation model. *Journal of Clinical Nursing*, 30(19-20), 2842–2853. 10.1111/jocn.1579133870550

Hemp, P. (2004). Presenteeism: At work-but out of it. *Harvard Business Review*, 82(10), 49–58. 15559575

Hobfoll, S. E. (2001). The Influence of culture, community, and the nested-self in the stress process: Advancing conservation of resources theory. *Applied Psychology*, 50(3), 33770. 10.1111/1464-0597.00062

Johansson, G., & Lundberg, I. (2004). Adjustment latitude and attendance requirements as determinants of sickness absence or attendance. Empirical tests of the illness flexibility model. *Social Science & Medicine*, 58(10), 1857–1868. 10.1016/S0277-9536(03)00407-615020004

Koopman, C., Pelletier, K. R., Murray, J. F., Sharda, C. E., Berger, M. L., Turpin, R. S., Hackleman, P., Gibson, P., Holmes, D. M., & Bendel, T. (2002). Stanford presenteeism scale: Health status and employee productivity. *Journal of Occupational and Environmental Medicine*, 44(1), 14–20. 10.1097/00043764-200201000-0000411802460

Kravina, L., Falco, A., Girardi, D., & De Carlo, N. A. (2010). Workaholism among management and workers in an Italian cooperative enterprise. *TPM. Testing, Psychometrics, Methodology in Applied Psychology*, 17, 201–216. 10.4473/TPM.17.4.2

Langseth-Eide, B. (2019). It's been a hard day's night and I've been working like a dog: Workaholism and work engagement in the JD-R model. *Frontiers in Psychology*, 10, 1444. 10.3389/fpsyg.2019.0144431293485

Mazzetti, G., Vignoli, M., Schaufeli, W., & Guglielmi, D. (2017). Work addiction and presenteeism: The buffering role of managerial support. *International Journal of Psychology*, 54(2), 174–179. Advance online publication. 10.1002/ijop.1244928791675

McGregor, A., Magee, C. A., Caputi, P., & Iverson, D. (2016). A job demands-resources approach to presenteeism. *Career Development International*, 21(4), 402418. 10.1108/CDI-01-2016-0002

Mokhtar, D., Abdullah, N.-A., & Roshaizad, N. (2020). Survey dataset on presenteeism, job demand and perceived job insecurity: The perspective of diplomatic officers. *Data in Brief*, 30, 105505. 10.1016/j.dib.2020.10550532368580

Ng, W. H., Sorensen, K. L., & Feldman, D. C. (2007). Dimensions, antecedents, and consequences of workaholism: A conceptual integration and extension. *Journal of Organizational Behavior*, 28(1), 111–136. 10.1002/job.424

Oates, W. E. (1971). *Confessions of a Workaholic: The Facts about Work Addiction*. World Publishing Company.

Pei, P., Lin, G., Li, G., Zhu, Y., & Xi, X. (2020). The association between doctors' presenteeism and job burnout: A cross-sectional survey study in China. *BMC Health Services Research*, 20(1), 1–7. 10.1186/s12913-020-05593-932746808

Schaufeli, W. B., Taris, T. W., & Bakker, A. B. (2008). It takes two to tango: Workaholism is working excessively and working compulsively. In Burke, R. J., & Cooper, C. L. (Eds.), *The long work hours culture: Causes, consequences and choices* (pp. 203–225). Emerald.

Smith, D. E., & Seymour, R. B. (2004). The nature of addiction. In Coombs, R. H. (Ed.), *Handbook of addictive disorders: A practical guide to diagnosis and treatment* (pp. 3–30). John Wiley & Sons, Inc.

Xie, J., Ifie, K., & Gruber, T. (2022). The dual threat of COVID-19 to health and job security–Exploring the role of mindfulness in sustaining frontline employee-related outcomes. *Journal of Business Research*, 146, 216–227. 10.1016/j.jbusres.2022.03.03035340762

Zhang, W., Bansback, N., & Anis, A. (2011). Measuring and valuing productivity loss due to poor health: A critical review. *Social Science & Medicine*, 72(2), 185–192. 10.1016/j.socscimed.2010.10.02621146909

Zhou, Q., Martinez, L. F., Ferreira, A. I., & Rodrigues, P. (2016). Supervisor support, role ambiguity and productivity associated with presenteeism: A longitudinal study. *Journal of Business Research*, 69(9), 3380–3387. 10.1016/j.jbusres.2016.02.006

Chapter 13
Educational Innovation in the Information Age:
AI Tutoring and Micro-Learning

Jihene Mrabet
Amity University, Dubai, UAE

Robert Studholme
Amity University, Dubai, UAE

Natoya Thompson
Fatima College of Health Sciences, UAE

ABSTRACT

AI tutoring is gaining importance in education due to remote and hybrid learning, where teachers may not provide the same level of individualized support. AI tutoring can fill this gap by providing tailored learning experiences, identifying areas of struggle, and providing targeted support. An exploratory research study investigated the effectiveness of AI tutoring in improving essay writing quality and regulating anxiety levels among university students. The experiment involved using ChatGPT as an English essay evaluator and suggestion provider and measuring students' anxiety levels pre- and post-AI usage. Results showed significant improvement in essay writing and anxiety management, but some students expressed skepticism about AI grading proficiency.

DOI: 10.4018/979-8-3693-3096-8.ch013

INTRODUCTION

According to Bloomberg (2023), the AI market in 2022 was valued at $40 billion and estimated to grow to $1.3 trillion within ten years. A less conservative estimate from (Srivastava, 2023) put the predicted 2030 market at $2 trillion. They go on to report that 40% of organizations plan significant investments in AI, expected to grow at a CAGR of 37.3% from 2023 to 2030.

Reasons given by business owners include the fact that 97% of them already see the benefits of ChatGPT in their businesses and over 60% believe AI will improve customer relationships. The results of this are not seen as the feared loss of human jobs, as they estimate that AI could create about 97 million new jobs. This is not a surprising result considering that 64% of businesses expect AI to boost productivity.

Appinventiv estimates the Chatbot market size to reach around $1.25 billion by 2025, while Bloomberg predicts the broader field of specialized generative AI assistant software will be $89 billion (ibid).

At the same time, rapid growth in the EdTech sector is being driven by AI trends that enhance student engagement. AI achieves this through personalized course content, interactive lectures, and gamified classroom experiences that focus on skill development. Consequently, the AI education market alone is anticipated to exceed $20 billion by 2027. Additionally, the global e-learning market's revenue is projected to reach $166.60 billion by 2023. (Statista). The numbers are huge and the conclusion obvious. AI is going to become a major part of our world.

The oldest member of our group can remember seeing one of the very first pocket calculators in the hands of his Mathematics teacher when he was around 13. He remembers visiting Newcastle University and its computer department at around the age of sixteen where a machine the size of a small van played rockets-landing-on-the-moon games. He recalls buying his first desktop computer in Japan during the 90s and running programmes for English language learners from floppy disks. He remembers the days when the smart phone was something used by the cast of Star Trek, rather than something small children regarded as a must have accessory. He now finds himself involved in research with a machine that is better than the Star Trek computer pretended to be. It is hard to find ways to describe the change in the world of education brought about by technology without falling into hyperbole.

Today, though, we seem to be facing an even more profound revolution: the emergence of AI tutoring. Those who know most about it think this leap is not merely evolutionary but revolutionary. AI tutoring, exemplified by technologies like ChatGPT, can already be described as having transcended the boundaries of traditional education. Where once students learned vocabulary from floppy–based spelling games, we now interact with AIs capable of personalized tutoring, adapting their teaching style to each learner's unique needs.

The shift from static, one-size-fits-all book-based educational materials to dynamic, AI-driven personalized learning is like the difference between the Wright brother's first flight and the Concorde. AI tutoring systems can analyze student responses, adapt to learning styles, and provide tailored feedback, something unimaginable a few decades ago.

In this new era, it is fair to say that AI tutors like ChatGPT are not just tools but collaborators in the educational process. They offer an interactive, responsive learning experience, bringing a level of engagement and personalization that traditional educational methods could never achieve. Teachers do not have the time or energy to give the personalized attention that the AI gives. We never make house calls at unsociable hours the night before a final exam. ChatGPT, on the other hand, will answer questions at any hour and at great length. Even Father Christmas could not be in as many houses at the same time, giving out so many gifts.

We are discovering more about the capabilities and potential of AI tutoring, and it is becoming increasingly clear that we are not just witnessing a change in educational tools but a fundamental shift in the way we teach and learn. The world described by science fiction is today's reality. We need to be looking forward to find our best path through it.

LITERATURE REVIEW

I. AI-Powered Education: Exploring Trends, Initiatives, and Challenges

The integration of Artificial Intelligence (AI) in education has become an increasingly prominent topic of discussion and research, reflecting the rapid advancements in technology and its transformative potential across various sectors. Within the unique context of the UAE, a nation renowned for its commitment to technological advancement and innovation, the adoption of AI in education is particularly pertinent. The allure of AI lies in its capacity to analyze vast amounts of data, adapt to individual learning styles, and provide real-time feedback, thus revolutionizing traditional teaching methodologies. As global trends in education undergo a paradigm shift, it is crucial to scrutinize these initiatives, discern the challenges encountered, and identify the opportunities that AI presents for fostering a more efficient and effective learning environment.

1. Key Trends and Developments in AI Integration

Recent research has highlighted key trends and developments in the use of AI in education. Luan (2020) and Ganga (2021) both emphasize the growing role of AI in assessment, individualized learning, and precision education, with a focus on intelligent tutors, evaluation, and learning analysis. Yousuf (2021) also presents a comprehensive overview that includes classroom monitoring, sentiment analysis and student grading.

In referencing the applications of AI in education (AIED), Paek (2021) highlights the existing category structure of intelligent tutoring systems (ITS), exploratory learning environments (ELE), and dialogue-based tutoring systems (DBTS). ITS such as MATHia and Cognitive Tutor at Carnegie Mellon University utilize domain, pedagogical, and learner models to create a customized learning path that provides step-by-step guidance and adapts to the individual needs of learners. ELEs promote active knowledge construction through open learning environments, correcting errors through automated feedback in an exploratory approach. Among the more popular ELEs are River City by Harvard University, Fractions Lab, and Betty's Brain. DBTS, such as Autotutor from the University of Memphis, Duolingo Chatbots, and IBM Watson Tutor, engages learners in dialogues using natural language processing to assess understanding and provide feedback.

While not explicitly designed as a tutoring system, ChatGPT, developed by OpenAI, is widely used for dialogue-based interactions in educational contexts. It uses natural language processing to engage in conversations and answer questions. Rahman and Watanobe (2023) discuss how students can benefit from ChatGPT by utilizing it for tasks such as solving intricate problems, seeking assistance with essay writing, and gaining insights into specific subjects, thereby enhancing their learning experience.

2. AI Initiatives in the UAE Education Sector

Within the education sector of the UAE, a range of AI initiatives and programs have been implemented in recent years. According to a report by the Oxford Business Group (2023), the government unveiled plans in March 2023 to implement AI chatbot tutors in the education sector. This program aims to enhance student learning by utilizing AI tutors to create educational content. The integration of online education tools is already underway in schools across the country, serving as a complementary resource to traditional classroom instruction.

Additionally, Pedró et al. (2019) cast the spotlight on the national initiative to implement a sophisticated data analytics platform across more than 1,200 schools and 70 higher education institutions, catering to a student population exceeding 1.2 million. This comprehensive system encompasses data related to curricula, teacher development, learning materials, financial aspects, operational metrics, performance reports, as well as feedback from educators, students, and parents. It also includes scores from international assessments such as PISA and TIMSS. Notably, the Ministry of Education in the UAE has established a dedicated data analytics section focused on developing machine learning algorithms to support strategic studies within the country's education system.

3. Challenges and Mitigating Strategies

While the benefits of using AI in education are compelling, assimilation is not without its challenges and opponents. The multifaceted resistance is fueled by concerns ranging from privacy, security, lack of trust, cheating, accessibility, fairness, and potential bias (Harry, 2023) to possible job displacement for educators and loss of human relationships (Al-Tkhayneh et al., 2023).

Successful implementation of AI in education requires careful consideration of these challenges and effective integration into current educational systems (Rizvi, 2023). Rahman and Watanobe (2023) suggest the use of mitigating measures such as the continued development of anti-plagiarism tools, better training data to reduce bias, and adopting appropriate measures to protect personal user data.

Despite these challenges, AI in education can contribute to sustainable development and the achievement of equitable, quality education for all (Pedró et al., 2019). The literature collectively underscores the transformative potential of AI in education while also pointing to the need for continued exploration and evaluation of its impact.

II. The Digital Writing Revolution: Assessing the Impact of ChatGPT and Other AIs

1. Understanding AI in Writing Assistance

When the authors began exploring the idea of using AI to assist in writing, ChatGPT was still only months old and research about it, necessarily, very sparse. Months later, there is an increasing quantity of research into its use as a tutor, though much of it seems undecided as to the efficacy of AI in helping students achieve better results. One possible reason for this is that much of the research has used Automated Writing Evaluation (AWE) tools. The authors have experience of using Class Companion with student groups who have found that it helps at a higher level with organization and relevance, but that it does not give assistance with more basic features such as sentence correctness. This higher level of feedback is undoubtedly of value for giving students a sense of what their audience finds valuable about their writing and where they found gaps in their ability to follow the logic etc, as evidenced by Hyland, (2016). For obvious reasons; however, those students who are having problems with sentence level construction are probably least able to use the feedback the AI that powers the AWE gives.

It is worth remembering that not all students at any level are proficient writers. The National Assessment of Educational Progress (NAEP) (2012) found less than a third of high school seniors were proficient writers. This is for native speakers. The problems faced by non-native speakers having to navigate the use of formal language for academic writing is the reason why most universities provide some form of writing support for students who are not native speakers.

ChatGPT, as many readers will already know, is capable of producing texts which aspiring writers could use as models to assist them in production of their own work. Gao et al (2023) demonstrated that it could produce abstracts for academic papers that journals are likely to accept due to their high quality. Similarly, Kung et al. (2023) demonstrated ChatGPT's ability to assist in the production of high quality research papers. Indeed, Yeadon et al (2023) demonstrated the ability of ChatGPT to produce short form physics essays that would achieve first class grades from an essay writing assignment from an accredited university physics module.

We fully expect that many readers will be able to add their own experiences of ChatGPT's abilities to generate above average answers to work they have assigned to students. It is often precisely the fact that the work is above average that prompts the teacher to suspect that ChatGPT has been used.

Not that copying models is, in itself, a bad method of learning the writer's craft. The Bronte sisters are famous for having lifted most of their inspiration and information from The Leeds Intelligencer and Blackwood's Edinburgh Magazine, to which their father subscribed. After reports of Lord Byron appeared in the magazine, Byronic characters began to appear in their books, Heathcliff being probably the most famous example (HistoryExtra, 2023). We doubt that many students using ChatGPT are aiming to follow the Bronte's, however.

2. AI Tools and Student Writing Development

As far back as 2019, (Parra G. & Calero S.) were using Grammarly as an intervention for student writing and finding that its ability to provide instant feedback on errors was beneficial to students, who are encouraged to note and self-correct their most common mistakes. Dizon and Gayed (2021) found that it had a significant effect on 'the grammatical accuracy, lexical richness, writing fluency, or syntactic complexity of L2 students' writing when compared to unassisted mobile writing.'

Zhang & Hyland (2018), make the important point that feedback has always been an important part of developing writing skills, but that its mere provision is not enough to ensure such development. Students need to engage with the feedback for it to be effective. Carless (2006) highlighted serious criticism that students often have of written teacher feedback. Teachers, especially those dealing with large classes, rarely have time to give detailed feedback on the work they are evaluating and their notes may not communicate the concepts to students struggling with the language.

Even before ChatGPT, Artificial Intelligence has been used to assist students in the writing process. As far back as 2009, Nagata developed a system called Robo-Sensei for teaching Japanese. This included writing practice at the sentence level. Lavolette et al (2015) examined the effect of using Criterion, a programme developed by Educational Testing Service, to see how accurate its reporting of errors was and how students reacted to it. Unsurprisingly, given the speed of change we see every day, the accuracy was not high. This is an important point as incorrect or insufficient identification of errors is not as useful to students. ChatGPT seems to be much more effective in this respect. Algaraady and Mahyoob, writing in Arab World English Journal (AWEJ), (2023) echoed the findings of Su et al. (2023) in finding LLMs to be superior to traditional grammar-checking software in identifying mistakes in second-language writing.

As noted, however, the value of ChatGPT as an aid to improving students' writing is, in the literature available at the time of writing, uncertain. Bašić et al (2023) performed a study with an experimental (using ChatGPT) and control group with both composing an essay on the topic of: The advantages and disadvantages of biometric identification in forensic sciences. The study found that the control group scored slightly better than the experimental group, who were allowed to use ChatGPT freely. The researchers freely admit that the result may have had something to do with the choice of topic being one not found in ChatGPT's database and the students' lack of familiarity with the AI.

Woo et al (2023) explored the use of AI in students' composition of stories and found that it did not universally benefit their writing scores. The ability of the individual writer and their confidence and familiarity with the use of AI all had major effects on what they produced.

Meanwhile, Wang et al (2020) explored the use of the eRevise automated writing evaluation system (AWE) and echoed the findings of Zhang & Hyland in that student use of the feedback provided led to a wide range of responses, some of which were actually worse than unguided composition.

Our study differs in that it refers specifically to a genre of writing undertaken by university students, the general essay, and defines exactly the ways in which the AI should be used. This specific design aims at improving the essay composition and mitigating the task related anxiety that would block the cognitive abilities of the students and hinder their academic success.

III. Exam Stress from Psychological Strains to Neurobiological Insights

Nowadays, stress has become an issue that negatively affects health. Regardless of their activities, people often find themselves experiencing stress due to the demands of their professional lives. This is particularly true when individuals prioritize their relationships with others while juggling responsibilities related to work and studies. Stress is defined as a perceived imbalance between the demands for survival and individuals' ability to adapt to these demands (Lazarus and Folkman, 1984). It manifests as both distress (such as anxiety and depression) and physical ailments (including headaches, neck pain, asthma, ulcers). There are diverse reasons that might provoke stress such as relationships issues, financial constraints or work related burdens.

Turning our attention towards students reveals evidence that they encounter identical situations challenging their psychological and academic stability, specifically in testing time. Exam anxiety, which refers to the fear or pressure associated with evaluations, is a common struggle faced by students worldwide. Recent studies and theories have attempted to explain the stress experienced by young people, who are likely undergoing significant physiological and psychological changes as they transition into adulthood. (Matud and Coll, 2020).

Arousal theory proposes that anxiety arises from physiological arousal during exams. Increased heart rate, sweaty palms and other physical responses would contribute to feelings of anxiety experienced by individuals, in exam environments (Dienstbier, 1989). According to trait anxiety theory, exam stress is closely related to an individual's inherent personality traits. Those with high trait anxiety may be more prone to experiencing stress in situations, including evaluations (Spielberger, 1972). Several factors contribute to the association between high trait anxiety and exam stress, such as: cognitive appraisal, physiological reactivity, attentional focus and poor coping strategies. Exam stress is connected to thought patterns and concerns about performance outcomes. Individuals may have self-defeating thoughts, such as the fear of failure or fixating on consequences, which contribute to increased levels of anxiety (Beck, 1976) that hinder the access to the stored information. Neurobiological research has advanced our understanding of exam stress by identifying brain regions associated with fear and stress responses. Research using functional magnetic resonance imaging (fMRI) has indicated that the amygdala and prefrontal cortex play a role, in processes related to anxiety (Bishop, 2007). According to Arden (2010), when negative self-confidence and/or self-esteem thoughts start to flow in the mind of the student, certain parts of the brain associated with emotions and stress can become active. The amygdala, a structure involved in how the brain responds to stressful situations, will be activated and will propagate feelings of threat leading to the release of stress hormones, like cortisol. High levels of cortisol for extended periods can impair how well the hippocampus, a region of the brain responsible for memory and retrieving information, functions making it harder for students to recall information efficiently. Moreover, cognitive processes associated with self-defeating thoughts, like thinking or excessive worrying, may involve another part of our brain called the cortex. This region is responsible for high-level functions such as decision making and controlling impulsive behavior. Persistent negative thought patterns could cause changes in cortex activity that can affect an individual's ability to regulate emotions effectively and stay focused, on tasks.

IV. Insights Into the Interplay of Exam Anxiety and Artificial Intelligence Advancements

According to Akunna and Coll (2022), this persistent exam related anxiety has led students to poor exam performance, depression and even suicide. According to The American Academy of Pediatrics, "AAP-AACAP-CHA Declaration of a National Emergency in Child and Adolescent Mental Health," (2021), suicide rates reached a very alarming level. Since 2018 in the US, it has become the second highest cause of death among teenagers aged 10 to 24 years old. Anxiety and depression rates kept escalating, increasing by almost 26 percent from 2016 to 2019 according to Lebrun-Harris and Coll (2022). According to a survey conducted in 2015 by the National College Health Assessment, an organization affiliated with the American College Health Association, 75% of college students have admitted to experiencing stress. Shockingly, out of those surveyed, 20% revealed that they have had thoughts related to suicide because of the stress they have been facing. The same research found that a substantial 87% of college students cited education as their major source of stress. College students face a range of stressors, such as managing a new workload, meeting rigorous study demands, balancing time effectively, navigating classroom competition, financial concerns, meeting family and professors' expectations and adapting to a new environment. The academic success and overall happiness of people are closely connected and, according to Pascoe and Coll (2020), academic stress is linked to motivation decrease, academic failure and elevated dropout percentages. According to Barbayannis and Coll (2022), there is a positive significant correlation between students suffering from high academic stress and unstable psychological health. While schools cannot solve all health-related problems, they can make an impact on students' wellbeing and academic achievements by collaborating with the community and utilizing different available resources.

Different government bodies, such as the North Carolina Department of Public Instruction, created a task force in 2017, known as "North Carolina's School Health Advisory Council" that carefully scrutinized the issues that students are facing and worked towards developing some strategies to prevent that chaos from spreading. Based on the work of health and academic experts, North Caroline implemented a law that required the State Board of Education to install in each school a specific mental health training program for teachers, counselors and administrators, shedding light on supporting systems and procedures.

In 2015, the World Health Organization and UNESCO initiated a joint project to establish global standards for Health Promoting Schools (HPS). This initiative emphasizes several key areas: integrating a life-course perspective to promote awareness from early childhood, advancing equity, adopting a culture-based approach, collaborating across various sectors to enhance wellbeing and academic success, and harmonizing the vision of the school community.

Unfortunately, according to the United Nations report issued in 2021, this initiative that included 90 countries all over the world was not implemented by most of the nations, thus thwarting the movement.

Luckmizankari (2017), found that undergraduate students at Eastern University tend to experience higher levels of stress during examinations. The researchers discovered that personal mindset and psychological wellbeing play the most important role in contributing to this exam related stress.

According to Osman and Afifi (2010), the support allocated to the mental health sector in the United Arab Emirates (UAE) is relatively limited considering the high prevalence of mental health disorders and the prevalence of resources and established mental health legislation. Moreover, mental health issues receive insufficient attention in research in UAE and some other Arabic countries. For example, between 1989 and 2008 only a small number (192) of studies were published addressing health in Gulf Cooperation Council countries with the UAE being the active contributor.

In the era of technology and Artificial Intelligence (AI), which is characterized by machines capable of perception, recognition, learning, reaction, and problem-solving, various sectors have adopted AI. These include information technology, healthcare, retail and e-commerce, banking and financial services, logistics and transportation, real estate, entertainment and gaming, manufacturing, the automotive industry, and media. Recently, the education sector has also begun integrating AI technologies.

Gona Sirwan and colleagues (2018) highlight several advantages of implementing AI in the education sector. These benefits include collecting data to develop predictive models for schools, creating learning processes tailored to students' emotional responses, developing personalized curricula and course selections, offering immediate feedback to teachers on the effectiveness of their teaching strategies, identifying and eliminating biases in instructional materials, and coaching students based on their performance. This approach ensures easier access to information and skills training for students. Microlearning would provide students with an upgraded gateway to knowledge assimilation and skills building respecting their own pace and fostering autonomous learning.

V. Methodology

1. Hypothesis

Using ChatGPT as an AI tutor would improve the writing skills of the student and would assist in decreasing achievement related stress.

2. Participants

The study participants were chosen using the convenience-sampling method because it was practical and accessible, within the research context. Convenient sampling involves selecting individuals who are readily available and willing to participate rather than using random or more complex sampling techniques. The participants were students aged 18 to 23 years old, from Amity University Dubai and Fatima College of Health Sciences. They included 69 undergraduate students (39 from psychology and 30 from English Language). Before participating in the study, all individuals received information about the purpose of the study, its procedures and any potential risks involved. Participants provided consent indicating his or her understanding of his or her participation and the confidentiality of their responses. We collected information such as age, gender and educational background to gain a comprehensive understanding of our participants' profiles. This information was used to identify any potential patterns within the data.

It is crucial to acknowledge that convenience sampling has its limitations. The non-random nature of this method can introduce selection bias potentially limiting the generalizability of our findings. Results will be interpreted with caution, taking into account these constraints and considering the context in which this study is conducted.

Figure 1. Participants' Gender Distribution

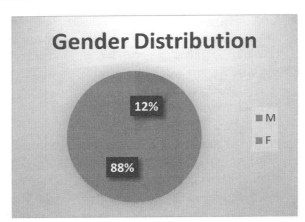

Figure 2. Participants' Age Distribution

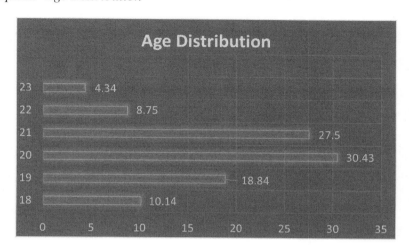

The sample of our research was selected per convenience and therefore, an equal distribution of gender could not be established. Our sample is represented by 88% of female students and 12% male students.

The age of the students participating to the research, vary from 18 to 23 years old and is distributed as follows: Twenty-year-olds constituted the majority with 30.43%, followed by 21-year-olds with 27.5%., 19-year-olds with 18.84%, 18-year-olds with 10.14%, 22-year-olds with 8.75%, and 23-year-olds with 4.34%..

3. Experiment Procedure

This research adopts an Experimental Research Design to explore the impact of utilizing AI (specifically ChatGPT) as a writing tutor. The study aims to investigate cause-and-effect relationships by altering one or more independent variables, in this case, the use of AI for writing assistance, and observing the subsequent effects on dependent variables, such as the quality of writing. Randomized controlled trials (RCTs) are a common experimental design. The students were seated in the classroom, the experiment was clearly explained and informed consent forms were collected. The experiment duration was of 2 hours, consisting of the following steps:

a. Pre-experiment survey:

A pre-experiment survey was distributed among the students measuring AI exposure among our participants.

b. The student answered the anxiety test "State-Trait Anxiety Inventory for Adult" (Charles D. Spielberger) for the first time

c. **Step 1**: A topic was suggested to the students and they were given 30 minutes to write an essay. The students had access to the internet to collect information if needed but copy pasting was prohibited and monitored through Turnitin. Any plagiarized document was excluded from the data collected.

After finishing their writing, the students submitted their essay on Turnitin and used the following prompt to have their writing evaluated by ChatGPT. IELTS standards.

Please evaluate the following according to the public rubric for IELTS type 2 writing tasks. Give a score and comments on each aspect and give an overall score.

d. **Step 2**: Students used ChatGPT to provide outlines for the given topic as per the prompts given previously.

Please generate an outline for an IELTS type 2 writing task on the following topic
The participants rewrote their essays according to the provided guidelines within a timeline of 30 minutes. They submitted the new essay in ChatGPT and again asked for IELTS evaluation.

e. **Step 3**: Participants asked ChatGPT to provide specific suggestions as per the given prompt to improve the clarity of their essay. They were given 30 minutes to complete their writings and submit it again for IELTS evaluation.
f. The students answered the anxiety test "State-Trait Anxiety Inventory for Adult" (Charles D. Spielberger) for the second time.
g. Post-experiment survey:

A post-experiment survey was distributed among the students measuring their feedback about the ability of ChatGPT to act as a tutor in improving English writing and reduce exam anxiety.

4. Measures

Participants were involved in a data collection process that included quantitative analysis and utilized two Likert scale surveys constructed for the purpose of the study. One of the surveys aimed at measuring the familiarity of students with AI usage and the second one the students' feedback about the role played by ChatGPT as an AI tutor.

In order to measure the assignment anxiety before and after resorting to the help of ChatGPT in writing the essay, we used "The State Trait Anxiety Inventory" (STAI).

a. The State Trait Anxiety Inventory

The State Trait Anxiety Inventory (STAI) created by Spielberger, Gorsuch, Lushene, Vagg and Jacobs in 1983 is widely used to measure both trait and state anxiety. It is primarily utilized in settings to diagnose anxiety disorders and distinguish them from syndromes. Moreover, researchers often employ the STAI, the Anxiety Form Y version to evaluate persons' distress in studies (Greene et al., 2017; Ugalde et al., 2014).

Anxiety Form Y consists of 20 items, for assessing both trait and state anxiety. State anxiety items capture feelings of tension and worry. On the other hand, trait anxiety items explore concerns and contentment while differentiating between stable and unsettled personality traits. Respondents rate each item on a scale of four points ranging from "Never" to "Always" with higher scores indicating higher levels of anxiety. The STAI is designed for individuals who have a sixth-grade reading level.

The STAI demonstrates reliability with consistency coefficients ranging from .86 to .95 and test-retest reliability coefficients ranging from.65 to.75, over a two-month period (Spielberger et al., 1983). In this study the test-retest coefficients varied from.69, to.89. The scales construct and concurrent validity have been strongly supported by evidence (Spielberger, 1989).

Moreover, the STAI has shown sensitivity in predicting persons' distress over time. Various studies have demonstrated its ability to detect changes in support systems, health status and individual characteristics (Elliott, Shewchuk, & Richards 2001; Shewchuk, Richards & Elliott 1998). This instrument not only serves as a tool but also provides valuable insights into the intricate dynamics of anxiety. It is a resource in both clinical and research settings.

b. ChatGPT

ChatGPT is a language model developed by OpenAI. It has advanced from GPT-2 to GPT-3, and then to its current form. The foundational GPT models were designed to mimic human-like text processing, but ChatGPT represents a leap forward in coherent text generation.

This development is largely a result of the rapid progress in artificial intelligence and natural language processing. Each version of the GPT model has demonstrated increasingly sophisticated language abilities. This testifies to both innovations in technology and the expanding quantity of text data these models learn from.

In educational contexts, ChatGPT is still in the process of carving out what seems to be a very versatile role. Its capacity to craft text, respond to queries, and simulate interactive dialogues makes it a powerful educational tool. It is employed for producing engaging learning materials, supporting language acquisition, and even acting as a tutor, providing explanations and feedback to students. ChatGPT can be used for personalized education as well, adapting to the unique learning styles and requirements of individual students.

The academic world is actively researching ChatGPT's role in education, exploring areas such as its potential to enrich learning experiences, its ethical application, and its integration into current educational paradigms. Despite its advantages, discussions continue about the challenges it presents, including maintaining content accuracy, addressing inherent biases, and its impact on conventional educational methodologies.

VI. Results

In our present research, we aim to find the impact of the use of ChatGPT (3.5) as an AI tutor on students' essays writing and exam anxiety management.

The experiment started with an AI exposure survey created to explore the familiarity of our students with artificial intelligence usage and its inclusion in education.

1. Pretest results of AI exposure:

The descriptive graphs show the answers of our students regarding their awareness and frequency of usage of AI.

Question 1

Figure 3. Percentage of AI powered writing tools

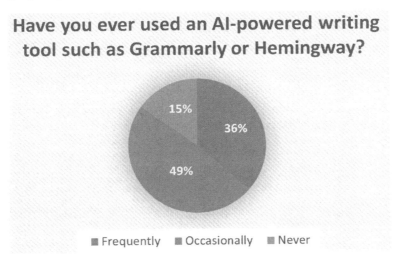

As shown in the above figure, almost half of our sample have been using AI-powered writing tools occasionally compared to 36% that do that frequently and only 15% that never have.

Question 2:

Figure 4. Perception about AI-powered writing tools

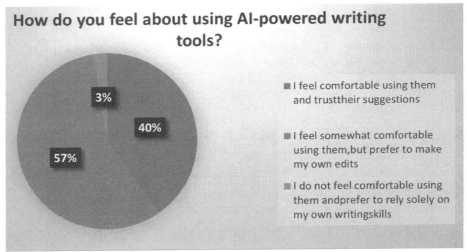

In the second question, the participants were questioned about their perception of using AI-powered writing tools. As displayed by figure 4, 40% of the participants feel comfortable using AI and accepting suggestions from it. Only 3% do not feel at ease resorting to AI while writing their essays and prefer using their own skills. The majority of our sample (57%) have a reserved position toward AI. They are not against using these tools, but they prefer making their own edits and not blindly follow the bot's suggestions.

Question 3:

Figure 5. Frequency of Chatbot or virtual assistant

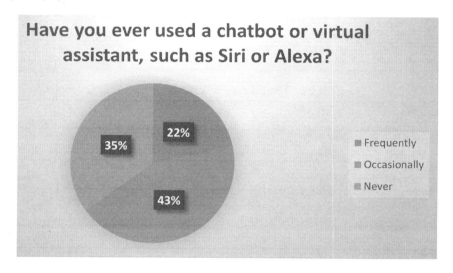

Our participants were questioned about the frequency of chatbot or virtual assistant usage and as shown in figure 5, the majority of our sample (43%) are using them occasionally while 22% do that frequently and 35% never do, an important percentage taking into consideration the pace at which AI is getting into our reality.

Question 4:

Figure 6. Frequency of usage of customer service chatbot or virtual assistant

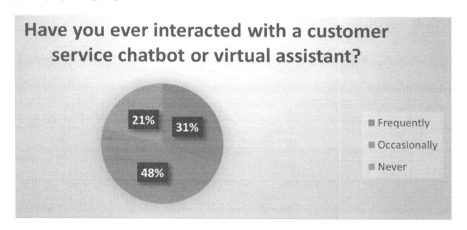

As per the findings shown in figure 6, the majority of the students interact occasionally with customer service chatbots or virtual assistants, 31% do that occasionally and 21% never did.

Question 5:

Figure 7. Efficiency perception of AI-powered writing tools by students

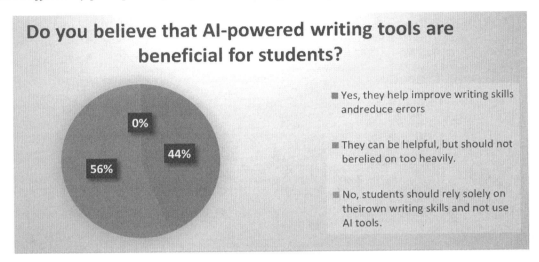

Through this question, the research team aimed at exploring the perception of students about the efficiency of AI-powered writing tools. The results showcased in figure 7 demonstrate that 44% believed that these writing tools are very helpful and could assist students to improve their writing skills and reduce errors. No students thought that these tools should never be used or that no assistance is needed. The majority of our sample (56%) expressed their willingness to resort to AI support but were still skeptical and cautious.

Question 6:

Figure 8. Frequency of usage of AI-powered tutor

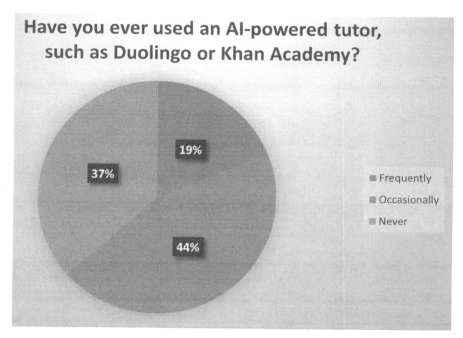

Students were questioned about their frequency of usage of micro learning AI-powered tools and the results reveal that the majority of our sample (44%) are occasionally doing it, only 19% are frequently using AI-powered tutors and 37% never have.

Question 7:

Figure 9. Comparison between AI-powered tutors and Human tutors

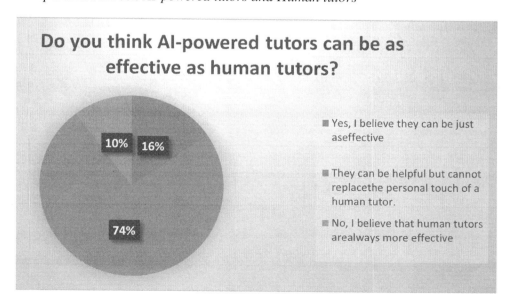

As displayed in the above figure (Figure 9), 16% of the students think that AI-powered tutors can be as effective as human tutors while 10% believe that human tutors will always be better than any AI-powered program. The majority of our sample (74%) consider that AI-powered tutors could be very helpful; however, there will be always a lack of a human touch.

Question 8:

Figure 10. Frequency of exposure to AI technology in academic settings

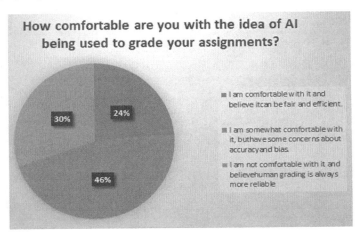

Participants were questioned about the frequency of exposure to AI technology in their classrooms and curricula. The majority of our students (57%) mentioned that this never happened to them during their academic journey, 34% stated that it happened occasionally and only 9% explained that they have been frequently exposed to AI technology.

Question 9:

Figure 11. Trust in AI powered tools for assignments grading

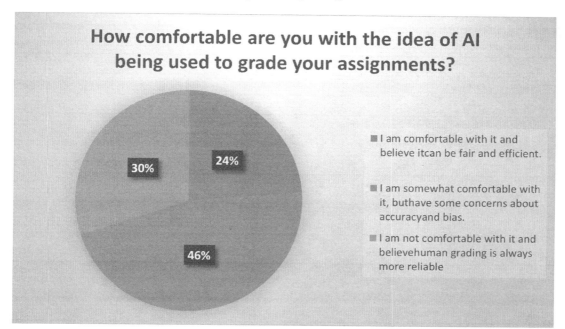

Trust in AI-powered tools as grading assistants for professors was differently represented among our sample. Only 24% of the students mentioned that they feel comfortable about AI programs grading their assignments and that they believe that it would be fair and efficient, while 30% choose the opposite direction insisting on the fact that AI programs will never be as reliable as humans regarding assignment grading. The majority of our sample (46%) commented that they might be comfortable with the idea of an AI program grading their assignment, but they were also skeptical about the accuracy of procedures.

Question 10:

Figure 12. Perception of the significance of AI in the future of education

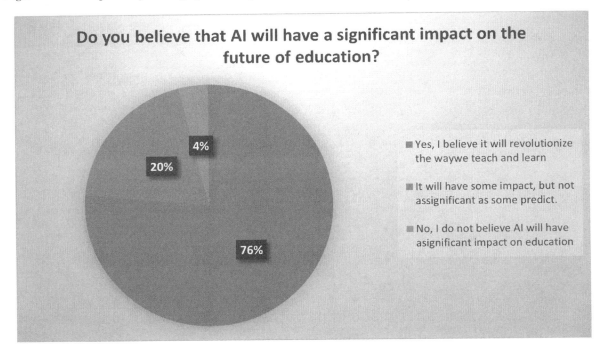

As shown in the above figure (Figure 11), 76% of our participants believe that introducing AI in education is not only inevitable but also would revolutionize the teaching strategies and pedagogies. Only 20% are doubtful about the significance it might have in the field of education and only 4% do not believe it would have any significant impact.

2. Essay Writing:

The essay writing part of the research was divided in three steps as explained previously in the methodology section.

-   **Phase One** consisted of spontaneous writing without the assistance of ChatGPT. An IELTS score was calculated assessing the quality of the students' writing.
-   **Phase Two** consisted of introducing ChatGPT as a tutor. The students requested specific outlines for the suggested topic and were encouraged to rewrite their essays according to the outlines given by the AI.
-   **Phase Three** consisted of copying the last essay, pasting it into ChatGPT and requesting the AI to provide the participant with specific suggestions improving clarity, style and word choices.

In order to measure the impact of ChatGPT on essay production, the difference between the IELTS scores from one phase to another phase was calculated and is displayed in the below figures.

After calculating the difference of scores between Phase One and Phase Two, the results highlight the positive impact of ChatGPT as a writing assistant. Indeed, as per the findings, 70.5% of the participants witnessed a significant improvement in IELTS scores (from 0.25 to 2.5). As per IELTS experts[1], it takes a person an average of three months English course preparation to be able to improve by half a band. Eighteen percent of our sample didn't improve their writing skills from Phase one to Phase two and 11.5% noticed a slight decrease in their scores (0.25 to 0.5) as shown by Figure 13.

Figure 13. The IELTS scores difference between Phase One and Phase Two

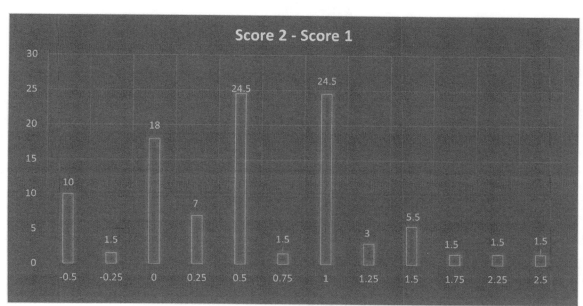

Moving to the third phase, data was collected from students and the difference between writing production in Phase 2 and Phase 3 was calculated and provided the following results. 61% of our participants increased their band scores by a minimum of 0.25 and maximum of 2, 32% didn't notice any band difference and 7% noticed a decrease in their IELTS scores (0.25 to 0.5) as shown in Figure 13.

Figure 14. The IELTS scores difference between Phase Three and Phase Two

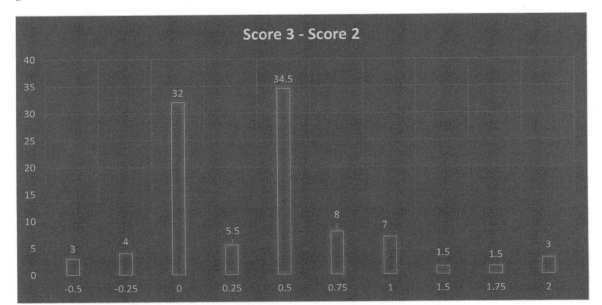

The below Figure 14 displays the difference of IELTS score between the last essays evaluation (after Phase Three) and the first spontaneous writing (without the assistance of ChatGPT).

The findings revealed that 84.5% of our sample improved their essay production with the assistance of ChatGPT by a minimum of 0.25 and a maximum of 4.25.

A better improvement is noticed among students that have initially low IELTS scores, below band 6 displayed as follow: one student had a score of 3.5, a second student had a score of 4, a third student had a score of 4.5, a fifth one had a score of 5 and one last student had a score of 5.5.

Only three students, that had an initial IELTS score superior to band 6 (7 and 8), showed a slight decrease in their essays production. Eight students did not notice any score improvement during the whole experiment. These participants already had a high IELTS score (Band 7 and 8).

Figure 15. The IELTS scores difference between Phase Three and Phase One

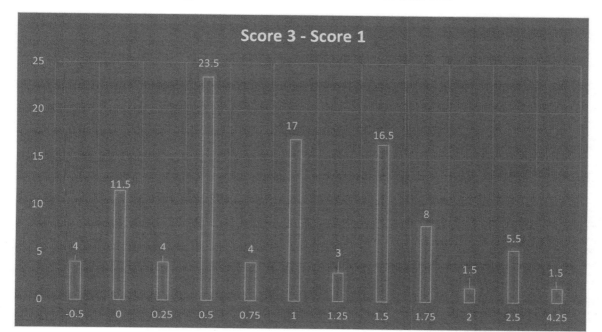

3. Anxiety Management:

The second objective of this research is to measure the impact of AI tutoring, through ChatGPT assistance during essay writing, on the anxiety level displayed by students during assignments.

The anxiety is measured during two times as clarified in the methodology section:

- Before Phase One (spontaneous essay writing)
- After Phase Three (After AI support)

A score difference is calculated at the end of the experiment between anxiety pretest and posttest. If the score is positive, it means that the student anxiety decreased while using ChatGPT for his assignment. In the opposite situation, if the difference is negative, it means that the anxiety level of the student increased during the experiment and that the assistance of the AI tutor could not help the participant manage his exam anxiety.

The below figure (Figure 15) displays the results of the difference between posttest and pretest for each student.

Figure 16. Anxiety state scores differences posttest-pretest

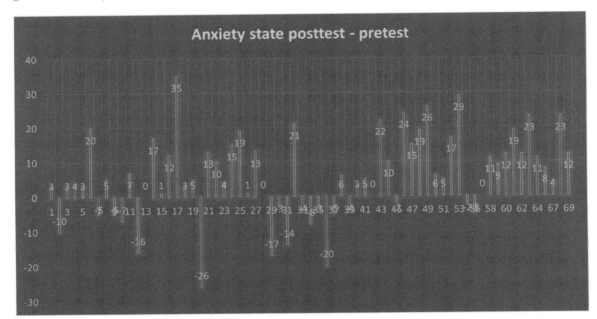

Among our participants, 65.2% had a positive difference posttest-pretest, which means that ChatGPT helped the majority of the students to feel less anxious about their assignment production as shown on figure 16. Only a small percentage of our sample (5.8%), 4 students out of 69 didn't witness any change in their anxiety level after the introduction of AI tutor. A non-negligible number of students (20) representing 29% of our sample, are showing negative difference posttest-pretest indicating that these participants anxiety level was heightened by the introduction of the AI tutor. In order to clarify this phenomenon, students were encouraged to provide feedback. The answers given revolve about the fatigability due to the length of the experiment, the lack of familiarity with ChatGPT, the lack of confidence in AI, the feeling that this kind of assistance might be unethical, the inhibition of creative expression and the need to resort to more human assistance characterized by empathy, better understanding of their weaknesses and strengths.

Figure 17. Student percentage of Anxiety scores difference posttest-pretest

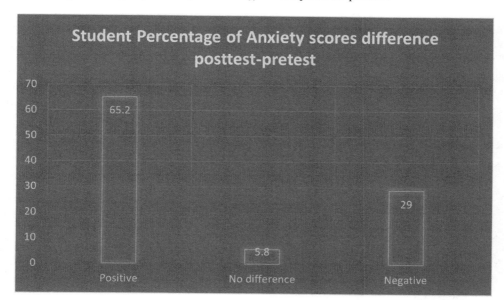

In order to assess the significance of the differences between anxiety score posttest versus anxiety score pretest, we displayed in figure 17, the anxiety fluctuation levels among our sample. The decrease or increase in anxiety is revealed as more significant if itsi the percentile the old and the new score belong to. The percentile should change from low average to average, from average to high or the opposite.

Figure 17 bars highlighted that 43.5% of our sample conserved scores at the average level despite the different fluctuations. Also 3% remain at the high percentile did not mark any alterations. However, 28% of our sample witnessed their anxiety level moving from a low percentile to average and therefore marking a lack of anxiety management during the experiment. On the other hand, 25% of our sample moved from high to average percentile testifying that using AI as a tutor could assist them in building independent learning and mitigate their exam anxiety by giving them guidelines and the needed strategies to succeed in their academic journey.

Figure 18. Anxiety level fluctuation pretest versus posttest

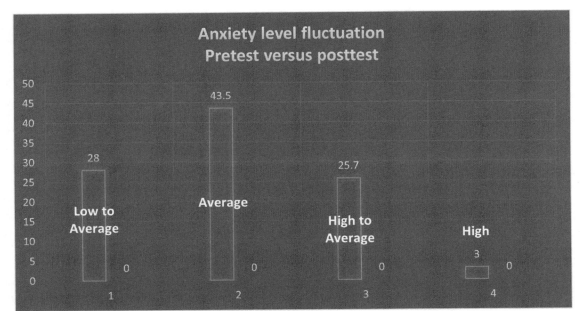

4. Posttest AI tutor Feedback:

The last part of our experiment was about feedback collection about the experiment and ChatGPT usage from our sample.

Question 1:

Figure 19. Perception of writing skills improvement after ChatGPT usage

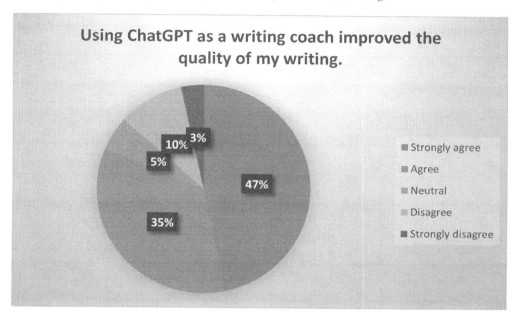

The student were questioned to which extend they agree that ChatGPT helped them improving their writing skills and the majority of the sample (strongly agree and agree) representing 82% affirmed that statement. Only 5% were neutral and 13% disagreed.

Question 2:

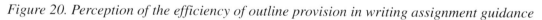

Figure 20. Perception of the efficiency of outline provision in writing assignment guidance

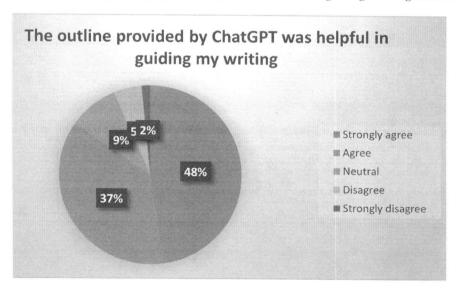

The majority of the participants (85%) believe that resorting to ChatGPT for outlines provision during their assignments was of great assistance. Only 9% were neutral and 7% disagreed.

Question 3:

Figure 21. Perception of the efficiency of ChatGPT in improving clarity and style of writings

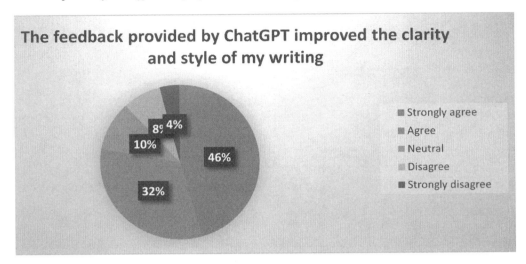

The majority of students (78%) state that ChatGPT, as an AI tutor, improved the clarity and style of their writings. Only 10% were neutral and 12% didn't think that ChatGPT was of any assistance concerning this matter.

Question 4:

Figure 22. The perception of ChatGPT efficiency in increasing writing abilities confidence

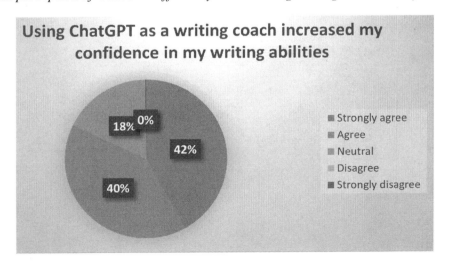

The majority of our sample (82%) mentioned that resorting to ChatGPT as a writing coach increased their confidence in their own writing abilities and only 18% were neutral concerning this matter.

Question 5:

Figure 23. Prospective students' enthusiasm about Employing ChatGPT as a Writing Coach

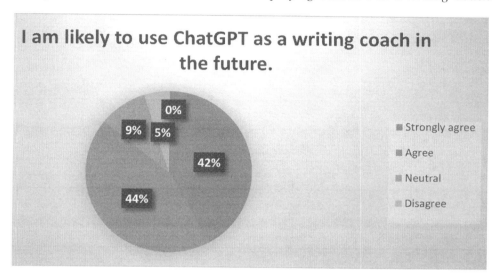

The majority of our sample (86%) affirmed that they will be using ChatGPT as a writing coach in the future. Only 9% were neutral and 5% disagreed.

Question 6:

Figure 24. Enhancing English Language Learning with ChatGPT as an AI coach

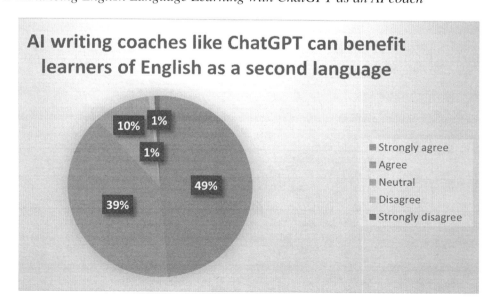

The majority of the participants (88%) mentioned that using ChatGPT as an AI tutor would enhance English language learning. Only 2% disagreed and 10% were neutral.

Question 7:

Figure 25. Challenges with ChatGPT as a Writing Coach

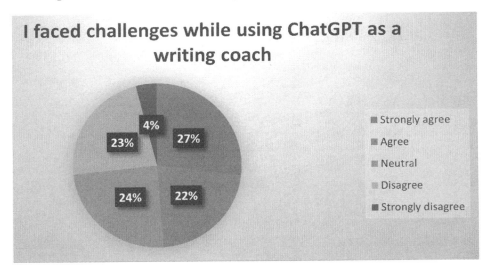

Even though the majority of the students were satisfied with ChatGPT as an AI tutor, many of them (49%) pointed out that they faced some challenges while using the AI-powered tool. Moreover, 24% were neutral and 27% disagreed and were very comfortable while using the Chatbot.

Question 8:

Figure 26. Students' recommendation of ChatGPT usage as a writing coach

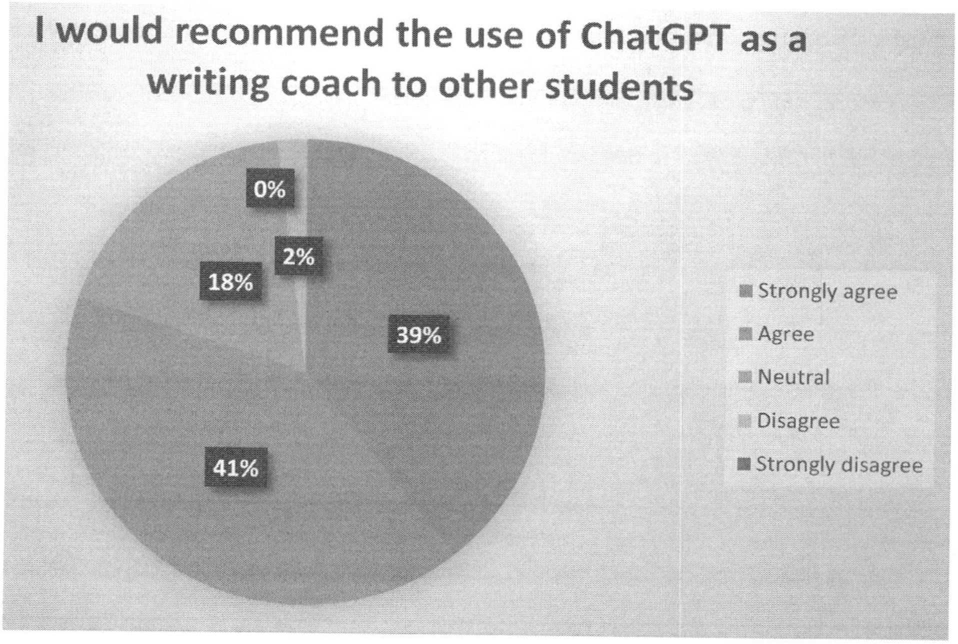

Among our participants, 80% recommended using ChatGPT as a writing tutor in order to assist in improving their essays quality and style. Only 2% didn't like the experiment and didn't express any will to recommend the Chatbot while 18% remained neutral.

Question 9:

Figure 27. Overall positive experiences utilizing ChatGPT as a writing coach

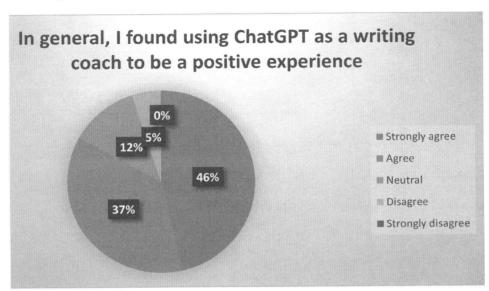

Students were also questioned about their overall experience while using ChatGPT as a writing tutor. The majority of our sample (83%), affirmed that it was a positive experience and that they would be repeating it. Only 5% didn't appreciate the assistance of ChatGPT as an AI tutor while 12% remained neutral.

Question 10:

Figure 28. Improving ChatGPT as a Writing Mentor

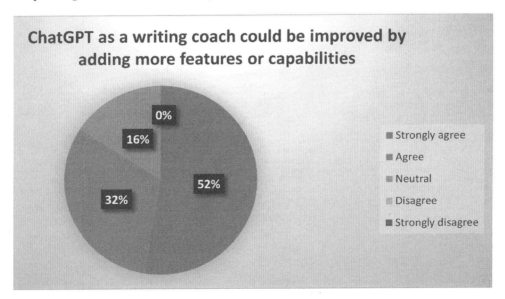

Many students were skeptical about adopting AI-powered program in assignment grading and essays guidance. Therefore, 84% of our sample stated that ChatGPT had to be improved in order to become an efficient writing tutor. The rest of the participants (16%) remained neutral and did not really have an opinion in this matter.

VI. Discussion

Use of ChatGPT as a tool by university students is something that, unsurprisingly, is becoming a popular topic to research. In looking at its use to improve their writing, we are not being particularly original – it is an obvious angle, especially considering that two of us are English/Communications lecturers. The interest in AI is a testament to the potential that teachers see in it, but its efficacy in bringing about tangible learning outcomes is a matter of debate.

Our study engaged 39 Psychology students from Amity University, Dubai, and 30 Emirati students studying English Language from Fatima College of Health Sciences in a structured writing exercise using ChatGPT, aiming to measure the practical impacts of AI-assisted writing on students of varied linguistic backgrounds. The process involved students writing essays, receiving AI-driven feedback, and revising their work accordingly. This methodology aligns with the growing body of research that emphasizes the importance of immediate, actionable feedback in the learning process (Zhang & Hyland, 2018; Carless, 2006).

A notable limitation of our study, as with many of its kind, lies in the essay topic. Feedback from participants suggested that a more personally relevant topic could have led to greater engagement and, potentially, more meaningful improvements in writing quality. (One student literally said that the problem was that we had asked a technology-based question that no one in their group would have any real interest in answering.) This highlights the nuanced relationship between student interest and writing performance, an aspect often overlooked in structured writing exercises. Furthermore, the exercise's time-constrained nature probably did induce fatigue, affecting the students' writing and revision capabilities.

Our student sample is a diverse one, including both native and non-native English speakers. This, in itself, adds another dimension of complexity. Studies have shown that non-native speakers face greater challenges in academic writing. These need tailored support (National Assessment of Educational Progress, 2012). This diversity, while it enriches the study, also complicates the interpretation of results, as improvements in writing could vary significantly based on initial proficiency levels.

Our use of ChatGPT reflects a shift from traditional Automated Writing Evaluation (AWE) tools. These often focus on higher-level writing aspects like organization and coherence (Gao et al, 2023; Kung, 2023). ChatGPT has shown promise in helping students with these more nuanced aspects of writing, such as style and clarity, however, its effectiveness in assisting with fundamental language issues is still not certain. We see this uncertainty echoed in the literature, where studies like those by Bašić et al (2023) and Woo et al (2023) present mixed findings on the efficacy of AI in improving writing skills.

Our study contributes to this ongoing dialogue by specifically focusing on general essay writing in a university setting and delineating clear parameters for AI usage. This specificity, we believe, provides valuable insights for educators and researchers seeking practical applications of ChatGPT in enhancing writing skills. We do not; however, believe that simply providing students with AI-generated feedback is a silver bullet that cures all ills. As Zhang & Hyland (2018) and Carless (2006) say, the effectiveness of feedback hinges on student engagement with it, an aspect that varies widely depending on the individuals and contexts involved.

In conclusion, our study shows the potential of ChatGPT as a tool for writing improvement. It also highlights the unavoidable complexities in its application. Diverse student backgrounds, the relevance of topic, and the individualized nature of writing skill development all play roles in determining how efficient AI-assisted writing exercises are. Against an evolving landscape of AI in education, we believe our findings offer a meaningful contribution to the conversation, pointing towards both the possibilities and the limitations of leveraging AI to enhance academic writing skills.

CONCLUSION

The study indicates that using ChatGPT as an AI tutor significantly improves students' writing skills. The evidence for this comes from increased IELTS scores on the part of most participants. Additionally, a majority of students reported reduced exam anxiety after using ChatGPT. We believe this shows its effectiveness in reducing academic stress.

However, the data reveals mixed perceptions about AI-powered writing tools among students. While a significant portion of the sample was comfortable using these tools and found them helpful, there was also a level of skepticism and preference for personal edits over complete reliance on AI suggestions. This highlights the need for a balanced approach in integrating AI into educational practices.

The study sample had a higher representation of female students and a majority in the 20-21 age range. This demographic distribution might influence the generalizability of the results, as different age groups and genders may have varied responses to AI tools and stress management techniques.

Despite the outcomes being very positive, nearly half of the students pointed out that they had had challenges in using ChatGPT. Some mentioned ethical concerns and a preference for more human, empathetic assistance. This suggests that while AI can be a valuable educational tool, it cannot fully replace the kind of support provided by human tutors.

The majority of students expressed willingness to use ChatGPT in the future. They also recognized the potential of AI in transforming the way they learn. However, there was a consensus on the need for further improvements in AI tutoring systems.

The research also underscores the broader issue of exam-related stress and its impact on mental health. This aligns with global trends of increasing anxiety and depression among students which many teachers will be familiar with and highlights the importance of addressing mental health needs in academic settings.

The study aligns with global initiatives like the Health Promoting Schools (HPS). We believe there is a need for educational policies that incorporate both mental health and AI technologies to enhance learning outcomes and student well-being.

Recommendations for Further Research

Future studies should aim for a more diverse sample in terms of gender, age, cultural background, and academic disciplines. At present we cannot generalize the findings and give insights into how different groups see and benefit from AI tools like ChatGPT.

Research to assess the long-term effects of using AI as a writing tutor on students' academic performance and mental health needs to be conducted. Ours lasted only two hours. Longitudinal studies could provide valuable data on whether the improvements in writing skills and reductions in exam anxiety are sustainable.

Our study did nothing to compare the effectiveness of AI tutoring with traditional human tutoring, though feedback suggested that students would trust something more human. This analysis could help identify areas where AI excels and where human intervention remains irreplaceable.

Looking at the use of AI tools in different educational settings, such as high schools, vocational training, and higher education, could give a broader understanding of its applicability and effectiveness.

Further research should investigate the ethical considerations and psychological impacts of relying on AI for educational purposes. Our students identified this as an issue. Dependency, privacy, and the effect on students' critical thinking and creativity are factors that need looking into.

It would be useful for teachers to know how AI tutoring can be tailored to individual learning styles and needs. That would include examining if AI can adapt to different learning paces, preferences, and challenges.

AI tutoring might help bridge educational gaps and provide support in under-resourced settings. Our study suggests this might be possible but does not answer the question of how to do it. Some students have learning disabilities or lack access to quality human tutors. AI as a means of alleviating this problem could be studied.

There is a well-recognized connection between academic stress and mental health, so research could explore how AI tools could be integrated with mental health support services.

REFERENCES

Ahmad, S. F., Rahmat, M. K., Mubarik, M. S., Alam, M. M., & Hyder, S. I. (2021). Artificial intelligence and its role in education. *Sustainability, 13*(22), 12902. 10.3390/su132212902

Akunna, L., Okesina, F., Ajiboye, S., & Monisola, E. (2022). Perception of undergraduates on study habit strategies for overcoming examination anxiety in Kwara, Nigeria. *Humanitas*, 19(2), 138–147. 10.26555/humanitas.v19i2.43

Al-Tkhayneh, K. M., Alghazo, E. M., & Tahat, D. (2023). The advantages and disadvantages of using artificial intelligence in education. *Journal of Educational and Social Research*, 13(4), 105–105. 10.36941/jesr-2023-0094

Algaraady, J., & Mahyoob, M. (n.d.). *CHATGPT's capabilities in spotting and analyzing writing errors experienced by EFL learners.* AWEJ. 10.24093/awej/call9.1

American Academy of Pediatrics. (2021, October 19). *AAP-AACAP-CHA Declaration of a National Emergency in Child and Adolescent Mental Health.* Retrieved from https://www.aap.org/en/advocacy/child-and-adolescent-healthy-mental-development/aap-aacap-cha-declaration-of-a-national-emergency-in-child-and-adolescent-mental-health/

American Psychological Association. (2020). *Stress in AmericaTM2020: A National Mental Health Crisis.* American Psychological Association.

Arden, J.-B. (2010). *Rewire your brain.* Wiley.

Barbayannis, G., Banddari, M., Zheng, X., Baquerizo, H., Pecor, K. W., & Ming, X. (2022). Academic Stress and Mental Well-Being in College Students: Correlations, Affected Groups, and COVID-19. *Frontiers in Psychology*, 13, 886344. Advance online publication. 10.3389/fpsyg.2022.88634435677139

Bašić, Ž., Banovac, A., Kružić, I., & Jerković, I. (2023, October 28). *CHATGPT-3.5 as writing assistance in students' essays.* Nature News. https://www.nature.com/articles/s41599-023-02269-7

Bishop, S.-J. (2007). Neurocognitive mechanisms of anxiety: An integrative account. *Trends in Cognitive Sciences*, 11(7), 307–316. 10.1016/j.tics.2007.05.00817553730

Carless, D. (2006). Differing perceptions in the feedback process. *Studies in Higher Education*, 31(2), 219–233. 10.1080/03075070600572132

Chinonso, O. E., Theresa, A. M.-E., & Aduke, T. C. (2023). ChatGPT for teaching, learning and research: Prospects and challenges. *Global Academic Journal of Humanities and Social Sciences*, 5(02), 33–40. 10.36348/gajhss.2023.v05i02.001

Dizon, G., & Gayed, J. M. (2023, April 25). Ex*amining the impact of Grammarly on the quality of mobile L2 writing.* Castledown. 10.29140/jaltcall.v17n2.336

Ganga, X. (2021, June 1). Educational Artificial Intelligence (EAI) Connotation, Key Technology and Application Trend -Interpretation and analysis of the two reports entitled "Preparing for the Future of Artificial Intelligence" and "The National Artificial Intelligence Research and Development Strategic Plan." *IEEE Xplore.* 10.1109/ICAA53760.2021.00046

Gao, C. A., Howard, F. M., Markov, N. S., Dyer, E. C., Ramesh, S., Luo, Y., & Pearson, A. T. (2023, April 26). *Comparing scientific abstracts generated by CHATGPT to real abstracts with detectors and blinded human reviewers.* Nature News. https://www.nature.com/articles/s41746-023-00819-6

Gona Sirwan, M., Karzan, W., & Sarkhell, S.-N. (2018). The Effectiveness of Microlearning to Improve Students' Learning Ability. *International Journal of Educational Research Review*, 3(3), 32–38. 10.24331/ijere.415824

Harry, A. (2023). Role of AI in education. *Interdiciplinary Journal and Hummanity*, 2(3), 260–268. 10.58631/injurity.v2i3.52

HistoryExtra. (2023, November 8). *The Brontës: The unfortunate and Unlikely tale of the world's "Greatest literary sisters."* https://www.historyextra.com/period/victorian/bronte-sisters-anne-charlotte-emily-who-were-they-house-famous-write-books/

Kung, T. H., Cheatham, M., Medenilla, A., Sillos, C., Leon, L. D., Elepaño, C., Madriaga, M., Aggabao, R., Diaz-Candido, G., Maningo, J., & Tseng, V. (2023, February 9). Performance of ChatGPT on USMLE: Potential for AI-assisted medical education using large language models. *PLOS Digital Health*, 2(2), e0000198. Advance online publication. 10.1371/journal.pdig.000019836812645

Lavolette, E., Polio, C., & Kahng, J. (2015). The accuracy of computer-assisted feedback and students' responses to it. *Language Learning & Technology*, 19(2), 50–68.

Lebrun-Harris, L.-A., Ghandour, R.-M., Kogan, M.-D., & Warren, M.-D. (2022). Five-Year Trends in US Children's Health and Well-being, 2016-2020. *JAMA Pediatrics*, 176(7), e220056. Advance online publication. 10.1001/jamapediatrics.2022.005635285883

Luan, H., Geczy, P., Lai, H., Gobert, J., Yang, S. J. H., Ogata, H., Baltes, J., Guerra, R., Li, P., & Tsai, C.-C. (2020). Challenges and future directions of big data and artificial intelligence in education. *Frontiers in Psychology, 11*. 10.3389/fpsyg.2020.580820

Luckmizankari, P. (2017). Factors Affecting On Examination Stress among Undergraduates: An Investigation from Eastern University. *Iconic Research and Engineering Journals*, 1(4), 9–15.

Matud, M. P., Díaz, A., Bethencourt, J. M., & Ibáñez, I. (2020). Stress and psychological distress in emerging adulthood: A gender analysis. *Journal of Clinical Medicine*, 9(9), 2859. 10.3390/jcm909285932899622

Nagata, N. (2013). Robo-sensei's NLP-based error detection and feedback generation. *CALICO Journal*, 26(3), 562–579. 10.1558/cj.v26i3.562-579

Online education - worldwide: Statista market forecast. (n.d.). *Statista*. https://www.statista.com/outlook/dmo/eservices/online-education/worldwide#analyst-opinion

Osman, O.-T., & Afifi, M. (2010). Troubled minds in the Gulf: Mental health research in the United Arab Emirates (1989–2008). *Asia-Pacific Journal of Public Health*, 22(3_suppl), 48S–53S. 10.1177/1010539510373025205666533

Oxford Business Group. (2023). *How generative AI could transform education in the GCC.* Oxford Business Group. https://oxfordbusinessgroup.com/articles-interviews/how-generative-ai-could-transform-education-in-the-gcc/

Paek, S., & Kim, N. (2021). Analysis of worldwide research trends on the impact of artificial intelligence in education. *Sustainability (Basel)*, 13(14), 7941. 10.3390/su13147941

Parra, G. L., & Calero, S. X. (2019, March 31). Automated writing evaluation tools in the improvement of the writing skill. *International Journal of Instruction*. https://eric.ed.gov/?id=EJ121102710.4324/9781315717203

Rahman, M., & Watanobe, Y. (2023). ChatGPT for education and research: Opportunities, threats, and strategies. *Applied Sciences (Basel, Switzerland)*, 13(9), 5783. 10.3390/app13095783

Rizvi, M. (2023). Exploring the landscape of artificial intelligence in education: Challenges and opportunities. *2023 5th International Congress on Human-Computer Interaction, Optimization and Robotic Applications (HORA)*, 1-3. 10.1109/HORA58378.2023.10156773

Spielberger, C.-D. (1972). *Anxiety: current trends in theory and research*. Academic Press.

Srivastava, S. (2023, November 27). *Top AI trends in 2023: Unveiling use cases across industries*. Appinventiv. https://appinventiv.com/blog/ai-trends/

Su, Y., Lin, Y., & Lai, C. (2023). Collaborating with CHATGPT in argumentative writing classrooms. *Assessing Writing*, 57, 100752. 10.1016/j.asw.2023.100752

Wang, E. L., Matsumura, L. C., Correnti, R., Litman, D., Zhang, H., Howe, E., Magooda, A., & Quintana, R. (2020). Erevis(ING): Students' revision of text evidence use in an automated writing evaluation system.*Assessing Writing*, 44, 100449. 10.1016/j.asw.2020.100449

Woo, D. J., Susanto, H., Yeung, C. H., Guo, K., & Fung, A. K. Y. (2023, March 10). *Exploring AI-generated text in student writing: How does AI help?* arXiv.org. https://arxiv.org/abs/2304.02478

Yeadon, W., Inyang, O.-O., Mizouri, A., Peach, A., & Testrow, C. P. (2023). The death of the short-form physics essay in the Coming Ai Revolution. *Physics Education*, 58(3), 035027. 10.1088/1361-6552/acc5cf

Yousuf, M., & Wahid, A. (2021, November 1). The role of artificial intelligence in education: Current trends and future prospects. *IEEE Xplore*. 10.1109/ICISCT52966.2021.9670009

Zhang, Z. (n.d.). *Student engagement with teacher and automated feedback on L2 ...* Assessing Writing. https://www.semanticscholar.org/paper/Student-engagement-with-teacher-and-automated-on-L2-Zhang-Hyland/da406dec79720a12d3b06a14bb71c4fab68acf83

ENDNOTE

[1]   IELTS. (2023, 1st of February). How long will it take to get the IELTS band score I need? Retrieved from https://ielts.org/news-and-insights/how-long-will-it-take-to-get-the-ielts-band-score-i-need#:~:text=If%20you're%20taking%20an,up%20to%20half%20a%20band

Chapter 14
An Empirical Analysis of CSR's Initiative on Employee Behaviour

Brahmmanand Sharma
https://orcid.org/0000-0001-6971-013X
School of Business, Galgotias University, Greater Noida, India

Navita Nathani
Prestige Institute of Management and Research, Gwalior, India

Kavita Sharma
Maldives Business School, Maldives

ABSTRACT

In today's competitive education industry, incorporating corporate social responsibility (CSR) has become a key strategy for enhancing performance and gaining a competitive edge. Previous research has shown that when academic industry implements CSR initiatives, it can positively influence employee engagement and result in beneficial behaviour. With this in mind, the purpose of the study was to investigate the CSR's initiative on employee behaviour in the academic sector. Using non-probability purposive sampling technique, the authors gathered data from 550 academic employees. Through analysis, the study assessed the ability of CSR to distinguish levels of employee engagement. Findings of the study demonstrated that company corporate social responsibility (CSR) initiatives hold immense power, reaching beyond mere employees behaviour. They possess the ability to greatly shape employee perceptions and actions towards the academic institutions.

INTRODUCTION

Corporate social responsibility (CSR) has transitioned from being a trendy term to becoming a crucial and necessary aspect of global company strategy. Micro-CSR, sometimes referred to as the micro-level of CSR or microfoundations of CSR, is a developing concept that plays a crucial role in comprehending the individual-level processes that influence CSR behaviour. It also aids in translating strategic board-

DOI: 10.4018/979-8-3693-3096-8.ch014

room CSR initiatives into practical duties. J. Iqbal, M. Aukhoon, and Z. A. Parray (2024). As firms recognise the significance of ethics and social duty, the concept of corporate social responsibility (CSR) has gained widespread acceptance. Corporate Social Responsibility (CSR) initiatives, which encompass activities related to environmental sustainability and community engagement, have an impact on both external and internal stakeholders, with a particular focus on employees (Gond et al., 2017). CSR can improve an organization stature in the eyes of the investment community, customers, employees and it is already influencing all its stakeholders' preferences. In order to address value creation efforts as part of the company's strategy, CSR (corporate social responsibility) should concentrate on the significant areas of interaction that exist between the firm and its main stakeholders. Moreover, CSR remains compelling differentiator, influencing both employees behaviour and corporate reputation. Though talented employees are demanding, they understand they must make a change, as well. The employees as internal customers expect companies to address social and environmental issues. Employees also seek more ways to engage in CSR efforts. According to the employees, they would be willing to volunteer their time and money for a cause, as well as make a donation to a charity that is backed by a firm that they have faith in. Corporate social responsibility (CSR) is closely linked to a company's reputation. Consumers are more likely to have a positive perception of companies that engage in social good, leading to increased trust and loyalty.(Kumar, V., & Pansari, A., 2016) However, it's crucial for companies to effectively communicate their CSR efforts. If communication is lacking, employees may not actively seek out information about these initiatives. To capture employee attention, companies should demonstrate exceptional CSR efforts that exceed industry standards. (please include more recent citation)

Corporate Social Responsibility (CSR) involves engaging both internal and external stakeholders. This allows educational institutions to better anticipate and adapt to rapidly evolving societal expectations and operating conditions. Social responsibility initiatives, such as employee and student engagement, foster long-term relationships and build trust that support sustainable business models. CSR also creates an atmosphere conducive to innovation and growth. Ultimately, CSR establishes core values that guide the creation of a cohesive society and facilitate the transition to a sustainable economic system.

Corporate Social Responsibility (CSR)

Corporate Social Responsibility involves ensuring that the company's operations have positive social and environmental impacts. Active CSR efforts aid businesses in the global market by overcoming cultural and social concerns. Considering the growing significance of Corporate Social Responsibility (CSR) for both organisations and society, as well as its capacity to contribute to the resolution of important challenges of the twenty-first century, it should not come as a surprise that this subject has gained a large amount of research attention (Villamor, G. B., & Wallace, L., 2024). CSR has been characterised in a number of different ways by researchers coming from a wide range of academic fields. A review conducted an analysis of various definitions of Corporate Social Responsibility (CSR) and identified five dimensions that were consistently mentioned: environmental (referring to the natural environment), social (relating to the relationship between business and society), economic (including socio-economic and financial aspects, as well as how CSR is described in terms of business operations), stakeholders (referring to groups with an interest in or impacted by the firm), and voluntariness (Glavas, A., 2024). According to the definitions of He, H., & Sutunyarak, C. (2024) CSR have been compiled based on research that was published between the years 1953 and 2024. Today, organisations separate CSR from philanthropy. When properly implemented, CSR should become engrained in a company's values and culture and positively impact business. CSR would be integrated into an organization's mission and marketing and advertising. Corporate social responsibility neglect threatens brand reputation and bottom line growth. Having a bad social and environmental reputation can hurt a company's profitability and success, as consumers want to buy products and services they believe in and work with ethical companies. CSR demands internal and external stakeholder involvement, which helps the organisation anticipate and capitalise on fast-changing social and operating situations. The core element of most successful business is excellent employees experience. Employees who are delighted are likely to continue the relationship with the firm (Cochran, 2007). The businesses firms which are socially responsible have the edge over other firms especially those which have socially irresponsible reputations. Among the various stakeholder groups, employees are the backbone of the business, and social-centric CSR initiatives impact the organization's performance significantly. The CSR strategies succeed when it benefits the employees.

Employees Engagement

According to Saks and Gruman (2024), employee engagement is defined as a heightened emotional connection with the organisation, which in turn leads to increased levels of dedication, support, and loyalty on the part of the employees. It is crucial to cultivate employee engagement, which is the cornerstone of long-term competitive advantage and organisational accomplishment (Bakker, 2022). Creating great employee experiences is essential for nurturing engagement. According to the findings of study, employee engagement is a psychological phenomena that has an effect on the loyalty of employees (Bowden, 2009). According to Bowden (2009), engagement for new workers means helping to cultivate loyalty, while for established employees, it involves working to maintain loyalty. The findings of additional research reveal that employee engagement is comprised of activities that go beyond merely executing duties. These behaviours demonstrate an employee's strong commitment to the organisation (Van den Broek et al., 2013). The authors Vivek et al. (2012) highlight the importance of employee involvement as a critical component in the process of developing relationships in the workplace. According to Vivek et al. (2012), strategic usage of it has the potential to efficiently attract, maintain, and increase staff interactions, which would ultimately result in the desired outcomes for the company concerned.

The findings of Kumar and Pansari (2016), which were published more recently, reveal that the happiness and emotional connection of employees have a significant impact on the level of employee engagement. It is possible that the factors that influence engagement will differ from person to person depending on their tastes and their level of connection with the organisation. Employee's engagement may also be described to such extent to which employees feel emotionally devoted and linked to an organisation and the goals that it strives to achieve. For example, research conducted by Gallup (1935) has demonstrated that employees who are totally involved in their work contribute substantially more to the income of an organisation than employees who are not engaged in their work. Organisations miss out on opportunities to interact with their employees and cultivate strong connections when they do not have a strategy in place to achieve employee engagement. A real focus on empathy, clarity, and simplicity in organisational interactions with employees can form the basis for effective engagement activities across a variety of industries, despite the fact that there is no strategy that is guaranteed to work for everyone.

REVIEW OF LITERATURE

The level of engagement of employees is a significant factor in determining the effectiveness of a business. According to Saks (2023), a study that was carried out between the years 2022 and 2024 reveals that efforts made by corporations to engage in Corporate Social Responsibility (CSR) can have a significant impact on motivating employees to work. As demonstrated by the research that Glavas and Kelley carried out in 2022, there is a significant and robust association between projects and the values that employees hold close to their hearts. Employees may experience a heightened sense of significance and, eventually, will be more involved in their work when they realise that their profession contributes to a larger purpose that goes beyond financial benefit. Moreover, corporate social responsibility (CSR) activities that engage employees in the decision-making process and volunteer opportunities are shown to have a significant impact on employee engagement according to Abeyton and Fonseca (2023). Given the chance to develop a sense of ownership and authority, employees develop a more profound allegiance to the company's social responsibility works.

In their article Maak and Spekman (2022) think about importance of employee perspective in implementing Corporate Social Responsibility (CSR) in company. On the other hand Puffer and Grandy (2024) found that employee engagement requires communicating clearly about CSR efforts. Moreover, an authentic approach is likely to be participative rather than observatory. Similarly, employee engagement may be enhanced through allowing them to chose GOPs. Recent research point to the capacity of CSR initiatives in enhancing engagement by underscoring transparency, authenticity, and employee involvement. Promotion of a sense of purpose, ownership, and connection to activities related to social responsibility can help businesses cultivate a workforce that is more engaged and productive.

Webster (1975) socially conscious consumer defined is an individual who considers what happens as a result of private consumption or who seeks changes for the society with his purchasing abilities at heart. Laroche et al. (2001), in their study aimed at profiling of green consumers, pointed that concerns over environment have resulted in a marketplace conscious of environment and consumers conscious of the impact of their purchasing behaviour over various ecological problems. Webb et al. (2007) argued that due to a drop in consumers' confidence in the frontrunners of major firms, individuals seek more socially and environmentally responsible behaviour from these firms which has resulted in higher number of American citizens to participate in responsible consumption. Thus, in a scenario so keenly attentive towards sensible consumption, firms engaging in active and consistent efforts towards catering to the social and environmental concerns have a higher chance of securing the mind share and consequently, the wallet share of its employees. Though, CSR based contributions would not be able to compensate for the compromises on service quality and brand image, the overall impact of the aforementioned three aspects clubbed together can outperform even the closest of competition and render a sustainable competitive advantage to the firm in the long run. Companies with visible and sincere sensitivity towards the environment and society stand to secure associations marked by respect and pride with its public. Moreover, CSR practices affect vital employee attitudes and responses as employees are more likely to form favourable notions about the organization which may lead to positive behavioural intentions towards organization, trust and more openness towards the firm. In the context of cause related marketing, Varadrajan and Menon (1988) underlined several advantages of such practices such as greater brand exposure and awareness, increased sales, defyingnegative publicity, repeat buying, etc. Wang et al. (2005); Brammer and Millington (2008)suggested that in the long run, socially responsible firms receive relatively better financialreturns. Becker Olsen et al. (2006); Curtis (2006); Du et al. (2007) declaimed favourable consumer thought process word of mouth and recommendations as the upshots for firmhaving CSR orientation. Wu et al. (2016) concluded that corporate social responsibility hasthe ability to exert positive impact over consumers' attitudes towards brand and brand imageand it stimulates consumers' purchase intention. Besides expediting the business interests ofthe firm, such encouraging rejoinder from the customers also help in framing and organizing successful customer engagement exercises at various levels which contribute in deepeningthe relationships between firm and the customers. The positive image developed andsustained through CSR initiatives transcends to the pre and post consumption stages ofcustomer company association and acts as an enabler of effective communication andinteractive exchanges at multiple platforms which build a powerful mechanism for employee engagement.

Corporate Social Responsibility and Employees Engagement: A Greater Good for a Greater Gain

Recent studies conducted over the course of the previous three years have consistently demonstrated that Corporate Social Responsibility (CSR) has a beneficial impact on employee engagement. Li, Li, and Fong (2021) argue that employees' perceptions of their organization's corporate social responsibility (CSR) initiatives greatly enhances their levels of both emotional and cognitive engagement. The same authors argue that when personal values are aligned with organizational ones, pride is nurtured among human resource staff which in turn gives them a sense belonging to their employer. The research conducted by Zhou et al. (2022) shown that corporate social responsibility (CSR) initiatives strengthen organisational commitment, which in turn improves engagement, notably through activities related to community involvement and environmental sustainability. According to Kim and Thapa (2023), individuals who believe the company provides them with support have a great effect on how the organization interacts with its workers. However, Zhou at al.'s (2022) study reveals that CSR programs enhance corporate commitment leading to increased involvement within operations basically surrounding the community work and employees. Specifically, when it comes to matters of corporate social responsibility concerning corporate social responsibility, the empirical studies undertaken by Singh, Gupta, and Sharma (2023) point out that it must be emphasized that CSR always stimulates involvement even though the types of activities favored by specific societies may not be the same. The research projects carried out on specific sectors of commerce, for example on the medical or technological sectors by Martinez & Perez (2022) as well as Lin & Lee (2023), provide more proof that establishment-based corporate social responsibility (CSR) programs greatly enhance worker loyalty and participation through such measures. Collectively, these findings indicate that incorporating corporate social responsibility (CSR) into fundamental business strategy is necessary in order to cultivate a workforce that is both engaged and motivated.

The discussion above chalks out a clear role of corporate social responsibility over various antecedents of employees engagement and does support a case of cause related internal marketing acting as a moderator of relationships between employees engagement and other employees variables such as employees satisfaction, trust, commitment, involvement, participation, etc. The antecedent role of these variables in determining the strength and success of employees engagement has been probed and proven by plethora of researches which clearly shows the path for effective implementation of employees engagement programs. employees engagement, primarily aimed at co-creation of mutual value, serves as a catalyst in creation of employees loyalty as the behavioural and attitudinal outcomes of employees engagement archetype the major manifestations of employees loyalty and therefore, holds immense value for a firm cognizant of the significance of securing employees loyalty in the long run. With the context of growing environmental concerns, more social consciousness, and the formation of movements aimed at protecting the planet, the significance of "Corporate Social Responsibility (CSR)" has been grown increasingly obvious in the arena of employee engagement as well as CSR. This is because CSR has become increasingly important in the context of employee engagement. Furthermore, recent company failures have brought to light the significance of ethical business practices notwithstanding their value. As a direct response to these trends, businesses of all sizes have acknowledged their social duties and taken steps to implement corporate social responsibility initiatives that are well-designed. Analysis of prior academic works as well as the business environment alludes to a positive relationship between corporate social responsibility (CSR) and sales increment as well as reputation enhancement of a firm. This makes it necessary for organizations to channel resources towards socially oriented and environmentally friendly projects. In their publication, H. L. Kim and C. Jeong (2020) argues that Companies that follow CSR best practices create trust with clients due to their ability to maintain an open communication channel. To increase employee engagement, companies should maximize their Corporate social responsibilities in order to unite the staff members around a single shared goal that encompasses the feeling of ownership at work. New research indicates that firms engaged in social good often trigger employee identification (Arli & Lasmono, 2010).The more organizations interact with employees and show commitment, the more it leads to increased employee participation in CSR. In addition, workers can participate in other areas concerning environmental and social concerns thus improving their satisfaction at work as well as positive feelings towards themselves Through corporate social responsibility (CSR), employees could also participate in volunteer activities. Business loyalty and affiliation are encouraged by these possibilities. Good way of increasing loyalty and retention among the staff. In terms of workforce engagement and loyalty, societal and environmental welfare investments benefit both the society and the enterprise. The companies which foster social responsibility and employee engagement can gain competitive advantage and make the world better off.

Employees are drawn to CSR in a variety of different ways. As a result of employees observing the corporate social responsibility (CSR) initiatives of an organisation, they develop a sense of emotional attachment to the organisation since they believe that the employees are acting on their behalf (Drumwright. M.E., & Braig. B.M., 2004). The individuals in question are of the opinion that the goals of the organisation and their own are identical. They enjoy being linked with the organisation and have the sense that they are a part of it, especially when they believe the organisation and themselves to be a single entity (S. Sen and C.B. Bhattacharya., 2016). Through corporate social responsibility (CSR), employees gain the assurance that their interests will not be exploited by the organisation, which in turn gives them the confidence to cultivate a close relationship with the company (Martínez, P. and del Bosque, 2013).

Initiatives that taken for Corporate Social Responsibility (CSR) play a crucial part in the process of cultivating emotional connections and engagement among employees. According to Lichtenstein, Drumwright, and Braig (2004), corporate social responsibility (CSR) initiatives not only foster feelings of warmth, unity, and reliability and trustworthiness among employees, but they also create similar attitudes inside the workforce. Employees have a stronger emotional connection with the firm because they experience a feeling of pride and connection to socially responsible organisations. They consider these organisations as champions for the welfare of society, which increases their connections to the company (Vlachos, 2012). According to Liu (2008), giving back to society not only increases happiness but also cultivates a sense of gratitude among employees towards their employer. This is something that should be taken into consideration. The findings of Romani (2013) provide more evidence that employees feel a sense of obligation to companies that are actively involved in supporting social causes. This results in a positive emotional response and a readiness to advocate for the organisation. Furthermore, employees experience sentiments of pride as a result of CSR initiatives (Chang, Kang, Ko, & Connaughton, 2017). This is because employees think of themselves as being associated with a firm that places a high priority on social responsibility. According to Perez (2015), despite the fact that corporate social responsibility (CSR) initiatives can elicit a range of feelings, the general attitude towards socially responsible businesses is typically favourable. The development of emotional ties is essential to the process of generating employee engagement (Pansari, 2017). This is because engaged employees demonstrate behaviours that are congruent with the interests of the firm. As Sashi (2012) explains, emotional attachment acts as a trigger for emotional and emotional development. Further highlighting the significance of emotional relationships in the workplace, Verleye (2014) conceptualises emotional intelligence as a sort of love that originates from affection among employees. According to Zainol, Omar, Osman, and Habidin (2016), CSR initiatives generate emotional responses among employees, which in turn contributes to employee engagement. Employees are said to identify with organisations that are reflective of their values and ideas, as stated by social identity theory (Stets & Burke, 2000) and self-categorization theory (Hornsey, 2008). According to Martínez and del Bosque (2013), employees build a sense of belonging and identity with organisations that prioritise corporate social responsibility (CSR). This is due to the fact that employees connect themselves with companies that are socially responsible. This alignment helps to cultivate a sense of unity and shared purpose among employees, which further enhances their engagement with the organisation.

In CSR and employee engagement, Webster (1975)'s idea of a socially conscious consumer can be applied to a socially conscious employee who examines how their workplace and company actions affect society. Roberts (1993)'s socially responsible consumer matches an engaged employee who wants to work for organisations with good social and environmental values. Laroche et al. (2001)'s emphasis on environmental concerns driving consumer behaviour might translate into employees who are more conscious of their workplace's social and environmental impact and choose companies that address these issues. In this context, companies that prioritise CSR activities to engage employees by addressing social and environmental issues will gain employee loyalty and commitment. Employees favour companies that show social responsibility, just as consumers want more from firms. While CSR programmes alone may not improve employee experience, they can motivate employees to stay engaged when combined with positive work environments and corporate cultures. Visible commitment to social and environmental causes inspires pride and respect in employees, increasing job satisfaction and dedication. CSR policies affect employee behaviour and staff opinions of their employer. CSR programmes can boost employees' faith in the company, pride in their work, and purpose in their jobs. Varadrajan and Menon (1988) and others found that CSR programmes boost employee engagement, job satisfaction, motivation, and company loyalty. Wang et al. (2005) and Brammer and Millington (2008) found that socially responsible companies have higher employee retention and a stronger workplace culture. Positive employee impressions from CSR programmes lead to positive word-of-mouth and referrals, according to Becker Olsen et al. (2006), Curtis (2006), and Du (2007). This positive feeling boosts the firm's reputation and capacity to attract and retain top talent. Finally, CSR programmes affect employees' brand and image impressions just as they do employee perceptions. This improves communication and interaction within the company, deepening employee relationships and increasing employee engagement. Corporate Social Responsibility (CSR) builds trust and strengthens connections, which boosts employee engagement. According to Morgan (1994)'s commitment-trust theory, trust is essential to good relationships. Employees and customers value reliability and feel safer working with a socially responsible organisation.

According to Palmatier et al. (2008), internal customers' trust in a socially responsible organisation leads to a readiness to build relationships, which can be applied to staff. According to Van Doorn (2011), CSR actions make a company seem more reliable, which increases employee engagement. Bowden (2009) says trust is essential to employee engagement. SR efforts foster employee engagement and connection building. Like building trust and rapport with employees, CSR creates trust and commitment among employees, promoting greater organisational engagement.

Ha(1): There exists a significant correlation between CSR initiatives (Community responsibility, Employee responsibility, Environmental responsibility, Investor responsibility, and Employees as internal customer responsibility) and employees engagement (additional loyalty, emotional attachment)

Ha(2): There is significant discriminating power in the CSR initiatives towards the employees engagement level

Objectives:

1. To measure the relationship between the CSR initiative and employee's engagement.
2. To measure the discriminating power of CSR initiative towards employee's engagement.

METHODOLOGY

The overall plan for conducting research is referred to as the research design. This approach outlines the procedures that are utilised to collect and analyse data in order to answer your research questions. This study involves assessing the perception level of employees towards CSR practices of institutional authority, their influence on employees engagement.As it attempts to measure the phenomena as they exist, causal research is used it is the most appropriate scientific method for collecting (survey research) data and analyzing the characteristics of the employees of the academic institutions. This study is carried out in India and nearby countries where the total number of academic institutions is 2529 which is 30% of all top higher education institutions. "The population of the study is confined to both public sector and private sector institutions. These institutions have their presence in urban, semi-urban and metropolitan location in the India and nearby countries. The CSR activities and CSR spending vary across India and nearby countries. Among the 29 public and private sector institutions nine institutions with the highest CSR spending were chosen for the study". Approximately there are6,000 employees in these countries of the chosen twenty nine institutions as the population is finite, non-probability sampling technique has been adopted for the study. The sample chosen were representative covering all the twenty nine institutions having equal members from selected of the study.

For the purpose of the sample study, employees were selected based on the length of time they had been working with their respective academic institutions. For the purpose of this study, which aimed to get a knowledge of the corporate social responsibility (CSR) policies of academic institutions, members of staff who were above the age of 25 and had been employed by the same academic institutions for a period of time more than one year were selected. It is possible for employees to take advantage of a wide range of institutional services, including possibilities for professional development and research, a variety of leave options, flexible working hours, and the ability to work five days annually. There is a presumption that a period of one year in which workers work with the same institutions will provide them with the opportunity to comprehend the corporate social responsibility activities in which the institution is involved. During a one-on-one conversation with the authority of the institution, the researcher was able to collect the approximate number of employees now employed by each of the institutions located throughout India and the nations that are close. The quantity of workers employed by the selected institutions was distinct from one another. In light of this, a representative sample of workers from each of the institutions was also collected, taking into account the total number of workers. For the purpose of selecting employees, the type of sampling technique that was utilised was proportionate stratified sampling.

The G Power analysis is what determines the size of the sample that will be used in this investigation (Faul, F., Erdfelder, E., Lang, A.-G., & Buchner, A., 2007). One of the capabilities of GPower 3 is the ability to do five distinct sorts of power analysis. The a priori, post hoc, compromise, criteria, and sensitivity power analyses are the ones that are being discussed here. Among these, the a priori power analysis is the one that is most pertinent to the determination of sample size. This is because it includes establishing the sample size that is necessary for any given power, alpha level, and effect size. Therefore, the sample size is determined to be 612 by taking into account the power, alpha level, and effect size that are stated for each of the statistical tests.

Data Collection

For the statistical study to be successful, the acquisition of data must be methodical. Both primary and secondary data sources are utilised by the researcher in order to fulfil the data collection process. Through the use of a standardised survey instrument that was administered to the respondent by the researcher, the direct personal interview served as the primary source of data for this study. Secondary data about CSR spending in institutions, Number, size of institutional authorising operations, employees base and employees size were collected from secondary sources like Higher Education Institutions website of India and nearby countries websites, government website, institutional authority information records, NGO box, India CSR, Karmayog CSR ranking and CMIE.

Table 1. Constructs and Measurements

S.No	Constructs	Dimension	Measurements
1.	CSR	CommunityResponsibility	Maignan & Ferrell (2004)
		EnvironmentResponsibility	
		EmployeeResponsibility	
		InvestorResponsibility	
		employeesasinternal CustomerResponsibility	
2.	Employees Engagement	Additional loyalty	Gallop Scale (2001)
		EmotionalAttachment	

Hypothesis of the Study

Ha(1): There exists a significant correlation between CSR (Community responsibility, Employee responsibility, Environmental responsibility, Investor responsibility,) and employees as internal customer engagement (additional loyalty, emotional attachment)

Ha(2): There is significant discriminating power in the CSR towards the Employees engagement level

RESULTS AND DISCUSSIONS

The Reliability-test was carried out with the purpose of determining whether or not the questionnaire that was constructed should be considered reliable, as well as determining how easy it was for respondents to answer the questionnaire. There are tests of reliability and validity carried out for each and every variable that is included in the study. When we talk about the reliability of the variables, we are referring to the accuracy with which the constructs measure the same phenomenon over and over again while yet allowing for some degree of fluctuation. The reliability of each construct in question is examined using Cronbach's alpha (Cronbach, 1951). It measures the interrelatedness of a set of items the alpha scores which greater than 0.7 is generally accepted as sufficient accuracy for a construct (Nunnally, 1978). "The composite reliability for internal consistency of the constructs was tested and was above 0.7. The value of Cronbach's Alpha for the whole items was found and represented in the below table which means that the instrument has a high level of consistency".

Table 2. Reliability of the Present Study's Constructs

S.No	Constructs	Dimension	Cronbach's Alpha
1.	CSR	CommunityResponsibility	0.942
		EnvironmentResponsibility	0.856
		EmployeeResponsibility	0.822
		InvestorResponsibility	0.815
		employeesasinternal CustomerResponsibility	0.910
2.	Employees Engagement	Additional loyalty	0.931
.		EmotionalAttachment	0.844

RESULTS AND DISCUSSIONS

Demographic Analysis

"The majority of the respondents (Employees) are female 362 (60.2%) and remaining are male 250(40.8%). Since sampling area in India and surrounding countries, the female employees of those countries are actively involved in the Self-help group activities and make frequent visit to the institutions. Majority of sample 432(70.6%) lies in the age group of 31-40 years, 28(4.6%) employees belong to the age group of 20-30 years, 123(20.1%) employees lie in the age group between 41-50 years, and 29(4.7%) belong to the senior age group more than 50 years. Majority of the respondents are married 427(69.8%), the remaining respondent is single 185(30.2%).In the income level distribution of the employees, majority 379(61.9%) of them belongs to 20001-25000 income group and the next level of income group is 25001-30000 which are 126 (20.6%)". Since this two income group level constitutes 80%. The majority of the age group of the employees are between 31-50 years and earn between 20000- 30000 per month.

Descriptive Analysis

Descriptive analysis provides valuable informationabout the nature of the employees group variability concerning the Perceived CSR and employees engagement data. The mean and standard deviation of all CSR and employees as internal customer engagement dimensions under study are as follows. The mean values of employees group representthe centre of gravity of distributionconcerning the Perceived CSR and employees engagement. The standard deviation value was computed to measure the dispersion.The questions with negative connotation were reverse coded. Since it is a five-point scale the standard for the mean is 3 Mean values above 3 meant that the employees showed a state of agreeableness with the constructs measured and the mean values less than 3 showed disagreeableness of the employees with regards to the factor measured.

Table 3. Descriptive statistics

S.No	Construct	Dimension	Employees	
			Mean	SD
1	Perceived CSR	CommunityResponsibility	3.97	0.62
		EnvironmentResponsibility	4.01	0.72
		EmployeeResponsibility	4.12	0.78
		InvestorResponsibility	4.07	0.68
		employeesasinternal CustomerResponsibility	3.56	0.84
2	Employees Engagement	Additional Loyalty	3.49	0.87
		Emotional Attachment	3.80	0.62

Table 3 "shows the mean and standard deviation of the *perceived corporate social responsibility* by the employees. employees as internal customer responsibility (Mean value= 4.12 and S.D= 0.78)had the highest mean when compared to the community responsibility.

(Mean value= 3.97 and S.D= 0.62), environmental responsibility (Mean value= 4.01 and S.D= 0.72), employee responsibility (Mean value= 4.07 and S.D= 0.68) and investor responsibility (Mean value= 3.56 and S.D= 0.84), the investor responsibility mean values was found to be the lowest, the employees is not aware of the Investor responsibility of the institutional authority CSR activity. The standard deviation is less than 1 for the entire sub-constructs which showed that the response of the entire employees did not vary much with the mean value". The construct *Employees engagement* had two sub-constructs Additional loyalty

($\mu = 3.49$), and emotional attachment ($\mu = 3.80$), comparing the two dimensions of employees engagement emotional attachment had the highest mean value which shows that the employees are emotionally attached and engaged with their institutional authority

Measuring the Relationship Between CSR and Employees Engagement

A correlation matrix was developed to find out if the independent and dependent constructs of have any relationship with eachother and among themselves; correlation also measures how far the constructs are linearly related to each other. Taking the CSR as an independent construct and employees engagement as dependent constructs bivariate correlation analysis was carried out.The Bivariate Pearson Correlation of independent construct CSR with dependent construct employees engagement is shown in the table 2.0

Ha(1): There exists a significant correlation between CSR (Community responsibility, Employee responsibility, Environmental responsibility, Investor responsibility, employees as internal customer responsibility) and employees engagement (additional loyalty, emotional attachment)

Table 4. Bivariate correlation between Corporate Social Responsibility and Employees Engagement

S.No	CSR	EMPLOYEES ENGAGEMENT			
		Additional Loyalty		Emotional Attachment	
1	COR	.16*	(.01)	.17*	(.00)
2	EMPR	.24*	(.00)	.17*	(.03)
3	ENVR	.19*	(.00)	.13*	(.02)
4	INVR	.17*	(.01)	.19*	(.00)
5	CUSTR	.25*	(.00)	.62*	(.00)

COR- community responsibility, EMPR- employee responsibility, ENVR- environmental responsibility, INVR- investor responsibility, CUSTR- employees as internal customer responsibility,

*Pearson correlation value, () Significance

From Table 4 it is evident that all the sub-constructs of CSR had significant (p <0.05) correlation with the all the sub-constructs of Employees engagement. So the alternate hypothesis is accepted and concluded that there is a relationship between CSR(Community responsibility, Employee responsibility, Environmental responsibility, Investor responsibility, employees as internal customer responsibility) and employees engagement (additional loyalty, emotional attachment). The employees responsibility had a high positive correlation with additional loyalty (r= 0.25) and emotional attachment (r=.62). So the employees loyalty and emotional attachment can be improved by the institutions, by enhancing employees responsibility initiatives which directly reach the target employees. Next to the employees as employee responsibility was correlated with employees engagement.

Assessing the CSR Determinants of Employees Engagement

A discriminant analysis was performed in order to determine the degree of discrimination available power of CSR on employees engagement. Discriminant analysis the dependent construct should be categorical variables and mutually exclusive, so the employees engagement construct is categorized into two groups as high and low, High indicates the high engagement level of employees and low indicates the low engagement level of employees.

Table 5. Eigenvalues

S.No	Construct	Definition	Sub construct	Measurement
1.	CSR (Corporate social responsibility)	Explore the organizations in their search to become more responsible towards the community responsibilities, environmental responsibilities, employee responsibilities, investor responsibility and employees as internal customer responsibilities	Community Responsibility, Environmental Responsibility, Employee Responsibility, Employees as internal Customer Responsibility	Maignan and Ferrell (2004) (5- point scale)
2.	Employees Engagement	It is defined as the extent to which employees are emotionally committed and attached towards an organization and its brand.	Additional loyalty, Emotional Attachment	Gallop scale (2001)

From above mentioned Table 5, it is seen that the resulted Eigenvalue .723, 72% of the variance in the employee engagement level caused by the Corporate social responsibility. Larger the Eigenvalue stronger the discriminant function. The correlation between the discriminant scores and the level of employee engagement (high or low) is the canonical correlation: the correlation between the two. Since the canonical correlation value is 0.648 is comparatively high compared with 1,so the corporate social responsibility discriminates the Employees engagement level.

Testing of Hypothesis

Ha (2): There is significant discriminating power in the CSR towards the Employees Engagement level

Table 6. Wilks Lambda

Test of Function	Wilks Lambda	Chi-Sqr	DF	Sig
1	0.58	330.46	5	`.000

Based on the data in Table 6, it is observed that the p-value is 0.000, which is lower than the significance level of 0.05. As a result, the null hypothesis is rejected, and the alternative hypothesis is accepted. This leads to the conclusion that there is a statistically significant ability to differentiate in the independent construct (CSR). Consequently, we can move forward with the development of the discriminant equation. The table4.0 reveals that the Wilks' Lambda value is 0.580 and the Chi-square value is 330.459 with 5 degrees of freedom, based on the levels of Employees engagement. Wilks' lambda serves as a measure of the effectiveness of each function in distinguishing cases into groups. Lower values of Wilks' lambda indicate a higher discriminatory ability of the function.

MEASURING THE RELATIVE IMPORTANCE OF EACH CSR SUB CONSTRUCT

Table 7. Standardized Canonical Discriminant Function Coefficients

S.No	CSR	Function
		1
1	Community Responsibility	.337
2	Environment Responsibility	.107
3	Employee Responsibility	.169
4	Investor Responsibility	.098
5	Employees as Internal Customer Responsibility	.951

From the above Table 7 by comparing the standard coefficient of each sub-construct of CSR, it is possible to identify which sub-construct of CSR discriminates the Employees engagement level. Employees as Internal Customer responsibility (.951) had a higher standardized discriminant coefficient, followed by the community responsibility (.337), so the employees and community responsibility of CSR construct have more discriminant power on employees engagement level when compared to other sub-construct of CSR. So this indicated that the employees responsibility and community responsibility activities of the institutional authority werethe best predictors of employees engagement.

Table 8. Unstandardized Canonical Discriminant Function Coefficients

S.No	CSR	Function
		1
1	Community Responsibility	.555
2	Environment Responsibility	.148
3	Employee Responsibility	.216
4	Investor Responsibility	.143
5	Employees as Internal Customer Responsibility	1.430
6	(Constant)	-7.019

From the above table 6.0 the unstandardised Canonical Discriminant Function Coefficients revealed and the Discriminant Function is derived as

$Z = -7.019 + .555$(Community responsibility) $+ .148$(Environmental responsibility) $+ .216$(Employee responsibility) $+ .143$(Investor responsibility) $+ 1.430$ (Employees as Internal Customer responsibility)

DECISION RULE

Table 9. Functions at Group centroids

S.No	Level of employees engagement	Function
		1
1	Low	-1.336
2	High	.539

The above Table 9 revealed the Group centroid scores of customer engagement level, the Group centroidscores gives the average discriminant score ofthe low and high employees' engagement level. The lower centroid score is -1.336 for the low of employees' engagement, and higher centroid score is .539 is for the high level of Employees engagement. The dividing point is calculated based on the high level (436), and low level (176) of employees' engagement concerning the centroid scores and decision rule classification were derived.

Dividing Rule

$$= \{(n1)\ (Lower\ Centriod) + (n2)\ (Higher\ Centriod)\}/\ \{n1 + n2\}$$

$$= \{(176)\ (-1.336) + (436)\ (.539)\}/\ \{176 + 376\}$$

$$= -.000215$$

Decision Rule Classification

Decision 1: -1.336<z<-.000215(Predict and classify low engagement level)
Decision 2: -.000215<z<.539 (Predict and classify High engagement level)

Table 10. Discriminant classification Results

S.No	Level of Employees' Engagement		Predicted Group Membership		Total
			Low	High	
1	Low	Count	139	37	176
2	High		69	367	436
3	Low	%	79.0	21.0	100.0
4	High		15.8	84.2	100.0

a. 82.7% of "original grouped cases correctly classified".

According to the data presented in Table 10, it can be seen that the discriminant function accurately identified 82.7% of the data as belonging to the High level and Low level of employee involvement and that this classification was accurate. At the level of employee engagement, it was discovered that out of

176 employees with a low level of engagement, 139 employees were accurately labelled as low level, while 37 people were incorrectly classified as high level. This was discovered in the context of the level of employee engagement. Furthermore, it was discovered that out of 436 employees have a high degree of engagement, 367 individuals have been appropriately classified as high level, while 69 employees have been incorrectly labelled as low level. In light of this, the accuracy of the model is regarded to be satisfactory. Clearly, this demonstrates that the discriminant function that was developed has an exceptional capacity for prediction; it has the potential to determine whether or not employees will be highly engaged or less engaged based on the activities that are related to corporate social responsibility.

CONCLUSION

Academic Institutions doing their CSR activities to take care of their stakeholders, which will be win- win situation for both institutions and stake holders and it benefits the both of them. The influence of corporate social responsibility (CSR) on employees extends beyond their decisions to stay with the company, and also affects their entire attitude and behaviour. Corporate Social Responsibility (CSR) elicits good emotions and fosters a sense of association between employees and the company, leading to increased engagement with socially responsible organisations. Engaged personnel exhibit a high level of commitment and loyalty to the organisation due to their strong affiliations with it. They exhibit higher levels of motivation while providing favourable recommendations for their organisation. Corporate Social Responsibility (CSR) not only provides the organisation with valuable information, but also improves employees' willingness to offer opinions. Employee Engagement is crucial in facilitating this process. Engaged personnel are motivated to improve the organisation and actively demonstrate supportive behaviours towards the organisation.

Implications

Improving employee services as they are internal customer too is the most obvious and best CSR practice that is overlooked by many academic institutions to engage their employees. Before any promotional aspects are introduced, it is essential to create a culture of approachable and amicable employees service in the institutions. An excellent employees services can go a long way as it considers every aspect of the institutional authority. It also help attracting potential new employees or serving a long term existing employees a new responsibilities and authorities. Institutions can improve employees service by responding to any requests or complaints quickly and promptly and by being polite, and treating employees with the dignity they build trust and congeniality at the institutional authority. Institutions earn their employees' loyalty through interaction by interaction. The prompt employees service, accessibility and overall experience serve to strengthen the academic institution's brand reputation. This, in turn, builds emotional bonds with employees in the long run. For institutions, consistent high performance is critical to employees' loyalty.

Scope for Further Research

The current investigation has been conducted with a restricted sample size. Moreover, it is possible to do the same study with a substantial sample size, allowing for the evaluation and comparison of the findings. The study focused exclusively on institutions, but it may be beneficial to include other industries that engage in corporate social responsibility (CSR) activities. Additionally, comparing CSR and employee engagement factors between private and public institutions, as well as examining additional employee attitude variables, could be considered for future research.

REFERENCES

Aguinis, H., & Glavas, A. (2019). On Corporate Social Responsibility, Sensemaking, and the Search for Meaningfulness Through Work. *Journal of Management*, 45(1), 105–128. 10.1177/0149206317691575

Aguinis, H., Rupp, D. E., & Glavas, A. (2024). Corporate social responsibility and individual behaviour. *Nature Human Behaviour*, 1–9.38233604

Becker-Olsen, K. L., Cudmore, B. A., & Hill, R. P. (2006). The impact of perceived corporate social responsibility on consumer behavior. *Journal of Business Research*, 59(1), 46–53. 10.1016/j.jbusres.2005.01.001

Bowden, J. L. H. (2009). The process of employees' engagement: A conceptual framework. *Journal of Marketing Theory and Practice*, 17(1), 63–74. 10.2753/MTP1069-6679170105

Bowden, P. (2022). *Employee engagement and how to achieve it*. Chartered Institute of Personnel and Development.

Brammer, S., Millington, A., & Rayton, B. (2007). The contribution of corporation social responsibility to organizational commitment. *International Journal of Human Resource Management*, 18(10), 1701–1719. 10.1080/09585190701570866

Chang, M. J., Kang, J. H., Ko, Y. J., & Connaughton, D. P. (2017). The effects of perceived team performance and social responsibility on pride and word-of-mouth recommendation. *Sport Marketing Quarterly*, 26, 31.

Cochran, P. L. (2007). The evolution of corporate social responsibility. *Business Horizons*, 50(6), 449–454. 10.1016/j.bushor.2007.06.004

Cronbach, L. J. (1951). Coefficient alpha and the internal structure of tests. *Psychometrika, 16*(3), 297-334.

Dessart, L., Veloutsou, C., & Morgan-Thomas, A. (2015). Consumer engagement in online brand communities: A social media perspective. *Journal of Product and Brand Management*, 24(1), 28–42. 10.1108/JPBM-06-2014-0635

Gallup Consulting. (2001). *Employees' engagement: What's Your Engagement Ratio?* Available at www.gallup.com/consulting/121901/Customer-Engagement-Overview-Brochure.aspx

Glavas, A., & Godwin, L. N. (2013). Is the Perception of 'Goodness' Good Enough? Exploring the Relationship Between Perceived Corporate Social Responsibility and Employee Organizational Identification. *Journal of Business Ethics*, 114(1), 15–27. 10.1007/s10551-012-1323-5

He, H., & Sutunyarak, C. (2024). Exploring the Impact of Perceived Corporate Social Responsibility on Employee Innovative Behaviour: The Mediating Role of Organizational Commitment. *Kurdish Studies*, 12(1), 3384–3407.

Hornsey, M. J. (2008). Social identity theory and self-categorization theory: A historical review. *Social and Personality Psychology Compass*, 2(1), 204–222. 10.1111/j.1751-9004.2007.00066.x

Hsieh, S. H., & Chang, A. (2016). The psychological mechanism of brand co-creation engagement. *Journal of Interactive Marketing*, 33, 13–26. 10.1016/j.intmar.2015.10.001

Jones, D. A., Willness, C. R., & Madey, S. (2014). Why Are Job Seekers Attracted by Corporate Social Performance? Experimental and Field Tests of Three Signal-Based Mechanisms. *Academy of Management Journal*, 57(2), 383–404. 10.5465/amj.2011.0848

Kim, H. L., Lee, Y., & Jeong, C. (2020). Effects of CSR on Employee Motivation and Service Performance in the Hotel Industry. *International Journal of Hospitality Management*, 88, 102–127.

Kumar, V., & Pansari, A. (2016). Competitive advantage through engagement. *JMR, Journal of Marketing Research*, 53(4), 497–514. 10.1509/jmr.15.0044

Laroche, M., Bergeron, J., & Barbaro-Forleo, G. (2001). Targeting Consumers Who Are Willing to pay more for Environmentally-Friendly Products. *Journal of Consumer Marketing*, 18(6), 503–520. 10.1108/EUM0000000006155

Leckie, C., Nyadzayo, M. W., & Johnson, L. W. (2016). Antecedents of consumer brand engagement and brand loyalty. *Journal of Marketing Management*, 32(5-6), 558–578. 10.1080/0267257X.2015.1131735

Lichtenstein, D. R., Drumwright, M. E., & Braig, B. M. (2004). The Effect of Corporate Social Responsibility on Customer Donations to Corporate-Supported Nonprofits. *Journal of Marketing*, 68(4), 16–32. 10.1509/jmkg.68.4.16.42726

Liu, W., & Aaker, J. (2008). The happiness of giving: The time-ask effect. *The Journal of Consumer Research*, 35(3), 543–557. 10.1086/588699

Maignan, I., & Ferrell, O. (2004). Corporate social responsibility and marketing: An integrative framework. *Journal of the Academy of Marketing Science*, 32(1), 3–19. 10.1177/0092070303258971

Martínez, P., & del Bosque, I. R. (2013). CSR and customer loyalty: The roles of trust, customer identification with the company and satisfaction. *International Journal of Hospitality Management*, 35, 89–99. 10.1016/j.ijhm.2013.05.009

Morgan, R. M., & Hunt, S. D. (1994). The commitment-trust theory of relationship marketing. *Journal of Marketing*, 58(3), 20–38. 10.1177/002224299405800302

Palmatier, R. W., Dant, R. P., Grewal, D., & Evans, K. R. (2006). Factors influencing the effectiveness of relationship marketing: A meta-analysis. *Journal of Marketing*, 70(4), 136–153. 10.1509/jmkg.70.4.136

Pansari, A., & Kumar, V. (2017). Employees' engagement: The construct, antecedents, and consequences. *Journal of the Academy of Marketing Science*, 45(3), 294–311. 10.1007/s11747-016-0485-6

Pérez, A., & Del Bosque, I. R. (2015). An integrative framework to understand how CSR affects customer loyalty through identification, emotions and satisfaction. *Journal of Business Ethics*, 129(3), 571–584. 10.1007/s10551-014-2177-9

Pivato, S., Misani, N., & Tencati, A. (2008). The impact of corporate social responsibility on consumer trust: The case of organic food. *Bus. Ethics. Business Ethics (Oxford, England)*, 17(1), 3–12. 10.1111/j.1467-8608.2008.00515.x

Roberts, J. A. (1993). Sex differences in socially responsible consumers' behavior. *Psychological Reports*, 73(1), 139–148. 10.2466/pr0.1993.73.1.139

Romani, S., Grappi, S., & Bagozzi, R. P. (2013). Explaining consumer reactions to corporate social responsibility: The role of gratitude and altruistic values. *Journal of Business Ethics*, 114(2), 193–206. 10.1007/s10551-012-1337-z

Roy, T. (2024). "We do care": The effects of perceived CSR on employee identification - empirical findings from a developing country. *Society and Business Review*, 19(1), 72–96. 10.1108/SBR-06-2021-0091

Saks, A. M., & Gruman, J. C. (2024). *Employee engagement: Antecedents and consequences* (2nd ed.). Edward Elgar Publishing.

Sashi, C. (2012). Customer engagement, buyer-seller relationships, and social media. *Management Decision*, 50(2), 253–272. 10.1108/00251741211203551

Sen, S., & Bhattacharya, C. B. (2001). Does doing good always lead to doing better? Consumer reactions to corporate social responsibility. *JMR, Journal of Marketing Research*, 38(2), 225–243. 10.1509/jmkr.38.2.225.18838

Van den Broek, J. D., Bakker, A. B., & De Boer, E. (2013). Current trends in employee engagement: A critical review of quantitative research. *Journal of Vocational Behavior*, 82(1), 1–10.

Van Doorn, J., Lemon, K. N., Mittal, V., Nass, S., Pick, D., Pirner, P., & Verhoef, P. C. (2010). Customer engagement behavior: Theoretical foundations and research directions. *Journal of Service Research*, 13(3), 253–266. 10.1177/1094670510375599

Van Doorn, J., Lemon, K. N., Mittal, V., Nass, S., Pick, D., Pirner, P., & Verhoef, P. C. (2010). Customer engagement behavior: Theoretical foundations and research directions. *Journal of Service Research*, 13(3), 253–266. 10.1177/1094670510375599

Varadarajan, R. P., & Menon, A. (1988). Cause-related marketing: A coalignment of marketing strategy and corporate philanthropy. *Journal of Marketing*, 52(3), 58–74. 10.1177/002224298805200306

Verleye, K., Gemmel, P., & Rangarajan, D. (2014). Managing engagement behaviors in a network of customers and stakeholders: Evidence from the nursing home sector. *Journal of Service Research*, 17(1), 68–84. 10.1177/1094670513494015

Villamor, G. B., & Wallace, L. (2024). Corporate social responsibility: Current state and future opportunities in the forest sector. *Corporate Social Responsibility and Environmental Management*, csr.2743. 10.1002/csr.2743

Vivek, S. D., Beatty, S. E., & Morgan, R. M. (2012). Customer engagement: Exploring customer relationships beyond purchase. *Journal of Marketing Theory and Practice*, 20(2), 122–146. 10.2753/MTP1069-6679200201

Vivek, S. D., Chandrasekhar, C. B., & Patnaik, S. (2012). The role of leadership styles in employee engagement. *The Journal of Applied Management and Entrepreneurship*, 17(2), 101–116.

Vlachos, P. A. (2012). Corporate social performance and consumer-retailer emotional attachment: The moderating role of individual traits. *European Journal of Marketing*, 46(11/12), 1559–1580. 10.1108/03090561211259989

Wang, H., Choi, J., & Li, J. (2008). Too little or too much? Untangling the relationship between corporate philanthropy and firm financial performance. *Organization Science*, 19(1), 143–159. 10.1287/orsc.1070.0271

Webb, D. J., Mohr, L. A., & Harris, K. E. (2008). A re-examination of socially responsible consumption and its measurement. *Journal of Business Research*, 61(2), 91–98. 10.1016/j.jbusres.2007.05.007

Webster, F. E.Jr. (1975). Determining the characteristics of the socially conscious consumer. *The Journal of Consumer Research*, 2(3), 188–196. 10.1086/208631

Zainol, Z., Omar, N. A., Osman, J., & Habidin, N. F. (2016). The Effect of Customer–Brand Relationship Investments 'Dimensions on Customer Engagement in Emerging Markets. *Journal of Relationship Marketing*, 15(3), 172–19. 10.1080/15332667.2016.1209051

Chapter 15
Financial Management Degree for Innovation–Driven Business:
Its Challenges and Prospects

Volha Rudkouskaya
http://orcid.org/0000-0002-0277-0741
Belarus State Economic University, Belarus

Firdous Ahmad Malik
https://orcid.org/0000-0002-7815-0143
University of People, USA

ABSTRACT

In today's rapidly evolving business landscape, where innovation is a key driver of success, the role of financial management is becoming increasingly crucial. This chapter delves into the unique challenges faced by financial managers in innovation-driven businesses, such as navigating uncertain market conditions, managing risk in high-growth environments, and allocating resources to support innovation initiatives. Despite these challenges, the prospects for individuals with a financial management degree in innovation-driven businesses are promising. Financial managers can play a pivotal role in driving innovation, fostering growth, and ensuring long-term sustainability. By understanding the specific financial needs and requirements of innovation-driven businesses, financial managers can contribute significantly to the success and competitiveness of their organizations. This chapter highlights the importance of a financial management degree in equipping professionals with the tools and expertise needed to thrive in the dynamic and fast-paced world of innovation-driven businesses.

DOI: 10.4018/979-8-3693-3096-8.ch015

1. INTRODUCTION

In today's rapidly changing business landscape, innovation has become a key driver of success for organizations across industries. As businesses strive to stay competitive and relevant in the market, the role of financial management in supporting and driving innovation has gained increasing importance.

A Financial Management Degree tailored for innovation-driven businesses equips professionals with the necessary skills and knowledge to navigate the unique challenges and capitalize on the prospects presented by this dynamic environment.

According to the Smith and Jones study (2018), financial managers in innovation-driven companies face a myriad of challenges, including the need to balance short-term financial goals with long-term innovation strategies. This balancing act requires a deep understanding of the financial implications of innovation initiatives and the ability to allocate resources effectively to support these endeavors.

Furthermore, research by Brown et al. (2019) highlights the importance of risk management in innovation-driven businesses. Financial managers must navigate the inherent uncertainties and risks associated with innovation, such as market volatility and technological disruptions, while ensuring the financial stability and sustainability of the organization. A Financial Management Degree specialized for innovation-driven businesses provides professionals with the tools and techniques to assess and mitigate these risks effectively.

In addition to challenges, there are also promising prospects for individuals with a Financial Management Degree in innovation-driven businesses. A study by Johnson and Smith (2020) suggests that financial managers who possess a deep understanding of innovation processes and technologies can drive value creation and competitive advantage for their organizations. By aligning financial strategies with innovation goals, these professionals can foster a culture of creativity and entrepreneurship within the organization.

Moreover, research by Lee et al. (2021) emphasizes the role of financial management in supporting the scalability and growth of innovation-driven businesses. Financial managers play a crucial role in securing funding for innovation projects, evaluating investment opportunities, and monitoring the financial performance of these initiatives. A Financial Management Degree tailored for innovation equips professionals with the expertise to make informed financial decisions that drive sustainable growth and profitability.

By understanding the unique financial needs and requirements of innovation-driven businesses, financial managers can drive value creation, foster growth, and ensure the long-term success of their organizations.

A financial management degree equips professionals with the necessary skills to effectively manage finances in innovative business environments. Here are the key aspects in financial management degree:

-   **Financial Analysis:** Financial analysis plays a crucial role in business decision-making by providing insights into a company's financial health and performance. It helps in evaluating profitability, liquidity, solvency, and efficiency, enabling informed strategic planning and resource allocation (Brigham & Ehrhardt, 2013). By analyzing financial statements, ratios, and trends, businesses can identify strengths, weaknesses, and areas for improvement. This information is vital for investors, creditors, and stakeholders to assess the company's viability and make informed investment decisions. Moreover, financial analysis aids in setting realistic goals, monitoring progress, and ensuring compliance with regulatory requirements. Overall, it is a fundamental tool for sustainable growth and success in the competitive business landscape (Palepu, et. al, 2013).

- **Investment Management:** Investment management is crucial for businesses as it involves strategically allocating funds to maximize returns while minimizing risks. By effectively managing investments in various assets such as stocks, bonds, and real estate, businesses can generate income, build wealth, and achieve long-term financial goals (Bodie & Marcus, 2018). It also helps in diversifying portfolios to spread risk and adapt to market fluctuations. Proper investment management enhances financial stability, supports expansion opportunities, and ensures sustainable growth (Fabozzi & Markowitz, 2011).

- **Risk Assessment:** Risk assessment is vital for innovative businesses as it helps identify potential threats and opportunities associated with new ventures. By evaluating and mitigating risks, companies can make informed decisions, allocate resources effectively, and enhance the success rate of innovative projects. Understanding the risks involved in implementing new ideas allows businesses to proactively manage uncertainties, adapt to changing market conditions, and maintain a competitive edge (Hillson & Murray-Webster, 2017). Through thorough risk assessment, businesses can minimize potential losses, optimize returns on investment, and foster a culture of innovation.

- **Corporate Finance:** Corporate finance plays a pivotal role in the success and sustainability of businesses by managing financial resources efficiently. It involves making strategic decisions related to funding, investment, and capital structure to maximize shareholder value (Berk & DeMarzo, 2016). Through corporate finance, companies can optimize their capital allocation, assess investment opportunities, and enhance profitability. Effective financial management ensures liquidity, solvency, and long-term growth, enabling businesses to navigate economic challenges and seize opportunities for expansion (Ross, et.al, 2016).

- **Cost control and Budgeting:** Budgeting is crucial for innovation-driven businesses as it provides a structured framework for allocating financial resources towards research, development, and implementation of new ideas. By setting aside funds specifically for innovation, companies can foster creativity, experimentation, and technological advancements (Palepu, et.al, 2013). A well-planned budget ensures that resources are utilized efficiently, risks are managed effectively, and innovation projects are aligned with strategic goals. Through budgeting, businesses can prioritize innovation initiatives, track performance metrics, and measure the return on investment in innovation (Kuczmarski & Kuczmarski, 2010).

- **Financial Reporting:** Mastering the art of preparing accurate financial statements is essential for innovation-driven businesses as it provides transparency and accountability in showcasing the financial performance and impact of innovation initiatives. Accurate and timely financial reports enable stakeholders to assess the effectiveness of investments in innovation, make informed decisions, and allocate resources strategically. By analyzing financial data related to innovation projects, businesses can identify trends, measure the return on investment, and adjust strategies accordingly. Effective financial reporting also enhances credibility with investors, partners, and regulators, fostering trust and confidence in the organization's innovation capabilities (Ittner, & Larcker, 2003).

- **Tax Planning:** Tax liabilities minimization for individuals and businesses can help optimize financial resources, incentivize innovation activities, and maximize tax benefits. By strategically planning for taxes, businesses can take advantage of various incentives, credits, and deductions specifically designed to support innovation and research and development efforts. Effective tax planning can reduce the overall tax burden, improve cash flow, and enhance profitability, allowing companies to reinvest savings into further innovation initiatives (Hasseldine & Li, 2017).

- **Strategic Financial Planning:** Developing long-term financial strategies to achieve organizational goals is essential as it aligns financial goals with innovation objectives, ensuring sustainable growth and competitive advantage. By integrating financial strategies with innovation initiatives, businesses can allocate resources effectively, manage risks, and capitalize on opportunities for growth (Dyreng, et.al, 2008). Strategic financial planning enables businesses to forecast future financial needs, evaluate investment options, and prioritize innovation projects that offer the highest potential return on investment (Kaplan & Norton, 2001). This approach fosters a culture of innovation, enhances financial performance, and positions the business for long-term success in dynamic markets.

- **Ethical Considerations:** It is essential for companies to prioritize ethical behavior to maintain trust with stakeholders and uphold their reputation. When making financial decisions, businesses must consider the impact on various stakeholders, such as employees, customers, and the community. Transparency, honesty, and fairness should guide financial decision-making processes to ensure that all parties involved are treated ethically (Crane & Matten, 2016).

- **Technology Integration:** By leveraging advanced tools and software, companies can streamline financial processes, improve decision-making, and drive sustainable growth. Automation of tasks such as budgeting, forecasting, and reporting reduces manual errors and increases efficiency. This allows financial teams to focus on strategic analysis and planning, leading to better insights and informed decisions (Simons, 2013).

Furthermore, technology integration enables real-time monitoring of financial data, providing businesses with accurate and up-to-date information to adapt quickly to market changes. Cloud-based solutions enhance collaboration among teams, regardless of geographical locations, fostering innovation and creativity. Implementing robust cybersecurity measures ensures the protection of sensitive financial information, safeguarding the business from cyber threats (Prasad & Green, 2015).

2 FINANCIAL MANAGEMENT EDUCATION: CONCEPT AND CONTEXT

2.1 Historical Context and Evolution of Financial Management Education

Financial management education has evolved significantly over the years, adapting to changes in the global economy, technological advancements, and shifting industry trends. In the past, financial management education was primarily focused on traditional accounting principles and basic financial concepts.

Historical outlook. The first mention of a financial degree (in our current understanding) in the world dates back to the establishment of the Wharton School of the University of Pennsylvania in the United States in 1881. At the same time, the roots of financial education are going far in the past.

During the 17th century in Europe, the field of financial management education was still in its early stages of development. The concept of modern finance as we know it today was just beginning to take shape, and formal education in financial management was limited. However, there were some key developments during this period that laid the foundation for future advancements in financial education.

One of the notable events in the 17th century that influenced financial management education was the establishment of the first modern stock exchange in Amsterdam in 1602. The Amsterdam Stock Exchange, known as the Beurs van Hendrick de Keyser, played a crucial role in the development of financial markets and investment practices. This early form of organized trading provided a platform for investors to buy and sell shares of joint-stock companies, paving the way for the growth of capital markets in Europe.

Another important aspect of financial management education in the 17th century was the emergence of prominent financial thinkers and theorists who contributed to the understanding of economic principles and financial practices. One such figure was Richard Cantillon, an Irish-French economist and author of the "Essay on the Nature of Trade in General" (1755). Cantillon's work laid the groundwork for modern economic theory and provided insights into the functioning of markets and the role of entrepreneurship in economic development.

In terms of formal education, universities in Europe began to offer courses in accounting and finance during the 17th century, although the curriculum was still relatively basic compared to modern standards. Students interested in financial management would study topics such as bookkeeping, arithmetic, and basic financial principles to prepare for careers in banking, trade, and commerce.

Overall, the 17th century marked a period of transition and growth in financial management education in Europe. While formal education in finance was limited compared to later centuries, the establishment of stock exchanges, the contributions of economic theorists, and the early development of financial markets all played a role in shaping the future of financial education.

During the 18th century, the field of financial management education was still in its infancy compared to today's standards. The concept of formal education in financial management as we know it today was not widespread during this period. However, there were significant developments in economic theory and financial practices that laid the groundwork for future advancements in the field.

One notable figure in the 18th century who made significant contributions to economic theory and financial management was Adam Smith. Smith, a Scottish economist and philosopher, published his seminal work "The Wealth of Nations" in 1776. In this book, Smith discussed the principles of free-market economics, division of labor, and the role of government in regulating economic activities. His ideas on the invisible hand and the importance of self-interest in driving economic growth had a profound impact on the development of modern financial management theories.

In terms of formal education, universities in Europe, particularly in countries like England, France, and Germany, began to offer courses in economics and finance during the 18th century. These courses often focused on topics such as trade, banking, and public finance, laying the foundation for future financial management education programs.

One example of an institution that played a role in financial education during this period was the University of Edinburgh in Scotland. The university offered courses in political economy, which encompassed topics related to finance and economic policy. Scholars like Adam Smith, who was a professor at the university, contributed to the development of economic thought and financial management principles.

In the 19th century, the field of Financial Management Education underwent significant developments that laid the foundation for modern financial education practices. During this time, the Industrial Revolution was in full swing, leading to rapid economic growth and the emergence of new financial institutions and practices. As a result, the need for individuals with specialized knowledge in financial management became increasingly apparent.

One of the key developments in financial management education during the 19th century was the establishment of business schools and universities offering courses in finance and accounting. These institutions provided students with the theoretical knowledge and practical skills needed to succeed in the rapidly evolving financial landscape. For example, the Wharton School of the University of Pennsylvania, founded in 1881, is widely regarded as the first business school in the United States and played a crucial role in shaping modern financial education.

Furthermore, the 19th century witnessed the rise of professional organizations and societies dedicated to promoting excellence in financial management. These organizations, such as the American Finance Association founded in 1939, provided a platform for professionals to exchange ideas, conduct research, and establish industry standards.

Overall, the 19th century was a pivotal period in the development of financial management education, laying the groundwork for the sophisticated financial education programs and practices that exist today. The establishment of business schools, the publication of influential works, and the formation of professional organizations all contributed to the professionalization of financial management and the cultivation of a skilled workforce capable of navigating the complexities of the modern financial world.

The main stages of modern world financial education formation can be summarized as follows:

1. Early 20th century: The first formal financial education programs began to emerge, focusing on basic financial concepts and skills.
2. 1940s-1960s: Financial education gained more recognition and was integrated into school curriculums in some countries.
3. 1970s-1990s: The rise of personal finance books, seminars, and workshops contributed to a growing interest in financial education among the general public. The 1980s saw a significant shift in financial management education with the introduction of computer technology and quantitative analysis tools. This led to the development of new courses in financial modeling, financial engineering, and financial derivatives.
4. 2000s-present: The digital age has revolutionized financial education, with online resources, apps, and platforms making it more accessible than ever before.

Today, financial management education covers a wide range of topics, including financial planning, investment management, risk management, and financial analysis. Students can pursue degrees in finance at the undergraduate and graduate levels, as well as professional certifications such as the Chartered Financial Analyst (CFA) designation.

Overall, the history of financial management education reflects the changing needs of the financial industry and the increasing importance of financial literacy in today's global economy both on the global and domestic levels.

2.2 Importance of Financial Management Degree on the Global and Domestic Levels

Financial management plays a crucial role in both international and domestic levels, as it involves the planning, organizing, directing, and controlling of financial activities within an organization. A financial management degree equips individuals with the necessary skills and knowledge to effectively manage finances, make informed decisions, and drive business growth.

On an international level, financial management is essential for multinational corporations operating in various countries. It helps in managing currency risks, navigating complex regulatory environments, and optimizing financial performance across different markets. A financial management degree provides professionals with a global perspective and the ability to adapt to diverse economic conditions.

At a domestic level, financial management is vital for businesses of all sizes to ensure sustainable growth and profitability. It involves budgeting, forecasting, financial analysis, and risk management to make strategic decisions that impact the organization's success. A financial management degree prepares individuals to handle financial challenges, drive innovation, and create value for stakeholders.

3. THE NEXUS BETWEEN FINANCIAL MANAGEMENT EDUCATION AND SUSTAINABLE DEVELOPMENT

3.1 Exploration of the Relationship Between Financial Management Education and Sustainable Development Goals

Financial management education plays a crucial role in promoting sustainable development by integrating principles of environmental, social, and governance (ESG) factors into financial decision-making. By incorporating sustainability concepts into financial practices, professionals can contribute to long-term value creation, risk mitigation, and ethical decision-making. This nexus highlights the importance of preparing future leaders with the knowledge and skills to drive positive change and address global challenges through sustainable financial management practices.

Sustainable development refers to meeting the needs of the present without compromising the ability of future generations to meet their own needs. It encompasses economic, social, and environmental dimensions, emphasizing the interconnectedness of these aspects. Financial management education plays a crucial role in advancing sustainable development by equipping individuals with the knowledge and skills to make informed financial decisions that consider these interconnected dimensions.

Financial management education also plays a role in promoting responsible investment practices. Responsible investing involves considering ESG factors when making investment decisions, with the goal of generating positive social and environmental impacts alongside financial returns. By educating individuals on responsible investment practices, financial management education can help drive capital towards sustainable and socially responsible projects.

Furthermore, financial management education can help individuals understand the importance of long-term value creation and risk management. Sustainable development requires a focus on long-term value creation rather than short-term gains. By incorporating sustainability principles into financial management practices, individuals can better assess and manage risks associated with environmental, social, and governance issues, ultimately leading to more resilient and sustainable financial systems.

In addition to financial decision-making, financial management education can also promote ethical leadership and corporate governance practices. Ethical leadership involves making decisions that consider the interests of all stakeholders, including employees, customers, communities, and the environment. By instilling ethical values in future financial leaders, financial management education can help create a culture of responsible and sustainable business practices.

SDG 1: No Poverty. SDG 1 aims to end poverty in all its forms by 2030, ensuring that all individuals have equal access to resources, opportunities, and basic services. A financial management degree equips individuals with the knowledge and skills necessary to address economic challenges, and create sustainable economic growth that can help lift people out of poverty. One key aspect of the relationship between a financial management degree and SDG 1 is the focus on economic empowerment. By understanding financial principles, individuals with a financial management degree can help empower marginalized communities and individuals living in poverty by providing them with access to financial resources, tools, and opportunities. This empowerment can enable individuals to start businesses, invest in education and healthcare, and build financial resilience, ultimately helping to break the cycle of poverty.

Financial management education also plays a crucial role in promoting financial inclusion, which is essential for achieving SDG 1. Financial inclusion refers to ensuring that all individuals, regardless of their income level, have access to affordable and appropriate financial services. Individuals with a financial management degree can work towards expanding financial services to underserved populations, promoting savings, credit, insurance, and other financial products that can help individuals build assets, manage risks, and improve their economic well-being.

Moreover, a financial management degree can help individuals understand the importance of sustainable economic growth in addressing poverty. Sustainable economic growth involves promoting inclusive and equitable economic development that benefits all members of society. By applying financial management principles, individuals can contribute to creating economic opportunities, promoting entrepreneurship, and fostering innovation that can drive economic growth and create jobs, ultimately reducing poverty levels.

Additionally, financial management education can help individuals address systemic issues that contribute to poverty, such as income inequality and lack of access to financial resources. By understanding financial systems, policies, and practices, individuals with a financial management degree can advocate for policies that promote social equity, fair distribution of resources, and financial stability, all of which are essential for reducing poverty and achieving SDG 1.

2. SDG2: Zero Hunger: aims to end hunger, achieve food security, improve nutrition, and promote sustainable agriculture by 2030. A financial management degree plays a crucial role in contributing to the achievement of this goal by addressing economic challenges, promoting investment in agriculture, and supporting sustainable food systems.

One key aspect of the relationship between a financial management degree and SDG 2 is the role of financial management in supporting agricultural development. Financial management skills are essential for managing resources effectively, making strategic investment decisions, and ensuring the financial sustainability of agricultural projects. Individuals with a financial management degree can help farmers and agricultural businesses access capital, manage risks, and improve productivity, ultimately contributing to food security and sustainable agriculture.

Sustainable food systems involve promoting environmentally friendly agricultural practices, reducing food waste, and ensuring equitable access to nutritious food for all. By applying financial management principles, individuals can support initiatives that promote sustainable agriculture, improve food distribution networks, and address food insecurity in vulnerable communities.

3. SDG8: Decent Work and Economic Growth: aims to promote sustained, inclusive, and sustainable economic growth, full and productive employment, and decent work for all. One of the key ways in which financial management contributes to SDG8 is through its role in promoting economic growth. By effectively managing financial resources, organizations can invest in new projects, expand their operations, and create job opportunities for individuals. This, in turn, helps to stimulate economic growth, increase productivity, and create a more prosperous society.

Additionally, financial management is essential for promoting decent work and employment opportunities. By ensuring that organizations have the financial resources needed to pay fair wages, provide benefits, and create a safe working environment, financial managers can help to promote decent work for all individuals. This includes ensuring that workers have access to training and development opportunities, as well as promoting diversity and inclusion in the workplace.

Furthermore, financial management plays a critical role in promoting sustainable economic growth. By making strategic investment decisions that take into account environmental and social factors, financial managers can help to ensure that economic growth is sustainable in the long term. This includes investing in renewable energy projects, promoting responsible business practices, and supporting initiatives that promote social inclusion and equality.

4. SDG9: Industry, Innovation and Infrastructure: Financial management skills are essential for effectively managing the financial resources required to support investments in infrastructure development and innovation within industries. By understanding financial principles, individuals with a financial management degree can help organizations secure funding for infrastructure projects, such as building sustainable transportation systems or upgrading technology in industries. Additionally, financial managers can support innovation by allocating resources towards research and development initiatives that drive technological advancements and improve industrial processes.

Case study: Belzarubezhstroy's experience demonstrates how a financial management degree can be instrumental in driving sustainable development initiatives that align with SDG9. Belzarubezhstroy is a renewable energy company that specializes in developing solar energy projects in emerging markets. The company is committed to promoting sustainable energy solutions and reducing carbon emissions to combat climate change. With the goal of expanding its operations and contributing to Sustainable Development Goal 9: Industry, Innovation, and Infrastructure, Belzarubezhstroy sought to secure financing for a new solar energy project in a developing country and appointed a team of financial managers with expertise in project finance and sustainable investments to lead the financing efforts. The financial managers conducted a thorough financial analysis to assess the feasibility of the project, taking into account factors such as construction costs, operational expenses, revenue projections, and potential risks.

The financial managers also explored various financing options, including debt financing, equity investments, and impact investing. The project involved the construction of a solar farm that would generate clean energy to power local communities, reduce reliance on fossil fuels, and create job opportunities in the region. They leveraged their financial management skills to structure a financing package that aligned with the company's sustainability goals and attracted investors interested in supporting renewable energy projects.

The financing package included a combination of debt financing from impact investors, equity investments from renewable energy funds, and grants from development organizations. The financial managers negotiated favorable terms that allowed Belzarubezhstroy to access the necessary capital to develop the project while ensuring a positive impact on the local economy and environment. The solar energy project not only contributed to reducing carbon emissions and increasing access to clean energy but also created opportunities for economic development and job creation in the community.

5. SDG12: Responsible Consumption and Production: A degree in financial management equips individuals with the knowledge and skills to make informed decisions regarding resource allocation, investment strategies, and financial planning. These skills are essential in driving sustainable practices within organizations and promoting responsible consumption and production patterns.

Financial management professionals play a key role in assessing the financial implications of sustainable initiatives, such as implementing green technologies, reducing waste, and promoting ethical sourcing practices. By incorporating environmental, social, and governance (ESG) factors into financial decision-making, they can help organizations align their financial goals with sustainable development objectives.

Furthermore, financial management degree holders can contribute to SDG12 by advocating for transparency and accountability in financial reporting. By ensuring that companies disclose their environmental and social impacts, financial professionals can help investors make informed decisions that support responsible consumption and production practices.

Case study: JSC «ENEF», a belarusian corporation in the consumer goods industry, recognized the importance of aligning its financial management practices with sustainable development goals, particularly SDG12: Responsible Consumption and Production. With a team of financial management professionals holding degrees in finance and accounting, the company embarked on a journey to integrate sustainability principles into its investment strategy.

The financial management team conducted a thorough analysis of the environmental and social impacts of its operations, supply chain, and products. They identified areas where the company could improve its responsible consumption and production practices, such as reducing waste, promoting energy efficiency, and sourcing ethically produced materials.

Using their financial expertise, the team developed a sustainable investment strategy that prioritized investments in green technologies, sustainable supply chain practices, and social impact initiatives. They conducted financial modeling to assess the long-term financial implications of these investments and demonstrated that sustainable practices could lead to cost savings, increased efficiency, and enhanced brand reputation.

Through their sustainable investment strategy, JSC «ENEF» was able to reduce its carbon footprint, minimize waste generation, and promote responsible consumption and production throughout its value chain. The financial management team played a crucial role in monitoring and evaluating the financial performance of these initiatives, ensuring that they were aligned with the company's overall financial goals.

As a result of their efforts, JSC «ENEF» not only achieved significant cost savings and operational efficiencies but also enhanced its reputation as a socially responsible company committed to sustainable development.

6. SDG13: Climate Action: One of the key ways in which financial management education contributes to SDG13 is through the integration of environmental, social, and governance (ESG) factors into financial decision-making. Financial management professionals are trained to assess the risks and opportunities associated with climate change, such as the impact of extreme weather events on business operations or the potential for investments in renewable energy technologies. By incorporating ESG considerations into investment strategies, financial management professionals can help organizations align their financial goals with climate action objectives.

Furthermore, financial management education can empower individuals to advocate for sustainable practices within organizations and to promote transparency and accountability in climate-related financial reporting. By ensuring that companies disclose their carbon emissions, climate-related risks, and mitigation strategies, financial professionals can help investors make informed decisions that support climate action initiatives.

4. CHALLENGES AND OPPORTUNITIES IN FINANCIAL MANAGEMENT EDUCATION FOR INNOVATION-DRIVEN BUSINESS

4.1 Challenges Faced by Financial Management Education

Here are main challenges that exist in today's world system of financial education:

1. **Lack of standardized curriculum:** The absence of a uniform curriculum across institutions and programs leads to inconsistencies in the knowledge and skills imparted to students. Different institutions and programs may cover varying topics and may not always align with the current financial landscape. This lack of consistency can lead to gaps in knowledge and skills among individuals seeking financial education.
2. **Rapidly evolving financial landscape:** The constant changes in financial products, services, and technologies make it challenging for educators to keep their curriculum up-to-date and relevant. As a result, students may not be adequately prepared to navigate the complexities of modern financial markets.
3. **Engagement and interest:** Financial management education can be perceived as dry or complex, leading to disinterest among learners and hindering effective engagement with the material. Educators must find innovative ways to make financial concepts more accessible and engaging to ensure that students retain the information and apply it in real-world scenarios.
4. **Practical application:** There is often a lack of emphasis on practical application in financial education, which can limit students' ability to apply theoretical knowledge in real-world scenarios. Hands-on experience, such as managing a mock investment portfolio or creating a budget, can help reinforce concepts and improve financial literacy.
5. **Accessibility:** Not all individuals have equal access to quality financial education, whether due to financial constraints, geographic location, or lack of awareness, leading to disparities in financial literacy. This disparity can perpetuate financial inequality and hinder individuals from making sound financial decisions.
6. **Technological advancements:** The integration of technology in financial services requires educators to adapt their teaching methods to incorporate digital tools and platforms effectively.
7. **Financial inclusion:** Ensuring that marginalized populations have access to financial education is crucial for promoting financial inclusion and reducing economic disparities.
8. **Behavioral biases:** Understanding and addressing behavioral biases in financial decision-making is essential for effective financial education.

9. **Globalization:** The interconnected nature of the global economy necessitates a broader understanding of international finance and economic systems in financial education programs.
10. **Regulatory changes:** Keeping pace with evolving financial regulations and compliance requirements poses a challenge for educators in providing accurate and up-to-date information to students.

Financial management education faces several challenges in providing effective and comprehensive instruction to students and the general public. Addressing these challenges will require collaboration among educators, policymakers, and industry stakeholders to develop standardized curriculum, incorporate practical application, enhance engagement strategies, and improve accessibility. By overcoming these obstacles, financial management education can better equip individuals with the knowledge and skills needed to navigate the complexities of the financial world and make informed decisions for their financial well-being. Addressing these challenges will require collaboration among educators, policymakers, industry stakeholders, and technology providers to enhance the effectiveness and accessibility of financial education worldwide. By recognizing and overcoming these obstacles, the world system of financial education can better equip individuals with the knowledge and skills needed to navigate the complexities of the financial world and make informed decisions for their financial well-being.

4.2 Prospects for Financial Management in Innovation-Driven Businesses

Despite challenges, the prospects for financial management professionals in innovation-driven businesses are promising, as they play a vital role in driving sustainable growth and success through effective financial strategies and decision-making.

1. **Integration of Sustainable Finance:** Future financial management education will place a greater emphasis on sustainable finance, incorporating environmental, social, and governance (ESG) factors into investment decisions.
2. **Technology Integration:** Financial management education will increasingly incorporate technology-driven tools and platforms, such as artificial intelligence and blockchain, to enhance financial analysis and decision-making processes.
3. **Data Analytics Skills:** Future financial management education will focus on developing strong data analytics skills to effectively analyze and interpret financial data for informed decision-making.
4. **Global Perspective:** Financial management education will emphasize a global perspective, preparing students to navigate the complexities of international markets and regulations.
5. **Interdisciplinary Approach:** Future financial management education will adopt an interdisciplinary approach, integrating knowledge from fields such as economics, psychology, and sociology to provide a holistic understanding of financial decision-making.
6. **Ethical Considerations:** Ethics and integrity will be core components of financial management education, emphasizing the importance of responsible and ethical financial practices.
7. **Risk Management Focus:** Future financial management education will place a strong emphasis on risk management, equipping students with the skills to identify, assess, and mitigate financial risks.
8. **Specialized courses on innovation finance:** There will be a greater emphasis on specialized courses that cover topics such as venture capital, crowdfunding, and innovation funding models to cater to the unique financial needs of innovation-driven businesses.

9. **Sustainability and ESG considerations:** Education in financial management for innovation-driven businesses will incorporate sustainability and environmental, social, and governance (ESG) considerations to align financial decisions with responsible business practices.

10. **Continuous Learning and upskilling:** Lifelong learning will be emphasized in financial management education, as the field continues to evolve rapidly with changing market dynamics and technological advancements.

11. **Industry Partnerships:** Financial management education will forge stronger partnerships with industry stakeholders, providing students with real-world experiences and opportunities for practical application of knowledge. Hands-on learning experiences, such as internships, case competitions, and industry projects, will be integrated into financial management education to provide students with practical skills and exposure to real-world business scenarios.

12. **Personalized Learning:** Future financial management education will offer personalized learning experiences, tailored to individual student needs and preferences, to enhance learning outcomes and career readiness.

5. CONCLUSION

In conclusion, a financial management degree plays a vital role in fostering innovation-driven businesses. By combining financial expertise with a strategic mindset, financial management professionals can help organizations navigate the complexities of the modern business landscape and drive innovation forward. Through effective financial planning, risk management, and investment strategies, they can support the development and implementation of innovative ideas that propel businesses towards growth and success.

Furthermore, financial management professionals are well-positioned to identify opportunities for innovation, assess their financial feasibility, and allocate resources effectively to bring these ideas to fruition. Their ability to analyze data, forecast trends, and make informed decisions enables them to support innovation initiatives that have the potential to transform industries and drive competitive advantage.

In today's rapidly evolving business environment, where innovation is a key driver of success, the importance of a financial management degree cannot be overstated. By equipping individuals with the skills and knowledge to navigate the intersection of finance and innovation, a financial management degree paves the way for businesses to thrive in an increasingly competitive and dynamic marketplace. Ultimately, the role of financial management in fostering innovation-driven businesses is essential for driving growth, creating value, and staying ahead of the curve in today's fast-paced business world.

REFERENCES

Berk, J., & DeMarzo, P. (2016). *Corporate Finance*. Pearson Education.

Bodie, Z., Kane, A., & Marcus, A. J. (2018). *Investments*. McGraw-Hill Education.

Brigham, E. F., & Ehrhardt, M. C. (2013). *Financial Management: Theory & Practice*. Cengage Learning.

Brown, C. (2019). Risk Management Strategies for Innovation-Driven Businesses. *International Journal of Financial Management*, 22(4), 112–125.

Cooper, R. G. (2008). Perspective: The Stage-Gate Idea-to-Launch Process—Update, What's New, and NexGen Systems. *Journal of Product Innovation Management*, 25(3), 213–232. 10.1111/j.1540-5885.2008.00296.x

Crane, A., & Matten, D. (2016). *Business ethics: Managing corporate citizenship and sustainability in the age of globalization*. Oxford University Press.

Dyreng, S. D., Hanlon, M., & Maydew, E. L. (2008). Long-Run Corporate Tax Avoidance. *The Accounting Review*, 83(1), 61–82. 10.2308/accr.2008.83.1.61

Epstein, M. J., & Buhovac, A. R. (2014). *Making Sustainability Work: Best Practices in Managing and Measuring Corporate Social, Environmental, and Economic Impacts*. Berrett-Koehler Publishers.

Fabozzi, F. J., & Markowitz, H. M. (2011). *The Theory and Practice of Investment Management: Asset Allocation, Valuation, Portfolio Construction, and Strategies*. John Wiley & Sons. 10.1002/9781118267028

Hasseldine, J., & Li, Z. (2017). Tax Planning and Corporate Social Responsibility. *Journal of Business Ethics*, 140(2), 245–260.

Hillson, D., & Murray-Webster, R. (2017). *Understanding and Managing Risk Attitude*. Routledge. 10.4324/9781315235448

Ittner, C. D., & Larcker, D. F. (2003). Coming Up Short on Nonfinancial Performance Measurement. *Harvard Business Review*, 81(11), 88–95. 14619154

Johnson, D., & Smith, E. (2020). Value Creation through Financial Management in Innovation-Driven Businesses. *Journal of Financial Innovation*, 18(3), 76–89.

Kaplan, R. S., & Norton, D. P. (2001). *The Strategy-Focused Organization: How Balanced Scorecard Companies Thrive in the New Business Environment*. Harvard Business Press. 10.1108/sl.2001.26129cab.002

Kuczmarski, T. D., & Kuczmarski, S. J. (2010). *Innovating the Corporation: Creating Value for Customers and Shareholders*. Business Expert Press.

Lee, F. (2021). Financial Management for Scalability and Growth in Innovation-Driven Businesses. *Journal of Innovation and Finance*, 25(1), 30–42.

Lozano, R. (2018). *Sustainability in Higher Education: A Call to Action*. Routledge.

March, J. G. (1991). Exploration and Exploitation in Organizational Learning. *Organization Science*, 2(1), 71–87. 10.1287/orsc.2.1.71

Palepu, K. G., Healy, P. M., & Peek, E. (2013). *Business Analysis and Valuation: Using Financial Statements*. Cengage Learning.

Prasad, A., & Green, P. (2015). *Impact of Technology Integration in Finance and Accounting: A Case Study of United Technologies Corporation*. Academic Press.

Ross, S. A., Westerfield, R. W., & Jaffe, J. (2016). *Corporate Finance*. McGraw-Hill Education.

Schaltegger, S., & Burritt, R. (2017). *Contemporary Environmental Accounting: Issues, Concepts and Practice*. Routledge. 10.4324/9781351282529

Simons, R. (2013). *Levers of Control: How Managers Use Innovative Control Systems to Drive Strategic Renewal*. Harvard Business Press.

Smith, A., & Jones, B. (2018). Financial Management Challenges in Innovation-Driven Businesses. *Journal of Innovation Finance*, 15(2), 45–58.

Chapter 16
Smart Cities:
Transforming Indian Cities Into Global Destinations

Taran Kaur
https://orcid.org/0000-0002-8527-9471
IILM Institute for Higher Education, India

Firdous Ahmad Malik
https://orcid.org/0000-0002-7815-0143
University of People, USA

Ivneet Kaur Walia
https://orcid.org/0009-0006-0215-1197
Rajiv Gandhi National University of Law, India

ABSTRACT

To provide people with a high-quality living, smart cities are modern urban conceptions. To achieve clever and sustainable practices, different technologies are conceptually grouped to form smart cities. As embodied by the four pillars of comprehensive development—institutional, physical, social, and economic infrastructure—urban planners' ultimate goal is to build the entire urban environment. The findings suggested various methods such as redevelopment, retrofitting, megaprojects, greenfield development, and unique projects for area-based development for projects having more than 500, 50, and 250 acres. Moreover, the pan development proposal is for the whole of the city by involving smart solutions to improve the infrastructure in cities. This study examines the various approaches towards smart cities in India. In addition to them, the current state and difficulties surrounding smart cities in India are also covered.

1. INTRODUCTION

The majority of Indian cities are distinguished by severe spatial, economic, and social dichotomies. In contrast, the conceptualization of the urban environment remains increasingly exclusive, disregarding or intensifying the myriad contradictions that have become intrinsic to our urban landscapes (Ahmed et al.,

DOI: 10.4018/979-8-3693-3096-8.ch016

2019). The marginalization and invisibility of the impoverished, as well as their increasing segregation and ghettoization, are consequences of state and non-state actors' acts of commission and omission (Agarwal, 2021). The prevalent paradigm of urbanization, which acknowledges the 'inevitability of urbanization' without scrutinizing its structural underpinnings or ramifications on the global ecosystem, has yielded several undesirable outcomes, including an increase in forced evictions, homelessness, inequality, and poverty. Conversely, state and policy interventions persist in being symptomatic as opposed to comprehensive and long-lasting. This exclusionary vision appears to be reinforced by the policy directives of the India Smart Cities Mission. According to a research report by Deloitte India (2019), the Smart Cities mission was officially launched in June 2015 with the purported objective of developing one hundred "smart cities" throughout the nation. The mission will reach its five-year milestone on June 25, 2020. Ever since its inception, it has generated both anticipation and doubt, skepticism and hope, uncertainty and optimism, with equal attention devoted to contemplating its possibilities and obstacles.

As per the Smart Cities Council, a smart city is an area that is improved in terms of sustainability, workability, and livability through the use of information and communications technology (ICT). "When investments in human and social capital, traditional (transport) and modern (ICT) communication infrastructure fuel sustainable economic growth and a high quality of life, while participatory government ensures prudent management of natural resources," according to Gupta and Singh (2020). This comprehensive definition effectively reconciles various economic and social requirements with the needs associated with urban development, while also including peripheral and underdeveloped cities. According to the website of the Business Dictionary, a developed urban area achieves a high standard of living and sustainable economic growth by excelling in several critical domains, including the economy, mobility, environment, people, and government.

Hence, how Smart Cities are conceptualized differs across cities and nations, contingent upon factors such as the degree of progress, propensity for transformation and adjustment, available resources, and the ambitions of the inhabitants of each locale (Jain, 2021). In developed nations, a smart city is an area where sustainable development is integrated with the enhancement of existing infrastructure via the application of information technology. Nevertheless, a distinct approach is taken within the Indian context. Given the prevalence of inadequate governance, institutional structures, and fundamental infrastructure in numerous cities, smart city endeavors will need to prioritize the provision of IT-enabled solutions to meet these requirements (Joshi & Rao, 2018).

As per the definition provided by the Ministry of Urban Development, a smart city is one in which urban planners strive to develop the entirety of the urban ecosystem—encompassing social, economic, physical, and institutional infrastructure—to meet the aspirations and requirements of the populace (Ministry of Housing and Urban Affairs, 2022). The physical infrastructure comprises high-speed broadband connectivity, multimodal public transportation, a power supply that is operational around the clock, and solid and liquid waste management systems that produce zero emissions. Inclusive development: affordable housing and night shelters; healthcare in all neighborhoods: telemedicine; entertainment and recreational facilities; cultural, athletic, and fitness centers; and social infrastructure comprise the social infrastructure. Skill development centers, incubators, trade facilitation and logistics centers, SME clusters, institutional finance/banking, working women's hostels, and creches comprise the economic infrastructure. Minimum governance, maximum governance, e-governance (online public service delivery 24/7), ease of doing business, citizen engagement, safety, security, enforcement, transparency and accountability, disaster management, and resilience are all components of the institutional infrastructure. Consequently, an inference that can be made from the Indian context is that "The overarching concept of smart cities is to enhance the quality of life for urban residents through the improvement of infrastructure and governance, while simultaneously implementing intelligent solutions to achieve sustainable development."

In 2015, the Smart Cities Mission was initiated by the Government of India to promote inclusive and sustainable urban development via the implementation of intelligent solutions (Kumar & Singh, 2020). An essential element of this undertaking is the area-based development strategy, which identifies and transforms into smart cities entire geographic regions within cities. The Smart Cities Mission (SCM) Guidelines, which dictated the process of developing Smart City Proposals, stipulated that every municipality must submit a proposal for a designated region under the heading Area Based Development and Pan City Initiative, incorporating a pan-city component with "smart solutions." These solutions encompass electronic service delivery, renewable energy sources, greenfield development, retrofitting, redevelopment, or a combination of these approaches. As stated by Kumar and Agarwal (2020), the implementation of an area-based development strategy facilitates focused interventions in urban services and infrastructure, which promotes economic expansion and resource optimization.

Moreover, Singh and Singh (2020) underscore the importance of smart city development at the area level in India, placing particular emphasis on the necessity of implementing context-specific solutions to tackle isolated urban issues. The authors contend that the implementation of an area-based approach in specific city zones enables the seamless incorporation of technology into urban governance, resulting in enhanced livability, sustainability, and economic productivity. Sharma and Gupta (2019) investigated the viability of redevelopment as a strategy to rejuvenate smart city urban areas in India that surpass 500 acres. This course investigates case studies and optimal strategies for optimizing land use and repurposing existing infrastructure to address the changing demands of urban populations. An examination of retrofitting as a methodology for undertakings spanning from 50 to 250 acres is conducted by Patel et al. (2020). The authors evaluate the viability and efficacy of improving urban services and infrastructure in well-established urban regions. Retrofitting strategies to enhance the resilience, sustainability, and viability of Indian cities are discussed in this article. Khan and Das (2021) conducted an analysis of the impetuses, obstacles, and results of over 500-acre megaprojects within smart cities in India, with a specific emphasis on such endeavors. They emphasize the significance of risk management, stakeholder engagement, and integrated planning in guaranteeing the success of megaprojects. Gupta and Jain (2022) conducted an assessment of greenfield development as a strategy for urban expansion, delving into the economic, social, and environmental consequences associated with the establishment of new cities or satellite towns. Approaches to fostering inclusive growth, sustainable land use, and biodiversity conservation in greenfield developments are examined in this article. In their investigation of innovative strategies for urban development, Mishra and Tiwari (2022) examine distinctive initiatives in Indian smart cities, including the preservation of cultural districts and waterfronts. This paper examines how placemaking, heritage preservation, and creativity contribute to the development of resilient and dynamic urban communities.

Notwithstanding the notable advancements achieved thus far in the advancement of smart cities in India, several obstacles continue to endure. As per the Ministry of Housing and Urban Affairs, Government of India (2022), the Smart Cities Mission has designated a cumulative count of one hundred smart cities for development as of March 2024. These urban areas have experienced progress in the domains of transportation, governance, technology integration, and infrastructure, thus establishing the foundation for a more intelligent and effective future for cities. On the contrary, Menon and Khanna (2018) highlight several obstacles that impede the execution of smart city initiatives in India. These include financial limitations, insufficient capabilities within urban local governing bodies, and insufficient engagement from the public. The authors emphasize the criticality of establishing innovative financing mechanisms and strengthening public-private partnerships to surmount these challenges and guarantee the long-term viability of smart city initiatives. Furthermore, in the realm of smart city development, the complexities inherent in integrating diverse stakeholders and harmonizing multiple agendas are underscored in a 2017 research report by the McKinsey Global Institute. They emphasize the necessity of adopting a comprehensive strategy that takes into account the environmental, social, and economic aspects of urban development, in addition to guaranteeing a fair allocation of intelligent solutions among various demographic groups.

A comprehensive literature review was conducted for this study, utilizing articles from the following nine databases: Web of Science, Taylor and Francis, Emerald Insight, Scopus, Science Direct, SAGE, Wiley, and IEEE Explore. 'Smart city' and sustainable infrastructure developments' are the terms that were employed in the selection process. This paper attempts to provide an answer to the overarching research question: What is the correlation between smart cities and the concepts of sustainable infrastructure development? To investigate this matter, the purpose of this study was to assess the current state of policies and challenges regarding sustainable infrastructure development in one hundred smart cities of India, concerning four pillars (social, economic, institutional, and physical infrastructural developments). The study is founded upon a contextual analysis of online publications spanning the years 2015 to 2023, including research papers, review articles, case studies written in the relevant field, and investigated reports disseminated by the Ministries of Urban Development and Housing and Urban Affairs.

This article examines the distinguishing characteristics of smart city development policies to illuminate the strategic decisions that must be made when outlining such a plan. Based on recent smart city literature and experience, the paper begins with a review and categorization of four sustainable infrastructure development pillars with a spatial reference. Following that, a discussion of the research methodology employed for data acquisition and the study's findings ensues. In the summary section, the practical implications and limitations of the study are ultimately outlined, in addition to suggestions for future research.

2. RESEARCH METHODOLOGY

An exploratory research design is utilized in this study, specifically, the literature review method proposed by Smith (2018). The purpose of this research is to examine the existing literature on smart city concepts and sustainable infrastructure development, as well as to determine the nature of their relationship. In addition, a qualitative research methodology was employed to achieve the stated objective, consisting of a systematic review of the literature found in various periodicals, websites (Ministry of Urban Development), and TED talks delivered by philosophers and CEOs of different companies. A total of 123 works of mainstream literature were examined. Table 1 details the search strategy implemented for the systematic review of the literature. The literature review was conducted utilizing the statistical software R. The study presents an analysis of the latest scholarly articles that center on the current state and obstacles faced by smart cities. An endeavor was undertaken to generate a word cloud comprising the most commonly encountered terms associated with the development of smart cities and sustainability.

Table 1. A List of Research Publications and Online Sources – Search Strategy

Type	Filters and Strings	Search Engine	Sub-Type	Total	Share (%)	Portion (%)
Journals, Conference papers	TOPIC: Smart Cities OR Features OR Policies OR Current Status OR Challenges OR Sustainable Infrastructure OR Socio-Economic Status of Smart Cities OR Promises Vs Performance of Smart Cities OR Environmental Sustainability OR Issues in Management of Smart Cities OR Smart Governance OR Smart Solutions based on IoT OR Indicators of Smart Cities OR Success Stories of Smart Cities in India OR Review of Smart Cities Mission OR Performance Assessment of Smart Cities Period: 2015-2023	Web of Science, Taylor and Francis, Emerald Insight, Scopus, Science Direct, SAGE, Wiley, IEEE Explore, Harvard Business Review	Journals (DOCUMENT TYPE: Article OR Conference Proceedings) Review Papers and White Paper Case Studies	45 22 11	37 19 9	65

continued on following page

Table 1. Continued

Type	Filters and Strings	Search Engine	Sub-Type	Total	Share (%)	Portion (%)
Online Sources	TOPIC Smart Cities OR Features OR Policies OR Current status OR Challenges OR Sustainable Infrastructure OR Promises Vs Performance of Smart Cities OR Environmental Sustainability OR Issues in Management of Smart Cities OR Smart Governance OR Smart Solutions based on IoT OR Indicators of Smart Cities OR Success Stories of Smart Cities in India Period: 2015-2023	McKinsey, Smart Cities World, Ministry of Housing and Urban Affairs, Deloitte State of Green, Chandigarhsmartcity. In, smartcityindore.org, Smart Cities Challenges in India	Research Reports Webpages TedTalks	12 15 9	8 12 7	27
Others	TOPIC: Issues in Management of Smart Cities OR Smart Governance OR Smart Solutions based on IoT OR Indicators of Smart Cities OR Success Stories of Smart Cities in India OR Review of Smart Cities Mission OR Performance Assessment of Smart Cities Period: 2015-2023	Shodhganaga, Online Repository Science Direct, IGI Global, Google Books, Taylor and Francis, Web of Science	Theses Book Chapters	2 7	2 6	8

Note: In the above table, the percentage of sub-type of publication is reflected in the 'share' column and the percentage on the type of publication is reflected in the 'proportion' column

The literature review serves as the foundation for scholarly writing. The review process enables researchers to acquaint themselves with the texts and identify the distinguished authors who have contributed to the field (Brown & Garcia, 2019). The literature review in this study employed a systematic analysis approach (Smith & Johnson, 2020). A total of nine prominent databases were queried for articles as part of the systematic review, including Web of Science, Taylor and Francis, Emerald Insight, Scopus, Science Direct, SAGE, Wiley, and IEEE Explore. The search criteria "sustainable infrastructure developments" and "smart city" were employed. Utilizing EndNote software aided in the compilation of data. We obtained a total of 173 documents following the verification of duplicates, which comprised research reports, articles, case studies, review papers, white papers, webpages, and case studies. A total of 135 were entirely accessible in electronic format. 123 documents were selected for reading by the researchers. We must read the complete texts of 123 documents after completing the abstracts. Following the perusal of these articles, an analysis was conducted to determine which ones presented information about sustainable infrastructure developments, government policies implemented, and the present state of challenges encountered by one hundred smart cities.

A comprehensive examination of the literature review was conducted utilizing the text analytical function in R software. Given that R is an open source of data analysis, it is a practical instrument for both quantitative and qualitative research (Smith, 2018). Following the extraction of words from the text data, the R-Studio software processed a total of 23321 words, excluding stop words, vacant spaces, and special characters. The word cloud that the software attempted to generate displays the most frequently used words about the topic, as illustrated in Figure 1. A comparison was also made between the text and positive and negative words. Comparative analysis revealed that the text of the literature review contained 167 negative words and 76 positive words. These are the fifteen most frequently extracted words from the literature.

- Development
- Sustainable
- Infrastructure
- Challenges
- Implementation
- Technology

    Planning

- Connectivity
- Innovation
- Governance
- Data
- Integration
- Environment
- Spatial
- Efficiency

Figure 1. Word Cloud for most frequently used words in literature review

land
rejuvenation energy
heritagesites innovation
acquisition implementation renewable
data connectivity sustainable participation
development challenges integration
efficiency india infrastructure environment
solution green spatial governance housing
smart technology
urban cities mobility
planning

3. RESULTS AND DISCUSSION

The findings of the systematic review of literature, which comprised 123 documents, are presented in this section. The discourse encompasses bibliometric data about scholarly investigations concerning smart city government policies, the advancement of sustainable infrastructure in smart cities, and the obstacles encountered by the smart city mission. The initial segment elucidates the correlation between smart cities and pertinent government policies. In the second section, the current state of smart city development about sustainable infrastructure is discussed. The challenges and concerns encountered by the smart cities mission in India are detailed in the third section.

Convergence With Related Policies

The SCM Guidelines propose that initiatives and programs implemented by the central and state administrations be complementary. The Guidelines explicitly advocate for the integration of initiatives proposed in the Smart City Proposal with other initiatives of the central government, which comprise:

Atal Mission for Rejuvenation and Urban Transformation (AMRUT)- An urban renewal initiative that was similarly introduced in 2015, AMRUT seeks to develop and upgrade physical infrastructure in 500 cities across the nation, including but not limited to water supply, sewerage, drainage, transportation, and green spaces. AMRUT has been allocated Rs 50,000 crore by the government over five years (Agarwal, 2021). The Pradhan Mantri Awas Yojana (Housing for All–2022) is a nationwide initiative that seeks to furnish housing for individuals classified as EWS and LIG. Its objectives for urban areas are to construct 10 million houses by 2022 (Kapoor, 2017), a figure that was reduced from the initial target of 20 million houses in 2015. The "Clean India Mission" (Swachh Bharat Mission/Abhiyan) is a nationwide initiative aimed at improving sanitation and hygiene conditions in India. One of the ways this is accomplished is by constructing latrines; the goal is to eliminate open defecation in the country by 2019 (Menon, 2018). HRIDAY, an initiative from the Ministry of Housing and Urban Development (MOHUD) in 2022, is designed to promote inclusive urban planning and the preservation of heritage cities. The Digital India Programme, established by the government (MOHUD, 2022) aims to expand internet connectivity and digital access for the entire population of India.

The proposals of all "smart cities" that have been shortlisted must include a section titled "Convergence Agenda." This section should delineate the funding schemes or programs from which the initiatives seek support, as well as the projected methodology for attaining convergence.

Sustainable Infrastructure Developments

An evaluation of every Smart City Proposal indicates that the favorable aspects of sustainable infrastructure advancements primarily pertain to inventive concepts that establish technological resolutions, foster the growth of renewable energy sources, advocate for environmental sustainability, and construct the "resilience" of urban areas (Housing and Land Rights Network). A few of the most significant areas of emphasis of the chosen "smart cities" are delineated.

Renewable Energy and "Green" Solutions: This is to ensure that all shortlisted cities maintain an emphasis on renewable energy utilization. To fulfill this requirement, Bhubaneswar has introduced a "Solar City Programme." This initiative is projected to produce 11 megawatts of energy, accounting for 11% of the city's total energy usage in 2020. Similar to how Bhubaneswar has pledged to implement disaster risk reduction strategies via a 'Future Proofing Sub-Plan,' Salem has devised a plan to reduce its carbon imprint by establishing "zero-emission zones" (Joshi & Rao, 2018).

Advancements in "Smart" Technology and Governance: Numerous municipalities are emphasizing critical technologies, including light-emitting diode (LED) lighting to substitute conventional street lights and water automatic transfer machines (ATMs). A 'common mobility card' has been proposed by Bengaluru, which would enable residents to utilize all modes of public transportation without the need for currency. According to Kapoor (2017), several cities, including Visakhapatnam, Amaravati, Dehradun, and Thiruvananthapuram, have prioritized the promotion of "good governance."

Transit-oriented development: Sustainable transport alternatives have been areas of emphasis for a number of the shortlisted cities to enhance mobility. As an illustration, the proposal put forth by Ludhiana places significant importance on enhancing transportation infrastructure, encompassing modes of non-motorized transport as well. In designated locations, street redesigns will prioritize pedestrian comfort, while dedicated bicycle lanes will be constructed. Electric rickshaws are anticipated to supplant auto-rickshaws, according to the Ministry of New and Renewable Energy. Urban areas such as Bengaluru, Pune, Bhopal, and Chennai have implemented public bicycle-sharing systems to reduce traffic congestion and foster the development of a sustainable urban transportation system (Mishra & Reddy, 2018).

Tourism and Economic Development: To stimulate economic growth, municipalities like Bareilly and Moradabad have focused on revitalizing the manufacturing industry. Bareilly's primary strategic objective is to establish the city as a center for the production of Zari handicrafts, as well as Manjha and Surma crafts. In contrast, Moradabad ventures towards establishing an artisans' manufacturing base and becoming a business brand for brass. Jalandhar is oriented towards the establishment of a "sports city" as its primary objective, whereas Kota aims to develop supportive infrastructure and infrastructure for resident students attending coaching centers throughout the city (Sharma & Das, 2019).

Enhanced Housing and Infrastructure: Indore has prioritized the improvement of health accessibility through the construction of a 50-bed "smart" health facility and education by equipping all high schools with Wi-Fi connectivity, "smart" classrooms, and other necessary facilities (Mishra & Reddy, 2018). Naya Raipur has put forth a proposition to create community schools consisting of one primary, two secondary, and one school dedicated to individuals with disabilities. In contrast, the proposal for Patna centers on the improvement of health and educational infrastructure, with a specific emphasis on enhancing female school enrollment (Joshi & Rao, 2018).

Area-based Development and Pan-city Initiatives: Pune's pan-city initiatives include "less is more" solutions based on information and communications technology (ICT). Through the implementation of a variety of ICT solutions, a total of nineteen solutions based on three themes—"smart" public transportation, intelligent traffic systems, and equitable water distribution—will be realized. To create a 'clean' city in mind, Nagpur intends to allocate resources towards the implementation of a tailored ICT-driven 'Smart Swachh City Solution' that will optimize waste management in the city. To implement ICT-based solutions, Nagpur has additionally made investments in a Unified Operations Command and Control Centre and a "Nagpur City Community Network" (Sharma & Das, 2019).

Priority for and Concentration on the Concerns of Marginalized Groups: Upon examining every Smart City Proposal, it becomes evident that the issues on women, sexual and religious minorities, and Scheduled Castes and Tribes—which are all marginalized and discriminated-against sectors of society— are not given due consideration or serious attention. Although 'gender equality' has been identified as a significant objective in the proposals of Bilaspur and Allahabad, the scope of these initiatives is limited to skill development and the provision of women's hostels and restrooms. There is no mention of domestic laborers in any of the 99 Smart City Proposals that were evaluated (Patel, 2021).

Challenges/Concerns That Must Be Addressed

The competitive format employed in the Smart Cities Challenge to select "smart cities" resulted in the selection of the most aesthetically pleasing city proposals rather than necessarily the most deserving or impoverished ones. Such an approach gives rise to erroneous priorities and disregards the authentic concerns and issues of individuals concerning sustainable urban development and the elimination of poverty (Sharma & Choudhary, 2021). The competition format additionally led to the involvement of private consulting firms, the majority of which were large multinational corporations, in the development of Smart City Proposals. These firms impose substantial consulting fees but may not be the most qualified to formulate a comprehensive, needs-driven proposal or vision of development that benefits the city's inhabitants. The shortlisted cities have failed to incorporate a human rights framework into their housing policies or establish safeguards to prevent infringements on the right to housing throughout the execution of 'smart city initiatives', including 'slum redevelopment/upgrading' projects (Patel & Shah, 2020). This disregard for human rights is evident in the forced evictions, forced land acquisition, and forced displacement that characterize these settlements.

Persisting Neglect of Rural-urban Linkages: The Mission egregiously disregards critical concerns about the involuntary relocation of individuals from rural to urban regions (Patel & Shah, 2020), as highlighted in Smart City Hub. Furthermore, it perpetuates the fallacious policy presumption that "urbanization is inevitable" in the absence of concerted efforts to mitigate forced population displacement to urban regions through investments in rural communities, responses to urgent land and agrarian crises, and the allocation of adequate financial resources and investment strategies towards rural development.

Challenges to Human Rights: One challenge is the absence of human rights standards to govern the selection and development of projects. This extends to areas such as housing, water, sanitation, health, and environmental sustainability. Without such standards, the Mission faces difficulties in effectively achieving its objectives and guaranteeing that the rights and entitlements of every resident of the city are respected (Ramaswamy, 2016). The National Institute for Transforming India (NITI Aayog) in India had previously expressed concern regarding the lack of standards in the Smart Cities Mission. The institute suggested that standards be established promptly to govern the design and implementation of transportation and housing and that these standards be regularly updated to reflect the most recent technological advancements (Sharma & Kumar, 2019).

Insufficient Information and Participation: As stated in the SCM Guidelines: "The formulation of the proposal will result in the formation of informed citizens." Using citizen consultations and the active involvement of various groups (e.g., Residents Welfare Associations, Tax Payers Associations, Senior Citizens, and Slum Dwellers Associations), the proposal will be initiated with the input and participation of citizens (Singh & Mishra, 2017). "Citizen-driven solutions will be generated and issues, needs, and priorities of citizens and groups of people will be identified during consultations." While nearly every municipality has claimed to involve residents in the development of Smart City Proposals, this information cannot be verified or evaluated to determine whether the concerns and issues raised by citizens during these consultations were incorporated into the final proposals.

Governance Mechanisms That Compete and Overlap: Elected local governments, municipal entities, and neighborhood committees (including mohalla sabhas) are granted authority by the Constitution (Seventy-fourth Amendment) Act 1992 to establish the governance framework for the city (Ramaswamy, 2016). The Smart Cities Mission infringes upon the stipulations of the Indian constitution and poses a threat to local democracy by establishing overlapping and competing mechanisms for local governance via the structure and authorities granted to the Special Purpose Vehicle (National Institute of Urban Affairs, 2018). In its operations, the Special Purpose Vehicle might circumvent or contest the authority of ULB and local administrations, or otherwise disregard their role. Although the SCM Guidelines provide a rationale for creating the Special Purpose Vehicle (SPHV) to guarantee impartial decision-making distinct from locally elected municipal bodies influenced by politics, this action is deemed to violate the constitution. The Minister of Housing and Urban Affairs reaffirmed, in response to a parliamentary inquiry, that the Special Purpose Vehicle must adhere to all regulatory and monitoring mechanisms stipulated in the Companies Act (Singh & Chatterjee, 2020).

Privacy Threats and Risks Associated with Digitalization: It is also necessary to evaluate the necessity and constraints of technology-driven "smart solutions" and the capacity of Indian cities to provide the necessary infrastructure to implement them. In situations where there is limited, erratic, or insufficient electricity supply in numerous cities, for instance, access to essential services for all residents should take precedence (Singh & Mishra, 2017).

Issue with PPP Model: The corporatization of urban areas is an aspect of the PPP model that may not consistently serve the needs and interests of marginalized and low-income populations. The justification for Public-Private Partnerships is rooted in the inefficiency and resource scarcity of the public sector. Even in the provision of fundamental services to impoverished communities at the local level, this type of PPP model incorporates an inherent mechanism to progress toward privatization (Singh & Chatterjee, 2020).

High Dependence on Foreign Investment: Securing foreign investment in the development and implementation of "smart city" initiatives is a primary objective of the Smart Cities Mission. A multitude of foreign governments and international agencies have been solicited for financial support, either to provide general assistance to the Mission or to finance specific city projects (Roy, 2019). Canada, China, France, Germany, Israel, Japan, South Korea, the Netherlands, Singapore, Spain, Sweden, Taiwan, the United Kingdom (UK), and the United States of America (USA) are among the nations that have expressed interest in investing in India's Smart Cities Mission (Verma & Rajput, 2018).

4. POLICY IMPLICATIONS

For the Smart Cities Mission to evaluate progress and the achievement of objectives and targets, enhanced mechanisms for project selection and delivery, in addition to a comprehensive monitoring and implementation framework, are necessary. The lack of a comprehensive assessment mechanism complicates the task of comprehending the accomplishments and methods of the Mission. Despite facing considerable criticism across multiple facets, the Smart Cities Missions have managed to identify and execute a handful of noteworthy projects and initiatives. The objective of a smart city is to consolidate information from various sources and produce practical intelligence that can inform decision-making processes to enhance public services and governance. Information and Communications Technology (ICT) serves as the foundational element of a comprehensive infrastructure framework and drives an integrated strategy towards "smartness."

5. CONCLUSION

The Housing and Land Rights Network's human rights analysis of the Smart Cities Mission demonstrates a conspicuous lack of adherence to a rights-based framework and disregard for the plight of the impoverished and marginalized in urban areas. A human rights-based framework for implementation and monitoring is essential for the Smart Cities Mission to evaluate the progress towards achieving its objectives, guarantee adherence to domestic and international legislation, and advance human rights and environmental sustainability through its projects. Without a monitoring mechanism, the Mission is unable to evaluate or appraise its progress.

In addition to economically disadvantaged sections/low-income communities, children, women, Scheduled Castes, Scheduled Tribes, homeless and landless persons, migrants, domestic workers, internally displaced persons, older persons, religious and sexual minorities, and persons with disabilities, the Mission must develop a special focus on the needs, concerns, and rights of these groups and individuals.

In all SCM cities, meaningful engagement and participation should take precedence over the selection and implementation of "smart city" initiatives. The involvement of individuals should not be considered solely a technical prerequisite. It must be sufficient, meaningful, and transparent, and it must be proactively solicited from all individuals whose lives may be directly or indirectly affected by the initiatives.

Before receiving approval, all Smart Cities Mission initiatives should be required to conduct an environmental impact assessment and a human rights-based impact assessment.

Greenfield urban development mustn't encroach upon rural development or the appropriation of agricultural land. Land that is forcibly acquired and causes involuntary displacement must never occur.

It is imperative to enhance the emphasis on ensuring sufficient affordable housing in all Smart City proposals in alignment with the objectives of PMAY/Housing for All–2022. Cities should establish explicit income-based criteria for 'affordable housing' to guarantee that it remains financially accessible to low-income populations.

Where applicable, the implementation of "smart city" initiatives must adhere to pre-existing city master plans. In municipalities lacking comprehensive master plans, it is advisable to commence participatory processes to formulate plans that accurately mirror the aspirations and requirements of the populace.

It is necessary to make sufficient investments in all Indian cities and villages to foster a balanced urban and rural development model. This could be accomplished via the Rurban Mission by investing adequately in rural areas and people after supporting a consultative process to identify the development needs of rural populations.

To ensure that inclusive city development benefits all segments of the population, technological and infrastructure advancements must be founded on thorough need assessments, explicit guidelines, and human rights standards (Singh & Sharma, 2021).

Precautions must be taken to safeguard the right to privacy and prevent data abuse and surveillance. India requires effective and suitably nuanced data legislation to counter the escalating risks posed by digitalization. Additionally, the government must increase its efforts to raise awareness of the associated risks and guarantee the responsible handling of data. Transparency, sufficient information, and prior consent are fundamental principles that must be maintained and respected.

REFERENCES

Agarwal, A. (2021). *Evaluating the Impact of Smart City Infrastructure on Quality of Life in Indian Cities* (Doctoral dissertation). Indian Institute of Technology, Bombay, India.

Ahmed, S., Basu, B., Ghosh, S., & Chakraborty, S. (2019). Area Based Development planning for smart cities in India. *Smart and Sustainable Built Environment*, 8(3), 312–331.

Brown, C. L., & Garcia, M. R. (2019). Utilizing R software for systematic literature reviews: A methodological approach. *Journal of Applied Research Methods*, 8(2), 78–94.

Deloitte India. (2019). *Smart Cities in India: A Roadmap for Digital Transformation.* Author.

Gupta, A., & Singh, H. (2020). IoT and Big Data Analytics in Smart Cities: A Survey of Indian Initiatives. *Journal of Big Data*, 7(1), 45.

Gupta, N., & Jain, V. (2022). Smart Waste Management in Indian Smart Cities: A Review of Technologies and Challenges. *Waste Management & Research*, 40(3), 215–230.

Jain, M. (2021). *Assessing the Impact of Smart City Initiatives on Sustainable Development Goals in India* (Master's thesis). Indian Institute of Management, Ahmedabad, India.

Joshi, M., & Rao, K. (2018). Smart Education Initiatives in Indian Smart Cities: Case Study of Pune. *Journal of Cases on Information Technology*, 20(3), 34–48.

Kapoor, S. (2017). *Reinventing Indian Cities through Smart Technologies* [TED Talk]. Retrieved from https://www.sciencedirect.com/ted-talks

Kumar, A., & Singh, R. (2020). Challenges of smart cities in India. International Journal of Management. *Technology and Engineering*, 10(1), 1134–1146.

Kumar, V., & Agarwal, S. (2020). Smart Healthcare Systems in Indian Smart Cities: Case Study of Bangalore. *Journal of Cases on Information Technology*, 22(4), 56–71.

McKinsey Global Institute. (2017). *India's Smart Cities: Opening Doors to Opportunity.* Author.

Menon, A., & Khanna, T. (2018). The Promise and Peril of India's Smart City Mission. *Harvard Business Review*. Retrieved from https://hbr.org/

Menon, N. (2018). *The Role of Innovation in Building Smart Cities* [TED Talk]. Retrieved from https://www.sciencedirect.com/ted-talks

Ministry of Electronics and Information Technology, Government of India. (n.d.). *Digital India: Smart Cities.* Retrieved from https://www.digitalindia.gov.in/

Ministry of Housing and Urban Affairs, Government of India (2022). *Smart Cities Mission.* Author.

Ministry of Housing and Urban Affairs, Government of India. (n.d.). *Smart Cities Mission.* Retrieved from https://smartcities.gov.in/

Ministry of New and Renewable Energy, Government of India. (n.d.). *Smart Cities Mission: Renewable Energy.* Retrieved from https://mnre.gov.in/

Mishra, S., & Reddy, G. R. (2018). Citizen Engagement in Indian Smart Cities: An Empirical Analysis. *Journal of Public Administration and Governance*, 8(1), 88–103.

National Institute of Urban Affairs. (2018). *Smart Cities in India: Status and Challenges*. Author.

Patel, R., & Shah, M. (2020). Smart Mobility Solutions in Indian Smart Cities: A Systematic Review. *Transport Reviews*, 40(5), 632–648.

Patel, S. (2021). *Smart Governance Framework for Indian Smart Cities* (Doctoral dissertation). University of Mumbai, Mumbai, India.

Ramaswamy, S. (2016). The Promise and Challenges of Smart Cities. *Harvard Business Review*. Retrieved from https://hbr.org/

Roy, S. (2019). *Harnessing Data for Smart Urban Development* [TED Talk]. Retrieved from https://www.sciencedirect.com/ted-talks

Sharma, M., & Choudhary, S. (2021). Challenges in the implementation of smart cities in India. *International Journal of Scientific and Engineering Research*, 12(4), 1–8.

Sharma, R., & Kumar, A. (2019). Smart Cities in India: A Review of Challenges and Opportunities. *Journal of Urban Technology*, 26(1), 45–62.

Sharma, S., & Das, A. (2019). Smart Energy Management in Indian Smart Cities: A Comprehensive Review. *Energy Sources. Part B, Economics, Planning, and Policy*, 14(8), 674–689.

Singh, P., & Chatterjee, S. (2020). Smart Cities in India: Progress, Challenges, and Future Directions. *International Journal of Urban and Regional Research*, 44(3), 567–589.

Singh, P., & Singh, J. (2020). Area Based Development for Smart Cities in India: Rejuvenating Urban Spaces. *Urban India*, 40(2), 17–29.

Singh, R., & Sharma, A. (2021). Role of Artificial Intelligence in Urban Planning: A Study of Indian Smart Cities. *Journal of Artificial Intelligence and Urban Planning*, 12(2), 123–138.

Singh, S., & Mishra, P. (2017). Cybersecurity Challenges in Indian Smart Cities: A Comprehensive Analysis. *IEEE Transactions on Dependable and Secure Computing*, 14(5), 498–513.

Smith, J. D., & Johnson, A. B. (2020). A systematic review of literature on data analysis techniques using R software. *Journal of Research Methods*, 15(3), 112–130.

Smith, P. A. (2018). The role of systematic review of literature as a tool in research synthesis. *Journal of Research Methods*, 12(4), 213–228.

Verma, R., & Rajput, A. (2018). Blockchain Technology for Smart Governance in Indian Smart Cities. *IEEE Transactions on Engineering Management*, 65(3), 378–392.

Chapter 17
Exploring the Landscape of Urban Development, Sustainability, and Smart Cities Research:
A Bibliometric Analysis

Chirra Baburao
https://orcid.org/0000-0003-4881-3708
GITAM School of Business, GITAM University (Deemed), India

P. Manjushree
GITAM School of Business, GITAM University (Deemed), India

Indukuri Bangar Raju
GITAM School of Business, GITAM University (Deemed), India

ABSTRACT

This bibliometric study explores the academic research on urban development, sustainability, and smart cities. It analyzes articles published from 2013 to 2023 and finds a growing interest in these areas. Research output has increased significantly, indicating a need for innovative and sustainable urban solutions. Using co-citation and co-occurrence network analysis, the study identifies dominant themes and shows a shift from traditional urban planning to contemporary sustainability and technological innovation. Italy is emerging as a leading contributor, with significant contributions from Brazil, China, and the UK. The results provide a comprehensive understanding of these research areas and offer valuable insights for stakeholders, including industry-academic partnerships, in creating sustainable and smart urban environments in the future.

DOI: 10.4018/979-8-3693-3096-8.ch017

1. INTRODUCTION

The topic of urban sustainability and smart cities has gained momentum in recent years. Researchers study urban development and sustainability, as well as the use of innovative technological solutions in smart cities (Qian et al., 2023; Vanli, 2023). These partnerships can advance urban development, sustainability, and smart cities research. To comprehensively address this investigation, we analyze annual production trends, author influence, and the application of Bradford Laws (Berger & Blanka, 2023; Qian et al., 2023; Vanli, 2023). We also examine the co-citation network to understand development patterns and shaping factors. By using co-occurrence network analysis, we aim to uncover prevailing themes, problems, and relationships (Jiang et al., 2023; Mangnus et al., 2022; Margherita et al., 2023). Thematic maps and trend analysis can provide a comprehensive understanding of the development of urban sustainability and smart cities in the literature. This method helps us identify significant themes and trends. We also investigate the influence of authors, countries, and sources in the discussion about urban sustainability and smart cities. We examine how their contributions have evolved and strengthened over time. This investigation focuses on key influencing factors in this area to understand the dynamics of influence. Our goal is to thoroughly analyze the history, current status, and future prospects of urban sustainability and smart cities. By analyzing development patterns, thematic trends, and influential contributors, we aim to improve our understanding of the complex relationship between urban development and sustainability. This understanding is facilitated by advances in smart city innovations and partnerships between industry and academia.

2. METHODOLOGY

2.1 Data Collection

To start the bibliometric analysis, we strategically chose keywords that are essential to our research focus. These keywords include "smart cities," "urban," "development," and "sustainability." We conducted a thorough search of academic literature using these keywords, resulting in a substantial pool of 1,290 relevant documents.

2.2 Data Refinement

In order to guarantee the relevance and specificity of our dataset, we implemented filters. Initially, we focused on articles to narrow down the pool of documents. As a result, we got a refined dataset comprising 609 documents. This meticulous process ensured that the selected papers were scholarly articles that aligned perfectly with our research objectives.

2.3 Subject Area Focus

In order to improve the accuracy of our dataset, we focused on documents specifically related to the fields of Business, Management, and Accounting, as well as Economics, Econometrics, and Finance. This careful selection process resulted in a final dataset of 126 documents. By employing this criterion, we ensured that the documents analyzed were directly relevant to our research topic of urban sustainability and smart cities within the context of these specific subject areas.This collection of 126 documents serves as the foundation for our bibliometric analysis, enabling us to explore the scholarly conversation surrounding urban sustainability and smart cities in the fields of Business, Management, and Accounting, as well as Economics, Econometrics, and Finance.

2.4 Search String

```
(TITLE-ABS-KEY ("Smart cities") AND TITLE-ABS-KEY (urban) AND TITLE-ABS-KEY
(development) AND TITLE-ABS-KEY (sustainability)) AND (LIMIT-TO (DOCTYPE,
"ar")) AND (LIMIT-TO (SUBJAREA, "BUSI") OR LIMIT-TO (SUBJAREA, "ECON"))
```

2.5 Analysis Tool

In order to perform analysis, the Bibilioshiny software is utilized as a bibliometric tool.

2.6. Research Objective

To explore scientific output, collaboration, and worldwide impact in the research landscape.

2.7 Research Questions

RQ1: How has scientific production evolved within the research landscape?
RQ:2 What was the Co-Occurrence Network within the Research landscape?
RQ:3 Which countries had the most influence on the research landscape?

3. DATA ANALYSIS

3.1 Evolution of Scientific Production

When analyzing the evolution of scientific production in urban sustainability and smart cities, we observe a diverse landscape of scholarly contributions. Some authors, such as AIRAKSINEN M and ANGELIDOU M, have experienced a decline in yearly citations. However, emerging authors like CELDRÁN-BERNABEU MA in 2023 have made a powerful impact with their high citation numbers. Authors like BIBRI SE and WANG C also show an upward trend in citations per year, indicating their growing influence in the field.On a country level, China has shown exponential growth in publications, starting from zero in 2013 and reaching 31 in 2023. This signifies a significant interest in and leadership in the field. The USA and Italy also exhibit steady growth in their contributions. Spain and Brazil have ramped up their efforts, with Brazil experiencing a rapid rise from zero articles in 2016 to 34 in 2023. Overall, the data highlights a dynamic and expanding field, with contributions from various authors and countries on the rise. The increasing global attention towards urban sustainability and smart cities indicates that there is a growing interest in this field, which presents a promising opportunity for further research and policy initiatives.

3.2 Co-Occurrence Network Analysis of Urban Sustainability and Smart Cities

Figure 1. Country scientific production

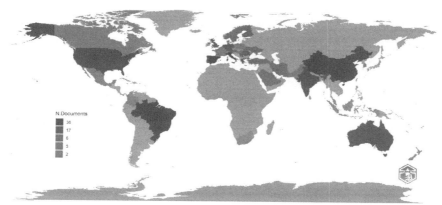

Source: Scopus

A detailed analysis of co-occurrence networks has been carried out in the field of urban sustainability and smart cities. This analysis aims to uncover the main themes, topics, and evolving relationships within this dynamic field. Among the clusters identified, "Sustainability" emerges as a central focus, appearing 31 times and indicating its significant role in scholarly discussions. The prominence of "Urban Development" and "Urban Planning," with 23 occurrences each, highlights the critical importance of transforming cities and planning efficiently to achieve sustainability goals. "Innovation" and "Decision Making," with ten occurrences each, demonstrate the ongoing exploration of innovative solutions and the importance of well-informed decisions in urban sustainability efforts. These clusters represent fundamental concepts and serve as pillars that have shaped the discourse on urban sustainability and smart cities. Measures of centrality, such as Betweenness Centrality, Closeness Centrality, and PageRank Centrality, provide further insights into the influence and interconnectedness of these themes within the scholarly network. Additionally, within this diverse range of research, clusters such as "Information and Communication Technology," "Technological Development," "Climate Change," "Stakeholder," and "Sustainable Development Goal" contribute to the multidimensional nature of the field. This analysis highlights the dynamic evolution of research themes and the complex relationships that define the intellectual landscape of urban sustainability and smart cities.

Figure 2. Authors' production over time

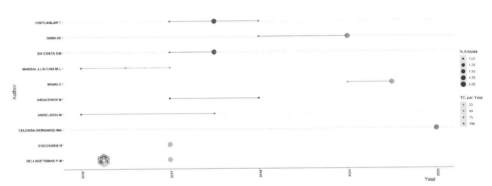

3.3 Analysis of Influential Countries in Urban Sustainability and Smart Cities

An extensive analysis has been conducted to determine the countries that have made the most significant contributions to the discourse on urban sustainability and smart cities. Italy emerges as a prominent leader with 24 articles, demonstrating a strong commitment to research in this field. Brazil and China closely follow with 10 and 8 articles respectively, highlighting their substantial contributions to the scholarly conversation. The United Kingdom, although contributing seven articles, stands out as all its contributions are single-authored, showcasing individual academic excellence. Australia and Greece have also made significant progress, each with six articles. Australia's research landscape is characterized by a collaborative approach, with a high Multiple Collaborative Papers (MCP) ratio of 0.667. On the other hand, Greece balances single-authored and collaborative work with an MCP ratio of 0.167. The Netherlands and Spain, each with five articles, exhibit distinct publishing patterns. The Netherlands strongly emphasizes collaboration, evident from its high MCP ratio of 0.6, while Spain's contributions are solely single-authored. In addition, Portugal and the USA have four articles in the field. Portugal demonstrates a substantial commitment to collaboration, boasting an MCP ratio of 0.75. In contrast, the USA's contributions are evenly distributed between single-authored and collaborative papers. Several other countries, including Austria, Finland, and Germany, have also played crucial roles in advancing research in urban sustainability and smart cities. Notably, Qatar and Saudi Arabia have achieved a high MCP ratio of 1, indicating solid collaborative efforts within their research communities. This analysis highlights the key players in this evolving discourse and sheds light on their collective tendencies and contributions to the scholarly landscape. It underscores the global nature of research in urban sustainability and smart cities, with various countries actively engaging in the conversation and shaping its trajectory.

Figure 3. Corresponding author's countries

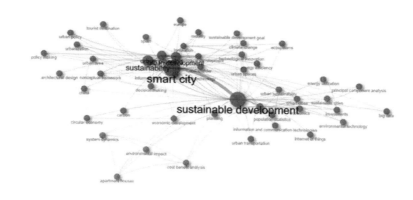

Source: Scopus

Figure 4. Cluster map

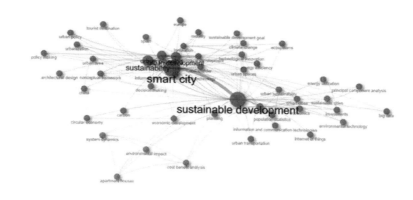

Source: Scopus

4. RESULTS

In our extensive bibliometric analysis, we thoroughly examined the landscape of research on urban development, sustainability, and smart cities. We focused on three key research questions. Firstly, we discovered a significant increase in scientific production in this field over time, with the number of articles steadily rising each year and reaching a peak of 23 in 2022. We also observed fluctuations in author impact, with the highest peaks occurring in 2017 and 2018. By using Bradford's Law, we identified the core journals in this domain. Additionally, we applied co-citation network analysis to identify important research clusters and influential documents. Secondly, we delved into the dominant themes and trends within this literature using co-occurrence network analysis. Our findings highlighted themes such as "sustainability," "urban development," and "urban planning" as central to this research. We were able to trace the evolution of these themes over time. We also found that themes like innovation, decision-making, and information and communication technology were evolving, providing valuable insights into the ever-changing research landscape of urban sustainability and smart cities.Lastly, we explored the contributions of influential authors, countries, and sources. Italy, Brazil, and China emerged as prominent countries in terms of scientific production, with Italy displaying a high Mean Citation Per Article (MCP) ratio. Several authors, including T. Yigitcanlar, M. Marsal-Llacuna, and M. Angelidou, made significant contributions to sustainable development, smart cities, and urban growth. Our analysis also showed how the contributions of different countries and authors evolved, reflecting the dynamic nature of research in this field. These results provide a comprehensive understanding of the research landscape on urban development, sustainability, and smart cities, shedding light on its growth, thematic shifts, and the key contributors driving advancements in the field.

5. DISCUSSION

This bibliometric analysis provide valuable insights into the changing landscape of research on urban sustainability and smart cities. Firstly, there has been a consistent increase in the number of published articles in this field, particularly from 2017 onwards, indicating a growing interest in urban sustainability and smart cities. This rise in research output aligns with the urgent need to address urban challenges in a world that is rapidly urbanizing. Through co-occurrence network analysis, key research themes and topics were identified. Sustainability, urban development, urban planning, and innovation emerged as the dominant themes, highlighting the ongoing focus on achieving sustainable urban environments through innovative planning and technology integration. These themes are closely connected to the goals of smart cities, emphasizing the significance of technology in urban sustainability. The distribution of research output across countries offers valuable insights into the global nature of this research. Italy, Brazil, China, and the United Kingdom are among the leading contributors, indicating their significant influence on the discourse of urban sustainability and smart cities. This diversity of contributors underscores the worldwide relevance of these topics and the necessity for international collaboration. Influential authors play a crucial role in shaping this research landscape. Authors like Yigitcanlar T, who have published multiple articles covering various aspects of smart cities and sustainability, demonstrate a multidimensional approach. Such authors make significant contributions to advancing knowledge in this multidisciplinary field. The interdisciplinary nature of research on urban sustainability and smart cities is evident through various keywords, topics, and themes. This multidisciplinary approach reflects the complex challenges of urbanization and the need to draw from multiple fields, such as urban planning, environmental science, technology, and economics. These findings have practical implications for policymakers and urban planners. Understanding the main themes and influential sources can help inform evidence-based policies and strategies for creating smart and sustainable cities. Collaboration among researchers, policymakers, and practitioners is crucial for implementing innovative solutions in urban development. As global urbanization continues to accelerate, research in urban sustainability and smart cities remains critical. Future research should focus on specific aspects such as the impact of emerging technologies, social equity in smart city development, and strategies for addressing environmental challenges. This will provide a comprehensive overview of the research landscape in urban sustainability and smart cities, offering insights that can guide future research and efforts to create sustainable and technologically advanced urban environments.

6. CONCLUSION

Study explores urban sustainability and smart cities, focusing on the role of industry-academia partnerships in promoting innovation and trade. The study shows that research in this field has grown in the past decade due to the integration of advanced technologies and the need to address environmental impacts. It identifies key journals and authors, highlighting the importance of collaboration and knowledge exchange between industry and academia. Sustainability is a central theme, emphasizing the balance between economic growth, social equity, and environmental responsibility. The study also emphasizes the increasing focus on climate change and stakeholder engagement, with industry-academia partnerships playing a crucial role. The analysis reveals a globally distributed knowledge network, with Italy, Brazil, China, and the UK being prominent contributors. Understanding the contributions of influential stakeholders, including industry-academia partnerships, is valuable for researchers, practitioners, and policymakers. This study has implications for academia, policymaking, and urban planning, providing insights for identifying research gaps, prioritizing areas of study, and implementing smart city solutions. The study underscores the importance of ongoing research and collaboration, particularly between industry and academia, to address urbanization challenges and ensure resilient, inclusive, and environmentally responsible cities.

7. LIMITATIONS

These limitations include limited data scope, potential errors in data quality, bias towards journal articles, influence of keyword selection, bias towards English publications, limited temporal scope, partial representation in co-citation analysis, interdisciplinary nature of the field, and lack of in-depth analysis of causal factors. However, the study still provides valuable insights into trends, key articles, influential sources, and global contributors. Researchers and policymakers should consider these limitations when interpreting the results and further exploring the topic.

8. FUTURE WORK

The study proposes various research directions to promote innovation and trade through industry-academic partnerships in urban development, sustainability and smart cities research. These directions include incorporating additional data sources to gain a better understanding of the professional literature, analyzing in multiple languages for inclusivity, and tracking the development of the field over time to identify emerging trends. The study also recommends examining interdisciplinary collaboration patterns between industry and academia, conducting region-specific analyses, and combining bibliometric analyzes with qualitative methods for a deeper understanding of research topics and trends. The study also suggests closing the gap between research and practice, developing visualization tools and using predictive analytics. Other research focuses include examining ethical and social implications, conducting intercultural studies, and researching public engagement and citizen participation. Pursuing these directions can provide valuable insights for science and practice and address the challenges of urbanization and sustainability in the 21st century. The study highlights the role of industry-academic partnerships in promoting these research directions.

REFERENCES

Ahvenniemi, H., Huovila, A., Pinto-Seppä, I., & Airaksinen, M. (2017). What are the differences between sustainable and smart cities? *Cities (London, England)*, 60, 234–245. 10.1016/j.cities.2016.09.009

Aina, Y. A. (2017). Achieving smart sustainable cities with GeoICT support: The Saudi evolving smart cities. *Cities (London, England)*, 71, 49–58. 10.1016/j.cities.2017.07.007

Allam, Z., & Dhunny, Z. A. (2019). On big data, artificial intelligence and smart cities. *Cities (London, England)*, 89, 80–91. 10.1016/j.cities.2019.01.032

Amendola, C., La Bella, S., Joime, G. P., Frattale Mascioli, F. M., & Vito, P. (2022). An Integrated Methodology Model for Smart Mobility System Applied to Sustainable Tourism. *Administrative Sciences*, 12(1), 40. Advance online publication. 10.3390/admsci12010040

Angelidou, M. (2015). Smart cities: A conjuncture of four forces. *Cities (London, England)*, 47, 95–106. 10.1016/j.cities.2015.05.004

Angelidou, M., Psaltoglou, A., Komninos, N., Kakderi, C., Tsarchopoulos, P., & Panori, A. (2018). Enhancing sustainable urban development through smart city applications. *Journal of Science and Technology Policy Management*, 9(2), 146–169. 10.1108/JSTPM-05-2017-0016

Anthony, B.Jr. (2023). The Role of Community Engagement in Urban Innovation Towards the Co-Creation of Smart Sustainable Cities. *Journal of the Knowledge Economy*. Advance online publication. 10.1007/s13132-023-01176-1

Anthopoulos, L. G., Pourzolfaghar, Z., Lemmer, K., Siebenlist, T., Niehaves, B., & Nikolaou, I. (2022). Smart cities as hubs: Connect, collect and control city flows. *Cities (London, England)*, 125, 103660. Advance online publication. 10.1016/j.cities.2022.103660

Antoniucci, V., D'Alpaos, C., & Marella, G. (2015). Energy saving in tall buildings: From urban planning regulation to smart grid building solutions. *International Journal for Housing Science and Its Applications*, 39(2), 101–110. https://www.scopus.com/inward/record.uri?eid=2-s2.0-84938378709&partnerID=40&md5=8e80f90dadb557f7b86f4d5a49a10ffe

Belanche, D., Casaló, L. V., & Orús, C. (2016). City attachment and use of urban services: Benefits for smart cities. *Cities (London, England)*, 50, 75–81. 10.1016/j.cities.2015.08.016

Berawi, M. A. (2022). New City Development: Creating a Better Future and Added Value. *International Journal of Technology*, 13(2), 225–228. 10.14716/ijtech.v13i2.5598

Berger, E. S. C., & Blanka, C. (2023). Comprehensive and multifaceted perspectives on sustainability, urban studies, and entrepreneurship. *Small Business Economics*. Advance online publication. 10.1007/s11187-023-00762-6

Bibri, S. E. (2021). The underlying components of data-driven smart sustainable cities of the future: A case study approach to an applied theoretical framework. *European Journal of Futures Research*, 9(1), 13. Advance online publication. 10.1186/s40309-021-00182-3

Bibri, S. E., & Krogstie, J. (2019). Generating a vision for smart sustainable cities of the future: A scholarly backcasting approach. *European Journal of Futures Research*, 7(1), 5. Advance online publication. 10.1186/s40309-019-0157-0

Blagojević, D., Nagy, I., Lukić, A., & Tešić, D. (2020). Adaptation To Climate Change Through Theories Of Urban Development. *DETUROPE, 12*(3), 37 – 57. https://www.scopus.com/inward/record.uri?eid= 2-s2.0-85103100540&partnerID=40&md5=ea2701a25107f58c081ae3169888269d

Cai, M., Kassens-Noor, E., Zhao, Z., & Colbry, D. (2023). Are smart cities more sustainable? An exploratory study of 103 U.S. cities. *Journal of Cleaner Production*, 416, 137986. Advance online publication. 10.1016/j.jclepro.2023.137986

Carter, E., Adam, P., Tsakis, D., Shaw, S., Watson, R., & Ryan, P. (2020). Enhancing pedestrian mobility in Smart Cities using Big Data. *Journal of Management Analytics*, 7(2), 173–188. 10.1080/23270012.2020.1741039

Carvalho, L., & Campos, J. B. (2013). Developing the PlanIT valley: A view on the governance and societal embedding of u-eco city pilots. *International Journal of Knowledge-Based Development*, 4(2), 109–125. 10.1504/IJKBD.2013.054089

Castanho, M. S., Ferreira, F. A. F., Carayannis, E. G., & Ferreira, J. J. M. (2021). SMART-C: Developing a "Smart City" Assessment System Using Cognitive Mapping and the Choquet Integral. *IEEE Transactions on Engineering Management*, 68(2), 562–573. 10.1109/TEM.2019.2909668

Cavalheiro, M. B., Joia, L. A., Cavalheiro, G. M. D. C., & Mayer, V. F. (2021). Smart tourism destinations: (mis)aligning touristic destinations and smart city initiatives. *BAR - Brazilian Administration Review*, 18(1), e190132. Advance online publication. 10.1590/1807-7692bar2021190132

Cebi, P. D., & Kozikoglu, N. (2015). Designing for the future of the city. *International Journal for Housing Science and Its Applications*, 39(2), 111–122. https://www.scopus.com/inward/record.uri?eid =2-s2.0-84938340285&partnerID=40&md5=87af1b9fd3482da61fac7febd6f7a3e7

Chan, C. S., & Tsun, W. Y. (2023). Unleashing the potential of local brand equity of Hong Kong as a green–creative–smart city. *Journal of Place Management and Development*. 10.1108/JPMD-12-2022-0122

Chang, D. L., Sabatini-Marques, J., da Costa, E. M., Selig, P. M., & Yigitcanlar, T. (2018). Knowledge-based, smart and sustainable cities: A provocation for a conceptual framework. *Journal of Open Innovation*, 4(1), 1–17. Advance online publication. 10.1186/s40852-018-0087-2

Coca-Stefaniak, J. A. (2020). Beyond smart tourism cities – towards a new generation of "wise" tourism destinations. *Journal of Tourism Futures*, 7(2), 251–258. 10.1108/JTF-11-2019-0130

Coccossis, H., Delladetsimas, P.-M., & Niavis, S. (2017). The challenge of incorporating smart city activities in medium-size cities: The case of Greece. *International Journal of Services Technology and Management*, 23(5–6), 381–402. 10.1504/IJSTM.2017.088947

Cravero, S. (2020). Methods, strategies and tools to improve citizens' engagement in the smart cities' context: A serious games classification [Metodi, strategie e strumenti per migliorare il coinvolgimento dei cittadini nelle smart cities: Una classificazione di Serious Games]. *Valori e Valutazioni, 2020*(24), 45 – 60. https://www.scopus.com/inward/record.uri?eid=2-s2.0-85087766230&partnerID=40&md5=9ffbae61e17fbff2618ab39989014165

Dana, L.-P., Salamzadeh, A., Hadizadeh, M., Heydari, G., & Shamsoddin, S. (2022). Urban entrepreneurship and sustainable businesses in smart cities: Exploring the role of digital technologies. *Sustainable Technology and Entrepreneurship*, 1(2), 100016. Advance online publication. 10.1016/j.stae.2022.100016

Dashkevych, O., & Portnov, B. A. (2023). Human-centric, sustainability-driven approach to ranking smart cities worldwide. *Technology in Society*, 74, 102296. Advance online publication. 10.1016/j.techsoc.2023.102296

Deakin, M., & Reid, A. (2018). Smart cities: Under-gridding the sustainability of city-districts as energy efficient-low carbon zones. *Journal of Cleaner Production*, 173, 39–48. 10.1016/j.jclepro.2016.12.054

Diána, E., & Mária, S. C. (2022). Assessing the links between the digital transformation and the sustainability transition in the capitals of the European Union [A digitális átalakulás és a fenntarthatósági átmenet összefüggéseinek értékelése az Európai Unió fővárosaiban]. *Teruleti Statisztika*, 62(6), 683–697. 10.15196/TS620603

Dickson, G., & Zhang, J. J. (2021). Sports and urban development: An introduction. *International Journal of Sports Marketing & Sponsorship*, 22(1), 1–9. 10.1108/IJSMS-11-2020-0194

Dupont, L., Morel, L., & Guidat, C. (2015). Innovative public-private partnership to support Smart City: The case of "Chaire REVES.". *Journal of Strategy and Management*, 8(3), 245–265. 10.1108/JSMA-03-2015-0027

Eichelberger, S., Peters, M., Pikkemaat, B., & Chan, C.-S. (2020). Entrepreneurial ecosystems in smart cities for tourism development: From stakeholder perceptions to regional tourism policy implications. *Journal of Hospitality and Tourism Management*, 45, 319–329. 10.1016/j.jhtm.2020.06.011

Esashika, D., Masiero, G., & Mauger, Y. (2021). An investigation into the elusive concept of smart cities: A systematic review and meta-synthesis. *Technology Analysis and Strategic Management*, 33(8), 957–969. 10.1080/09537325.2020.1856804

Farid, A. M., Alshareef, M., Badhesha, P. S., Boccaletti, C., Cacho, N. A. A., Carlier, C.-I., Corriveau, A., Khayal, I., Liner, B., Martins, J. S. B., Rahimi, F., Rossett, R., Schoonenberg, W. C. H., Stillwell, A., & Wang, Y. (2021). Smart City Drivers and Challenges in Urban-Mobility, Health-Care, and Inter-dependent Infrastructure Systems. *IEEE Potentials*, 40(1), 11–16. 10.1109/MPOT.2020.3011399

Ferreira, A. C. D., Titotto, S. L. M. C., & Akkari, A. C. S. (2022). Urban Agriculture 5.0: An Exploratory Approach to the Food System in a Super Smart Society. International Journal of Mathematical. *Engineering and Management Sciences*, 7(4), 455–475. 10.33889/IJMEMS.2022.7.4.030

Galeeva, A., Mingazova, N., & Gilmanshin, I. (2014). Sustainable urban development: Urban green spaces and water bodies in the city of Kazan, Russia. *Mediterranean Journal of Social Sciences*, 5(24), 356–360. 10.5901/mjss.2014.v5n24p356

Gao, C., Gao, C., Song, K., & Fang, K. (2020). Pathways towards regional circular economy evaluated using material flow analysis and system dynamics. *Resources, Conservation and Recycling*, 154, 104527. Advance online publication. 10.1016/j.resconrec.2019.104527

García-Fuentes, M. Á., & de Torre, C. (2017). Towards smarter and more sustainable cities: The re-mourban model. *Entrepreneurship and Sustainability Issues*, 4(3), 328–338. 10.9770/jesi.2017.4.3S(8)

Gimpel, H., Graf-Drasch, V., Hawlitschek, F., & Neumeier, K. (2021). Designing smart and sustainable irrigation: A case study. *Journal of Cleaner Production*, 315, 128048. Advance online publication. 10.1016/j.jclepro.2021.128048

Glebova, I. S., Yasnitskaya, Y. S., & Maklakova, N. V. (2014). Assessment of cities in Russia according to the concept of "smart city" in the context of the application of information and communication technologies. *Mediterranean Journal of Social Sciences,* 5(18), 55 – 60. 10.5901/mjss.2014.v5n18p55

Goel, R. K., Yadav, C. S., & Vishnoi, S. (2021). Self-sustainable smart cities: Socio-spatial society using participative bottom-up and cognitive top-down approach. *Cities (London, England)*, 118, 103370. Advance online publication. 10.1016/j.cities.2021.103370

Grindsted, T. S., Christensen, T. H., Freudendal-Pedersen, M., Friis, F., & Hartmann-Petersen, K. (2022). The urban governance of autonomous vehicles – In love with AVs or critical sustainability risks to future mobility transitions. *Cities (London, England)*, 120, 103504. Advance online publication. 10.1016/j.cities.2021.103504

Guerra, I., Borges, F., Padrão, J., Tavares, J., & Padrão, M. H. (2017). Smart cities, smart tourism? The case of the city of Porto. *Revista Galega de Economia,* 26(2), 129 – 142. https://www.scopus.com/inward/record.uri?eid=2-s2.0-85061032204&partnerID=40&md5=53340c00f01ed8ce67e24ad121953ba2

Gupta, A., Panagiotopoulos, P., & Bowen, F. (2023). Developing Capabilities in Smart City Ecosystems: A multi-level approach. *Organization Studies*, 44(10), 1703–1724. Advance online publication. 10.1177/01708406231164114

Houston, L., Gabrys, J., & Pritchard, H. (2019). Breakdown in the Smart City: Exploring Workarounds with Urban-sensing Practices and Technologies. *Science, Technology & Human Values*, 44(5), 843–870. 10.1177/0162243919852677

Huk, K., & Agata, G. (2021). Impact of private transport on the environment and society in the concept of city logistics and life cycle assessment. *Acta Logistica*, 8(3), 287–295. 10.22306/al.v8i3.251

Huovila, A., Bosch, P., & Airaksinen, M. (2019). Comparative analysis of standardized indicators for Smart sustainable cities: What indicators and standards to use and when? *Cities (London, England)*, 89, 141–153. 10.1016/j.cities.2019.01.029

Ibănescu, B.-C., Bănică, A., Eva, M., & Cehan, A. (2020). The puzzling concept of smart city in central and eastern europe: A literature review designed for policy development. *Transylvanian Review of Administrative Sciences*, 16(61), 70–87. 10.24193/tras.61E.4

Ionescu, R.-V., Zlati, M. L., & Antohi, V.-M. (2023). Smart cities from low cost to expensive solutions under an optimal analysis. *Financial Innovation*, 9(1), 60. Advance online publication. 10.1186/s40854-023-00448-836883188

Ivars-Baidal, J. A., Celdrán-Bernabeu, M. A., Femenia-Serra, F., Perles-Ribes, J. F., & Vera-Rebollo, J. F. (2023). Smart city and smart destination planning: Examining instruments and perceived impacts in Spain. *Cities (London, England)*, 137, 104266. Advance online publication. 10.1016/j.cities.2023.104266

Ivars-Baidal, J. A., Vera-Rebollo, J. F., Perles-Ribes, J., Femenia-Serra, F., & Celdrán-Bernabeu, M. A. (2023). Sustainable tourism indicators: What's new within the smart city/destination approach? *Journal of Sustainable Tourism*, 31(7), 1556–1582. 10.1080/09669582.2021.1876075

Jiang, Z., Zhang, X., Zhao, Y., Li, C., & Wang, Z. (2023). The impact of urban digital transformation on resource sustainability: Evidence from a quasi-natural experiment in China. *Resources Policy*, 85, 103784. Advance online publication. 10.1016/j.resourpol.2023.103784

Khozhylo, I., Lipovska, N., Chernysh, O., Antonova, O., Diegtiar, O., & Dmytriieva, O. (2022). Implementation of smart-city tools as a response to challenges in socio-humanitarian field in Ukrainian metropolises. *Acta Logistica*, 9(1), 23–30. 10.22306/al.v9i1.262

Koch, F., Beyer, S., & Chen, C.-Y. (2023). Monitoring the Sustainable Development Goals in cities: Potentials and pitfalls of using smart city data. *GAIA - Ecological Perspectives for Science and Society*, 32, 47 – 53. 10.14512/gaia.32.S1.8

Koens, K., Melissen, F., Mayer, I., & Aall, C. (2021). The Smart City Hospitality Framework: Creating a foundation for collaborative reflections on overtourism that support destination design. *Journal of Destination Marketing & Management*, 19, 100376. Advance online publication. 10.1016/j.jdmm.2019.100376

Komninos, N., & Tsarchopoulos, P. (2013). Toward Intelligent Thessaloniki: From an Agglomeration of Apps to Smart Districts. *Journal of the Knowledge Economy*, 4(2), 149–168. 10.1007/s13132-012-0085-8

Krishankumar, R., Ecer, F., Mishra, A. R., Ravichandran, K. S., Gandomi, A. H., & Kar, S. (2022). A SWOT-Based Framework for Personalized Ranking of IoT Service Providers With Generalized Fuzzy Data for Sustainable Transport in Urban Regions. *IEEE Transactions on Engineering Management*, 1–14. 10.1109/TEM.2022.3204695

Kroh, J., & Schultz, C. (2023). The more the better? The role of stakeholder information processing in complex urban innovation projects for green transformation. *International Journal of Project Management*, 41(3), 102466. Advance online publication. 10.1016/j.ijproman.2023.102466

Kudva, S., & Ye, X. (2017). Smart cities, big data, and sustainability union. *Big Data and Cognitive Computing*, 1(1), 1–13. 10.3390/bdcc1010004

Kumar, H., Singh, M. K., Gupta, M. P., & Madaan, J. (2020). Moving towards smart cities: Solutions that lead to the Smart City Transformation Framework. *Technological Forecasting and Social Change*, 153, 119281. Advance online publication. 10.1016/j.techfore.2018.04.024

Kurniawan, T. A., Maiurova, A., Kustikova, M., Bykovskaia, E., Othman, M. H. D., & Goh, H. H. (2022). Accelerating sustainability transition in St. Petersburg (Russia) through digitalization-based circular economy in waste recycling industry: A strategy to promote carbon neutrality in era of Industry 4.0. *Journal of Cleaner Production*, 363, 132452. Advance online publication. 10.1016/j.jclepro.2022.132452

Kutty, A. A., Kucukvar, M., Onat, N. C., Ayvaz, B., & Abdella, G. M. (2023). Measuring sustainability, resilience and livability performance of European smart cities: A novel fuzzy expert-based multi-criteria decision support model. *Cities (London, England)*, 137, 104293. Advance online publication. 10.1016/j.cities.2023.104293

Lata, S., Jasrotia, A., & Sharma, S. (2022). Sustainable development in tourism destinations through smart cities: A case of urban planning in Jammu City. *Enlightening Tourism*, 12(2), 661–690. 10.33776/et.v12i2.6911

Lee, J. H., Hancock, M. G., & Hu, M.-C. (2014). Towards an effective framework for building smart cities: Lessons from Seoul and San Francisco. *Technological Forecasting and Social Change*, 89, 80–99. 10.1016/j.techfore.2013.08.033

Linde, L., Sjödin, D., Parida, V., & Wincent, J. (2021). Dynamic capabilities for ecosystem orchestration A capability-based framework for smart city innovation initiatives. *Technological Forecasting and Social Change*, 166, 120614. Advance online publication. 10.1016/j.techfore.2021.120614

Liu, J., Chen, N., Chen, Z., Xu, L., Du, W., Zhang, Y., & Wang, C. (2022). Towards sustainable smart cities: Maturity assessment and development pattern recognition in China. *Journal of Cleaner Production*, 370, 133248. Advance online publication. 10.1016/j.jclepro.2022.133248

Lopez-Carreiro, I., Monzon, A., Lopez, E., & Lopez-Lambas, M. E. (2020). Urban mobility in the digital era: An exploration of travellers' expectations of MaaS mobile-technologies. *Technology in Society*, 63, 101392. Advance online publication. 10.1016/j.techsoc.2020.101392

Lorquet, A., & Pauwels, L. (2020). Interrogating urban projections in audio-visual 'smart city' narratives. *Cities (London, England)*, 100, 102660. Advance online publication. 10.1016/j.cities.2020.102660

Lyaskovskaya, E. A., Khudyakova, T. A., & Shmidt, A. V. (2022). Improving the Ranking of Russian Smart Cities [СОВЕршЕнСТВОВАнИЕ рЕйТИнгА рОССИйСКИх умных гОрОДОВ]. *Economy of Regions*, 18(4), 1046–1061. 10.17059/ekon.reg.2022-4-6

Lytras, M. D., Visvizi, A., Chopdar, P. K., Sarirete, A., & Alhalabi, W. (2021). Information Management in Smart Cities: Turning end users' views into multi-item scale development, validation, and policy-making recommendations. *International Journal of Information Management*, 56, 102146. Advance online publication. 10.1016/j.ijinfomgt.2020.102146

Macke, J., Casagrande, R. M., Sarate, J. A. R., & Silva, K. A. (2018). Smart city and quality of life: Citizens' perception in a Brazilian case study. *Journal of Cleaner Production*, 182, 717–726. 10.1016/j.jclepro.2018.02.078

Macke, J., Rubim Sarate, J. A., & de Atayde Moschen, S. (2019). Smart sustainable cities evaluation and sense of community. *Journal of Cleaner Production*, 239, 118103. Advance online publication. 10.1016/j.jclepro.2019.118103

Magliacani, M. (2023). How the sustainable development goals challenge public management. Action research on the cultural heritage of an Italian smart city. *The Journal of Management and Governance*, 27(3), 987–1015. 10.1007/s10997-022-09652-7

Manate, D., Lile, R., Rad, D., Szentesi, S.-G., & Cuc, L. D. (2023). An analysis of the concept of green buildings in Romania in the context of the energy paradigm change in the EU [Tvariųjų pastatų sampratos rumunijoje analizė: Energetikos paradigma pokyčių es kontekste]. *Transformations in Business & Economics*, 22(1), 115–129. https://www.scopus.com/inward/record.uri?eid=2-s2.0-85153742642&partnerID=40&md5=8f5e2638cd62236415818c9004346527

Mangnus, A. C., Vervoort, J. M., Renger, W.-J., Nakic, V., Rebel, K. T., Driessen, P. P. J., & Hajer, M. (2022). Envisioning alternatives in pre-structured urban sustainability transformations: Too late to change the future? *Cities (London, England)*, 120, 103466. Advance online publication. 10.1016/j.cities.2021.103466

Marchetti, D., Oliveira, R., & Figueira, A. R. (2019). Are global north smart city models capable to assess Latin American cities? A model and indicators for a new context. *Cities (London, England)*, 92, 197–207. 10.1016/j.cities.2019.04.001

Margherita, E. G., Escobar, S. D., Esposito, G., & Crutzen, N. (2023). Exploring the potential impact of smart urban technologies on urban sustainability using structural topic modelling: Evidence from Belgium. *Cities (London, England)*, 141, 104475. Advance online publication. 10.1016/j.cities.2023.104475

Marsal-Llacuna, M.-L., Colomer-Llinàs, J., & Meléndez-Frigola, J. (2015). Lessons in urban monitoring taken from sustainable and livable cities to better address the Smart Cities initiative. *Technological Forecasting and Social Change, 90*(PB), 611 – 622. 10.1016/j.techfore.2014.01.012

Marsal-Llacuna, M.-L., & Segal, M. E. (2016). The Intelligenter Method (I) for making "smarter" city projects and plans. *Cities (London, England)*, 55, 127–138. 10.1016/j.cities.2016.02.006

Marsal-Llacuna, M.-L., & Segal, M. E. (2017). The Intelligenter Method (II) for "smarter" urban policy-making and regulation drafting. *Cities (London, England)*, 61, 83–95. 10.1016/j.cities.2016.05.006

Matos, F., Vairinhos, V. M., Dameri, R. P., & Durst, S. (2017). Increasing smart city competitiveness and sustainability through managing structural capital. *Journal of Intellectual Capital*, 18(3), 693–707. 10.1108/JIC-12-2016-0141

Morales-Pinzón, T., Rieradevall, J., Gasol, C. M., & Gabarrell, X. (2015). Modelling for economic cost and environmental analysis of rainwater harvesting systems. *Journal of Cleaner Production*, 87(C), 613–626. 10.1016/j.jclepro.2014.10.021

Mosannenzadeh, F., Bisello, A., Vaccaro, R., D'Alonzo, V., Hunter, G. W., & Vettorato, D. (2017). Smart energy city development: A story told by urban planners. *Cities (London, England)*, 64, 54–65. 10.1016/j.cities.2017.02.001

Nederhand, J., Avelino, F., Awad, I., De Jong, P., Duijn, M., Edelenbos, J., Engelbert, J., Fransen, J., Schiller, M., & Van Stapele, N. (2023). Reclaiming the city from an urban vitalism perspective: Critically reflecting smart, inclusive, resilient and sustainable just city labels. *Cities (London, England)*, 137, 104257. Advance online publication. 10.1016/j.cities.2023.104257

Neves, F. T., de Castro Neto, M., & Aparicio, M. (2020). The impacts of open data initiatives on smart cities: A framework for evaluation and monitoring. *Cities (London, England)*, 106, 102860. Advance online publication. 10.1016/j.cities.2020.102860

Nunes, S. A. S., Ferreira, F. A. F., Govindan, K., & Pereira, L. F. (2021). "Cities go smart!": A system dynamics-based approach to smart city conceptualization. *Journal of Cleaner Production*, 313, 127683. Advance online publication. 10.1016/j.jclepro.2021.127683

Palumbo, R., Manesh, M. F., Pellegrini, M. M., Caputo, A., & Flamini, G. (2021). Organizing a sustainable smart urban ecosystem: Perspectives and insights from a bibliometric analysis and literature review. *Journal of Cleaner Production*, 297, 126622. Advance online publication. 10.1016/j.jclepro.2021.126622

Parada, J. (2017). Social innovation for "smart" territories: Fiction or reality? [Innovaciones sociales para territorios "inteligentes": ¿Ficción o realidad?]. *Problemas del Desarrollo*, 48(190), 11–35. 10.1016/j.rpd.2017.06.002

Pardo-García, N., Simoes, S. G., Dias, L., Sandgren, A., Suna, D., & Krook-Riekkola, A. (2019). Sustainable and Resource Efficient Cities platform – SureCity holistic simulation and optimization for smart cities. *Journal of Cleaner Production*, 215, 701–711. 10.1016/j.jclepro.2019.01.070

Pasquinelli, C., & Trunfio, M. (2020). Reframing urban overtourism through the Smart-City Lens. *Cities (London, England)*, 102, 102729. Advance online publication. 10.1016/j.cities.2020.102729

Praharaj, S., & Han, H. (2019). Cutting through the clutter of smart city definitions: A reading into the smart city perceptions in India. City. *Cultura e Scuola*, 18, 100289. Advance online publication. 10.1016/j.ccs.2019.05.005

Qian, H., Wu, J., & Zheng, S. (2023). Entrepreneurship, sustainability, and urban development. *Small Business Economics*. Advance online publication. 10.1007/s11187-023-00761-7

Richter, M. A., Hagenmaier, M., Bandte, O., Parida, V., & Wincent, J. (2022). Smart cities, urban mobility and autonomous vehicles: How different cities needs different sustainable investment strategies. *Technological Forecasting and Social Change*, 184, 121857. Advance online publication. 10.1016/j.techfore.2022.121857

Romão, J., Kourtit, K., Neuts, B., & Nijkamp, P. (2018). The smart city as a common place for tourists and residents: A structural analysis of the determinants of urban attractiveness. *Cities (London, England)*, 78, 67–75. 10.1016/j.cities.2017.11.007

Ruso, J., Horvat, A., & Maričić, M. (2019). Do international standards influence the development of smart regions and cities? [Utječu li međunarodni standardi na razvoj pametnih regija i gradova?]. *Zbornik Radova Ekonomskog Fakulteta u Rijeci*, 37(2), 629–652. 10.18045/zbefri.2019.2.629

Saha, A. R., & Singh, N. (2017). Smart cities for a sustainable future: Can Singapore be a model for Delhi? *International Journal of Economic Research*, 14(18), 367–379. https://www.scopus.com/inward/record.uri?eid=2-s2.0-85040189243&partnerID=40&md5=b243ff5ff749469abc2be93625464072

Sarif, M., & Gupta, R. D. (2022). Spatiotemporal mapping of Land Use/Land Cover dynamics using Remote Sensing and GIS approach: A case study of Prayagraj City, India (1988–2018). *Environment, Development and Sustainability*, 24(1), 888–920. 10.1007/s10668-021-01475-0

Savchenko, A. B., & Borodina, T. L. (2020). Green and Digital Economy for Sustainable Development of Urban Areas. *Regional Research of Russia*, 10(4), 583–592. 10.1134/S2079970520040097

Schiller, F. (2016). Urban transitions: Scaling complex cities down to human size. *Journal of Cleaner Production*, 112, 4273–4282. 10.1016/j.jclepro.2015.08.030

Shao, Q.-G., Jiang, C.-C., Lo, H.-W., & Liou, J. J. H. (2023). Establishing a sustainable development assessment framework for a smart city using a hybrid Z-fuzzy-based decision-making approach. *Clean Technologies and Environmental Policy*, 25(9), 3027–3044. Advance online publication. 10.1007/s10098-023-02547-7

Stanković, J., Džunić, M., Džunić, Ž., & Marinković, S. (2017). A multi-criteria evaluation of the European cities' smart performance: Economic, social and environmental aspects [Višekriterijska evaluacija pametnih performansi Europskih gradova: Gospodarski, socijalni i okolišni aspekti]. *Zbornik Radova Ekonomskog Fakulteta u Rijeci*, 35(2), 519–550. 10.18045/zbefri.2017.2.519

Tajani, F., & Morano, P. (2015). An evaluation model of the financial feasibility of social housing in urban redevelopment. *Property Management*, 33(2), 133–151. 10.1108/PM-02-2014-0007

Trindade, E. P., Hinnig, M. P. F., da Costa, E. M., Marques, J. S., Bastos, R. C., & Yigitcanlar, T. (2017). Sustainable development of smart cities: A systematic review of the literature. *Journal of Open Innovation*, 3(3), 1–14. Advance online publication. 10.1186/s40852-017-0063-2

Tura, N., & Ojanen, V. (2022). Sustainability-oriented innovations in smart cities: A systematic review and emerging themes. *Cities (London, England)*, 126, 103716. Advance online publication. 10.1016/j.cities.2022.103716

Valdez, A.-M., Cook, M., Langendahl, P.-A., Roby, H., & Potter, S. (2018). Prototyping sustainable mobility practices: User-generated data in the smart city. *Technology Analysis and Strategic Management*, 30(2), 144–157. 10.1080/09537325.2017.1297399

Vanli, T. (2023). Can systemic governance of smart cities catalyse urban sustainability? *Environment, Development and Sustainability*. Advance online publication. 10.1007/s10668-023-03601-6

Visvizi, A., & Lytras, M. D. (2018). Rescaling and refocusing smart cities research: From mega cities to smart villages. *Journal of Science and Technology Policy Management*, 9(2), 134–145. 10.1108/JSTPM-02-2018-0020

Wang, C., Martínez, O. S., & Crespo, R. G. (2021). Improved hybrid fuzzy logic system for evaluating sustainable transportation systems in smart cities. *International Journal of Shipping and Transport Logistics*, 13(5), 554–568. 10.1504/IJSTL.2021.117295

Wang, Y., Hao, H., & Wang, C. (2022). Preparing Urban Curbside for Increasing Mobility-on-Demand Using Data-Driven Agent-Based Simulation: Case Study of City of Gainesville, Florida. *Journal of Management Engineering*, 38(3). Advance online publication. 10.1061/(ASCE)ME.1943-5479.0001021

Warnecke, D., Wittstock, R., & Teuteberg, F. (2019). Benchmarking of European smart cities – a maturity model and web-based self-assessment tool. Sustainability Accounting. *Management and Policy Journal*, 10(4), 654–684. 10.1108/SAMPJ-03-2018-0057

White, L., & Burger, K. (2022). Understanding Frameworking for Smart and Sustainable City Development: A configurational approach. *Organization Studies*. Advance online publication. 10.1177/01708406221099694

Yigitcanlar, T., Kamruzzaman, M., Buys, L., Ioppolo, G., Sabatini-Marques, J., da Costa, E. M., & Yun, J. J. (2018). Understanding 'smart cities': Intertwining development drivers with desired outcomes in a multidimensional framework. *Cities (London, England)*, 81, 145–160. 10.1016/j.cities.2018.04.003

Yigitcanlar, T., Wilson, M., & Kamruzzaman, M. (2019). Disruptive impacts of automated driving systems on the built environment and land use: An urban planner's perspective. *Journal of Open Innovation*, 5(2), 24. Advance online publication. 10.3390/joitmc5020024

Zaidan, E., Ghofrani, A., Abulibdeh, A., & Jafari, M. (2022). Accelerating the Change to Smart Societies-a Strategic Knowledge-Based Framework for Smart Energy Transition of Urban Communities. *Frontiers in Energy Research*, 10, 852092. Advance online publication. 10.3389/fenrg.2022.852092

Compilation of References

Aan Alten, D. C., Phielix, C., Janssen, J., & Kester, L. (2020). Self-regulated learning support in flipped learning videos enhances learning outcomes. *Computers & Education*, 158, 104000. 10.1016/j.compedu.2020.104000

Abid, M. A., Shafique, F., Zahid, M., Mehmood, S., & Asim, N. (2023). *Impact of Social Media Influencers on Consumers Purchase Intentions to Buy Pakistani Food: Investigating The Mediating Role Of Consumer Attitude*. Academic Press.

Acuña, M. A. O., de Almeida Filho, A. T., & Ramos, F. S. (2024). Modelling the triple helix system innovation of the main economies from Latin America: A coalitional game theory approach. *Scientometrics*. Advance online publication. 10.1007/s11192-024-05020-4

Adan, N., Douni, R., & Hashim, H. A. (2021). Industry Perception on the Implementation of Work-Based Learning (WBL) in Politeknik Ibrahim Sultan. *Politeknik & Kolej Komuniti.Journal of Social Sciences and Humanities*, 6(1), 87–98.

Adeel, A., Batool, S., & Kee, D. M. H. (2023). Why cognitive absorption is not enough: The role of knowledge absorption capacity and technological opportunity for individual learning. *Asian Academy of Management Journal*, 28(2), 239–274. 10.21315/aamj2023.28.2.9

Adeel, A., Sarminah, S., Jie, L., Kee, D. M. H., Qasim, D. Y., & Alghafes, R. A. (2023). When procrastination pays off: Role of knowledge sharing ability, autonomous motivation, and task involvement for employee creativity. *Heliyon*, 9(10), e19398. 10.1016/j.heliyon.2023.e1939837767479

Agarwal, A. (2021). *Evaluating the Impact of Smart City Infrastructure on Quality of Life in Indian Cities* (Doctoral dissertation). Indian Institute of Technology, Bombay, India.

Agarwal, R., & Mehrotra, A. (2023). Work-stress content analysis using social media data. *FIIB Business Review*.

Aguinis, H., & Glavas, A. (2019). On Corporate Social Responsibility, Sensemaking, and the Search for Meaningfulness Through Work. *Journal of Management*, 45(1), 105–128. 10.1177/0149206317691575

Aguinis, H., Rupp, D. E., & Glavas, A. (2024). Corporate social responsibility and individual behaviour. *Nature Human Behaviour*, 1–9.38233604

Ahmad, S. F., Rahmat, M. K., Mubarik, M. S., Alam, M. M., & Hyder, S. I. (2021). Artificial intelligence and its role in education. *Sustainability*, 13(22), 12902. 10.3390/su132212902

Ahmad, A., Khan, M. N., & Haque, M. A. (2019). Employer branding aids in enhancing employee attraction and retention. *Journal of Asia-Pacific Business*, 21(1), 27–38. 10.1080/10599231.2020.1708231

Ahmad, M. F. B., & Abd Rashid, K. A. (2011). Lecturers' Industrial Attachment Programme to increase Lecturers' Soft Skill and Technological Competencies for Global Stability and Security. *Journal of Sustainable Development*, 4(1), 281.

Ahmed, G. K., Khedr, E. M., Hamad, D. A., Meshref, T. S., Hashem, M. M., & Aly, M. M. (2021). Long-term impact of COVID-19 infection on sleep and mental health: A cross-sectional study. *Psychiatry Research*, 114243. Advance online publication. 10.1016/j.psychres.2021.11424334673325

Ahmed, M. M. (2021). ICT-enhanced instruction in COVID-19 lockdown: A conceptual paper. *International Journal of Case Studies in BusinessIT and Education*, 5(2), 386–398.

Ahmed, S., Basu, B., Ghosh, S., & Chakraborty, S. (2019). Area Based Development planning for smart cities in India. *Smart and Sustainable Built Environment*, 8(3), 312–331.

Ahvenniemi, H., Huovila, A., Pinto-Seppä, I., & Airaksinen, M. (2017). What are the differences between sustainable and smart cities? *Cities (London, England)*, 60, 234–245. 10.1016/j.cities.2016.09.009

Aina, Y. A. (2017). Achieving smart sustainable cities with GeoICT support: The Saudi evolving smart cities. *Cities (London, England)*, 71, 49–58. 10.1016/j.cities.2017.07.007

Aini, W., Kustono, D., Dardiri, A., & Kamdi, W. (2016). Work-based learning for enhancing the capacity of engagement: Lesson from stakeholders perspective literature. In *AIP Conference Proceedings* (Vol. 1778, No. 1, p. 030052). AIP Publishing LLC.

Aithal, P., & Maiya, A. K. (2023). Innovations in Higher Education Industry—Shaping the Future. *International Journal of Case Studies in Business, IT, and Education*, 7(4), 283–311. 10.47992/IJCSBE.2581.6942.0321

Ajzen, I. (1991). The theory of planned behavior. *Organizational Behavior and Human Decision Processes*, 50(2), 179–211. 10.1016/0749-5978(91)90020-T

Akhtar, F., & Malik, A. (2023). Education and Skills Development: Empowering Youth for Pakistan's Future Workforce. *Pakistan Research Letter*, 1(3), 151-159.

Akunna, L., Okesina, F., Ajiboye, S., & Monisola, E. (2022). Perception of undergraduates on study habit strategies for overcoming examination anxiety in Kwara, Nigeria. *Humanitas*, 19(2), 138–147. 10.26555/humanitas.v19i2.43

Algaraady, J., & Mahyoob, M. (n.d.). *CHATGPT's capabilities in spotting and analyzing writing errors experienced by EFL learners*. AWEJ. 10.24093/awej/call9.1

Ali, L. (2019). The Design of Curriculum, Assessment and Evaluation in Higher Education with Constructive Alignment. *Journal of Education and e-learning Research*, 5(1), 72–78. 10.20448/journal.509.2018.51.72.78

AlKandari, N. Y. (2020). Students anxiety experiences in higher education institutions. In *Anxiety The new achievements*. IntechOpen.

Allam, Z., & Dhunny, Z. A. (2019). On big data, artificial intelligence and smart cities. *Cities (London, England)*, 89, 80–91. 10.1016/j.cities.2019.01.032

Alpaydın, U. A. R., & Fitjar, R. D. (2024). How do university-industry collaborations benefit innovation? Direct and indirect outcomes of different collaboration types. *Growth and Change*, 12721(2). Advance online publication. 10.1111/grow.12721

Alpaydın, Y., & Kültür, K. (2022). Improving the Transition from Higher Education to Employment: A Review of Current Policies. In Akgün, B., & Alpaydın, Y. (Eds.), *Education Policies in the 21st Century*. Maarif Global Education Series. 10.1007/978-981-19-1604-5_5

Alshare, K., & Sewailem, M. F. (2018). A gap analysis of business students' skills in the 21st century: A case study of Qatar. *Academy of Educational Leadership Journal*, 22(1), 1–22.

Al-Tkhayneh, K. M., Alghazo, E. M., & Tahat, D. (2023). The advantages and disadvantages of using artificial intelligence in education. *Journal of Educational and Social Research*, 13(4), 105–105. 10.36941/jesr-2023-0094

Amaral, G. F., Gomide, L. M., Batista, M. D., Píccolo, P. D., Teles, T. B., Oliveira, P. M., & Pereira, M. A. (2008). SintomasdepressivosEmacadêmicos de medicina Da Universidade federal de Goiás: Um estudo de prevalência. *Revista de Psiquiatria do Rio Grande do Sul, 30*(2), 124-130. doi:10.1590/s0101-81082008000300008

Amendola, C., La Bella, S., Joime, G. P., Frattale Mascioli, F. M., & Vito, P. (2022). An Integrated Methodology Model for Smart Mobility System Applied to Sustainable Tourism. *Administrative Sciences, 12*(1), 40. Advance online publication. 10.3390/admsci12010040

American Academy of Pediatrics. (2021, October 19). *AAP-AACAP-CHA Declaration of a National Emergency in Child and Adolescent Mental Health*. Retrieved from https://www.aap.org/en/advocacy/child-and-adolescent-healthy-mental-development/aap-aacap-cha-declaration-of-a-national-emergency-in-child-and-adolescent-mental-health/

American Psychological Association. (2020). *Stress in AmericaTM2020: A National Mental Health Crisis*. American Psychological Association.

Amin, A. (2007). Re-thinking the Urban Social. *City (London, England), 11*(1), 100–114. 10.1080/13604810701200961

Anderson, P. M., Butcher, K. F., & Levine, P. B. (2003). Maternal employment and overweight children. *Journal of Health Economics, 22*(3), 477–504. 10.1016/S0167-6296(03)00022-512683963

Andreassen, C. S., Pallesen, S., Moen, B. E., Bjorvatn, B., Waage, S., & Schaufeli, W. B. (2018). Workaholism and negative work-related incidents among nurses. *Industrial Health, 56*(5), 2017–0223. 10.2486/indhealth.2017-022329760300

Angelidou, M. (2015). Smart cities: A conjuncture of four forces. *Cities (London, England), 47*, 95–106. 10.1016/j.cities.2015.05.004

Angelidou, M., Psaltoglou, A., Komninos, N., Kakderi, C., Tsarchopoulos, P., & Panori, A. (2018). Enhancing sustainable urban development through smart city applications. *Journal of Science and Technology Policy Management, 9*(2), 146–169. 10.1108/JSTPM-05-2017-0016

Angold, A., & Costello, E. J. (2001). The epidemiology of depression in children and adolescents. *The Depressed Child and Adolescent, 2*, 143-178.

Anjum, T., Farrukh, M., Heidler, P., & Díaz Tautiva, J. A. (2020). Entrepreneurial intention: Creativity, entrepreneurship, and university support. *Journal of Open Innovation, 7*(1), 11. 10.3390/joitmc7010011

Ankrah, S., & AL-Tabbaa, O. (2015). Universities–industry collaboration: A systematic review. *Scandinavian Journal of Management, 31*(3), 387–408. 10.1016/j.scaman.2015.02.003

Anthony, B.Jr. (2023). The Role of Community Engagement in Urban Innovation Towards the Co-Creation of Smart Sustainable Cities. *Journal of the Knowledge Economy*. Advance online publication. 10.1007/s13132-023-01176-1

Anthopoulos, L. G., Pourzolfaghar, Z., Lemmer, K., Siebenlist, T., Niehaves, B., & Nikolaou, I. (2022). Smart cities as hubs: Connect, collect and control city flows. *Cities (London, England), 125*, 103660. Advance online publication. 10.1016/j.cities.2022.103660

Antoniucci, V., D'Alpaos, C., & Marella, G. (2015). Energy saving in tall buildings: From urban planning regulation to smart grid building solutions. *International Journal for Housing Science and Its Applications, 39*(2), 101–110. https://www.scopus.com/inward/record.uri?eid=2-s2.0-84938378709&partnerID=40&md5=8e80f90dadb557f7b86f4d5a49a10ffe

Arden, J.-B. (2010). *Rewire your brain*. Wiley.

Arnett, J. J. (2000). Emerging adulthood: A theory of development from the late teens through the twenties. *The American Psychologist, 55*(5), 469–480. 10.1037/0003-066X.55.5.46910842426

Aronsson, G., Gustafsson, K., & Dallner, M. (2000). Sick but yet at work. An empirical study of sickness presenteeism. *Journal of Epidemiology and Community Health*, 54(7), 502–509. 10.1136/jech.54.7.50210846192

Atkinson, G. (2016). *Work-Based Learning and Work-Integrated Learning: Fostering Engagement with Employers*. National Centre for Vocational Education Research Ltd.

Auerbach, R. P., Alonso, J., Axinn, W. G., Cuijpers, P., Ebert, D. D., Green, J. G., Hwang, I., Kessler, R. C., Liu, H., Mortier, P., Nock, M. K., Pinder-Amaker, S., Sampson, N. A., Aguilar-Gaxiola, S., Al-Hamzawi, A., Andrade, L. H., Benjet, C., Caldas-de-Almeida, J. M., Demyttenaere, K., & Bruffaerts, R. (2016). Mental disorders among college students in the World Health Organization World Mental Health Surveys. *Psychological Medicine*, 46(14), 2955–2970. 10.1017/S0033291716001665 27484622

Avery, G. C., & Bergsteiner, H. (2011). Sustainable leadership practices for enhancing business resilience and performance. *Strategy and Leadership*, 39(3), 5–15. 10.1108/10878571111128766

Aziz, H. (2018, October 3). Graduate skills gap. *New Straits Times*. Retrieved from https://www.nst.com.my/education/2018/10/417327/graduate-skills-gap

Baber, P., Baber, R., & Di Virgilio, F. (2023a). Exploring the relationship between workplace spirituality, spiritual survival and innovative work behavior among healthcare professionals. *International Journal of Healthcare Management*, 1–12. 10.1080/20479700.2023.2199555

Baber, R., Baber, P., & Sanyal, A. (2023b). Power and Politics: A Case of Hotel Amada. *FIIB Business Review*, 12(3), 238–242. 10.1177/23197145221139687

Baber, R., Upadhyay, Y., & Kaurav, R. P. S. (2017). Individuals' Motivation for Joining a Social Group: Examining Their Homogeneity. *Asia-Pacific Journal of Management Research and Innovation*, 13(1-2), 43–51. 10.1177/2319510X18760616

Bacikova-Sleskova, M., Benka, J., & Orosova, O. (2014). Parental employment status and adolescents' health: The role of financial situation, parent-adolescent relationship and adolescents' resilience. *Psychology & Health*, 30(4), 400–422. 10.1080/08870446.2014.976645 25322966

Backhaus, K., & Tikoo, S. (2004). Conceptualizing and researching employer branding. *Career Development International*, 9(5), 501–517. 10.1108/13620430410550754

Bag, S. D., Kilby, C. J., Kent, J. N., Brooker, J., & Sherman, K. A. (2022). Resilience, self-compassion, and indices of psychological wellbeing: A not so simple set of relationships. *Australian Psychologist*, 57(4), 249–257. 10.1080/00050067.2022.2089543

Bahuguna, P. C., Bangwal, D., & Kumar, R. (2023). Talent management and its impact on organizational commitment: An empirical investigation of Indian hospitality industry. *FIIB Business Review*, 12(2), 176–192. 10.1177/23197145221101436

Bäker, A., & Natter, M. (2022). Improving gig worker performance and retention on staffing platforms. *Proceedings - Academy of Management*, 2022(1). 10.5465/AMBPP.2022.227

Bandura, A. (1986). *Social foundations of thought and action: A social cognitive theory*. Prentice Hall.

Banker, D. V., & Bhal, K. T. (2020). Understanding compassion from practicing managers' perspective: Vicious and virtuous forces in business organizations. *Global Business Review*, 21(1), 262–278. 10.1177/0972150917749279

Bansal, P. (2023). AI design of Ride-hailing Platforms : A feminist analysis of workers' precarity. In *Amsterdam University Press eBooks*. 10.5117/9789463728386_ch01

Barbayannis, G., Banddari, M., Zheng, X., Baquerizo, H., Pecor, K. W., & Ming, X. (2022). Academic Stress and Mental Well-Being in College Students: Correlations, Affected Groups, and COVID-19. *Frontiers in Psychology*, 13, 886344. Advance online publication. 10.3389/fpsyg.2022.88634435677139

Barnard, A., & Simbhoo, N. (2014). South African managers in public service: On being authentic. *International Journal of Qualitative Studies on Health and Well-being*, 9(1), 20630. 10.3402/qhw.v9.2063024434054

Barnes, T., Pashby, I., & Gibbons, A. (2002). Effective university–industry interaction: A multi-case evaluation of collaborative R&D projects. *European Management Journal*, 20(3), 272–285. 10.1016/S0263-2373(02)00044-0

Barney, J. (1991). Firm Resources and Sustained Competitive Advantage. *Journal of Management*, 17(1), 99–120. 10.1177/014920639101700108

Bartlett, S., & Ross, J. (2022). Mental health and wellbeing of tertiary learners: What do we need to know? *Contemporary Research Topics, 66.*

Bashar, S. (2023, July 17). The Gig Economy and AI: How Artificial Intelligence is Changing Freelancing. *Medium*. https://medium.com/@saikat.ipe92/the-gig-economy-and-ai-how-artificial-intelligence-is-changing-freelancing-1039ed9d2533

Bašić, Ž., Banovac, A., Kružić, I., & Jerković, I. (2023, October 28). *CHATGPT-3.5 as writing assistance in students' essays.* Nature News. https://www.nature.com/articles/s41599-023-02269-7

Basri, M., Husain, B., & Modayama, W. (2021). University students' perceptions in implementing asynchronous learning during Covid-19 era. *Metathesis: Journal of English Language, Literature, and Teaching*, 4(3), 263–276. 10.31002/metathesis.v4i3.2734

Becker-Olsen, K. L., Cudmore, B. A., & Hill, R. P. (2006). The impact of perceived corporate social responsibility on consumer behavior. *Journal of Business Research*, 59(1), 46–53. 10.1016/j.jbusres.2005.01.001

Behere, A. P., Basnet, P., & Campbell, P. (2017). Effects of family structure on mental health of children: A preliminary study. *Indian Journal of Psychological Medicine*, 39(4), 457–463. 10.4103/0253-7176.21176728852240

Behl, A., Sampat, B., & Raj, S. (2021). Productivity of gig workers on crowdsourcing platforms through artificial intelligence and gamification: A multi-theoretical approach. *The TQM Journal*. Advance online publication. 10.1108/TQM-07-2021-0201

Bekkers, R., & Bodas Freitas, I. M. (2008). Analysing knowledge transfer channels between universities and industry: To what degree do sectors also matter? *Research Policy*, 37(10), 1837–1853. 10.1016/j.respol.2008.07.007

Belanche, D., Casaló, L. V., & Orús, C. (2016). City attachment and use of urban services: Benefits for smart cities. *Cities (London, England)*, 50, 75–81. 10.1016/j.cities.2015.08.016

Belwal, S., Al Maqbali, A. A. H., & Belwal, R. (2023). Understanding the Impact of Occupational Stress on the Home Environment: Evidence from Oman. *FIIB Business Review*, 12(3), 263–278. 10.1177/23197145221132064

Berawi, M. A. (2022). New City Development: Creating a Better Future and Added Value. *International Journal of Technology*, 13(2), 225–228. 10.14716/ijtech.v13i2.5598

Berbegal-Mirabent, J., Sánchez García, J. L., & Ribeiro-Soriano, D. E. (2015). University–industry partnerships for the provision of R&D services. *Journal of Business Research*, 68(7), 1407–1413. 10.1016/j.jbusres.2015.01.023

Berger, E. S. C., & Blanka, C. (2023). Comprehensive and multifaceted perspectives on sustainability, urban studies, and entrepreneurship. *Small Business Economics*. Advance online publication. 10.1007/s11187-023-00762-6

Berk, J., & DeMarzo, P. (2016). *Corporate Finance*. Pearson Education.

Bhandari, R. (2023). Bridging the skills gap: Fuelling careers and the economy in Malaysia. *Economist Impact*. Retrieved from https://impact.economist.com/perspectives/talent-education/bridging-skills-gap-fuelling-careers-and-economy-malaysia

Bibri, S. E. (2021). The underlying components of data-driven smart sustainable cities of the future: A case study approach to an applied theoretical framework. *European Journal of Futures Research*, 9(1), 13. Advance online publication. 10.1186/s40309-021-00182-3

Bibri, S. E., & Krogstie, J. (2019). Generating a vision for smart sustainable cities of the future: A scholarly backcasting approach. *European Journal of Futures Research*, 7(1), 5. Advance online publication. 10.1186/s40309-019-0157-0

Bishop, S.-J. (2007). Neurocognitive mechanisms of anxiety: An integrative account. *Trends in Cognitive Sciences*, 11(7), 307–316. 10.1016/j.tics.2007.05.00817553730

Blagojević, D., Nagy, I., Lukić, A., & Tešić, D. (2020). Adaptation To Climate Change Through Theories Of Urban Development. *DETUROPE*, *12*(3), 37 – 57. https://www.scopus.com/inward/record.uri?eid=2-s2.0-85103100540&partnerID=40&md5=ea2701a25107f58c081ae3169888269d

Blanco, C., Okuda, M., Wright, C., Hasin, D. S., Grant, B. F., Liu, S., & Olfson, M. (2008). The mental health of college students and their non-college-attending peers: Results from the National Epidemiologic Study on Alcohol and Related Conditions. *Archives of General Psychiatry*, 65(12), 1429–1437. 10.1001/archpsyc.65.12.142919047530

Block, F., & Keller, M. R. (1970). Where Do Innovations Come From? Transformations in the US National Innovation System, 1970-2006. *Innovation*.

Bodie, Z., Kane, A., & Marcus, A. J. (2018). *Investments*. McGraw-Hill Education.

Bornstein, M. H., Cote, L. R., & Venuti, P. (2001). Parenting beliefs and behaviors in northern and southern groups of Italian mothers of young infants. *Journal of Family Psychology*, 15(4), 663–675. 10.1037/0893-3200.15.4.66311770473

Bowden, J. L. H. (2009). The process of employees' engagement: A conceptual framework. *Journal of Marketing Theory and Practice*, 17(1), 63–74. 10.2753/MTP1069-6679170105

Bowden, P. (2022). *Employee engagement and how to achieve it*. Chartered Institute of Personnel and Development.

Boyd-Franklin, N. (2003). *Black families in therapy*. Guildford Press.

Bozkurt, A. (2022). Resilience, Adaptability, and Sustainability of Higher Education: A Systematic Mapping Study on the Impact of the Coronavirus (COVID-19) Pandemic and the Transition to the New Normal. *Journal of Learning for Development*, 9(1), 1–16. 10.56059/jl4d.v9i1.590

Brammer, S., Millington, A., & Rayton, B. (2007). The contribution of corporation social responsibility to organizational commitment. *International Journal of Human Resource Management*, 18(10), 1701–1719. 10.1080/09585190701570866

Brandao, T. (2023, November 9). *The future of work: Navigating benefits and challenges ahead*. Sesame HR. https://www.sesamehr.com/blog/future-work/

Bratman, G. N., & Alvarez, H. O. (2021). Psychological impacts from COVID-19 among university students: Risk factors across seven states in the United States. *PLoS One*, 16(1), e0245327. 10.1371/journal.pone.024532733411812

Bridger, R. (2008). *Introduction to ergonomics*. Crc Press.

Bridges, D. (2000). Back to the Future : The higher education curriculum in the 21st century. *Cambridge Journal of Education*, 30(1), 37–55. 10.1080/03057640050005762

Briggs-Gowan, M. J., Carter, A. S., Bosson-Heenan, J., Guyer, A. E., & Horwitz, S. M. (2006). Are infant-toddler social-emotional and behavioral problems transient? *Journal of the American Academy of Child and Adolescent Psychiatry*, 45(7), 849–858. 10.1097/01.chi.0000220849.48650.5916832322

Brigham, E. F., & Ehrhardt, M. C. (2013). *Financial Management: Theory & Practice*. Cengage Learning.

Broadbent, E., Kumar, V., Li, X., Sollers, J.III, Stafford, R. Q., MacDonald, B. A., & Wegner, D. M. (2013). Robots with display screens: A robot with a more humanlike face display is perceived to have more mind and a better personality. *PLoS One*, 8(8), e72589. 10.1371/journal.pone.007258924015263

Brody, G. H., Stoneman, Z., & Burke, M. (1987). Child temperaments, maternal differential behavior, and sibling relationships. *Developmental Psychology*, 23(3), 354–362. 10.1037/0012-1649.23.3.354

Brown, M. (2023, June 2). *How AI programs are threatening the future of the gig industry - Jarvee*. Jarvee. https://jarvee .com/how-ai-programs-are-threatening-the-future-of-the-gig-industry/

Brown, C. (2019). Risk Management Strategies for Innovation-Driven Businesses. *International Journal of Financial Management*, 22(4), 112–125.

Brown, C. L., & Garcia, M. R. (2019). Utilizing R software for systematic literature reviews: A methodological approach. *Journal of Applied Research Methods*, 8(2), 78–94.

Bruffaerts, R., Mortier, P., Kiekens, G., Auerbach, R. P., Cuijpers, P., Demyttenaere, K., & Kessler, R. C. (2018). Mental health problems in college freshmen: Prevalence and academic functioning. *Journal of Affective Disorders*, 225, 97–103. 10.1016/j.jad.2017.07.04428802728

Bruneel, J., D'Este, P., & Salter, A. (2010). Investigating the factors that diminish the barriers to university–industry collaboration. *Research Policy*, 39(7), 858–868. 10.1016/j.respol.2010.03.006

Bstieler, L., Hemmert, M., & Barczak, G. (2015). Trust formation in university-industry collaborations in the US biotechnology industry: IP policies, shared governance, and champions. *Journal of Product Innovation Management*, 32(1), 111–121. 10.1111/jpim.12242

Burbidge, J. G. (2013). *Effect of sibling relationships on well-being and depression in adults with and without developmental disabilities*. Queen's University.

Burov, O. (2020). Human Factors/Ergonomics in eWorld: Methodology, Techniques and Applications. In Karwowski, W., Trzcielinski, S., & Mrugalska, B. (Eds.), *Advances in Manufacturing, Production Management and Process Control. AHFE 2019. Advances in Intelligent Systems and Computing* (Vol. 971). Springer. 10.1007/978-3-030-20494-5_43

Cai, M., Kassens-Noor, E., Zhao, Z., & Colbry, D. (2023). Are smart cities more sustainable? An exploratory study of 103 U.S. cities. *Journal of Cleaner Production*, 416, 137986. Advance online publication. 10.1016/j.jclepro.2023.137986

Carayannis, E. G., & Campbell, D. F. (2018). *Smart quintuple helix innovation systems: How social ecology and environmental protection are driving innovation, sustainable development and economic growth*. Springer.

Carless, D. (2006). Differing perceptions in the feedback process. *Studies in Higher Education*, 31(2), 219–233. 10.1080/03075070600572132

Carrington, M. J., Neville, B. A., & Whitwell, G. J. (2010). Why ethical consumers don't walk their talk: Towards a framework for understanding the gap between the ethical purchase intentions and actual buying behaviour of ethically minded consumers. *Journal of Business Ethics*, 97(1), 139–158. 10.1007/s10551-010-0501-6

Carter, E., Adam, P., Tsakis, D., Shaw, S., Watson, R., & Ryan, P. (2020). Enhancing pedestrian mobility in Smart Cities using Big Data. *Journal of Management Analytics*, 7(2), 173–188. 10.1080/23270012.2020.1741039

Carvalho, L., & Campos, J. B. (2013). Developing the PlanIT valley: A view on the governance and societal embedding of u-eco city pilots. *International Journal of Knowledge-Based Development*, 4(2), 109–125. 10.1504/IJKBD.2013.054089

Caspi, A., Begg, D., Dickson, N., Harrington, H., Langley, J., Moffitt, T. E., & Silva, P. A. (1997). Personality differences predict health-risk behaviors in young adulthood: Evidence from a longitudinal study. *Journal of Personality and Social Psychology*, 73(5), 1052–1063. 10.1037/0022-3514.73.5.10529364760

Castanho, M. S., Ferreira, F. A. F., Carayannis, E. G., & Ferreira, J. J. M. (2021). SMART-C: Developing a "Smart City" Assessment System Using Cognitive Mapping and the Choquet Integral. *IEEE Transactions on Engineering Management*, 68(2), 562–573. 10.1109/TEM.2019.2909668

Castillo, L. G., & Schwartz, S. J. (2013). Introduction to the Special Issue on College Student Mental Health. *Journal of Clinical Psychology*, 69(4), 291–297. 10.1002/jclp.2197223381839

Casuso-Holgado, M. J., Moreno-Morales, N., Labajos-Manzanares, M. T., & Montero-Bancalero, F. J. (2019). The association between perceived health symptoms and academic stress in Spanish higher education students. *European Journal of Education and Psychology*, 12(2), 109–123. 10.30552/ejep.v12i2.277

Cavalheiro, M. B., Joia, L. A., Cavalheiro, G. M. D. C., & Mayer, V. F. (2021). Smart tourism destinations: (mis)aligning touristic destinations and smart city initiatives. *BAR - Brazilian Administration Review*, 18(1), e190132. Advance online publication. 10.1590/1807-7692bar2021190132

CBI & Pearson. (2016). *The right combination: CBI/Pearson education and skills survey*. Retrieved from www.cbi.org .uk/cbi-prod/assets/File/pdf/cbi-education-and-skills- survey2016.pdf

Cebi, P. D., & Kozikoglu, N. (2015). Designing for the future of the city. *International Journal for Housing Science and Its Applications*, 39(2), 111–122. https://www.scopus.com/inward/record.uri?eid=2-s2.0-84938340285&partnerID=40 &md5=87af1b9fd3482da61fac7febd6f7a3e7

Chamorro-premuzic, T., & Frankiewicz, B. (2019, January 14). Does Higher Education Still Prepare People for Jobs? *Harvard Business Review*. https://hbr.org/2019/01/does-higher-education-still-prepare-people-for-jobs

Chamorro-premuzic, T., & Frankiewicz, B. (2019, January 7). Does Higher Education Still Prepare People for Jobs? *Harvard Business Review*.

Chan, C. S., & Tsun, W. Y. (2023). Unleashing the potential of local brand equity of Hong Kong as a green–creative–smart city. *Journal of Place Management and Development*. 10.1108/JPMD-12-2022-0122

Chang, D. L., Sabatini-Marques, J., da Costa, E. M., Selig, P. M., & Yigitcanlar, T. (2018). Knowledge-based, smart and sustainable cities: A provocation for a conceptual framework. *Journal of Open Innovation*, 4(1), 1–17. Advance online publication. 10.1186/s40852-018-0087-2

Chang, M. J., Kang, J. H., Ko, Y. J., & Connaughton, D. P. (2017). The effects of perceived team performance and social responsibility on pride and word-of-mouth recommendation. *Sport Marketing Quarterly*, 26, 31.

Chan, Y. F., & Balaraman, S. (2019). Strategies to Close the Knowledge Gap of New Engineers in The Automotive Industry in Malaysia. *International Journal of Academic Research in Business and Social Sciences, 9*(13), 270-283.

Chen, L., Wu, Q., & Jiang, L. (2022). Impact of environmental concern on ecological purchasing behavior: The moderating effect of Prosociality. *Sustainability (Basel)*, 14(5), 3004. 10.3390/su14053004

Chen, M. F., & Tung, P. J. (2014). Developing an extended theory of planned behavior model to predict consumers' intention to visit green hotels. *International Journal of Hospitality Management*, 36, 221–230. 10.1016/j.ijhm.2013.09.006

Chinonso, O. E., Theresa, A. M.-E., & Aduke, T. C. (2023). ChatGPT for teaching, learning and research: Prospects and challenges. *Global Academic Journal of Humanities and Social Sciences*, 5(02), 33–40. 10.36348/gajhss.2023.v05i02.001

Choi, H. J. (2021). Effect of chief executive officer's sustainable leadership styles on organization members' psychological well-being and organizational citizenship behavior. *Sustainability (Basel)*, 13(24), 13676. 10.3390/su132413676

Christensen, C. M., & Raynor, M. E. (2011). The innovator's solution. *Journal of the American College of Radiology*, 8(6), 382. 10.1016/j.jacr.2011.03.004

Cicirelli, V. G. (1989). Feelings of attachment to siblings and well-being in later life. *Psychology and Aging*, 4(2), 211–216. 10.1037/0882-7974.4.2.2112789748

Cignitas, C. P., Arevalo, J. A. T., & Crusells, J. V. (2022). *The effect of strategy performance management methods on employee wellbeing: A case study analyzing the effects of balanced scorecard*. Academic Press.

Coca-Stefaniak, J. A. (2020). Beyond smart tourism cities – towards a new generation of "wise" tourism destinations. *Journal of Tourism Futures*, 7(2), 251–258. 10.1108/JTF-11-2019-0130

Coccossis, H., Delladetsimas, P.-M., & Niavis, S. (2017). The challenge of incorporating smart city activities in medium-size cities: The case of Greece. *International Journal of Services Technology and Management*, 23(5–6), 381–402. 10.1504/IJSTM.2017.088947

Cochran, P. L. (2007). The evolution of corporate social responsibility. *Business Horizons*, 50(6), 449–454. 10.1016/j.bushor.2007.06.004

Cohen, J. (2013). *Statistical power analysis for the behavioral sciences*. Academic press. 10.4324/9780203771587

Colombo, M. G., & Delmastro, M. (2002). How effective are technology incubators? *Research Policy*, 31(7), 1103–1122. 10.1016/S0048-7333(01)00178-0

Connell, J., Brazier, J., O'Cathain, A., Lloyd-Jones, M., & Paisley, S. (2012). Quality of Life of people with mental health problems: A synthesis of qualitative research. *Health and Quality of Life Outcomes*, 10(1), 138. 10.1186/1477-7525-10-13823173689

Connelly, B. S., & McAbee, S. T. (2024). Reputations at work: Origins and outcomes of shared person perceptions. *Annual Review of Organizational Psychology and Organizational Behavior*, 11(1), 251–278. 10.1146/annurev-orgpsych-110721-022320

Cooper, R. G. (2008). Perspective: The Stage-Gate Idea-to-Launch Process—Update, What's New, and NexGen Systems. *Journal of Product Innovation Management*, 25(3), 213–232. 10.1111/j.1540-5885.2008.00296.x

Corsi, C., & Prencipe, A. (2016). Improving Innovation in University Spin-Offs: The Fostering Role of University and Region. *Journal of Technology Management & Innovation*, 11(2), 13–21. 10.4067/S0718-27242016000200002

Costa, E. F., Rocha, M. M., Santos, A. T., Melo, E. V., Martins, L. A., & Andrade, T. M. (2014). Common mental disorders and associated factors among final-year healthcare students. *Revista da Associação Médica Brasileira*, 60(6), 525–530. 10.1590/1806-9282.60.06.00925650851

Costarelli, S., & Colloca, P. (2007). The moderation of ambivalence on attitude–intention relations as mediated by attitude importance. *European Journal of Social Psychology*, 37(5), 923–933. 10.1002/ejsp.403

Côté, K., Lauzier, M., & Stinglhamber, F. (2021). The relationship between presenteeism and job satisfaction: A mediated moderation model using work engagement and perceived organizational support. *European Management Journal*, 39(2), 270–278. 10.1016/j.emj.2020.09.001

Crane, A., & Matten, D. (2016). *Business ethics: Managing corporate citizenship and sustainability in the age of globalization*. Oxford University Press.

Cravero, S. (2020). Methods, strategies and tools to improve citizens' engagement in the smart cities' context: A serious games classification [Metodi, strategie e strumenti per migliorare il coinvolgimento dei cittadini nelle smart cities: Una classificazione di Serious Games]. *Valori e Valutazioni, 2020*(24), 45 – 60. https://www.scopus.com/inward/record.uri?eid=2-s2.0-85087766230&partnerID=40&md5=9ffbae61e17fbff2618ab39989014165

Creswell, J. (2003). *Research Design: Qualitative, Quantitative and Mixed Methods* (2nd ed.). Sage Publications.

Cronbach, L. J. (1951). Coefficient alpha and the internal structure of tests. *Psychometrika, 16*(3), 297-334.

Cropley, D. H. (2015). *Creativity in engineering: Novel solutions to complex problems. Explorations in creativity research*. Elsevier Academic Press. 10.1016/B978-0-12-800225-4.00002-1

Dana, L.-P., Salamzadeh, A., Hadizadeh, M., Heydari, G., & Shamsoddin, S. (2022). Urban entrepreneurship and sustainable businesses in smart cities: Exploring the role of digital technologies. *Sustainable Technology and Entrepreneurship*, 1(2), 100016. Advance online publication. 10.1016/j.stae.2022.100016

Daradkeh, M., & Mansoor, W. (2023). The impact of network orientation and entrepreneurial orientation on startup innovation and performance in emerging economies: The moderating role of strategic flexibility. *Journal of Open Innovation*, 9(1), 100004. 10.1016/j.joitmc.2023.02.001

Dashiff, C., DiMicco, W., Myers, B., & Sheppard, K. (2009). Poverty and Adolescent Mental Health. *Journal of Child and Adolescent Psychiatric Nursing*, 22(1), 23–32. 10.1111/j.1744-6171.2008.00166.x19200289

Dashkevych, O., & Portnov, B. A. (2023). Human-centric, sustainability-driven approach to ranking smart cities worldwide. *Technology in Society*, 74, 102296. Advance online publication. 10.1016/j.techsoc.2023.102296

DaSilva, C. M., & Trkman, P. (2014). Business Model: What It Is and What It Is Not. *Long Range Planning*, 47(6), 379–389. 10.1016/j.lrp.2013.08.004

De Von, H. A., Block, M. E., Moyle-Wright, P., Ernst, D. M., Hayden, S. J., Lazzara, D. J., Savoy, S. M., & Kostas-Polston, E. (2007). A psychometric toolbox for testing validity and reliability. *Journal of Nursing Scholarship*, 39(2), 155–164. 10.1111/j.1547-5069.2007.00161.x17535316

Deakin, M., & Reid, A. (2018). Smart cities: Under-gridding the sustainability of city-districts as energy efficient-low carbon zones. *Journal of Cleaner Production*, 173, 39–48. 10.1016/j.jclepro.2016.12.054

Deb, S., Strodl, E., & Sun, J. (2015). Academic Stress, Parental Pressure, Anxiety and Mental Health among Indian High School Students. *International Journal of Psychology and Behavioral Sciences*, 5(1), 26–34.

Deery, S., Walsh, J., & Zatzick, C. D. (2014). A moderated mediation analysis of job demands, presenteeism, and absenteeism. *Journal of Occupational and Organizational Psychology*, 87(2), 352–369. 10.1111/joop.12051

DeHart, T., Pelham, B. W., & Tennen, H. (2006). What lies beneath: Parenting style and implicit self-esteem. *Journal of Experimental Social Psychology*, 42(1), 1–17. 10.1016/j.jesp.2004.12.005

Delhi Showcases Over, I. I. T. (n.d.). *80 Technologies Developed by its Researchers at 4th Industry Day.*https://home.iitd.ac.in/show.php?id=149&in_sections=Press

Deloitte India. (2019). *Smart Cities in India: A Roadmap for Digital Transformation.* Author.

Demerouti, E., Le Blanc, P. M., Bakker, A. B., Schaufeli, W. B., & Hox, J. (2009). Present but sick: A three-wave study on job demands, presenteeism and burnout. *Career Development International*, 14(1), 50–68. 10.1108/13620430910933574

Dessart, L., Veloutsou, C., & Morgan-Thomas, A. (2015). Consumer engagement in online brand communities: A social media perspective. *Journal of Product and Brand Management*, 24(1), 28–42. 10.1108/JPBM-06-2014-0635

Di Fabio, A., & Peiró, J. M. (2018). Human Capital Sustainability Leadership to promote sustainable development and healthy organizations: A new scale. *Sustainability (Basel)*, 10(7), 2413. 10.3390/su10072413

Di Maria, E., De Marchi, V., & Spraul, K. (2019). Who benefits from university–industry collaboration for environmental sustainability? *International Journal of Sustainability in Higher Education*, 20(6), 1022–1041. 10.1108/IJSHE-10-2018-0172

Diamantopoulos, A., Riefler, P., & Roth, K. P. (2008). Advancing formative measurement models. *Journal of Business Research*, 61(12), 1203–1218. 10.1016/j.jbusres.2008.01.009

Diána, E., & Mária, S. C. (2022). Assessing the links between the digital transformation and the sustainability transition in the capitals of the European Union [A digitális átalakulás és a fenntarthatósági átmenet összefüggéseinek értékelése az Európai Unió fővárosaiban]. *Teruleti Statisztika*, 62(6), 683–697. 10.15196/TS620603

Dickson, G., & Zhang, J. J. (2021). Sports and urban development: An introduction. *International Journal of Sports Marketing & Sponsorship*, 22(1), 1–9. 10.1108/IJSMS-11-2020-0194

Divaris, K., Mafla, A. C., Villa-Torres, L., Sánchez-Molina, M., Gallego-Gómez, C. L., Vélez-Jaramillo, L. F., & Polychronopoulou, A. (2013). Psychological distress and its correlates among dental students: A survey of 17 Colombian dental schools. *BMC Medical Education*, 13(1), 91. Advance online publication. 10.1186/1472-6920-13-9123802917

Dizon, G., & Gayed, J. M. (2023, April 25). Exa*mining the impact of Grammarly on the quality of mobile L2 writing.* Castledown. 10.29140/jaltcall.v17n2.336

Dorsey, S., Lucid, L., Murray, L., Bolton, P., Itemba, D., Manongi, R., & Whetten, K. (2015). A qualitative study of mental health problems among orphaned children and adolescents in Tanzania. *The Journal of Nervous and Mental Disease*, 203(11), 864–870. 10.1097/NMD.0000000000000038826488916

Drysdale, M. T. B., & McBeath, M. (2018). Motivation, self-efficacy and learning strategies of university students participating in work-integrated learning. *Journal of Education and Work*, 31(5–6), 478–488. 10.1080/13639080.2018.1533240

Duggan, J., Sherman, U., Carbery, R., & McDonnell, A. (2021). Boundaryless careers and algorithmic constraints in the gig economy. *International Journal of Human Resource Management*, 33(22), 4468–4498. 10.1080/09585192.2021.1953565

Dul, J., Bruder, R., Buckle, P., Carayon, P., Falzon, P., Marras, W.S., Wilson, J.R. & van der Doelen, B.A. (2012). Strategy for human factors/ergonomics: developing the discipline and profession. *Ergonomics, 55*(4), 377-95. 10.1080/00140139.2012.661087

Dupont, L., Morel, L., & Guidat, C. (2015). Innovative public-private partnership to support Smart City: The case of "Chaire REVES.". *Journal of Strategy and Management*, 8(3), 245–265. 10.1108/JSMA-03-2015-0027

Dutton, J. E., Lilius, J. M., & Kanov, J. M. (2007). The transformative potential of compassion at work. *Handbook of transformative cooperation: New designs and dynamics, 1*, 107-126.

Dutton, J. E., Lilius, J. M., & Kanov, J. M. (2007). The transformative potential of compassion at work. In Piderit, S. K., Fry, R. E., & Cooperrider, D. L. (Eds.), *Handbook of transformative cooperation: New designs and dynamics* (pp. 107–124). Stanford University Press. 10.1515/9781503625969-006

Dwairy, M., & Menshar, K. E. (2006). Parenting style, individuation, and mental health of Egyptian adolescents. *Journal of Adolescence*, 29(1), 103–117. 10.1016/j.adolescence.2005.03.00216338432

Dye, C. (2008). Health and urban living. *Science*, 319(5864), 766–769. 10.1126/science.115019818258905

Dyreng, S. D., Hanlon, M., & Maydew, E. L. (2008). Long-Run Corporate Tax Avoidance. *The Accounting Review*, 83(1), 61–82. 10.2308/accr.2008.83.1.61

Eichelberger, S., Peters, M., Pikkemaat, B., & Chan, C.-S. (2020). Entrepreneurial ecosystems in smart cities for tourism development: From stakeholder perceptions to regional tourism policy implications. *Journal of Hospitality and Tourism Management*, 45, 319–329. 10.1016/j.jhtm.2020.06.011

Eisenberg, D., Hunt, J., & Speer, N. (2012). Help-seeking for mental health on college campuses: Review of evidence and next steps for research and practice. *Harvard Review of Psychiatry*, 20(4), 222–232. 10.3109/10673229.2012.712 83922894731

Ek Styvén, M., Näppä, A., Mariani, M., & Nataraajan, R. (2022). Employee perceptions of employers' creativity and innovation: Implications for employer attractiveness and branding in tourism and hospitality. *Journal of Business Research*, 141, 290–298. 10.1016/j.jbusres.2021.12.038

El Ansari, W., & Stock, C. (2010). Isthe health andwellbeing of university students associated with their academic performance? Cross sectional findings from the United Kingdom. *International Journal of Environmental Research and Public Health*, 7(2), 509–527. 10.3390/ijerph702050920616988

Elani, H. W., Allison, P. J., Kumar, R. A., Mancini, L., Lambrou, A., & Bedos, C. (2014). A systematic review of stress in dental students. *Journal of Dental Education*, 78(2), 226–242. http://www.jdentaled.org/ content/78/2/226.full.pdf+html. 10.1002/j.0022-0337.2014.78.2.tb05673.x24489030

Elardo-Zabala. (2021). The Leadership Styles of the Local Universities and Colleges' Administrators. *International Journal of Educational Management and Development Studies, 2*(2), 20-37.

Elayan, M. B. (2022). Transformation of Human Resources Management Solutions as a strategic tool for GIG workers contracting. In *IGI Global eBooks* (pp. 711–734). 10.4018/978-1-6684-3873-2.ch038

El-Said, O. A. (2020). Impact of online reviews on hotel booking intention: The moderating role of brand image, star category, and price. *Tourism Management Perspectives*, 33, 100604. 10.1016/j.tmp.2019.100604

Epstein, M. J., & Buhovac, A. R. (2014). *Making Sustainability Work: Best Practices in Managing and Measuring Corporate Social, Environmental, and Economic Impacts*. Berrett-Koehler Publishers.

Erevik, E. K., Pallesen, S., Vedaa, Ø., Andreassen, C. S., Dhir, A., & Torsheim, T. (2020). General and alcohol-related social media use and mental health: A large-sample longitudinal study. *International Journal of Mental Health and Addiction*, 19(6), 1991–2002. 10.1007/s11469-020-00296-y

Ergonomics—Physiopedia. (n.d.). Retrieved 23 December 2023, from https://www.physio-pedia.com/Ergonomics

Ergün, H. S., & Kuşcu, Z. K. (2013). Innovation orientation, market orientation and e-loyalty: Evidence from Turkish e-commerce customers. *Procedia: Social and Behavioral Sciences*, 99, 509–516. 10.1016/j.sbspro.2013.10.520

Esashika, D., Masiero, G., & Mauger, Y. (2021). An investigation into the elusive concept of smart cities: A systematic review and meta-synthesis. *Technology Analysis and Strategic Management*, 33(8), 957–969. 10.1080/09537325.2020.1856804

Escorpizo, R. (2008). Understanding work productivity and its application to work-related musculoskeletal disorders. *International Journal of Industrial Ergonomics*, 38(3-4), 291–297. 10.1016/j.ergon.2007.10.018

Etzkowitz, H. (2004). The evolution of the entrepreneurial university. *International Journal of Technology and Globalisation*, 1(1), 64–77. 10.1504/IJTG.2004.004551

Etzkowitz, H. (2013). Anatomy of the entrepreneurial university. *Social Sciences Information. Information Sur les Sciences Sociales*, 52(3), 486–511. 10.1177/0539018413485832

Etzkowitz, H., & Leydesdorff, L. (2000). Leydesdorff, L. The triple helix: An evolutionary model of innovations. *Research Policy*, 29(2), 243–255. 10.1016/S0048-7333(99)00063-3

Etzkowitz, H., & Leydesdorff, L. (2000). The dynamics of innovation: From National Systems and "Mode 2" to a Triple Helix of university-industry-government relations. *Research Policy*, 29(2), 109–123. 10.1016/S0048-7333(99)00055-4

European Association of Research & Technology Organization. (2014). *The TRL Scale as Research & Innovation Policy Tool.* EARTO Recommendations.

Eusof, N. S. (2024). Hays: Skill shortages a burden to Malaysian employers. *The Edge Malaysia.* Retrieved from https://theedgemalaysia.com/article/hays-skill-shortages-burden-malaysian-employers

Fabozzi, F. J., & Markowitz, H. M. (2011). *The Theory and Practice of Investment Management: Asset Allocation, Valuation, Portfolio Construction, and Strategies.* John Wiley & Sons. 10.1002/9781118267028

Farid, A. M., Alshareef, M., Badhesha, P. S., Boccaletti, C., Cacho, N. A. A., Carlier, C.-I., Corriveau, A., Khayal, I., Liner, B., Martins, J. S. B., Rahimi, F., Rossett, R., Schoonenberg, W. C. H., Stillwell, A., & Wang, Y. (2021). Smart City Drivers and Challenges in Urban-Mobility, Health-Care, and Interdependent Infrastructure Systems. *IEEE Potentials*, 40(1), 11–16. 10.1109/MPOT.2020.3011399

Farooq, M. S., Salam, M., Fayolle, A., Jaafar, N., & Ayupp, K. (2018). Impact of service quality on customer satisfaction in Malaysia airlines: A PLS-SEM approach. *Journal of Air Transport Management*, 67, 169–180. 10.1016/j.jairtraman.2017.12.008

Farooq, M. S., Salam, M., Jaafar, N., Fayolle, A., Ayupp, K., Radovic-Markovic, M., & Sajid, A. (2017). Acceptance and use of lecture capture system (LCS) in executive business studies: Extending UTAUT2. *Interactive Technology and Smart Education*, 14(4), 329–348. 10.1108/ITSE-06-2016-0015

Fergusson, D. M., Woodward, L. J., & Horwood, L. J. (2013). Risk factors and life processes associated with the onset of suicidal behaviour during adolescence and early adulthood. *Psychological Medicine*, 30(1), 23–39. 10.1017/S003329179900135X10722173

Ferreira, A. C. D., Titotto, S. L. M. C., & Akkari, A. C. S. (2022). Urban Agriculture 5.0: An Exploratory Approach to the Food System in a Super Smart Society. International Journal of Mathematical. *Engineering and Management Sciences*, 7(4), 455–475. 10.33889/IJMEMS.2022.7.4.030

Fornell, C., & Larcker, D. F. (1981). Evaluating structural equation models with unobservable variables and measurement error. *JMR, Journal of Marketing Research*, 18(1), 39–50. 10.1177/002224378101800104

Frackiewicz, M. (2023). *Transforming the Gig Economy with AI: Top Opportunities.* Retrieved from https://ts2.space/en/transforming-the-gig-economy-with-ai-top-opportunities/#gsc.tab=00

Frąckiewicz, M. (2023a, May 19). *How AI is Shaping the Future of Work: Profitable Gig Economy Opportunities*. TS2 SPACE. https://ts2.space/en/how-ai-is-shaping-the-future-of-work-profitable-gig-economy-opportunities/#gsc.tab=0

Frąckiewicz, M. (2023b, July 27). *AI in the Gig Economy: Opportunities and Challenges for Workers and Businesses*. TS2 SPACE. https://ts2.space/en/ai-in-the-gig-economy-opportunities-and-challenges-for-workers-and-businesses/#gsc.tab=0

Franco, M., & Haase, H. (2015). University–industry cooperation: Researchers' motivations and interaction channels. *Journal of Engineering and Technology Management*, 36, 41–51. 10.1016/j.jengtecman.2015.05.002

Frissen, A., van Os, J., Lieverse, R., Habets, P., Gronenschild, E., & Marcelis, M. (2017). No evidence of association between childhood urban environment and cortical thinning in psychotic disorder. *PLoS One*, 12(1), e0166651. 10.1371/journal.pone.016665128045900

Galeeva, A., Mingazova, N., & Gilmanshin, I. (2014). Sustainable urban development: Urban green spaces and water bodies in the city of Kazan, Russia. *Mediterranean Journal of Social Sciences*, 5(24), 356–360. 10.5901/mjss.2014.v5n24p356

Gallagher, S. E., & Savage, T. (2023). Challenge-based learning in higher education: An exploratory literature review. *Teaching in Higher Education*, 28(6), 1135–1157. 10.1080/13562517.2020.1863354

Gallup Consulting. (2001). *Employees' engagement: What's Your Engagement Ratio?* Available at www.gallup.com/consulting/121901/Customer-Engagement-Overview-Brochure.aspx

Gandhi, M. M. (2014). Industry-academia collaboration in India: Recent initiatives, issues, challenges, opportunities and strategies. *The Business & Management Review*, 5(2), 45.

Ganga, X. (2021, June 1). Educational Artificial Intelligence (EAI) Connotation, Key Technology and Application Trend -Interpretation and analysis of the two reports entitled "Preparing for the Future of Artificial Intelligence" and "The National Artificial Intelligence Research and Development Strategic Plan." *IEEE Xplore*. 10.1109/ICAA53760.2021.00046

Gao, C. A., Howard, F. M., Markov, N. S., Dyer, E. C., Ramesh, S., Luo, Y., & Pearson, A. T. (2023, April 26). *Comparing scientific abstracts generated by CHATGPT to real abstracts with detectors and blinded human reviewers*. Nature News. https://www.nature.com/articles/s41746-023-00819-6

Gao, C., Gao, C., Song, K., & Fang, K. (2020). Pathways towards regional circular economy evaluated using material flow analysis and system dynamics. *Resources, Conservation and Recycling*, 154, 104527. Advance online publication. 10.1016/j.resconrec.2019.104527

Garbie, I. (2017). Identifying challenges facing manufacturing enterprises toward implementing sustainability in newly industrialized countries. *Journal of Manufacturing Technology Management*, 28(7), 928–960. 10.1108/JMTM-02-2017-0025

García-Fuentes, M. Á., & de Torre, C. (2017). Towards smarter and more sustainable cities: The remourban model. *Entrepreneurship and Sustainability Issues*, 4(3), 328–338. 10.9770/jesi.2017.4.3S(8)

García, O. F., Serra, E., Zacarés, J. J., & García, F. (2018). Parenting styles and short- and long-term socialization outcomes: A study among Spanish adolescents and older adults. *Psychosocial Intervention*, 27(3), 153–161. 10.5093/pi2018a21

Ghazali, G., & Bennett, D. (2017). Employability for music graduates : Malaysian educational reform and the focus on generic skills. *International Journal of Music Education*, 35(4), 588–600. 10.1177/0255761416689844

Gillet, N., Austin, S., Fernet, C., Sandrin, E., Lorho, F., Brault, S., Becker, M., & Aubouin Bonnaventure, J. (2021). Workaholism, presenteeism, work–family conflicts and personal and work outcomes: Testing a moderated mediation model. *Journal of Clinical Nursing*, 30(19-20), 2842–2853. 10.1111/jocn.1579133870550

Gimpel, H., Graf-Drasch, V., Hawlitschek, F., & Neumeier, K. (2021). Designing smart and sustainable irrigation: A case study. *Journal of Cleaner Production*, 315, 128048. Advance online publication. 10.1016/j.jclepro.2021.128048

Glasscock, D. J., Andersen, J. H., Labriola, M., Rasmussen, K., & Hansen, C. D. (2013). Can negative life events and coping style help explain socioeconomic differences in perceived stress among adolescents? A cross-sectional study based on the West Jutland cohort study. *BMC Public Health*, 13(1), 532. 10.1186/1471-2458-13-53223724872

Glavas, A., & Godwin, L. N. (2013). Is the Perception of 'Goodness' Good Enough? Exploring the Relationship Between Perceived Corporate Social Responsibility and Employee Organizational Identification. *Journal of Business Ethics*, 114(1), 15–27. 10.1007/s10551-012-1323-5

Glebova, I. S., Yasnitskaya, Y. S., & Maklakova, N. V. (2014). Assessment of cities in Russia according to the concept of "smart city" in the context of the application of information and communication technologies. *Mediterranean Journal of Social Sciences, 5*(18), 55 – 60. 10.5901/mjss.2014.v5n18p55

Goel, R. K., Yadav, C. S., & Vishnoi, S. (2021). Self-sustainable smart cities: Socio-spatial society using participative bottom-up and cognitive top-down approach. *Cities (London, England)*, 118, 103370. Advance online publication. 10.1016/j.cities.2021.103370

Gold, A. (2016, July 12). *Why self-esteem is important for mental health.* Retrieved from https://www.nami.org/Blogs/NAMI-Blog/July-2016/Why-Self-Esteem-Is-Important-for-Mental-Health

Gona Sirwan, M., Karzan, W., & Sarkhell, S.-N. (2018). The Effectiveness of Microlearning to Improve Students' Learning Ability. *International Journal of Educational Research Review*, 3(3), 32–38. 10.24331/ijere.415824

Gorączkowska, J. (2020). Enterprise innovation in technology incubators and university business incubators in the context of Polish industry. *Oeconomia Copernicana*, 11(4), 799–817. 10.24136/oc.2020.032

Goswami, I., Mittal, A., Kumar, V., Verma, P., & Mer, A. (2024). Analysing the role of total rewards and compensation in increasing employee motivation. *Int. J. Business Excellence.*

Grahn, P., & Stigsdotter, U. A. (2003). Landscape planning and stress. *Urban Forestry & Urban Greening*, 2(1), 1–18. 10.1078/1618-8667-00019

Graner, K. M., Moraes, A. B., Torres, A. R., Lima, M. C., Rolim, G. S., & Ramos-Cerqueira, A. T. (2018). Prevalence and correlates of common mental disorders among dental students in Brazil. *PLoS One*, 13(9), e0204558. 10.1371/journal.pone.020455830261025

Greyvenstein, H., & Cilliers, F. (2012). Followership's experiences of organisational leadership: A systems psychodynamic perspective. *SA Journal of Industrial Psychology*, 38(2), 1–10. 10.4102/sajip.v38i2.1001

Grilli, L., & Marzano, R. (2023). Bridges over troubled water: Incubators and start-ups' alliances. *Technovation*, 121, 102689. 10.1016/j.technovation.2022.102689

Grimaldi, R., & Grandi, A. (2005). Business incubators and new venture creation: An assessment of incubating models. *Technovation*, 25(2), 111–121. 10.1016/S0166-4972(03)00076-2

Grindsted, T. S., Christensen, T. H., Freudendal-Pedersen, M., Friis, F., & Hartmann-Petersen, K. (2022). The urban governance of autonomous vehicles – In love with AVs or critical sustainability risks to future mobility transitions. *Cities (London, England)*, 120, 103504. Advance online publication. 10.1016/j.cities.2021.103504

Grosemans, I., Coertjens, L., & Kyndt, E. (2020). Work-related learning in the transition from higher education to work: The role of the development of self-efficacy and achievement goals. *The British Journal of Educational Psychology*, 90(1), 19–42. 10.1111/bjep.1225830506557

Guerra, I., Borges, F., Padrão, J., Tavares, J., & Padrão, M. H. (2017). Smart cities, smart tourism? The case of the city of Porto. *Revista Galega de Economia, 26*(2), 129 – 142. https://www.scopus.com/inward/record.uri?eid=2-s2.0 -85061032204&partnerID=40&md5=53340c00f01ed8ce67e24ad121953ba2

Guerrero, M., Cunningham, J. A., & Urbano, D. (2015). Economic impact of entrepreneurial universities' activities: An exploratory study of the United Kingdom. *Research Policy*, 44(3), 748–764. 10.1016/j.respol.2014.10.008

Gupta & Mehtani. (2015). Parenting Style and Psychological Well-Being among Adolescents: A Theoretical Perspective. *ZENITH International Journal of Multidisciplinary Research, 5*(2), 74-84.

Gupta, A., Panagiotopoulos, P., & Bowen, F. (2023). Developing Capabilities in Smart City Ecosystems: A multi-level approach. *Organization Studies*, 44(10), 1703–1724. Advance online publication. 10.1177/01708406231164114

Gupta, A., & Singh, H. (2020). IoT and Big Data Analytics in Smart Cities: A Survey of Indian Initiatives. *Journal of Big Data*, 7(1), 45.

Gupta, N., & Jain, V. (2022). Smart Waste Management in Indian Smart Cities: A Review of Technologies and Challenges. *Waste Management & Research*, 40(3), 215–230.

Gustavsson, M., & Lundqvist, D. (2021). Learning conditions supporting the management of stressful work. *Journal of Workplace Learning*, 33(2), 81–94. 10.1108/JWL-09-2019-0116

Gu, Y., & Su, D. (2018). I*nnovation orientations, external partnerships, and start-ups' performance of low-carbon ventures.Journal of Cleaner Production*, 194, 69–77. 10.1016/j.jclepro.2018.05.017

Haghighi, M., & Gerber, M. (2019). Does mental toughness buffer the relationship between perceived stress, depression, burnout, anxiety, and sleep? *International Journal of Stress Management*, 26(3), 297–305. 10.1037/str0000106

Hair, J. F.Jr, Howard, M. C., & Nitzl, C. (2020). Assessing measurement model quality in PLS-SEM using confirmatory composite analysis. *Journal of Business Research*, 109, 101–110. 10.1016/j.jbusres.2019.11.069

Hair, J. F.Jr, Hult, G. T. M., Ringle, C., & Sarstedt, M. (2016). *A Primer on Partial Least Squares Structural Equation Modeling (PLS-SEM)*. Sage Publications.

Hair, J. F.Jr, Matthews, L. M., Matthews, R. L., & Sarstedt, M. (2017). PLS-SEM or CB-SEM: Updated guidelines on which method to use. *International Journal of Multivariate Data Analysis*, 1(2), 107–123. 10.1504/IJMDA.2017.087624

Hair, J. F., Risher, J. J., Sarstedt, M., & Ringle, C. M. (2019). When to use and how to report the results of PLS-SEM. *European Business Review*, 31(1), 2–24. 10.1108/EBR-11-2018-0203

Hallinger, P., & Suriyankietkaew, S. (2018). Science mapping of the knowledge base on sustainable leadership, 1990–2018. *Sustainability (Basel)*, 10(12), 4846. 10.3390/su10124846

Hamid, M. S. A., Islam, R., & Hazilah, A. M. N. (2014). Malaysian graduates' employability skills enhancement : An application of the importance performance analysis. *Journal for Global Business Advancement*, 7(3), 181–197. 10.1504/JGBA.2014.064078

Hanaysha, J. R., Al-Shaikh, M. E., Joghee, S., & Alzoubi, H. M. (2022). Impact of innovation capabilities on business sustainability in small and medium enterprises. *FIIB Business Review*, 11(1), 67–78. 10.1177/23197145211042232

Han, J. H. (2020). The effects of personality traits on subjective well-being and behavioral intention associated with serious leisure experiences. *J. Asian Fin. Econ. Bus.*, 7(5), 167–176. 10.13106/jafeb.2020.vol7.no5.167

Harden, N. (2012). The End of the University as We Know It - The American Interest. In *The American Interest* (Volume 8, pp. 54–62). https://www.the-american-interest.com/2012/12/11/the-end-of-the-university-as-we-know-it/

Hardjom, S., & Haryono, S., & Bashor, K. (2021). The Role of Coping Strategies in Achieving Psychological Well Being in Students During the Covid-19 Pandemic with Religiosity as a Moderator Variable. *Psychology and Education*, 58(5), 25–34.

Hargreaves, A., & Fink, D. (2007). *Sustainable leadership*. John Wiley.

Harris, M. (2023, August 18). *The rise of Flexibility: Navigating the gig economy in recruitment - Hirebee*. Hirebee. https://hirebee.ai/blog/what-is-employer-branding-what-to-pay-attention-to/the-rise-of-flexibility-navigating-the-gig-economy-in-recruitment/

Harry, A. (2023). Role of AI in education. *Interdiciplinary Journal and Hummanity*, 2(3), 260–268. 10.58631/injurity.v2i3.52

Harvey, L. (2001). Defining and measuring employability. *Quality in Higher Education*, 7(2), 97–109. 10.1080/13538320120059990

Hasseldine, J., & Li, Z. (2017). Tax Planning and Corporate Social Responsibility. *Journal of Business Ethics*, 140(2), 245–260.

Héder, M. (2017). From NASA to EU: The evolution of the TRL scale in Public Sector Innovation. *The Innovation Journal*, 22(2), 1–23. https://eprints.sztaki.hu/9204/

He, H., & Sutunyarak, C. (2024). Exploring the Impact of Perceived Corporate Social Responsibility on Employee Innovative Behaviour: The Mediating Role of Organizational Commitment. *Kurdish Studies*, 12(1), 3384–3407.

Hemmert, M., Bstieler, L., & Okamuro, H. (2014). Bridging the cultural divide: Trust formation in university–industry research collaborations in the US, Japan, and South Korea. *Technovation*, 34(10), 605–616. 10.1016/j.technovation.2014.04.006

Hemp, P. (2004). Presenteeism: At work-but out of it. *Harvard Business Review*, 82(10), 49–58.15559575

Hendriks, M., Burger, M., Rijsenbilt, A., Pleeging, E., & Commandeur, H. (2020). Virtuous leadership: A source of employee well-being and trust. *Management Research Review*, 43(8), 951–970. 10.1108/MRR-07-2019-0326

Henseler, J., & Fassott, G. (2010). Testing moderating effects in PLS path models: an illustration of available procedures. In *Handbook of Partial Least Squares* (pp. 713–735). Springer. 10.1007/978-3-540-32827-8_31

Henseler, J., Ringle, C. M., & Sarstedt, M. (2015). A new criterion for assessing discriminant validity in variance-based structural equation modeling. *Journal of the Academy of Marketing Science*, 43(1), 115–135. 10.1007/s11747-014-0403-8

Hernandez, M. (2012). Toward an understanding of the psychology of stewardship. *Academy of Management Review*, 37(2), 172–193. 10.5465/amr.2010.0363

Herrera, R., Berger, U., Genuneit, J., Gerlich, J., Nowak, D., Schlotz, W., & Radon, K. (2017). Chronic stress in young German adults: Who is affected? A prospective cohort study. *International Journal of Environmental Research and Public Health*, 14(11), 1325. 10.3390/ijerph1411132529088088

Hewitt-Dundas, N., Gkypali, A., & Roper, S. (2019). Does learning from prior collaboration help firms to overcome the 'two-worlds' paradox in university-business collaboration? *Research Policy*, 48(5), 1310–1322. 10.1016/j.respol.2019.01.016

Hillson, D., & Murray-Webster, R. (2017). *Understanding and Managing Risk Attitude*. Routledge. 10.4324/9781315235448

HistoryExtra. (2023, November 8). *The Brontës: The unfortunate and Unlikely tale of the world's "Greatest literary sisters."* https://www.historyextra.com/period/victorian/bronte-sisters-anne-charlotte-emily-who-were-they-house-famous-write-books/

Hobfoll, S. E. (2001). The Influence of culture, community, and the nested-self in the stress process: Advancing conservation of resources theory. *Applied Psychology*, 50(3), 33770. 10.1111/1464-0597.00062

Hong, W., & Su, Y.-S. (2013) The effect of institutional proximity in non-local university–industry collaborations: an analysis based on Chinese patent data. *Res Policy, 42*, 454–464. 10.1016/j.respol.2012.05.012

Hoppe, D. (2018). Linking employer branding and internal branding: Establishing perceived employer brand image as an antecedent of favourable employee brand attitudes and behaviours. *Journal of Product &amp. Journal of Product and Brand Management*, 27(4), 452–467. 10.1108/JPBM-12-2016-1374

Hornsey, M. J. (2008). Social identity theory and self-categorization theory: A historical review. *Social and Personality Psychology Compass*, 2(1), 204–222. 10.1111/j.1751-9004.2007.00066.x

Hou, B., Hong, J., Wang, H., & Zhou, C. (2019). Academia-industry collaboration, government funding and innovation efficiency in Chinese industrial enterprises. *Technology Analysis and Strategic Management*, 31(6), 692–706. 10.1080/09537325.2018.1543868

Houston, L., Gabrys, J., & Pritchard, H. (2019). Breakdown in the Smart City: Exploring Workarounds with Urban-sensing Practices and Technologies. *Science, Technology & Human Values*, 44(5), 843–870. 10.1177/0162243919852677

Howell, K. (2013). *An Introduction to the Philosophy of Methodology*. SAGE Publications. 10.4135/9781473957633

Howell, R., Kern, M., & Lyubomirsky, S. (2007). Health benefits: Meta-analytically determining the impact of well-being on objective health outcomes. *Health Psychology Review*, 1(1), 83–136. 10.1080/17437190701492486

Hsieh, S. H., & Chang, A. (2016). The psychological mechanism of brand co-creation engagement. *Journal of Interactive Marketing*, 33, 13–26. 10.1016/j.intmar.2015.10.001

Huang, C., Hsieh, Y., Shen, A., Wei, H., Feng, J., Hwa, H., & Feng, J. (2019). Relationships between parent-reported parenting, child-perceived parenting, and children's mental health in Taiwanese children. *International Journal of Environmental Research and Public Health*, 16(6), 1049. 10.3390/ijerph1606104930909532

Huk, K., & Agata, G. (2021). Impact of private transport on the environment and society in the concept of city logistics and life cycle assessment. *Acta Logistica*, 8(3), 287–295. 10.22306/al.v8i3.251

Hu, L. T., & Bentler, P. M. (1999). Cutoff criteria for fit indexes in covariance structure analysis: Conventional criteria versus new alternatives. *Structural Equation Modeling*, 6(1), 1–55. 10.1080/10705519909540118

Hunt, J., & Eisenberg, D. (2010). Mental health problems and help-seeking behavior among college students. *The Journal of Adolescent Health*, 46(1), 3–10. 10.1016/j.jadohealth.2009.08.00820123251

Huovila, A., Bosch, P., & Airaksinen, M. (2019). Comparative analysis of standardized indicators for Smart sustainable cities: What indicators and standards to use and when? *Cities (London, England)*, 89, 141–153. 10.1016/j.cities.2019.01.029

Hu, X., Chong, H. Y., & Wang, X. (2019). Sustainability perceptions of off-site manufacturing stakeholders in Australia. *Journal of Cleaner Production*, 227, 346–354. 10.1016/j.jclepro.2019.03.258

Ibănescu, B.-C., Bănică, A., Eva, M., & Cehan, A. (2020). The puzzling concept of smart city in central and eastern europe: A literature review designed for policy development. *Transylvanian Review of Administrative Sciences*, 16(61), 70–87. 10.24193/tras.61E.4

Ibrahim, D. H. M., & Mahyuddin, M. Z. (2017). *Youth Unemployment in Malaysia : Developments and Policy Considerations*. Retrieved from https://www.bnm.gov.my/files/publication/ar/en/2016/cp04_003_box.pdf

Ibrahim, A., Kelly, S., & Glazebrook, C. (2011). Analysis of an Egyptian study on the socioeconomic distribution of depressive symptoms among undergraduates. *Social Psychiatry and Psychiatric Epidemiology*, 47(6), 927–937. 10.1007/s00127-011-0400-x21626055

Ionescu, R.-V., Zlati, M. L., & Antohi, V.-M. (2023). Smart cities from low cost to expensive solutions under an optimal analysis. *Financial Innovation*, 9(1), 60. Advance online publication. 10.1186/s40854-023-00448-836883188

Iqbal, Q., & Ahmad, N. H. (2021). Sustainable development: The colors of sustainable leadership in learning organization. *Sustainable Development (Bradford)*, 29(1), 108–119. 10.1002/sd.2135

Ismail, A. (2018). *HEBATising FUTURE TALENTS USM style* [Powerpoint slides]. Retrieved from https://cdae.usm.my/index.php/programmes/academic-excellence/competition

Ismail, S., Mohamad, M. M., Omar, N., Heong, Y. M., & Kiong, T. T. (2015). A Comparison of The Work-Based Learning Models and Implementation in Training Institutions. *Procedia: Social and Behavioral Sciences*, 204, 282–289. 10.1016/j.sbspro.2015.08.153

Ittner, C. D., & Larcker, D. F. (2003). Coming Up Short on Nonfinancial Performance Measurement. *Harvard Business Review*, 81(11), 88–95.14619154

Ivars-Baidal, J. A., Celdrán-Bernabeu, M. A., Femenia-Serra, F., Perles-Ribes, J. F., & Vera-Rebollo, J. F. (2023). Smart city and smart destination planning: Examining instruments and perceived impacts in Spain. *Cities (London, England)*, 137, 104266. Advance online publication. 10.1016/j.cities.2023.104266

Ivars-Baidal, J. A., Vera-Rebollo, J. F., Perles-Ribes, J., Femenia-Serra, F., & Celdrán-Bernabeu, M. A. (2023). Sustainable tourism indicators: What's new within the smart city/destination approach? *Journal of Sustainable Tourism*, 31(7), 1556–1582. 10.1080/09669582.2021.1876075

Jackson, D., Shan, H., & Meek, S. (2022). Employer development of professional capabilities among early career workers and implications for the design of work-based learning. *International Journal of Management Education*, 20(3), 100692. 10.1016/j.ijme.2022.100692

Jackson, P., Mavi, R. K., Suseno, Y., & Standing, C. (2018, February). University–industry collaboration within the triple helix of innovation: The importance of mutuality. *Science & Public Policy*, 45(1), 142. 10.1093/scipol/scx093

Jacobsen, C. (2023, August 25). *Article*. Mexico Business. https://mexicobusiness.news/entrepreneurs/news/navigating-challenges-and-opportunities-ai-freelancing

Jain, M. (2021). *Assessing the Impact of Smart City Initiatives on Sustainable Development Goals in India* (Master's thesis). Indian Institute of Management, Ahmedabad, India.

Jamil, F., Ismail, K., & Mahmood, N. (2015). A review of commercialization tools: University incubators and technology parks. *International Journal of Economics and Financial Issues*, 5(Special Issue), 223–228.

Jarrahi, M. H., & Sutherland, W. (2019). Algorithmic Management and Algorithmic Competencies: Understanding and appropriating algorithms in gig work. In *Lecture Notes in Computer Science* (pp. 578–589). 10.1007/978-3-030-15742-5_55

Jaškevičiūtė, V. (2021). Trust in organization effect on the relationship between HRM practices and employee well-being. *SHS Web of Conferences*.

Jiang, Z., Zhang, X., Zhao, Y., Li, C., & Wang, Z. (2023). The impact of urban digital transformation on resource sustainability: Evidence from a quasi-natural experiment in China. *Resources Policy*, 85, 103784. Advance online publication. 10.1016/j.resourpol.2023.103784

Johansson, G., & Lundberg, I. (2004). Adjustment latitude and attendance requirements as determinants of sickness absence or attendance. Empirical tests of the illness flexibility model. *Social Science & Medicine*, 58(10), 1857–1868. 10.1016/S0277-9536(03)00407-615020004

Johnson, D. S. (2020). Public versus private employees: A perspective on the characteristics and implications. *FIIB Business Review*, 9(1), 9–14. 10.1177/2319714519901081

Johnson, D., & Smith, E. (2020). Value Creation through Financial Management in Innovation-Driven Businesses. *Journal of Financial Innovation*, 18(3), 76–89.

Johnston, V., Jull, G., Souvlis, T., & Jimmieson, N. L. (2010). Interactive effects from self-reported physical and psychosocial factors in the workplace on neck pain and disability in female office workers. *Ergonomics*, 53(4), 502–513. 10.1080/00140130090349069220309746

Jonathan, L. Y., & Laik, M. N. (2019). Using experiential learning theory to improve teaching and learning in higher education. *European Journal of Social Sciences Education and Research*, 6(1), 123. 10.26417/ejser.v6i1.p123-132

Jones, D. A., Willness, C. R., & Madey, S. (2014). Why Are Job Seekers Attracted by Corporate Social Performance? Experimental and Field Tests of Three Signal-Based Mechanisms. *Academy of Management Journal*, 57(2), 383–404. 10.5465/amj.2011.0848

Joshi, G., Teferi, M. Y., Miller, R., Jamali, S., Groesbeck, M., Van Tol, J., McLaughlin, R., Vardeny, Z. V., Lupton, J. M., Malissa, H., & Boehme, C. (2018). High-Field magnetoresistance of organic semiconductors. *Physical Review Applied*, 10(2), 024008. Advance online publication. 10.1103/PhysRevApplied.10.024008

Joshi, M., & Rao, K. (2018). Smart Education Initiatives in Indian Smart Cities: Case Study of Pune. *Journal of Cases on Information Technology*, 20(3), 34–48.

Jouybari, L., Manchri, H., Sanagoo, A., Sabzi, Z., & Jafari, S. Y. (2017). Hamideh Manchri, Akram Sanagoo, Leila Jouybari, Zahra Sabzi, Seyyed Yaghob Jafari (2016). The relationship between mental health status with academic performance and demographic factors among students of university of medical sciences. *Journal of Nursing and Midwifery Sciences*, 4(1), 8–13. 10.18869/acadpub.jnms.4.1.8

Jun, W. H., & Lee, G. (2017). Comparing anger, anger expression, life stress and social support between Korean female nursing and general university students. *Journal of Advanced Nursing*, 73(12), 2914–2922. 10.1111/jan.1335428556972

Jussila, J., Raitanen, J., Partanen, A., Tuomela, V., Siipola, V., & Kunnari, I. (2020). Rapid product development in university-industry collaboration: Case study of a smart design project. *Technology Innovation Management Review*, 10(3), 49–59. 10.22215/timreview/1336

Kaltiainen, J., & Hakanen, J. J. (2023). Why increase in telework may have affected employee well-being during the COVID-19 pandemic? The role of work and non-work life domains. *Current Psychology (New Brunswick, N.J.)*, 1–19.36718392

Kamath, M., & Kumar, A. (2023). 7 E's of Constructivism in E-learning Skills of University Faculty. (n.d.). International Journal of Case Studies in Business. *IT and Education*, 7(1), 62–73.

Kang, B. (2021). *How the COVID-19 Pandemic Is Reshaping the Education Service* (Lee, J., & Han, S. H., Eds.)., 10.1007/978-981-33-4126-5_2

Kantabutra, S., & Avery, G. (2013). Sustainable leadership: Honeybee practices at a leading Asian industrial conglomerate. *Asia-Pacific Journal of Business Administration*, 5(1), 36–56. 10.1108/17574321311304521

Kaplan, R. S., & Norton, D. P. (2001). *The Strategy-Focused Organization: How Balanced Scorecard Companies Thrive in the New Business Environment*. Harvard Business Press. 10.1108/sl.2001.26129cab.002

Kaplan, R., & Kaplan, S. (2011). Well-being, Reasonableness, and the Natural Environment. *Applied Psychology. Health and Well-Being*, 3(3), 304–321. Advance online publication. 10.1111/j.1758-0854.2011.01055.x

Kapoor, S. (2017). *Reinventing Indian Cities through Smart Technologies* [TED Talk]. Retrieved from https://www.sciencedirect.com/ted-talks

Kashive, N., Khanna, V. T., & Bharthi, M. N. (2020). Employer branding through crowdsourcing: Understanding the sentiments of employees. *Journal of Indian Business Research*, 12(1), 93–111. 10.1108/JIBR-09-2019-0276

Kasriel, S. (2018, October 31). The future of work won't be about college degrees, it will be about job skills. *CNBC*. Retrieved from https://www.cnbc.com/2018/10/31/the-future-of-work-wont-be-about-degrees-it-will-be-about-skills.html

Kazemi, M., Ansari, A., Allah Tavakoli, M., & Karimi, S. (2004). The Effect of the Recitation of Holy Quran on Mental Health in Nursing Students of Rafsanjan University of Medical Sciences. *JRUMS*, 3(1), 52-57. http://journal.rums.ac.ir/article-1-53-en.html

Kee, D. M. H., Al-anesi, M., Chandran, S., Elanggovan, H., Nagendran, B., & Mariappan, S. (2021). COVID-19 as a double-edged sword: The perfect opportunity for GrabFood to optimize its performance. *Journal of the Community Development in Asia*, 4(1), 53–65. 10.32535/jcda.v4i1.998

Kee, D. M. H., Anwar, A., Shern, L. Y., & Gwee, S. L. (2023). Course quality and perceived employability of Malaysian youth: The mediating role of course effectiveness and satisfaction. *Education and Information Technologies*, 28(10), 1–8. 10.1007/s10639-023-11737-1

Kefelew, E., Hailu, A., Kote, M., Teshome, A., Dawite, F., & Abebe, M. (2023). Prevalence and associated factors of stress and anxiety among female employees of hawassa industrial park in sidama regional state, Ethiopia. *BMC Psychiatry*, 23(1), 103. 10.1186/s12888-023-04575-536774468

Kerpelman, J. L., Eryigit, S., & Stephens, C. J. (2008). African American adolescents' future education orientation: Associations with self efficacy, ethnic identity, and perceived parental support. *Journal of Youth and Adolescence*, 37(8), 997–1008. 10.1007/s10964-007-9201-7

Kerr, M., Stattin, H., & Ozdemir, M. (2012). Perceived parenting style and adolescent adjustment: Revisiting directions of effects and the role of parental knowledge. *Developmental Psychology*, 48(6), 1540–1553. 10.1037/a002772022448987

Kessler, R. C., Amminger, G. P., Aguilar-Gaxiola, S., Alonso, J., Lee, S., & Ustun, T. B. (2007). Age of onset of mental disorders: A review of recent literature. *Current Opinion in Psychiatry*, 20(4), 359–364. 10.1097/YCO.0b013e32816e-bc8c17551351

Keys, J., Dempster, M., Jackson, J., Williams, M., & Coyle, S. (2021). The psychosocial impact of losing an eye through traumatic injury and living with prosthetic restoration: A thematic analysis. *Acta Psychologica*, 219, 103383. 10.1016/j.actpsy.2021.10338334352606

Khampirat, B., Pop, C., & Bandaranaike, S. (2019). The effectiveness of work-integrated learning in developing student work skills: A case study of Thailand. *International Journal of Work-Integrated Learning*, 20, 126–146.

Khan, F., & Mer, A. (2023). Embracing artificial intelligence technology: Legal implications with special reference to european union initiatives of data protection. In *Digital Transformation, Strategic Resilience, Cyber Security and Risk Management* (pp. 119-141). Emerald Publishing Limited.

Khatri, P., & Gupta, P. (2022). Impact of Workplace Spirituality on Employee Well-Being: The Mediating Role of Organizational Politics. *FIIB Business Review*.

Khozhylo, I., Lipovska, N., Chernysh, O., Antonova, O., Diegtiar, O., & Dmytriieva, O. (2022). Implementation of smart-city tools as a response to challenges in socio-humanitarian field in Ukrainian metropolises. *Acta Logistica*, 9(1), 23–30. 10.22306/al.v9i1.262

Kimberly, J. R., & Bouchikhi, H. (2016). Disruption on Steroids: Sea Change in the Worlds of Higher Education in General and Business Education in Particular. *Journal of Leadership & Organizational Studies*, 23(1), 5–12. 10.1177/1548051815606434

Kim, H. L., Lee, Y., & Jeong, C. (2020). Effects of CSR on Employee Motivation and Service Performance in the Hotel Industry. *International Journal of Hospitality Management*, 88, 102–127.

Kim, J., & Tummala-Narra, P. (2022). Rise of anti-Asian violence and the COVID-19 pandemic for Asian Americans. *Asian American Journal of Psychology*, 13(3), 217–219. 10.1037/aap0000301

Knight, B., Mitrofanov, D., & Netessine, S. (2023). The impact of AI technology on the productivity of gig economy workers. *Social Science Research Network*. 10.2139/ssrn.4372368

Koch, F., Beyer, S., & Chen, C.-Y. (2023). Monitoring the Sustainable Development Goals in cities: Potentials and pitfalls of using smart city data. *GAIA - Ecological Perspectives for Science and Society*, 32, 47 – 53. 10.14512/gaia.32.S1.8

Koens, K., Melissen, F., Mayer, I., & Aall, C. (2021). The Smart City Hospitality Framework: Creating a foundation for collaborative reflections on overtourism that support destination design. *Journal of Destination Marketing & Management*, 19, 100376. Advance online publication. 10.1016/j.jdmm.2019.100376

Kolb, M., Fröhlich, L., & Schmidpeter, R. (2017). Implementing sustainability as the new normal: Responsible management education – From a private business school's perspective. *International Journal of Management Education*, 15(2), 280–292. 10.1016/j.ijme.2017.03.009

Komninos, N., & Tsarchopoulos, P. (2013). Toward Intelligent Thessaloniki: From an Agglomeration of Apps to Smart Districts. *Journal of the Knowledge Economy*, 4(2), 149–168. 10.1007/s13132-012-0085-8

Konstantinou, I., & Miller, E. (2021). Self-managed and Work-Based Learning: Problematising The Workplace–Classroom Skills Gap. *Journal of Work-Applied Management*.

Koopman, C., Pelletier, K. R., Murray, J. F., Sharda, C. E., Berger, M. L., Turpin, R. S., Hackleman, P., Gibson, P., Holmes, D. M., & Bendel, T. (2002). Stanford presenteeism scale: Health status and employee productivity. *Journal of Occupational and Environmental Medicine*, 44(1), 14–20. 10.1097/00043764-200201000-0000411802460

Krabbendam, L., & van Os, J. (2005). Schizophrenia and urbanicity: A major environmental influence–conditional on genetic risk. *Schizophrenia Bulletin*, 31(4), 795–799. 10.1093/schbul/sbi06016150958

Kravina, L., Falco, A., Girardi, D., & De Carlo, N. A. (2010). Workaholism among management and workers in an Italian cooperative enterprise. *TPM. Testing, Psychometrics, Methodology in Applied Psychology*, 17, 201–216. 10.4473/TPM.17.4.2

Krishankumar, R., Ecer, F., Mishra, A. R., Ravichandran, K. S., Gandomi, A. H., & Kar, S. (2022). A SWOT-Based Framework for Personalized Ranking of IoT Service Providers With Generalized Fuzzy Data for Sustainable Transport in Urban Regions. *IEEE Transactions on Engineering Management*, 1–14. 10.1109/TEM.2022.3204695

Kroh, J., & Schultz, C. (2023). The more the better? The role of stakeholder information processing in complex urban innovation projects for green transformation. *International Journal of Project Management*, 41(3), 102466. Advance online publication. 10.1016/j.ijproman.2023.102466

Kuczmarski, T. D., & Kuczmarski, S. J. (2010). *Innovating the Corporation: Creating Value for Customers and Shareholders*. Business Expert Press.

Kudva, S., & Ye, X. (2017). Smart cities, big data, and sustainability union. *Big Data and Cognitive Computing*, 1(1), 1–13. 10.3390/bdcc1010004

Kulkarni, J. (2008). Women's Mental Health. *The Australian and New Zealand Journal of Psychiatry*, 42(1), 1–2. 10.1080/00048670701762662 18058437

Kulkarni, R. (2019). https://www.peoplematters.in/article/training-development/training-for-the-gig-economy-the-ld-way-23904

Kumar, A., & Singh, R. (2020). Challenges of smart cities in India. International Journal of Management. *Technology and Engineering*, 10(1), 1134–1146.

Kumar, H., Singh, M. K., Gupta, M. P., & Madaan, J. (2020). Moving towards smart cities: Solutions that lead to the Smart City Transformation Framework. *Technological Forecasting and Social Change*, 153, 119281. Advance online publication. 10.1016/j.techfore.2018.04.024

Kumar, M. H., & Baliya, J. N. (2017). Study on mental health among college students with respect to their cognitive styles. International Journal of Law. *Psychology and Human Life*, 4(2), 8–13.

Kumar, V., & Agarwal, S. (2020). Smart Healthcare Systems in Indian Smart Cities: Case Study of Bangalore. *Journal of Cases on Information Technology*, 22(4), 56–71.

Kumar, V., & Pansari, A. (2016). Competitive advantage through engagement. *JMR, Journal of Marketing Research*, 53(4), 497–514. 10.1509/jmr.15.0044

Kung, T. H., Cheatham, M., Medenilla, A., Sillos, C., Leon, L. D., Elepaño, C., Madriaga, M., Aggabao, R., Diaz-Candido, G., Maningo, J., & Tseng, V. (2023, February 9). Performance of ChatGPT on USMLE: Potential for AI-assisted medical education using large language models. *PLOS Digital Health*, 2(2), e0000198. Advance online publication. 10.1371/journal.pdig.000019836812645

Kuok, A. C., & Rashidnia, J. (2019). College students' attitudes toward counseling for mental health issues in two developing Asian countries. *Spiritual Psychology and Counseling*, 4(1), 67–84. 10.37898/spc.2019.4.1.0056

Kurniawan, T. A., Maiurova, A., Kustikova, M., Bykovskaia, E., Othman, M. H. D., & Goh, H. H. (2022). Accelerating sustainability transition in St. Petersburg (Russia) through digitalization-based circular economy in waste recycling industry: A strategy to promote carbon neutrality in era of Industry 4.0. *Journal of Cleaner Production*, 363, 132452. Advance online publication. 10.1016/j.jclepro.2022.132452

Kusumasondjaja, S., Shanka, T., & Marchegiani, C. (2012). Credibility of online reviews and initial trust: The roles of reviewer's identity and review valence. *Journal of Vacation Marketing*, 18(3), 185–195. 10.1177/1356766712449365

Kutty, A. A., Kucukvar, M., Onat, N. C., Ayvaz, B., & Abdella, G. M. (2023). Measuring sustainability, resilience and livability performance of European smart cities: A novel fuzzy expert-based multi-criteria decision support model. *Cities (London, England)*, 137, 104293. Advance online publication. 10.1016/j.cities.2023.104293

Lakshmi, V., & Narain, S. (2014). *Manual for Stress Scale SS-LVNS*. National Psychological Corporation.

Lang, J., Li, Y., Cheng, C., Cheng, X. Y., & Chen, F. Y. (2023). Are algorithmically controlled gig workers deeply burned out? An empirical study on employee work engagement. *BMC Psychology*, 11(1), 354. Advance online publication. 10.1186/s40359-023-01402-037876010

Langseth-Eide, B. (2019). It's been a hard day's night and I've been working like a dog: Workaholism and work engagement in the JD-R model. *Frontiers in Psychology*, 10, 1444. 10.3389/fpsyg.2019.0144431293485

Larkin, M. (2014). *Building successful partnerships between academia and industry*. Elsevierconnect.

Laroche, M., Bergeron, J., & Barbaro-Forleo, G. (2001). Targeting Consumers Who Are Willing to pay more for Environmentally-Friendly Products. *Journal of Consumer Marketing*, 18(6), 503–520. 10.1108/EUM0000000006155

Lata, S., Jasrotia, A., & Sharma, S. (2022). Sustainable development in tourism destinations through smart cities: A case of urban planning in Jammu City. *Enlightening Tourism*, 12(2), 661–690. 10.33776/et.v12i2.6911

Lau, Y., & Yin, L. (2011). Maternal, obstetric variables, perceived stress and health-related quality of life among pregnant women in Macao, China. *Midwifery*, 27(5), 668–673. 10.1016/j.midw.2010.02.00820466467

Lavie, D., Stettner, U., & Tushman, M. L. (2010). Exploration and exploitation within and across organizations. *The Academy of Management Annals*, 4(1), 109–155. 10.5465/19416521003691287

Lavolette, E., Polio, C., & Kahng, J. (2015). The accuracy of computer-assisted feedback and students' responses to it. *Language Learning & Technology*, 19(2), 50–68.

Lebrun-Harris, L.-A., Ghandour, R.-M., Kogan, M.-D., & Warren, M.-D. (2022). Five-Year Trends in US Children's Health and Well-being, 2016-2020. *JAMA Pediatrics*, 176(7), e220056. Advance online publication. 10.1001/jamapediatrics.2022.005635285883

Leckie, C., Nyadzayo, M. W., & Johnson, L. W. (2016). Antecedents of consumer brand engagement and brand loyalty. *Journal of Marketing Management*, 32(5-6), 558–578. 10.1080/0267257X.2015.1131735

Lee, C., Lee, D., & Sho, M. (2020). Effect of efficient triple-helix collaboration on organizations based on their stage of growth. *Journal of Engineering and Technology Management*, 58, 101604. 10.1016/j.jengtecman.2020.101604

Lee, F. (2021). Financial Management for Scalability and Growth in Innovation-Driven Businesses. *Journal of Innovation and Finance*, 25(1), 30–42.

Lee, H. W. (2017). Sustainable leadership: An empirical investigation of its effect on organizational effectiveness1. *International Journal of Organization Theory and Behavior*, 20(4), 419–453. 10.1108/IJOTB-20-04-2017-B001

Lee, J. H., Hancock, M. G., & Hu, M.-C. (2014). Towards an effective framework for building smart cities: Lessons from Seoul and San Francisco. *Technological Forecasting and Social Change*, 89, 80–99. 10.1016/j.techfore.2013.08.033

Leigh, J., Bowen, S., & Marlatt, G. A. (2005). Spirituality, mindfulness and substance abuse. *Addictive Behaviors*, 30(7), 1335–1341. 10.1016/j.addbeh.2005.01.01016022930

Leszczyńska, D., & Khachlouf, N. (2018). How proximity matters in interactive learning and innovation: A study of the Venetian glass industry. *Industry and Innovation*, 25(9), 874–896. 10.1080/13662716.2018.1431524

Leten, B., Landoni, P., & Van Looy, B. (2014). Science or graduates: How do firms benefit from the proximity of universities? *Research Policy*, 43(8), 1398–1412. 10.1016/j.respol.2014.03.005

Li, T. J., Lu, Y., Clark, J., Chen, M., Cox, V. S., Meng, J., Yang, Y., Kay, T., Wood, D., & Brockman, J. B. (2022). A Bottom-Up End-User Intelligent Assistant Approach to Empower Gig Workers against AI Inequality. *arXiv (Cornell University)*. /arxiv.2204.1384210.1145/3533406.3533418

Lichtenstein, D. R., Drumwright, M. E., & Braig, B. M. (2004). The Effect of Corporate Social Responsibility on Customer Donations to Corporate-Supported Nonprofits. *Journal of Marketing*, 68(4), 16–32. 10.1509/jmkg.68.4.16.42726

Lilius, J. M., Worline, M. C., Maitlis, S., Kanov, J., Dutton, J. E., & Frost, P. (2008). The contours and consequences of compassion at work. *Journal of Organizational Behavior: The International Journal of Industrial. Journal of Organizational Behavior*, 29(2), 193–218. 10.1002/job.508

Lima, M. C., Domingues, M. D., & Cerqueira, A. T. (2006). Prevalência E fatores de risco para transtornos mentais comuns entre estudantes de medicina. *Revista de Saude Publica*, 40(6), 1035–1041. 10.1590/S0034-89102006000700011117173160

Lim, Y. M., Lee, T. H., Yap, C. S., & Ling, C. C. (2016). Employability skills, personal qualities, and early employment problems of entry-level auditors: Perspectives from employers, lecturers, auditors, and students. *Journal of Education for Business*, 91(4), 185–192. 10.1080/08832323.2016.1153998

Linde, L., Sjödin, D., Parida, V., & Wincent, J. (2021). Dynamic capabilities for ecosystem orchestration A capability-based framework for smart city innovation initiatives. *Technological Forecasting and Social Change*, 166, 120614. Advance online publication. 10.1016/j.techfore.2021.120614

Lindholdt, L., Labriola, M., Andersen, J. H., Kjeldsen, M. M. Z., Obel, C., & Lund, T. (2022). Perceived stress among adolescents as a marker for future mental disorders: A prospective cohort study. *Scandinavian Journal of Public Health*, 50(3), 412–417. 10.1177/140349482199371933641501

Lindqvist, H., Weurlander, M., Barman, L., Wernerson, A., & Thornberg, R. (2023). Work-based learning partnerships: Mentor-teachers' perceptions of student teachers' challenges. *Educational Research*, 65(3), 392–407. 10.1080/00131881.2023.2234384

Lin, H., Zhang, M., Gursoy, D., & Fu, X. (2019). Impact of tourist-to-tourist interaction on tourism experience: The mediating role of cohesion and intimacy. *Annals of Tourism Research*, 76, 153–167. 10.1016/j.annals.2019.03.009

Link, B., & Phelan, J. (1995). Social Conditions As Fundamental Causes of Disease. *Journal of Health and Social Behavior*, 35, 80–94. 10.2307/26269587560851

Liu, J., Chen, N., Chen, Z., Xu, L., Du, W., Zhang, Y., & Wang, C. (2022). Towards sustainable smart cities: Maturity assessment and development pattern recognition in China. *Journal of Cleaner Production*, 370, 133248. Advance online publication. 10.1016/j.jclepro.2022.133248

Liu, J., Sekine, M., Tatsuse, T., Fujimura, Y., Hamanishi, S., & Zheng, X. (2015). Association among number, order and type of siblings and adolescent mental health at age 12. *Pediatrics International*, 57(5), 849–855. 10.1111/ped.1262925808043

Liu, W., & Aaker, J. (2008). The happiness of giving: The time-ask effect. *The Journal of Consumer Research*, 35(3), 543–557. 10.1086/588699

Liu, Y., Lou, B., Zhao, X., & Li, X. (2023). Unintended consequences of advances in matching technologies: Information revelation and strategic participation on GIG-Economy platforms. *Management Science*. Advance online publication. 10.1287/mnsc.2023.4770

Lobato, D., Faust, D., & Spirito, A. (1988). Examining the effects of chronic disease and disability on children's sibling relationships. *Journal of Pediatric Psychology*, 13(3), 389–407. 10.1093/jpepsy/13.3.3893058922

Lopez-Carreiro, I., Monzon, A., Lopez, E., & Lopez-Lambas, M. E. (2020). Urban mobility in the digital era: An exploration of travellers' expectations of MaaS mobile-technologies. *Technology in Society*, 63, 101392. Advance online publication. 10.1016/j.techsoc.2020.101392

Lorquet, A., & Pauwels, L. (2020). Interrogating urban projections in audio-visual 'smart city' narratives. *Cities (London, England)*, 100, 102660. Advance online publication. 10.1016/j.cities.2020.102660

Lozano, R. (2018). *Sustainability in Higher Education: A Call to Action*. Routledge.

Luan, H., Geczy, P., Lai, H., Gobert, J., Yang, S. J. H., Ogata, H., Baltes, J., Guerra, R., Li, P., & Tsai, C.-C. (2020). Challenges and future directions of big data and artificial intelligence in education. *Frontiers in Psychology, 11*. 10.3389/fpsyg.2020.580820

Luckmizankari, P. (2017). Factors Affecting On Examination Stress among Undergraduates: An Investigation from Eastern University. *Iconic Research and Engineering Journals*, 1(4), 9–15.

Lukat, J., Margraf, J., Lutz, R., van der Veld, W. M., & Becker, E. S. (2016). Psychometric properties of the Positive Mental Health Scale (PMH-scale). *BMC Psychology*, 4(1), 8. 10.1186/s40359-016-0111-x26865173

Lyaskovskaya, E. A., Khudyakova, T. A., & Shmidt, A. V. (2022). Improving the Ranking of Russian Smart Cities [СОВЕршЕнСТВОВАнИЕ рЕйТИнгА рОССИйСКИх умных гОрОДОВ]. *Economy of Regions*, 18(4), 1046–1061. 10.17059/ekon.reg.2022-4-6

Lytras, M. D., Visvizi, A., Chopdar, P. K., Sarirete, A., & Alhalabi, W. (2021). Information Management in Smart Cities: Turning end users' views into multi-item scale development, validation, and policy-making recommendations. *International Journal of Information Management*, 56, 102146. Advance online publication. 10.1016/j.ijinfomgt.2020.102146

Macke, J., Casagrande, R. M., Sarate, J. A. R., & Silva, K. A. (2018). Smart city and quality of life: Citizens' perception in a Brazilian case study. *Journal of Cleaner Production*, 182, 717–726. 10.1016/j.jclepro.2018.02.078

Macke, J., Rubim Sarate, J. A., & de Atayde Moschen, S. (2019). Smart sustainable cities evaluation and sense of community. *Journal of Cleaner Production*, 239, 118103. Advance online publication. 10.1016/j.jclepro.2019.118103

Magliacani, M. (2023). How the sustainable development goals challenge public management. Action research on the cultural heritage of an Italian smart city. *The Journal of Management and Governance*, 27(3), 987–1015. 10.1007/s10997-022-09652-7

Maignan, I., & Ferrell, O. (2004). Corporate social responsibility and marketing: An integrative framework. *Journal of the Academy of Marketing Science*, 32(1), 3–19. 10.1177/0092070303258971

Malaysian Productivity Corporation. (2017). *Productivity report 2016/2017*. Retrieved from https://www.mpc.gov.my/wp-content/uploads/2017/05/Productivity-Report-2017.pdf

Malik, A., Budhwar, P., & Srikanth, N. R. (2020). Gig Economy, 4IR and Artificial Intelligence: Rethinking Strategic HRM. In *Emerald Publishing Limited eBooks* (pp. 75–88). 10.1108/978-1-83867-223-220201005

Mallick, S. (2023, December 14). *People matters - Interstitial site — People matters*. People Matters. https://www.peoplematters.in/article/hr-technology/mastering-gig-economy-recruitment-retention-39779

Manate, D., Lile, R., Rad, D., Szentesi, S.-G., & Cuc, L. D. (2023). An analysis of the concept of green buildings in Romania in the context of the energy paradigm change in the EU [Tvariųjų pastatų sampratos rumunijoje analizė: Energetikos paradigma pokyčių es kontekste]. *Transformations in Business & Economics*, 22(1), 115–129. https://www.scopus.com/inward/record.uri?eid=2-s2.0-85153742642&partnerID=40&md5=8f5e2638cd62236415818c9004346527

Mangnus, A. C., Vervoort, J. M., Renger, W.-J., Nakic, V., Rebel, K. T., Driessen, P. P. J., & Hajer, M. (2022). Envisioning alternatives in pre-structured urban sustainability transformations: Too late to change the future? *Cities (London, England)*, 120, 103466. Advance online publication. 10.1016/j.cities.2021.103466

Mankins, J. C. (1995). *Technology readiness levels: A white paper*. http://www. hq. nasa. gov/office/codeq/trl/trl. Pdf

Manning, N. (2019). Sociology, biology and mechanisms in urban mental health. Social Theory & Health. *Journal of Marriage and Family*, 82(1), 198–223.

Manrique-de-Lara, P., & Viera-Armas, M. (2019). Does ethical leadership motivate followers to participate in delivering compassion? *Journal of Business Ethics*, 154(1), 195–210. 10.1007/s10551-017-3454-1

Marchetti, D., Oliveira, R., & Figueira, A. R. (2019). Are global north smart city models capable to assess Latin American cities? A model and indicators for a new context. *Cities (London, England)*, 92, 197–207. 10.1016/j.cities.2019.04.001

March, J. G. (1991). Exploration and exploitation in organizational learning. *Organization Science*, 2(1), 71–87. 10.1287/orsc.2.1.71

Margherita, E. G., Escobar, S. D., Esposito, G., & Crutzen, N. (2023). Exploring the potential impact of smart urban technologies on urban sustainability using structural topic modelling: Evidence from Belgium. *Cities (London, England)*, 141, 104475. Advance online publication. 10.1016/j.cities.2023.104475

Mariani, K., & Lozada, F. V. (2023). The use of AI and algorithms for decision-making in workplace recruitment practices. *Journal of Student Research*, 12(1). Advance online publication. 10.47611/jsr.v12i1.1855

Marr, B. (2023, February 9). The future of work: Are traditional degrees still worthwhile? *Forbes*. https://www.forbes.com/sites/bernardmarr/2023/02/09/the-future-of-work-are-traditional-degrees-still-worthwhile/?sh=440803591bfe

Marsal-Llacuna, M.-L., Colomer-Llinàs, J., & Meléndez-Frigola, J. (2015). Lessons in urban monitoring taken from sustainable and livable cities to better address the Smart Cities initiative. *Technological Forecasting and Social Change*, 90(PB), 611 – 622. 10.1016/j.techfore.2014.01.012

Marsal-Llacuna, M.-L., & Segal, M. E. (2016). The Intelligenter Method (I) for making "smarter" city projects and plans. *Cities (London, England)*, 55, 127–138. 10.1016/j.cities.2016.02.006

Marsal-Llacuna, M.-L., & Segal, M. E. (2017). The Intelligenter Method (II) for "smarter" urban policy-making and regulation drafting. *Cities (London, England)*, 61, 83–95. 10.1016/j.cities.2016.05.006

Martinez, I., & Garcia, J. F. (2007). Impact of parenting styles on adolescents' self-esteem and internalization of values in Spain. *The Spanish Journal of Psychology*, 10(2), 338–348. 10.1017/S1138741600006600117992960

Martínez, P., & del Bosque, I. R. (2013). CSR and customer loyalty: The roles of trust, customer identification with the company and satisfaction. *International Journal of Hospitality Management*, 35, 89–99. 10.1016/j.ijhm.2013.05.009

Martínez-Plumed, F., Gómez, E., & Hernández-Orallo, J. (2021). Futures of artificial intelligence through technology readiness levels. *Telematics and Informatics*, 58, 101525. 10.1016/j.tele.2020.101525

Martin, G., Gollan, P. J., & Grigg, K. (2011). Is there a bigger and better future for employer branding? Facing up to innovation, corporate reputations and wicked problems in SHRM. *International Journal of Human Resource Management*, 22(17), 3618–3637. 10.1080/09585192.2011.560880

Mathiesen, K. S., & Sanson, A. (2000). Dimensions of early childhood behavior problems: Stability and predictors of change from 18 to 30 months. *Journal of Abnormal Child Psychology*, 28(1), 15–31. 10.1023/A:1005165916906107772347

Matos, F., Vairinhos, V. M., Dameri, R. P., & Durst, S. (2017). Increasing smart city competitiveness and sustainability through managing structural capital. *Journal of Intellectual Capital*, 18(3), 693–707. 10.1108/JIC-12-2016-0141

Matsouka, K., & Mihail, D. M. (2016). Graduates' employability : What do graduates and employers think? *Industry and Higher Education*, 30(5), 321–326. 10.1177/0950422216663719

Matud, M. P., Díaz, A., Bethencourt, J. M., & Ibáñez, I. (2020). Stress and psychological distress in emerging adulthood: A gender analysis. *Journal of Clinical Medicine*, 9(9), 2859. 10.3390/jcm909285932899622

Maynard, D.-M., & Fayombo, G. (2015). Influence of Parental Employment Status on Caribbean Adolescents' Self-Esteem. *International Journal of School and Cognitive Psychology.*, 2, 1–6. 10.4172/1234-3425.1000123

Mazzetti, G., Vignoli, M., Schaufeli, W., & Guglielmi, D. (2017). Work addiction and presenteeism: The buffering role of managerial support. *International Journal of Psychology*, 54(2), 174–179. Advance online publication. 10.1002/ijop.1244928791675

McDonnell, A., Carbery, R., Burgess, J., & Sherman, U. (2021). Technologically mediated human resource management in the gig economy. *International Journal of Human Resource Management*, 32(19), 3995–4015. 10.1080/09585192.2021.1986109

McGregor, A., Magee, C. A., Caputi, P., & Iverson, D. (2016). A job demands-resources approach to presenteeism. *Career Development International*, 21(4), 402418. 10.1108/CDI-01-2016-0002

McHale, S. M., Updegraff, K. A., & Whiteman, S. D. (2012, October 1). Sibling Relationships and Influences in Childhood and. Adolescence. *Journal of Marriage and Family*, 74(5), 913–930. 10.1111/j.1741-3737.2012.01011.x24653527

McKinsey Global Institute. (2017). *India's Smart Cities: Opening Doors to Opportunity*. Author.

McNall, L. A., & Michel, J. S. (2016). The relationship between student core self-evaluations, support for school, and the work–school interface. *Community Work & Family*, 20(3), 253–272. 10.1080/13668803.2016.1249827

Meijerink, J. G. (2021). Talent management in the gig economy. In *Routledge eBooks* (pp. 98–121). 10.4324/9780429265440-6-6

Menon, A., & Khanna, T. (2018). The Promise and Peril of India's Smart City Mission. *Harvard Business Review*. Retrieved from https://hbr.org/

Menon, N. (2018). *The Role of Innovation in Building Smart Cities* [TED Talk]. Retrieved from https://www.sciencedirect.com/ted-talks

Mer, A., & Srivastava, A. (2023). Employee Engagement in the New Normal: Artificial Intelligence as a Buzzword or a Game Changer? In *The Adoption and Effect of Artificial Intelligence on Human Resources Management, Part A* (pp. 15-46). Emerald Publishing Limited

Mer, A., & Virdi, A. S. (2022). Artificial intelligence disruption on the brink of revolutionizing HR and marketing functions. *Impact of artificial intelligence on organizational transformation*, 1-19.

Mer, A., & Virdi, A. S. (2023). Navigating the paradigm shift in HRM practices through the lens of artificial intelligence: A post-pandemic perspective. *The Adoption and Effect of Artificial Intelligence on Human Resources Management, Part A*, 123-154.

Mer, A., & Virdi, A. S. (2024). Fostering Creativity, Innovative Service Behaviour, and Performance Among Entrepreneurs in the VUCA World Through Employee Engagement Practices. In *VUCA and Other Analytics in Business Resilience, Part A* (pp. 59-76). Emerald Publishing Limited.

Mer, A. (2023). Artificial Intelligence in Human Resource Management: Recent Trends and Research Agenda. *Digital Transformation, Strategic Resilience. Cyber Security and Risk Management*, 111, 31–56.

Mer, A., & Vijay, P. (2021). Towards enhancing work engagement in the service sector in India: A conceptual model. In *Doing business in emerging markets* (pp. 118–135). Routledge India. 10.4324/9781003199168-7

Mer, A., & Virdi, A. S. (2024). Decoding the Challenges and Skill Gaps in Small-and Medium-Sized Enterprises in Emerging Economies: A Review and Research Agenda. *Contemporary Challenges in Social Science Management: Skills Gaps and Shortages in the Labour Market*, 112, 115–134. 10.1108/S1569-37592024000112B007

Migliore, M. C., Ricceri, F., Lazzarato, F., & d'Errico, A. (2021). Impact of different work organisational models on gender differences in exposure to psychosocial and ergonomic hazards at work and in mental and physical health. *International Archives of Occupational and Environmental Health*, 94(8), 1889–1904. 10.1007/s00420-021-01720-z34050822

Miller, F. M. (2015). Ad authenticity: An alternative explanation of advertising's effect on established brand attitudes. *Journal of Current Issues and Research in Advertising*, 36(2), 177–194. 10.1080/10641734.2015.1023871

Miner, J. L., & Clarke-Stewart, K. A. (2008). Trajectories of externalizing behavior from age 2 to age 9: Relations with gender, temperament, ethnicity, parenting, and rater. *Developmental Psychology*, 44(3), 771–786. 10.1037/0012-1649.44.3.77118473643

Ministry of Electronics and Information Technology, Government of India. (n.d.). *Digital India: Smart Cities*. Retrieved from https://www.digitalindia.gov.in/

Ministry of Housing and Urban Affairs, Government of India (2022). *Smart Cities Mission*. Author.

Ministry of Housing and Urban Affairs, Government of India. (n.d.). *Smart Cities Mission*. Retrieved from https://smartcities.gov.in/

Ministry of New and Renewable Energy, Government of India. (n.d.). *Smart Cities Mission: Renewable Energy*. Retrieved from https://mnre.gov.in/

Mishra, S., & Reddy, G. R. (2018). Citizen Engagement in Indian Smart Cities: An Empirical Analysis. *Journal of Public Administration and Governance*, 8(1), 88–103.

Moffitt, T. E., & Scott, S. (2008). Conduct disorders of childhood and adolescence. In *Rutter's child and adolescent psychiatry* (5th ed.). Blackwell Publishing Ltd. 10.1002/9781444300895.ch35

Mohamad, M. H., Baidi, N., & Nor, H. N. A. (2018). The relationship between mental health, stress and academic performance among college student. *The European Proceedings of Social & Behavioural Sciences*. 10.15405/epsbs.2018.07.02.60

Mohamad, M. M., Ismail, S., & Faiz, N. S. M. (2021). A tie between educational institution and industry: A66 case study of benefit from work-based learning. *Journal of Technical Education and Training*, 13(1), 128–138.

Mohd Salleh, N., Mapjabil, J., & Legino, R. (2019). Graduate Work-Readiness in Malaysia: Challenges, Skills and Opportunities. In Dhakal, S., Prikshat, V., Nankervis, A., & Burgess, J. (Eds.), *The Transition from Graduation to Work: Challenges and Strategies in the Twenty-First Century Asia Pacific and Beyond* (pp. 125–142). Springer Singapore. 10.1007/978-981-13-0974-8_8

Mohsin, F., Md Isa, N., Awee, A., & Purhanudin, N. (2022). Growing Gigs: A Conceptual Report on Job Autonomy and Work Engagement on Gig Workers' Performance. *International Journal Of Advanced Research In Economics And Finance*, 4(1), 144–156.

Mokhtar, D., Abdullah, N.-A., & Roshaizad, N. (2020). Survey dataset on presenteeism, job demand and perceived job insecurity: The perspective of diplomatic officers. *Data in Brief*, 30, 105505. 10.1016/j.dib.2020.10550532368580

Mokhtar, M. M., Rosenthal, D. A., Hocking, J. S., & Satar, N. A. (2013). Bridging the gap: Malaysian youths and the pedagogy of school-based sexual health education. *Procedia: Social and Behavioral Sciences*, 85, 236–245. 10.1016/j.sbspro.2013.08.355

Möller, E. L., Nikolić, M., Majdandžić, M., & Bögels, S. M. (2016). Associations between maternal and paternal parenting behaviors, anxiety and its precursors in early childhood: A meta-analysis. *Clinical Psychology Review*, 45, 17–33. 10.1016/j.cpr.2016.03.00226978324

Monroe, S. M., Slavich, G. M., & Georgiades, K. (2009). The social environment and life stress in depression. In Gotlib, I. H., & Hammen, C. L. (Eds.), *Handbook of depression and its treatment* (2nd ed., pp. 340–360). Guilford Press.

Moos, D. C., & Bonde, C. (2016). Flipping the classroom: Embedding self-regulated learning prompts in videos. Technology. *Knowledge and Learning*, 21(2), 1–18. 10.1007/s10758-015-9269-1

Morales-Pinzón, T., Rieradevall, J., Gasol, C. M., & Gabarrell, X. (2015). Modelling for economic cost and environmental analysis of rainwater harvesting systems. *Journal of Cleaner Production*, 87(C), 613–626. 10.1016/j.jclepro.2014.10.021

Morgan, R. M., & Hunt, S. D. (1994). The commitment-trust theory of relationship marketing. *Journal of Marketing*, 58(3), 20–38. 10.1177/002224299405800302

Mork, R., Falkenberg, H. K., Fostervold, K. I., & Throud, H. M. S. (2018). Visual and psychological stress during computer work in healthy, young females—Physiological responses. *International Archives of Occupational and Environmental Health*, 91(7), 811–830. 10.1007/s00420-018-1324-529850947

Morley, D. A. (2018). *Enhancing Employability in Higher Education through Work Based Learning*. Palgrave Macmillan. 10.1007/978-3-319-75166-5

Morrissette, P. J. (1994). The holocaust of first nation people: Residual effects on parenting and treatment implications. *Contemporary Family Therapy*, 16(5), 381–392. 10.1007/BF02197900

Morrissey, C. A. (2019). The Digital Transformation of Management Education - A Peer-Reviewed Academic Articles. *Graziadio Business Review, 22*(1). https://gbr.pepperdine.edu/2019/03/the-digital-transformation-of-management-education/

Morris, T. H. (2022). How Creativity Is Oppressed through Traditional Education. *On the Horizon*, 30(3), 133–140. 10.1108/OTH-09-2022-124

Morsing, M. (2021). PRME – principles for responsible management education. *Responsible Management Education*, 3–12. 10.4324/9781003186311-2

Mortier, P., Demyttenaere, K., Auerbach, R. P., Green, J. G., Kessler, R. C., & Kiekens, G.. (1981). The impact of lifetime suicidality on academic performance in college freshmen. *Journal of Affective Disorders*, 2015(186), 254–260.26254617

Mosannenzadeh, F., Bisello, A., Vaccaro, R., D'Alonzo, V., Hunter, G. W., & Vettorato, D. (2017). Smart energy city development: A story told by urban planners. *Cities (London, England)*, 64, 54–65. 10.1016/j.cities.2017.02.001

Mudambi & Schuff. (2010). Research note: What makes a helpful online review? A study of customer reviews on amazon. com. *MIS Quarterly, 34*(1), 185. 10.2307/20721420

Mukerjee, D. (n.d.). *How AI is fuelling the rise of gig economy.* People Matters. Retrieved December 7, 2023, from https://www.peoplematters.in/article/hr-technology/how-leena-ai-is-helping-employees-become-more-productive-23737

Mukerjee, S. (2014). Agility: A crucial capability for universities in times of disruptive change and innovation. *Australian Universities Review*, 56(1), 56–60.

Muldoon, J., & Rækstad, P. (2022). Algorithmic domination in the gig economy. *European Journal of Political Theory*, 22(4), 587–607. 10.1177/14748851221082078

Mullen, P. R., Morris, C., & Lord, M. (2017). The experience of ethical dilemmas, burnout, and stress among practicing counselors. *Counseling and Values*, 62(1), 37–56. 10.1002/cvj.12048

Mungila Hillemane, B. S. (2020). Technology business incubators in India: What determines their R&D contributions to the national economy? *International Journal of Innovation Science*, 12(4), 385–408. 10.1108/IJIS-03-2020-0020

Munni. (2018). A Study of Academic Anxiety in Relation to Mental Health in Adolescents. *International Journal of Current Research and Review*. DOI: 10.7324/IJCRR.2018.1066

Muris, P., van den Broek, M., Otgaar, H., Oudenhoven, I., & Lennartz, J. (2018). Good and bad sides of self-compassion: A face validity check of the self-compassion scale and an investigation of its relations to coping and emotional symptoms in non-clinical adolescents. *Journal of Child and Family Studies*, 27(8), 2411–2421. 10.1007/s10826-018-1099-z30100697

Muscio, A., & Vallanti, G. (2014). Perceived obstacles to university–industry collaboration: Results from a qualitative survey of Italian academic departments. *Industry and Innovation*, 21(5), 410–429. 10.1080/13662716.2014.969935

Musset, P. (2019). *Improving work-based learning in schools.* OECD Social, Employment and Migration Working Papers, No. 233, OECD Publishing. 10.1787/1815199X

Myoken, Y. (2013). The role of geographical proximity in university and industry collaboration: Case study of Japanese companies in the UK. *International Journal of Technology Transfer and Commercialisation*, 12(1/2/3), 43–61. 10.1504/IJTTC.2013.064170

Nagata, N. (2013). Robo-sensei's NLP-based error detection and feedback generation. *CALICO Journal*, 26(3), 562–579. 10.1558/cj.v26i3.562-579

Nardi, P. (2006). *Doing Survey Research. A Guide to Quantitative Methods.* Pearson Education.

Nass, C., & Moon, Y. (2000). Machines and mindlessness: Social responses to computers. *The Journal of Social Issues*, 56(1), 81–103. 10.1111/0022-4537.00153

National Institute of Urban Affairs. (2018). *Smart Cities in India: Status and Challenges.* Author.

Nederhand, J., Avelino, F., Awad, I., De Jong, P., Duijn, M., Edelenbos, J., Engelbert, J., Fransen, J., Schiller, M., & Van Stapele, N. (2023). Reclaiming the city from an urban vitalism perspective: Critically reflecting smart, inclusive, resilient and sustainable just city labels. *Cities (London, England)*, 137, 104257. Advance online publication. 10.1016/j.cities.2023.104257

Nedregård, T., & Olsen, R. (2014). *Studentenes Helse- OgTrivselsundersøkelse SHOT 2014.* Available at: http://www.vtbergen.no/wp-content/uploads/2013/10/VT0614_6214_SHoT2014.pdf

Neff, K. D., & Costigan, A. P. (2014). Self-Compassion, Wellbeing, and Happiness: Mitgefühl mit sich selbst. *Wohlbefinden und Glücklichsein.Psychologie in Österreich*, 2, 114–119.

Nerdrum, P., Rustoen, T., & Helge Roinstead, M. (2009). Psychological distress among nursing, physiotherapy, and occupational therapy students: A longitudinal and predictive study. *Scandinavian Journal of Educational Research*, 53(4), 363–378. 10.1080/00313830903043133

Netemeyer, R. G., Bearden, W. O., & Sharma, S. (2003). *Scaling procedures: Issues and applications*. Sage Publications.

Netemeyer, R., Bearden, W., & Sharma, S. (2003). *Scaling Procedures: Issues and Applications*. Sage Publications. 10.4135/9781412985772

Neves, F. T., de Castro Neto, M., & Aparicio, M. (2020). The impacts of open data initiatives on smart cities: A framework for evaluation and monitoring. *Cities (London, England)*, 106, 102860. Advance online publication. 10.1016/j.cities.2020.102860

Nguyen, H. M., & Nguyen, L. V. (2022). Employer attractiveness, employee engagement and employee performance. *International Journal of Productivity and Performance Management*, 72(10), 2859–2881. 10.1108/IJPPM-04-2021-0232

Ng, W. H., Sorensen, K. L., & Feldman, D. C. (2007). Dimensions, antecedents, and consequences of workaholism: A conceptual integration and extension. *Journal of Organizational Behavior*, 28(1), 111–136. 10.1002/job.424

Norlander, P., Jukić, N., Varma, A., & Nestorov, S. (2021). The effects of technological supervision on gig workers: Organizational control and motivation of Uber, taxi, and limousine drivers. *International Journal of Human Resource Management*, 32(19), 4053–4077. 10.1080/09585192.2020.1867614

Nottingham, P. (2016). The use of work-based learning pedagogical perspectives to inform flexible practice within higher education. *Teaching in Higher Education*, 21(7), 790–806. 10.1080/13562517.2016.1183613

Nunes, S. A. S., Ferreira, F. A. F., Govindan, K., & Pereira, L. F. (2021). "Cities go smart!": A system dynamics-based approach to smart city conceptualization. *Journal of Cleaner Production*, 313, 127683. Advance online publication. 10.1016/j.jclepro.2021.127683

Nyemba, W. R., Mbohwa, C., & Carter, K. F. (2021). *Bridging the Academia Industry Divide: Innovation and Industrialisation Perspective Using Systems Thinking Research in Sub-Saharan Africa*. Springer. 10.1007/978-3-030-70493-3

O'Donnell, M. L., Schaefer, I., Varker, T., Kartal, D., Forbes, D., Bryant, R. A., & Steel, Z. (2017). A systematic review of person-centered approaches to investigating patterns of trauma exposure. *Clinical Psychology Review*, 57, 208–225. 10.1016/j.cpr.2017.08.00928919323

Oates, W. E. (1971). *Confessions of a Workaholic: The Facts about Work Addiction*. World Publishing Company.

OECD. (2015). *OECD science, technology and industry scoreboard 2015: innovation for growth and society*. OECD.

Okolie, U. C., Nwosu, H. E., & Mlanga, S. (2019). Graduate employability: How the higher education institutions can meet the demand of the labour market. *Higher Education, Skills and Work-Based Learning*, 2042–3896. 10.1108/HESWBL-09-2018-0089

Oliveira, M., Proença, T., & Ferreira, M. R. (2021). Do corporate volunteering programs and perceptions of corporate morality impact perceived employer attractiveness? *Social Responsibility Journal*, 18(7), 1229–1250. 10.1108/SRJ-03-2021-0109

Online education - worldwide: Statista market forecast. (n.d.). *Statista*. https://www.statista.com/outlook/dmo/eservices/online-education/worldwide#analyst-opinion

Organisation for Economic Cooperation and Development (OECD). (2018). *The future of education and skills: Education 2030*. OECD Education Working Papers.

Osman, O.-T., & Afifi, M. (2010). Troubled minds in the Gulf: Mental health research in the United Arab Emirates (1989–2008). *Asia-Pacific Journal of Public Health*, 22(3_suppl), 48S–53S. 10.1177/1010539510373302520566533

Oxford Business Group. (2023). *How generative AI could transform education in the GCC*. Oxford Business Group. https://oxfordbusinessgroup.com/articles-interviews/how-generative-ai-could-transform-education-in-the-gcc/

Özcan, F., & Elçi, M. (2020). Employees' perception of CSR affecting employer brand, brand image, and corporate reputation. *SAGE Open*, 10(4). 10.1177/2158244020972372

Paek, S., & Kim, N. (2021). Analysis of worldwide research trends on the impact of artificial intelligence in education. *Sustainability (Basel)*, 13(14), 7941. 10.3390/su13147941

Paetzold, F., & Busch, T. (2014). Unleashing the powerful few: Sustainable investing behaviour of wealthy private investors. *Organization & Environment*, 27(4), 347–367. 10.1177/1086026614555991

Palepu, K. G., Healy, P. M., & Peek, E. (2013). *Business Analysis and Valuation: Using Financial Statements*. Cengage Learning.

Palmatier, R. W., Dant, R. P., Grewal, D., & Evans, K. R. (2006). Factors influencing the effectiveness of relationship-marketing: A meta-analysis. *Journal of Marketing*, 70(4), 136–153. 10.1509/jmkg.70.4.136

Palumbo, R., Manesh, M. F., Pellegrini, M. M., Caputo, A., & Flamini, G. (2021). Organizing a sustainable smart urban ecosystem: Perspectives and insights from a bibliometric analysis and literature review. *Journal of Cleaner Production*, 297, 126622. Advance online publication. 10.1016/j.jclepro.2021.126622

Pansari, A., & Kumar, V. (2017). Employees' engagement: The construct, antecedents, and consequences. *Journal of the Academy of Marketing Science*, 45(3), 294–311. 10.1007/s11747-016-0485-6

Parada, J. (2017). Social innovation for "smart" territories: Fiction or reality? [Innovaciones sociales para territorios "inteligentes": ¿Ficción o realidad?]. *Problemas del Desarrollo*, 48(190), 11–35. 10.1016/j.rpd.2017.06.002

Paramita, D. (2020). Digitalization in Talent acquisition : A Case study of AI in Recruitment. *SciSpace - Paper*. https://typeset.io/papers/digitalization-in-talent-acquisition-a-case-study-of-ai-in-2cde0gvcal

Pardo-García, N., Simoes, S. G., Dias, L., Sandgren, A., Suna, D., & Krook-Riekkola, A. (2019). Sustainable and Resource Efficient Cities platform – SureCity holistic simulation and optimization for smart cities. *Journal of Cleaner Production*, 215, 701–711. 10.1016/j.jclepro.2019.01.070

Parra, G. L., & Calero, S. X. (2019, March 31). Automated writing evaluation tools in the improvement of the writing skill. *International Journal of Instruction*. https://eric.ed.gov/?id=EJ1211027 10.4324/9781315717203

Pasquinelli, C., & Trunfio, M. (2020). Reframing urban overtourism through the Smart-City Lens. *Cities (London, England)*, 102, 102729. Advance online publication. 10.1016/j.cities.2020.102729

Patel, S. (2021). *Smart Governance Framework for Indian Smart Cities* (Doctoral dissertation). University of Mumbai, Mumbai, India.

Patel, R., & Shah, M. (2020). Smart Mobility Solutions in Indian Smart Cities: A Systematic Review. *Transport Reviews*, 40(5), 632–648.

Peen, J., Schoevers, R. A., Beekman, A. T., & Dekker, J. (2010). The current status of urbanrural differences in psychiatric disorders. *Acta Psychiatrica Scandinavica*, 121(2), 84–93. 10.1111/j.1600-0447.2009.01438.x19624573

Pei, P., Lin, G., Li, G., Zhu, Y., & Xi, X. (2020). The association between doctors' presenteeism and job burnout: A cross-sectional survey study in China. *BMC Health Services Research*, 20(1), 1–7. 10.1186/s12913-020-05593-932746808

Pereira, D., Leitão, J., Oliveira, T., & Peirone, D. (2023). Proposing a holistic research framework for university strategic alliances in sustainable entrepreneurship. *Heliyon*, 9(5), e16087. 10.1016/j.heliyon.2023.e1608737215802

Pérez, A., & Del Bosque, I. R. (2015). An integrative framework to understand how CSR affects customer loyalty through identification, emotions and satisfaction. *Journal of Business Ethics*, 129(3), 571–584. 10.1007/s10551-014-2177-9

Perkmann, M., Neely, A., & Walsh, K. (2011). How should firms evaluate success in university–industry alliances? A performance measurement system. *R & D Management*, 41(2), 202–216. 10.1111/j.1467-9310.2011.00637.x

Perkmann, M., Tartari, V., McKelvey, M., Autio, E., Broström, A., D'Este, P., Fini, R., Geuna, A., Grimaldi, R., Hughes, A., Krabel, S., Kitson, M., Llerena, P., Lissoni, F., Salter, A., & Sobrero, M. (2013). Academic engagement and commercialisation: A review of the literature on university– industry relations. *Research Policy*, 42(2), 423–442. 10.1016/j.respol.2012.09.007

Perusso, A., & Wagenaar, R. (2023). Electronic work-based learning (eWBL): A framework for trainers in companies and higher education. *Studies in Higher Education*, 1–17. 10.1080/03075079.2023.2280193

Philbin, S. P. (2010). Developing and Managing University-Industry Research Collaborations through a Process Methodology/Industrial Sector Approach. *The Journal of Research Administration*, 41(3), 51–68.

Piercy, C. W., & Carr, C. T. (2020). Employer reviews may say as much about the employee as they do the employer: Online disclosures, organizational attachments, and unethical behavior. *Journal of Applied Communication Research*, 48(5), 577–597. 10.1080/00909882.2020.1812692

Piko, B.F., & Balazs, M.A. (2012). Control or involvement? Relationship between authoritative parenting style and adolescent depressive symptomology. *Eur Child Adolesc Psychiatry, 21*, 149–155.

Pitt, B. (2020). *The study of how XR technologies impact the retail industry, now and in the future*. Academic Press.

Piva, E., & Rossi-Lamastra, C. (2013). Systems of indicators to evaluate the performance of university–industry alliances: A review of the literature and directions for future research. *Measuring Business Excellence*, 17(3), 40–54. 10.1108/MBE-01-2013-0004

Pivato, S., Misani, N., & Tencati, A. (2008). The impact of corporate social responsibility on consumer trust: The case of organic food. *Bus. Ethics. Business Ethics (Oxford, England)*, 17(1), 3–12. 10.1111/j.1467-8608.2008.00515.x

Pletcher, S. N. (2023). Practical and Ethical Perspectives on AI-Based Employee Performance Evaluation. *OSF Preprints*. 10.31219/osf.io/29yej

Podsakoff, P. M., MacKenzie, S. B., Lee, J. Y., & Podsakoff, N. P. (2003). Common method biases in behavioral research: A critical review of the literature and recommended remedies. *The Journal of Applied Psychology*, 88(5), 879–903. 10.1037/0021-9010.88.5.87914516251

Pokhrel, S., & Chhetri, R. (2021). A Literature Review on Impact of COVID-19 Pandemic on Teaching and Learning. *Higher Education for the Future*, 8(1), 133–141. 10.1177/2347631120983481

Poston, R. S., & Richardson, S. M. (2011). Designing an academic project management program: A collaboration between a university and a PMI chapter. *Journal of Information Systems Education*, 22, 55–72.

Prabu, S., (2015). A Study on Academic Stress among Higher Secondary Students. *International Journal of Humanities and Social Science Invention*.

Pradhan, D. (2022, September 14). *Gig economy and AI's role in making the gig model thrive | FuseMachines Insights.* Fusemachines. https://insights.fusemachines.com/a-new-era-of-gig-workers-and-ais-role-in-making-the-gig-model-thrive/

Praharaj, S., & Han, H. (2019). Cutting through the clutter of smart city definitions: A reading into the smart city perceptions in India. City. *Cultura e Scuola*, 18, 100289. Advance online publication. 10.1016/j.ccs.2019.05.005

Prasad, A., & Green, P. (2015). *Impact of Technology Integration in Finance and Accounting: A Case Study of United Technologies Corporation.* Academic Press.

Preacher, K. J., & Hayes, A. F. (2008). Asymptotic and resampling strategies for assessing and comparing indirect effects in multiple mediator models. *Behavior Research Methods*, 40(3), 879–891. 10.3758/BRM.40.3.87918697684

Psychiatrists TRCo. (2011). *Mental health of students in higher education.* Author.

PWC. (2020). *Harnessing Education in the New Economy: Private Higher Education Investments in Malaysia.* PricewaterhouseCoopers. https://www.pwc.com/my/en/assets/publications/2020/pwc-harnessing-education-in-the-new-economy.pdf

PWC. (2022). *Impact on the Higher Education Sector.* https://www.pwc.com/sg/en/publications/a-resilient-tomorrow-COVID-19-response-and-transformation/higher-education.html

Qian, C., & Kee, D. M. H. (2023). Exploring the path to enhance employee creativity in Chinese MSMEs: The influence of individual and team learning orientation, transformational leadership, and creative self-efficacy. *Information (Basel)*, 14(8), 449. 10.3390/info14080449

Qian, H., Wu, J., & Zheng, S. (2023). Entrepreneurship, sustainability, and urban development. *Small Business Economics*. Advance online publication. 10.1007/s11187-023-00761-7

Rahim, H. F., Mooren, T. T., van den Brink, F., Knipscheer, J. W., & Boelen, P. A. (2021). Cultural identity conflict and psychological well-being in bicultural young adults: Do self-concept clarity and self-esteem matter? *The Journal of Nervous and Mental Disease*, 209(7), 525–532. 10.1097/NMD.00000000000133234009862

Rahman, M., & Watanobe, Y. (2023). ChatGPT for education and research: Opportunities, threats, and strategies. *Applied Sciences (Basel, Switzerland)*, 13(9), 5783. 10.3390/app13095783

Rajalo, S., & Vadi, M. (2017). University-industry innovation collaboration: Reconceptualization. *Technovation*, 62–63(April), 42–54. 10.1016/j.technovation.2017.04.003

Ramaswamy, S. (2016). The Promise and Challenges of Smart Cities. *Harvard Business Review*. Retrieved from https://hbr.org/

Rashid, S., & Yadav, S. S. (2020). Impact of COVID-19 Pandemic on Higher Education and Research. *Indian Journal of Human Development*, 14(2), 340–343. 10.1177/0973703020946700

Rasoolimanesh, S. M., Ringle, C. M., Jaafar, M., & Ramayah, T. (2017). Urban vs. rural destinations: Residents' perceptions, community participation and support for tourism development. *Tourism Management*, 60, 147–158. 10.1016/j.tourman.2016.11.019

Reeves, B., & Nass, C. (1996). *The media equation: How people treat computers, television, and new media like real people.* Academic Press.

Reiss, F. (2013). Socioeconomic inequalities and mental health problems in children and adolescents: A systematic review. *Social Science & Medicine*, 90, 24–31. 10.1016/j.socscimed.2013.04.02623746605

Ren, X., Wang, X., & Sun, H. (2020). Key person ethical decision-making and substandard drugs rejection intentions. *PLoS One*, 15(3), e0229412. 10.1371/journal.pone.022941232191721

Renzenbrink, I. (2011). The inhospitable hospital. *Illness, Crises, and Loss*, 19(1), 27–39. 10.2190/IL.19.1.c

Richter, M. A., Hagenmaier, M., Bandte, O., Parida, V., & Wincent, J. (2022). Smart cities, urban mobility and autonomous vehicles: How different cities needs different sustainable investment strategies. *Technological Forecasting and Social Change*, 184, 121857. Advance online publication. 10.1016/j.techfore.2022.121857

Richter, N. F., Cepeda-Carrión, G., Roldán Salgueiro, J. L., & Ringle, C. M. (2016). European management research using partial least squares structural equation modeling (PLS-SEM). *European Management Journal*, 34(6), 589–597. 10.1016/j.emj.2016.08.001

Rizvi, M. (2023). Exploring the landscape of artificial intelligence in education: Challenges and opportunities. *2023 5th International Congress on Human-Computer Interaction, Optimization and Robotic Applications (HORA)*, 1-3. 10.1109/HORA58378.2023.10156773

Roach, B., Goodwin, N., & Nelson, J. (2019). *Consumption and the consumer society*. Global Development and Environment Institute, Tufts University.

Roberts, J. A. (1993). Sex differences in socially responsible consumers' behavior. *Psychological Reports*, 73(1), 139–148. 10.2466/pr0.1993.73.1.139

Romani, S., Grappi, S., & Bagozzi, R. P. (2013). Explaining consumer reactions to corporate social responsibility: The role of gratitude and altruistic values. *Journal of Business Ethics*, 114(2), 193–206. 10.1007/s10551-012-1337-z

Romão, J., Kourtit, K., Neuts, B., & Nijkamp, P. (2018). The smart city as a common place for tourists and residents: A structural analysis of the determinants of urban attractiveness. *Cities (London, England)*, 78, 67–75. 10.1016/j.cities.2017.11.007

Roy, S. (2019). *Harnessing Data for Smart Urban Development* [TED Talk]. Retrieved from https://www.sciencedirect.com/ted-talks

Roy, T. (2024). "We do care": The effects of perceived CSR on employee identification - empirical findings from a developing country. *Society and Business Review*, 19(1), 72–96. 10.1108/SBR-06-2021-0091

Rubin, A. (1982). *Research and Therapy*. New York: Wiley.

Rural and Appalachian Youth and Families Consortium. (1996). Parenting practices and interventions among marginalized families in Appalachia: building on family strengths. *Fam Relat, 45*, 387–396.

Ruso, J., Horvat, A., & Maričić, M. (2019). Do international standards influence the development of smart regions and cities? [Utječu li međunarodni standardi na razvoj pametnih regija i gradova?]. *Zbornik Radova Ekonomskog Fakulteta u Rijeci*, 37(2), 629–652. 10.18045/zbefri.2019.2.629

Ryan, R. M., & Deci, E. L. (2001). On happiness and human potentials: A review of research on hedonic and eudaimonic wellbeing. *Annual Review of Psychology*, 52(1), 141–166. 10.1146/annurev.psych.52.1.14111148302

Rybnicek, R., & Königsgruber, R. (2019). What makes industry—University collaboration succeed? A systematic review of the literature. *Journal of Business Economics*, 89(2), 221–250. 10.1007/s11573-018-0916-6

Sabeh, H. N., Husin, M. H., Kee, D. M. H., Baharudini, A. H., & Abdullah, R. (2021). A systematic review of the DeLone and McLean model of information systems success in an e-learning context (2010-2020). *IEEE Access : Practical Innovations, Open Solutions*, 9, 81210–81235. 10.1109/ACCESS.2021.3084815

Sadeghinehijad, Z. (2022, April 22). *COVID-19, the digital revolution, and the value proposition of future business schools: Insights from UNPRME*. UBSS Publication. https://www.ubss.edu.au/articles/2022/april/COVID-19-the-digital-revolution-and-the-value-proposition-of-future-business-schools-insights-from-unprme/

Sady, M., Żak, A., & Rzepka, K. (2019). The role of universities in sustainability-oriented competencies development: Insights from an empirical study on Polish universities. *Administrative Sciences*, 9(3), 62. 10.3390/admsci9030062

Saha, A. R., & Singh, N. (2017). Smart cities for a sustainable future: Can Singapore be a model for Delhi? *International Journal of Economic Research*, 14(18), 367–379. https://www.scopus.com/inward/record.uri?eid=2-s2.0-85040189243&partnerID=40&md5=b243ff5ff749469abc2be93625464072

Said, D., Kypri, K., & Bowman, J. (2013). Risk factors for mental disorder among university students in Australia: Findings from a web-based cross-sectional survey. *Social Psychiatry and Psychiatric Epidemiology*, 48(6), 935–944. 10.1007/s00127-012-0574-x22945366

Saks, A. M., & Gruman, J. C. (2024). *Employee engagement: Antecedents and consequences* (2nd ed.). Edward Elgar Publishing.

Santiago, C. D., Etter, E. M., Wadsworth, M. E., & Raviv, T. (2012, May). Predictors of responses to stress among families coping with poverty-related stress. *Anxiety, Stress, and Coping*, 25(3), 239–258. 10.1080/10615806.2011.58334721614698

Sareen, J., Afifi, T. O., McMillan, K. A., & Asmundson, G. J. (2011). Relationship between household income and mental disorders: Findings from a population-based longitudinal study. *Archives of General Psychiatry*, 68(4), 419–427. 10.1001/archgenpsychiatry.2011.1521464366

Sarif, M., & Gupta, R. D. (2022). Spatiotemporal mapping of Land Use/Land Cover dynamics using Remote Sensing and GIS approach: A case study of Prayagraj City, India (1988–2018). *Environment, Development and Sustainability*, 24(1), 888–920. 10.1007/s10668-021-01475-0

Sashi, C. (2012). Customer engagement, buyer-seller relationships, and social media. *Management Decision*, 50(2), 253–272. 10.1108/00251741211203551

Saunders, M., Lewis, P., & Thornhill, A. (2012). *Research Methods for Business Students* (6th ed.). Pearson Education.

Savchenko, A. B., & Borodina, T. L. (2020). Green and Digital Economy for Sustainable Development of Urban Areas. *Regional Research of Russia*, 10(4), 583–592. 10.1134/S2079970520040097

Scambler & Scambler. (2015). Theorizing health inequalities: The untapped potential of dialectical critical realism. *Social Theory & Health 13, 3*(4), 340–354.

Schaltegger, S., & Burritt, R. (2017). *Contemporary Environmental Accounting: Issues, Concepts and Practice*. Routledge. 10.4324/9781351282529

Schaufeli, W. B., Taris, T. W., & Bakker, A. B. (2008). It takes two to tango: Workaholism is working excessively and working compulsively. In Burke, R. J., & Cooper, C. L. (Eds.), *The long work hours culture: Causes, consequences and choices* (pp. 203–225). Emerald.

Schiller, F. (2016). Urban transitions: Scaling complex cities down to human size. *Journal of Cleaner Production*, 112, 4273–4282. 10.1016/j.jclepro.2015.08.030

Schmidt, G. B., Philip, J., Van Dellen, S. A., & Islam, S. (2022). Gig worker organizing: Toward an adapted Attraction-Selection-Attrition framework. *Journal of Managerial Psychology*, 38(1), 47–59. 10.1108/JMP-09-2021-0531

Scholtz, D. (2020). Assessing workplace-based learning. *International Journal of Work-Integrated Learning*.

Schwab, D. P. (2013). *Research methods for organizational studies.* Psychology Press. 10.4324/9781410611284

Scott, D. (2020). Creatively expanding research from work-based learning. *Journal of Work-Applied Management*, 12(2), 115–125. 10.1108/JWAM-03-2020-0015

Segrin, C. (2017). Indirect effects of social skills on health through stress and loneliness. *Health Communication*, 34(1), 118–124. 10.1080/10410236.2017.138443429053380

Sellenthin, M. O. (2011). Factors that impact on university–industry collaboration: Empirical evidence from Sweden and Germany. *Business and Economic Review*, 54, 81–100.

Sen, S., & Bhattacharya, C. B. (2001). Does doing good always lead to doing better? Consumer reactions to corporate social responsibility. *JMR, Journal of Marketing Research*, 38(2), 225–243. 10.1509/jmkr.38.2.225.18838

Serbanica, C. M., Constantin, D. L., & Dragan, G. (2015). University–industry knowledge transfer and network patterns in Romania: Does knowledge supply fit SMEs' regional profiles? *European Planning Studies*, 23(2), 292–310. 10.1080/09654313.2013.862215

Shalender, K. (2022). *Key Variables in Team Dynamics in Small Businesses and Start-ups* (pp. 141-153). World Scientific Publishing Co. Pte. Ltd. 10.1142/9789811239212_0007

Shankar, N. L., & Park, C. L. (2016). Effects of stress on students' physical and mental health and academic success. *International Journal of School & Educational Psychology*, 4(1), 5–9. 10.1080/21683603.2016.1130532

Shanmugam, M. (2017, March 25). Unemployment among graduates needs to be sorted out fast. *The Star Online*. Retrieved from https://www.thestar.com.my/business/business-news/2017/03/25/unemployment-among-graduates-needs-to-sorted-out-fast/

Shao, Q.-G., Jiang, C.-C., Lo, H.-W., & Liou, J. J. H. (2023). Establishing a sustainable development assessment framework for a smart city using a hybrid Z-fuzzy-based decision-making approach. *Clean Technologies and Environmental Policy*, 25(9), 3027–3044. Advance online publication. 10.1007/s10098-023-02547-7

Shapiro, D. L., & Kirkman, B. (2018). *It's Time to Make Business School Research More Relevant.* Harvard Business Review. https://hbr.org/2018/07/its-time-to-make-business-school-research-more-relevant

Sharma, M., & Choudhary, S. (2021). Challenges in the implementation of smart cities in India. *International Journal of Scientific and Engineering Research*, 12(4), 1–8.

Sharma, P. (2023). Industry-Academia Collaboration in India: Recent Initiatives, Issues, Challenges, Opportunities and Strategies. *Vidhyayana-An International Multidisciplinary Peer-Reviewed E-Journal*, 8(s16), 888–909.

Sharma, R., & Kumar, A. (2019). Smart Cities in India: A Review of Challenges and Opportunities. *Journal of Urban Technology*, 26(1), 45–62.

Sharma, S., & Das, A. (2019). Smart Energy Management in Indian Smart Cities: A Comprehensive Review. *Energy Sources. Part B, Economics, Planning, and Policy*, 14(8), 674–689.

Sharma, S., & Lenka, U. (2019). Exploring linkages between unlearning and relearning in organizations. *The Learning Organization*, 26(5), 500–517. 10.1108/TLO-10-2018-0164

Shaw, D. S., Gilliom, M., Ingoldsby, E. M., & Nagin, D. S. (2003). Trajectories leading to school-age conduct problems. *Developmental Psychology*, 39(2), 189–200. 10.1037/0012-1649.39.2.18912661881

Shaw, D., & Shiu, E. (2002). An assessment of ethical obligation and self-identity in ethical consumer decision-making: A structural equation modelling approach. *International Journal of Consumer Studies*, 26(4), 286–293. 10.1046/j.147 0-6431.2002.00255.x

Sherman, A. M., Lansford, J. E., & Volling, B. L. (2006). Sibling relationships and best friendships in young adulthood: Warmth, conflict, and well-being. *Personal Relationships*, 13(2), 151–165. 10.1111/j.1475-6811.2006.00110.x

Shrout, P. E., & Bolger, N. (2002). Mediation in experimental and non-experimental studies: New procedures and recommendations. *Psychological Methods*, 7(4), 422–445. 10.1037/1082-989X.7.4.42212530702

Shuck, B., Alagaraja, M., Immekus, J., Cumberland, D., & Honeycutt-Elliott, M. (2019). Does compassion matter in leadership? A two-stage sequential equal status mixed method exploratory study of compassionate leader behavior and connections to performance in human resource development. *Human Resource Development Quarterly*, 30(4), 537–564. 10.1002/hrdq.21369

Silva, A. G., Cerqueira, A. T., & Lima, M. C. (2014). Social support and common mental disorder among medical students. *Revista Brasileira de Epidemiologia*, 17(1), 229–242. 10.1590/1415-790X201400010018ENG24896795

Simons, R. (2013). *Levers of Control: How Managers Use Innovative Control Systems to Drive Strategic Renewal*. Harvard Business Press.

Simpson, P. M., Siguaw, J. A., & Enz, C. A. (2006). Innovation orientation outcomes: The good and the bad. *Journal of Business Research*, 59(10-11), 1133–1141. 10.1016/j.jbusres.2006.08.001

Singh, M., Mittal, M., Mehta, P., & Singla, H. (2021). Personal values as drivers of socially responsible investments: A moderation analysis. *Review of Behavioral Finance*, 13(5), 543–565. 10.1108/RBF-04-2020-0066

Singh, P., & Chatterjee, S. (2020). Smart Cities in India: Progress, Challenges, and Future Directions. *International Journal of Urban and Regional Research*, 44(3), 567–589.

Singh, P., Narasuman, S., & Thambusamy, R. X. (2012). Refining teaching and assessment methods in fulfilling the needs of employment : A Malaysian perspective. *Futures*, 44(2), 136–147. 10.1016/j.futures.2011.09.006

Singh, P., & Singh, J. (2020). Area Based Development for Smart Cities in India: Rejuvenating Urban Spaces. *Urban India*, 40(2), 17–29.

Singh, R. P., & Banerjee, N. (2018). Exploring the influence of celebrity credibility on brand attitude, advertisement attitude and purchase intention. *Global Business Review*, 19(6), 1622–1639. 10.1177/0972150918794974

Singh, R., & Sharma, A. (2021). Role of Artificial Intelligence in Urban Planning: A Study of Indian Smart Cities. *Journal of Artificial Intelligence and Urban Planning*, 12(2), 123–138.

Singh, S., & Mishra, P. (2017). Cybersecurity Challenges in Indian Smart Cities: A Comprehensive Analysis. *IEEE Transactions on Dependable and Secure Computing*, 14(5), 498–513.

Skovgaard, A. M., Houmann, T., Christiansen, E., Landorph, S., Jørgensen, T., Olsen, E. M., Heering, K., Kaas-Nielsen, S., Samberg, V., & Lichtenberg, A. (2007). 2008 The prevalence of mental health problems in children 11/2 years of age – the copenhagen child cohort 2000. *Journal of Child Psychology and Psychiatry, and Allied Disciplines*, 48(1), 62–70. 10.1111/j.1469-7610.2006.01659.x17244271

Smetana, J. G. (2017). Current research on parenting styles, dimensions, and beliefs. *Current Opinion in Psychology*, 15, 19–25. 10.1016/j.copsyc.2017.02.01228813261

Smith, A., & Jones, B. (2018). Financial Management Challenges in Innovation-Driven Businesses. *Journal of Innovation Finance*, 15(2), 45–58.

Smith, D. E., & Seymour, R. B. (2004). The nature of addiction. In Coombs, R. H. (Ed.), *Handbook of addictive disorders: A practical guide to diagnosis and treatment* (pp. 3–30). John Wiley & Sons, Inc.

Smith, J. D., & Johnson, A. B. (2020). A systematic review of literature on data analysis techniques using R software. *Journal of Research Methods*, 15(3), 112–130.

Smith, P. A. (2018). The role of systematic review of literature as a tool in research synthesis. *Journal of Research Methods*, 12(4), 213–228.

Solis, M., & Silveira, S. (2020). Technologies for chemical recycling of household plastics – A technical review and TRL assessment. *Waste Management (New York, N.Y.)*, 105, 128–138. 10.1016/j.wasman.2020.01.03832058902

Sparks, B. A., & Browning, V. (2011). The impact of online reviews on hotel booking intentions and perception of trust. *Tourism Management*, 32(6), 1310–1323. 10.1016/j.tourman.2010.12.011

Spielberger, C.-D. (1972). *Anxiety: current trends in theory and research*. Academic Press.

Squires, L. R., Hollett, K. B., Hesson, J., & Harris, N. (2020). Psychological distress, emotion dysregulation, and coping behaviour: A theoretical perspective of problematic smartphone use. *International Journal of Mental Health and Addiction*, 19(4), 1284–1299. 10.1007/s11469-020-00224-0

Srivastava, S. (2023, November 27). *Top AI trends in 2023: Unveiling use cases across industries*. Appinventiv. https://appinventiv.com/blog/ai-trends/

Stallmann, H. M. (2008). Prevalence of psychological distress in university students: Implications for service delivery. *Australian Family Physician*, 37, 673–677.18704221

Stanković, J., Džunić, M., Džunić, Ž., & Marinković, S. (2017). A multi-criteria evaluation of the European cities' smart performance: Economic, social and environmental aspects [Višekriterijska evaluacija pametnih performansi Europskih gradova: Gospodarski, socijalni i okolišni aspekti]. *Zbornik Radova Ekonomskog Fakulteta u Rijeci*, 35(2), 519–550. 10.18045/zbefri.2017.2.519

Steel, Z., Marnane, C., Iranpour, C., Chey, T., Jackson, J. W., Patel, V., & Silove, D. (2014). The global prevalence of common mental disorders: A systematic review and meta-analysis 1980–2013. *International Journal of Epidemiology*, 43(2), 476–493. 10.1093/ije/dyu03824648481

Steinberg, L. (2001). We know some things: Parent–adolescent relationships in retrospect and prospect. *Journal of Research on Adolescence*, 11(1), 1–19. 10.1111/1532-7795.00001

Steinmo, M., & Rasmussen, E. (2016). How firms collaborate with public research organizations: The evolution of proximity dimensions in successful innovation projects. *Journal of Business Research*, 69(3), 1250–1259. 10.1016/j.jbusres.2015.09.006

Stewart, . (2018). https://hbr.org/2018/11/how-our-careers-affect-our-children

Stockman, S., Van Hoye, G., & da Motta Veiga, S. (2020). Negative word-of-mouth and applicant attraction: The role of employer brand equity. *Journal of Vocational Behavior*, 118, 103368. 10.1016/j.jvb.2019.103368

Storrie, K., Ahern, K., & Tuckett, A. (2010). A systematic review: Students with mental health problems-A growing problem. *International Journal of Nursing Practice*, 16(1), 1–6. 10.1111/j.1440-172X.2009.01813.x20158541

Stress. (n.d.). Retrieved 23 December 2023, from https://www.apa.org/topics/stress

Stress: Signs, Symptoms, Management & Prevention. (n.d.). Retrieved 23 December 2023, from https://my.clevelandclinic.org/health/articles/11874-stress

Subbiah, R. (2023). Gig economy. *International Journal for Multidisciplinary Research*, 5(1), 1638. Advance online publication. 10.36948/ijfmr.2023.v05i01.1638

Subramani, C., & Kadhiravan, S. (2017). Academic stress and mental health among high school students. *Indian Journal of Applied Research*, 7(5), 404–406.

Su, L., Yang, Q., Swanson, S. R., & Chen, N. C. (2021). The impact of online reviews on destination trust and travel intention: The moderating role of online review trustworthiness. *Journal of Vacation Marketing*, 28(4), 406–423. 10.1177/13567667211063207

Supriadi, A., Permana, I., Afandi, D. R., Arisondha, E., & Kusumaningsih, A. (2024). The Triple Helix Model: University-Industry-Government Collaboration and Its Role in Smes Innovation and Development. *International Journal of Economic Literature*, 2(1), 75–90.

SuSarla, A., Barua, A., & Whinston, A. (2003). Under-Standing The Service Component of Application Service Provision: An Empirical Analysis of Satisfaction With ASP Services. *MISOudrierty, 27*(1).

Su, T. (2022). Does family cohesion moderate the relationship between acculturative stress and depression among Asian American immigrants? *Asian American Journal of Psychology*, 13(2), 141–148. 10.1037/aap0000227

Su, Y., Lin, Y., & Lai, C. (2023). Collaborating with CHATGPT in argumentative writing classrooms. *Assessing Writing*, 57, 100752. 10.1016/j.asw.2023.100752

Tajani, F., & Morano, P. (2015). An evaluation model of the financial feasibility of social housing in urban redevelopment. *Property Management*, 33(2), 133–151. 10.1108/PM-02-2014-0007

Tajeri, B. (2010). *A survey on the influence of mothers' employment on behavioral and educational performance of children*. Available from http://pooyamoshavereh.persianblog.ir/post/82

Talbot, J. (2017). Curriculum Design For The Post-Industrial Society: The Facilitation Of Individually Negotiated Higher Education In Work-Based Learning Shell Frameworks In The United Kingdom. *The Journal of Educational Research*, 11(2).

Tan, S. (2019, April 18). Malaysian Fresh Graduates Can't Secure High-Paying Jobs as They Lack Digital Skills. *World of Buzz*. Retrieved from https://www.worldofbuzz.com/msian-fresh-graduates-cant-secure-high-paying-jobs-as-they-lack-digital-skills/

Tan, A. Y. T., Chew, E., & Kalavally, V. (2017). The expectations gap for engineering field in Malaysia in the 21st century. *On the Horizon*, 25(2), 131–138. 10.1108/OTH-12-2015-0071

Taylor, A. F., Kuo, F. E., & Sullivan, W. C. (2001). Coping with ADD: The surprising connection to green play settings. *Environment and Behavior*, 33(1), 54–77. 10.1177/00139160121972864

Taylor, A. F., Wiley, A., Kuo, F. E., & Sullivan, W. C. (1998). Growing up in the inner city: Green spaces as places to grow. *Environment and Behavior*, 30(1), 3–27. 10.1177/0013916598301001

Terry, A., & Rory, M. (2012). Disruptive pedagogies and technologies in universities. *Journal of Educational Technology & Society*, 15(4), 380–389.

Thoits, P.A. (1982). Life stress, social support, and psychological vulnerability: epidemiological considerations. *J Community Psychol., 10*(4), 341–362.

Thomas, E., Faccin, K., & Asheim, B. T. (2021). Universities as orchestrators of the development of regional innovation ecosystems in emerging economies. *Growth and Change*, 52(2), 770–789. 10.1111/grow.12442

Thurber, C. A., & Walton, E. A. (2012). Homesickness and adjustment in university students. *Journal of American College Health*, 60(5), 415–419. 10.1080/07448481.2012.67352022686364

Tian, L., Chen, G., Wang, S., Liu, H., & Zhang, W. (2012). Effects of parental support and friendship support on loneliness and depression during early and middle adolescence. *Acta Psychologica Sinica*, 44(7), 944–956. 10.3724/SP.J.1041.2012.00944

Toorani, H., & Khorshidi, A. (2012). Introduction to Work-based Learning. *Journal of Educational and Management Studies.*, 2(1), 1–6.

Tountopoulou, M., Vlachaki, F., Daras, P., Vretos, N., & Christoforidis, A. (2021). Indirect skill assessment using AI technology. *Advances in Social Sciences Research Journal*, 8(4), 723–737. 10.14738/assrj.84.10077

Trindade, E. P., Hinnig, M. P. F., da Costa, E. M., Marques, J. S., Bastos, R. C., & Yigitcanlar, T. (2017). Sustainable development of smart cities: A systematic review of the literature. *Journal of Open Innovation*, 3(3), 1–14. Advance online publication. 10.1186/s40852-017-0063-2

Tripathi, M. A., Tripathi, R., Yadav, U. S., & Shastri, R. K. (2022). Gig Economy: Reshaping strategic HRM in the era of industry 4.0 and Artificial intelligence. *ResearchGate*. https://www.researchgate.net/publication/360258253_Gig_Economy_Reshaping_Strategic_HRM_In_The_Era_of_Industry_40_and_Artificial_Intelligence/comments

Tripp, C., Jensen, T. D., & Carlson, L. (1994). The effects of multiple product endorsements by celebrities on consumers' attitudes and intentions. *The Journal of Consumer Research*, 20(4), 535–547. 10.1086/209368

Trkman, P. (2019). Value proposition of business schools: More than meets the eye. In *International Journal of Management Education* (Vol. 17, Issue 3). 10.1016/j.ijme.2019.100310

Tsui, A. S. (2013). The Spirit of Science and Socially Responsible Scholarship. *Management and Organization Review*, 9(3), 375–394. 10.1111/more.12035

Tura, N., & Ojanen, V. (2022). Sustainability-oriented innovations in smart cities: A systematic review and emerging themes. *Cities (London, England)*, 126, 103716. Advance online publication. 10.1016/j.cities.2022.103716

Um, N. (2023). Predictors affecting effects of virtual influencer advertising among college students. *Sustainability (Basel)*, 15(8), 6388. 10.3390/su15086388

UN. (2007). *The principles for responsible management education*. United Nations. https://www.unprme.org/resource-docs/PRME.pdf

US Department of Transport, Federal Highway Administration (2017), *Technology Readiness Level Guidebook*, FHWA-HRT-17-047.

Valdez, A.-M., Cook, M., Langendahl, P.-A., Roby, H., & Potter, S. (2018). Prototyping sustainable mobility practices: User-generated data in the smart city. *Technology Analysis and Strategic Management*, 30(2), 144–157. 10.1080/09537325.2017.1297399

Van den Broek, J. D., Bakker, A. B., & De Boer, E. (2013). Current trends in employee engagement: A critical review of quantitative research. *Journal of Vocational Behavior*, 82(1), 1–10.

Van Doorn, J., Lemon, K. N., Mittal, V., Nass, S., Pick, D., Pirner, P., & Verhoef, P. C. (2010). Customer engagement behavior: Theoretical foundations and research directions. *Journal of Service Research*, 13(3), 253–266. 10.1177/1094670510375599

Van Veldhoven, M., & Peccei, R. (Eds.). (2014). *Well-being and performance at work: The role of context*. Psychology Press. 10.4324/9781315743325

Vanli, T. (2023). Can systemic governance of smart cities catalyse urban sustainability? *Environment, Development and Sustainability*. Advance online publication. 10.1007/s10668-023-03601-6

Varadarajan, R. P., & Menon, A. (1988). Cause-related marketing: A coalignment of marketing strategy and corporate philanthropy. *Journal of Marketing*, 52(3), 58–74. 10.1177/002224298805200306

Varma, C., & Malik, S. (2023). *TVET in the 21st Century: A Focus on Innovative Teaching and Competency Indicators*. IntechOpen.

Venkat, M. V. V., Khan, S. R. K., Gorkhe, M. D., Reddy, M. K. S., & Rao, S. P. (2023). Fostering Talent Stability: A Study on Evaluating the Influence of Competency Management on Employee Retention in the Automotive Industry. *Remittances Review, 8*(4).

Verger, P., Guagliardo, V., Gilbert, F., Rouillon, F., & Kovess-Masfety, V. (2010). Psychiatric disorders in students in six French universities: 12-month prevalence, comorbidity, impairment, and help-seeking. *Social Psychiatry and Psychiatric Epidemiology*, 45(2), 189–199. 10.1007/s00127-009-0055-z19381424

Verleye, K., Gemmel, P., & Rangarajan, D. (2014). Managing engagement behaviors in a network of customers and stakeholders: Evidence from the nursing home sector. *Journal of Service Research*, 17(1), 68–84. 10.1177/1094670513494015

Verma, B., & Srivastava, A. (2023). Impact of different dimensions of globalisation on firms' performance: An unbalanced panel-data study of firms operating in India. *World Review of Entrepreneurship, Management and Sustainable Development*, 19(3-5), 360–378. 10.1504/WREMSD.2023.130618

Verma, P., Nankervis, A., Priyono, S., Mohd Salleh, N., Connell, J., & Burgess, J. (2018). Graduate work-readiness challenges in the Asia-Pacific region and the role of HRM. *Equality, Diversity and Inclusion*, 37(2), 121–137. 10.1108/EDI-01-2017-0015

Verma, R., & Rajput, A. (2018). Blockchain Technology for Smart Governance in Indian Smart Cities. *IEEE Transactions on Engineering Management*, 65(3), 378–392.

Vik, J., Melås, A. M., Stræte, E. P., & Søraa, R. A. (2021). Balanced readiness level assessment (BRLa): A tool for exploring new and emerging technologies. *Technological Forecasting and Social Change*, 169, 120854. 10.1016/j.techfore.2021.120854

Villamor, G. B., & Wallace, L. (2024). Corporate social responsibility: Current state and future opportunities in the forest sector. *Corporate Social Responsibility and Environmental Management*, csr.2743. 10.1002/csr.2743

Vincent-Höper, S., & Stein, M. (2019). The role of leaders in designing employees' work characteristics: Validation of the health-and development-promoting leadership behavior questionnaire. *Frontiers in Psychology*, 10, 1049. 10.3389/fpsyg.2019.0104931156499

Visvizi, A., & Lytras, M. D. (2018). Rescaling and refocusing smart cities research: From mega cities to smart villages. *Journal of Science and Technology Policy Management*, 9(2), 134–145. 10.1108/JSTPM-02-2018-0020

Vivek, S. D., Beatty, S. E., & Morgan, R. M. (2012). Customer engagement: Exploring customer relationships beyond purchase. *Journal of Marketing Theory and Practice*, 20(2), 122–146. 10.2753/MTP1069-6679200201

Vivek, S. D., Chandrasekhar, C. B., & Patnaik, S. (2012). The role of leadership styles in employee engagement. *The Journal of Applied Management and Entrepreneurship*, 17(2), 101–116.

Vlachos, P. A. (2012). Corporate social performance and consumer-retailer emotional attachment: The moderating role of individual traits. *European Journal of Marketing*, 46(11/12), 1559–1580. 10.1108/03090561211259989

Wadsworth, M. E., & Achenbach, T. M. (2005, December). Explaining the link between low socioeconomic status and psychopathology: Testing two mechanisms of the social causation hypothesis. *Journal of Consulting and Clinical Psychology*, 73(6), 1146–1153. 10.1037/0022-006X.73.6.114616392987

Wagner, D., Vollmar, G., & Wagner, H. T. (2014). The impact of information technology on knowledge creation: An affordance approach to social media. *Journal of Enterprise Information Management*, 27(1), 31–44. 10.1108/JEIM-09-2012-0063

Wahl, C., Hultquist, T. B., Struwe, L., & Moore, J. (2018). Implementing a peer support network to promote compassion without fatigue. *The Journal of Nursing Administration*, 48(12), 615–621. 10.1097/NNA.0000000000000069130431516

Wallerstein, J. S., & Kelly, J. B. (1980). The effects of parental divorce: Experiences of the child in later latency. In Hartog, J. (Ed.), *4s. The Anatomy of Lonelinex*. International Universities Press.

Wang, C., Martínez, O. S., & Crespo, R. G. (2021). Improved hybrid fuzzy logic system for evaluating sustainable transportation systems in smart cities. *International Journal of Shipping and Transport Logistics*, 13(5), 554–568. 10.1504/IJSTL.2021.117295

Wang, E. L., Matsumura, L. C., Correnti, R., Litman, D., Zhang, H., Howe, E., Magooda, A., & Quintana, R. (2020). Erevis(ING): Students' revision of text evidence use in an automated writing evaluation system. *Assessing Writing*, 44, 100449. 10.1016/j.asw.2020.100449

Wang, H., Choi, J., & Li, J. (2008). Too little or too much? Untangling the relationship between corporate philanthropy and firm financial performance. *Organization Science*, 19(1), 143–159. 10.1287/orsc.1070.0271

Wang, S., Lilienfeld, S. O., & Rochat, P. (2015). The uncanny valley: Existence and explanations. *Review of General Psychology*, 19(4), 393–407. 10.1037/gpr0000056

Wang, Y., Hao, H., & Wang, C. (2022). Preparing Urban Curbside for Increasing Mobility-on-Demand Using Data-Driven Agent-Based Simulation: Case Study of City of Gainesville, Florida. *Journal of Management Engineering*, 38(3). Advance online publication. 10.1061/(ASCE)ME.1943-5479.0001021

Warnecke, D., Wittstock, R., & Teuteberg, F. (2019). Benchmarking of European smart cities – a maturity model and web-based self-assessment tool. Sustainability Accounting. *Management and Policy Journal*, 10(4), 654–684. 10.1108/SAMPJ-03-2018-0057

Watisin, W. (2017). *Pelaksanaan program pembelajaran berasaskan kerja politeknik bersama industri* (Doctoral dissertation, Universiti Tun Hussein Onn Malaysia).

Webb, D. J., Mohr, L. A., & Harris, K. E. (2008). A re-examination of socially responsible consumption and its measurement. *Journal of Business Research*, 61(2), 91–98. 10.1016/j.jbusres.2007.05.007

Webster, F. E.Jr. (1975). Determining the characteristics of the socially conscious consumer. *The Journal of Consumer Research*, 2(3), 188–196. 10.1086/208631

What is the gig economy? (2023, August 2). McKinsey & Company. https://www.mckinsey.com/featured-insights/mckinsey-explainers/what-is-the-gig-economy

White, L., & Burger, K. (2022). Understanding Frameworking for Smart and Sustainable City Development: A configurational approach. *Organization Studies*. Advance online publication. 10.1177/01708406221099694

Wig, N. (2012). Chapter-60 a model for rural psychiatric Services Raipur rani experience. *Community Mental Health in India*, 603-616. 10.5005/jp/books/11688_60

Wilkins, A. J., O'Callaghan, M. J., Najman, J. M., Bor, W., Williams, G. M., & Shuttlewood, G. (2004). Early childhood factors influencing health-related quality of life in adolescents at 13 years. *Journal of Paediatrics and Child Health*, 40(3), 102–111. 10.1111/j.1440-1754.2004.00309.x15009573

Williams, P. D., Williams, A. R., Graff, J. C., Hanson, S., Stanton, A., Hafeman, C., Liebergen, A., Leuenberg, K., Setter, R. K., Ridder, L., Curry, H., Barnard, M., & Sanders, S. (2003). A community-based intervention for siblings and parents of children with chronic illness or disability: The ISEE Study. *The Journal of Pediatrics*, 143(3), 386–393. 10.1067/S0022-3476(03)00391-314517525

Williams, P., McDonald, P., & Mayes, R. (2021). Recruitment in the gig economy: Attraction and selection on digital platforms. *International Journal of Human Resource Management*, 32(19), 4136–4162. 10.1080/09585192.2020.1867613

Wong, K. K. K. (2016). Mediation analysis, categorical moderation analysis, and higher-order constructs modeling in partial least squares structural equation modeling (PLS-SEM): A B2B example using SmartPLS. *Marketing Bulletin*, 26(1), 1–22.

Woo, D. J., Susanto, H., Yeung, C. H., Guo, K., & Fung, A. K. Y. (2023, March 10). *Exploring AI-generated text in student writing: How does AI help?* arXiv.org. https://arxiv.org/abs/2304.02478

Wood, A. J., Graham, M., Lehdonvirta, V., & Hjorth, I. (2018). Good gig, Bad gig: Autonomy and algorithmic control in the global gig economy. *Work, Employment and Society*, 33(1), 56–75. 10.1177/0950017018785616308864 60

Wood, J. J., McLeod, B. D., Sigman, M., Hwang, W.-C., & Chu, B. C. (2003). Parenting and childhood anxiety: Theory, empirical findings, and future directions. *Journal of Child Psychology and Psychiatry, and Allied Disciplines*, 44(1), 134–151. 10.1111/1469-7610.0010612553416

Wu, T.-T., Lee, H.-Y., Li, P.-H., Huang, C.-N., & Huang, Y.-M. (2023). Promoting Self-Regulation Progress and Knowledge Construction in Blended Learning via ChatGPT-Based Learning Aid. *Journal of Educational Computing Research*, 61(8), 3–31. 10.1177/07356331231191125

Xie, J., Ifie, K., & Gruber, T. (2022). The dual threat of COVID-19 to health and job security–Exploring the role of mindfulness in sustaining frontline employee-related outcomes. *Journal of Business Research*, 146, 216–227. 10.1016/j.jbusres.2022.03.03035340762

Xin, S., & Park, T. (2024). The roles of big businesses and institutions in entrepreneurship: A cross-country panel analysis. *Journal of Innovation & Knowledge*, 9(1), 100457. 10.1016/j.jik.2023.100457

Yadav, R., & Pathak, G. S. (2016). Young consumers' intention towards buying green products in a developing nation: Extending the theory of planned behavior. *Journal of Cleaner Production*, 135, 732–739. 10.1016/j.jclepro.2016.06.120

Yang, H., Bin, P., & He, A. J. (2020). Opinions from the epicenter: An online survey of university students in Wuhan amidst the COVID-19 outbreak1. *Journal of Chinese Governance*, 5(2), 234–248. 10.1080/23812346.2020.1745411

Yang, L., Zhao, Y., Wang, Y., Liu, L., Zhang, X., Li, B., & Cui, R. (2015). The effects of psychological stress on depression. *Current Neuropharmacology*, 13(4), 494–504. 10.2174/1570159X1304150831150507264 12069

Yankson, B., Berkoh, E., Hussein, M., & Dadson, Y. (2024).The Role of Industry-Academia Partnerships Can Play in Cybersecurity: Exploring Collaborative Approaches to Address Cybercrime. In *International Conference on Cyber Warfare and Security* (Vol. 19, No. 1, pp. 26-33). 10.34190/iccws.19.1.2169

Yavuz, B., & Dilmaç, B. (2020). The relationship between psychological hardiness and mindfulness in University students: The role of spiritual well-being. *Spiritual Psychology and Counseling*, 5(3), 257–271. 10.37898/spc.2020.5.3.090

Yeadon, W., Inyang, O.-O., Mizouri, A., Peach, A., & Testrow, C. P. (2023). The death of the short-form physics essay in the Coming Ai Revolution. *Physics Education*, 58(3), 035027. 10.1088/1361-6552/acc5cf

Yigitcanlar, T., Kamruzzaman, M., Buys, L., Ioppolo, G., Sabatini-Marques, J., da Costa, E. M., & Yun, J. J. (2018). Understanding 'smart cities': Intertwining development drivers with desired outcomes in a multidimensional framework. *Cities (London, England)*, 81, 145–160. 10.1016/j.cities.2018.04.003

Yigitcanlar, T., Wilson, M., & Kamruzzaman, M. (2019). Disruptive impacts of automated driving systems on the built environment and land use: An urban planner's perspective. *Journal of Open Innovation*, 5(2), 24. Advance online publication. 10.3390/joitmc5020024

Yoong, D., Don, Z. M., & Foroutan, M. (2017). Prescribing roles in the employability of Malaysian graduates. *Journal of Education and Work*, 30(4), 432–444. 10.1080/13639080.2016.1191626

Yousuf, M., & Wahid, A. (2021, November 1). The role of artificial intelligence in education: Current trends and future prospects. *IEEE Xplore*. 10.1109/ICISCT52966.2021.9670009

Yusof, M. F. M., Wong, A., Ahmad, G., Aziz, R. C., & Hussain, K. (2020). Enhancing Hospitality and Tourism Graduate Employability Through The 2u2i Program. *Worldwide Hospitality and Tourism Themes*.

Zahir, I. (2022). *What the Post-COVID-19 world could look like for business schools*. Chartered Association of Business Schools. https://charteredabs.org/what-the-post-COVID-19-world-could-look-like-for-business-schools/

Zaidan, E., Ghofrani, A., Abulibdeh, A., & Jafari, M. (2022). Accelerating the Change to Smart Societies- a Strategic Knowledge-Based Framework for Smart Energy Transition of Urban Communities. *Frontiers in Energy Research*, 10, 852092. Advance online publication. 10.3389/fenrg.2022.852092

Zainol, Z., Omar, N. A., Osman, J., & Habidin, N. F. (2016). The Effect of Customer–Brand Relationship Investments 'Dimensions on Customer Engagement in Emerging Markets. *Journal of Relationship Marketing*, 15(3), 172–19. 10.1080/15332667.2016.1209051

Zeidan, S., & Bishnoi, M. M. (2020). An effective framework for bridging the gap between industry and academia. *International Journal on Emerging Technologies*, 11(3), 454–461. https://www.education.gov.in/nep/about-nep

Zessin, U., Dickhäuser, O., & Garbade, S. (2015). The relationship between self-compassion and well-being: A meta-analysis. *Applied Psychology. Health and Well-Being*, 7(3), 340–364. 10.1111/aphw.1205126311196

Zhang, Z. (n.d.). S*tudent engagement with teacher and automated feedback on L2* ... Assessing Writing. https://www.semanticscholar.org/paper/Student-engagement-with-teacher-and-automated-on-L2-Zhang-Hyland/da406dec79720a12d3b06a14bb71c4fab68acf83

Zhang, A., Boltz, A., Lynn, J., Wang, C., & Lee, M. K. (2023). Stakeholder-Centered AI Design: Co-Designing Worker Tools with Gig Workers through Data Probes. *CHI '23: Proceedings of the 2023 CHI Conference on Human Factors in Computing Systems*. 10.1145/3544548.3581354

Zhang, W., Bansback, N., & Anis, A. (2011). Measuring and valuing productivity loss due to poor health: A critical review. *Social Science & Medicine*, 72(2), 185–192. 10.1016/j.socscimed.2010.10.02621146909

Zhou, J., & Wang, M. (2023). The role of government-industry-academia partnership in business incubation: Evidence from new R&D institutions in China. *Technology in Society*, 72, 102194. 10.1016/j.techsoc.2022.102194

Zhou, Q., Martinez, L. F., Ferreira, A. I., & Rodrigues, P. (2016). Supervisor support, role ambiguity and productivity associated with presenteeism: A longitudinal study. *Journal of Business Research*, 69(9), 3380–3387. 10.1016/j.jbusres.2016.02.006

Zhou, S., Da, S., Guo, H., & Zhang, X. (2018). Work–Family Conflict and Mental Health Among Female Employees: A Sequential Mediation Model via Negative Affect and Perceived Stress. *Frontiers in Psychology*, 9, 544. 10.3389/fpsyg.2018.0054429719522

Zivin, K., Eisenberg, D., Gollust, S. E., & Golberstein, E. (2009). Persistence of mental health problems and needs in a college student population. *Journal of Affective Disorders*, 117(3), 180–185. 10.1016/j.jad.2009.01.00119178949

About the Contributors

Nishant Joshi is currently the Director, of Prestige Institute of Management and Research, Gwalior. He is credited with bringing the Institue into NIRF(National Institutional Ranking Frame Work, Govt. of India) top 125 Management Institutions in India also during his tenure the institution's gross enrolment improved to record high with teaching and learning at the core of its activities. He is PhD in International Marketing from the coveted 'Banasthali Vidhyapeeth', Rajasthan a NIRF top 50 University Ranked Globally by QSS and Times. He is an author and has been a faculty of International Business. He is also the Professional Director of HF Universal Private Limited an INR.100 Crore turnover Company and the Managing Director of PRO AGRI COM TRADE FZCO, Dubai, UAE. He has extensive experience in marketing and trading Agricultural Commodities for Food and Feed needs. His area of operations is West Asia and North Africa.

Firdous Ahmad Malik was born in India and is currently employed by the University of People as an Assistant Professor of Economics (instructor), Department of Management. Currently he is perceiving Post Doctoral research at Amity Dubai University. Before that, he was a research fellow at the National Institute of Public Finance and Policy (NIPFP) in Delhi, India. Prior to this, he was a senior research associate at the O.P. Jindal Global University in Sonipat, Haryana's Jindal Center for the Global South. From Babasaheb Bhimrao Ambedkar University in Lucknow, India, he received his Ph.D. He has a Master's in Economics from the University of Kashmir and an MPhil in Economics from Babasaheb Bhimrao Ambedkar University Lucknow. Microfinance, financial inclusion, and financial literacy are his main areas of study interest. He has articles in journals that are Scopus-indexed from Springer, Elsevier, Taylor Francis, and others. Moreover, he has published more than six books which includes the first book on "Financial Inclusion Schemes in India" published by Springer released. His second book, "Financial Behaviour of Urban Destitutes in India," by Notion Press. Third book, "Health System in Jammu and Kashmir Challenges and Opportunities," is published by Shineeks. His Fourth book, "Asymmetry of Information and Lending Risk Livelihood Pattern of Street Vendors in India," is published by Booksclinic. The fifth book, "Linkage Between Interest Rate Policy and Macro Economic Variables Issues and Concerns of Indian Economy," is published by Booksclinic. The sixth book, "Repatriation Management and Competency Transfer in a Culturally", is published by Springer. His forthcoming books are Economics of Financial Inclusion to be published by Routledge Publication and Fostering Industry-Academia Partnerships for Innovation-Driven Trade by IGI publication. Microfinance, Development Economics, Monetary Economics, and Public Finance are areas of expertise. To promote research among the upcoming young generation, Dr. Firdous at present is associated with specific international organizations viz. Young Scholars Initiative (YSI). He further keeps on contributing and promoting research by participating as a presenter and along with serving as session chair, review panelists in national and international conferences across the globe. For his tireless contribution to promoting young researchers, he has been awarded by the Jindal Center for Global South two best paper presentations and AIBPM Malaysian conference organizers as a best reviewer award in June 2023.

Chanda Gulati is Associate Professor of Human Resource Management working with Prestige Institute of Management and Research, Gwalior. She has more than 12 years of experience in academics and 2.5 years of corporate experience. She obtained her Ph.D. from Jiwaji University and MBA in HR Specialization from VIT University. She has published papers and case studies in ABDC, Scopus, Web of Sciences and Routledge. She has edited seven books. She is a MOOC content writer for E-pathshala platform of MHRD. She has chaired sessions in overseas conference. She is an active lifetime member of ISTD (Treasurer- Gwalior Chapter). She is member of review boards of many journals including SAJM, Sanchayan, GSSS of Jindal Global University, SAJM, etc. Her areas of interests are human resource management, industrial relations and organizational behaviour.

Abhay Dubey is Associate Professor in Marketing at Prestige Institute of Management and Research, Gwalior. He has more than 10 years of experience in academics. Earlier he was employed with Madhya Pradesh Chamber of Commerce and Industries, Gwalior, and Nai Dunia Media Pvt. Ltd. as Senior Event Manager. He has authored/co-authored more than 28 publications in various known International and National Journals and conference proceedings. He has also presented his research papers and cases in more than 15 international and National academic and professional conferences. He has conducted 3 research consultancy projects as Coordinator and Co-coordinator for Gwalior Based organizations like Hotel Central park, Rotary International and Dainik Bhaskar.

* * *

Saurabh Agarwala is working as Assistant General Manager in Research and Development division at Engineers India Limited. A Chemical Engineer by qualification, he completed his B.Tech in Chemical Engineering from Meerut University followed by M.S. in Chemical Engineering from Washington University in St. Louis, US. He has over 15 years of work experience including research work in areas such as oil and gas, biomedical engineering and environmental sciences. He has worked extensively on technology development for LPG treatment units and Hydroprocessing of Kerosene streams. He has authored/ co-authored patents in these fields. He holds experience in operations of Gas Cracker plant and has been involved in commissioning & troubleshooting activities for various units. He is also a Bureau of Energy Efficiency (BEE)-India certified Energy Manager and has been involved in Energy Efficiency evaluation of Petrochemical Plants.

Moniruzz Aman has 20+ years of working experience in consulting, teaching, and advising in Business Planning & Development, Supply Chain, Finance, Auditing and Business Analysis and also a Regular Member of CFA Institute USA and Associate Member of IMM Malaysia and a Regular member of Dhaka Taxes Bar, PhD Scholar in Putra Business School, UPM and CSCM from Bangladesh Institute of Supply Chain Management and IBA

Shweta Arora, Associate Professor at Graphic Era Hill University, Bhimtal Campus holds Ph.D. (English), M.A. (English), B.Sc. degrees. She holds her Ph.D in English Literature from Kumaun University. She has more than 21 years of teaching experience. She has served as Head, Professional Communication and PDP Department at Graphic Era Hill University, Bhimtal Campus. She has also worked as Assistant Professor and Head, Professional Communication Dept at Apex Institute of Technology, (AICTE Approved Affiliated to Mahamaya Technical University), in the Department of Applied Sciences Kaushalganj, Rampur (UP). Prior to this, she worked as a Contract Lecturer in G.B. Pant University of Agriculture and Technology, in the Department of Social Science and Humanities, Pantnagar. She has also worked in Ashok Leyland with NTTF (Nettur Technical Training Foundation). Dr. Arora has 31 scopus indexed research publications in National and International journals, conference proceedings and book chapters to her credit. She has also authored a book entitled "Professional Communication: Practical Workbook". She has also published 2 patents on "High Speed Seed Ball Dispersal" and "Oil Melting Electric Strip/Jacket Band" She has actively mentored students for writing and publishing research papers. She is a member of All India English Language Teachers Association.

Prerana Baber, lecturer at SoS in Management, Jiwaji University, Gwalior, Madhya Pradesh. India. She specializes in managerial decision-making, research methodology, and social media marketing. Dr. Prerana Baber has more than 15 published papers in national and international journals. She has attended and presented articles at national and international conferences.

Ruturaj Baber is an Associate Professor of Management from the School of Business & Management, Christ University, NCR. He specializes in fields like consumer decision-making, research methodology and market orientation. He has more than 50 papers in national and international journals and conference proceedings.

Chirra Baburao is enthusiastic about IT entrepreneurship. He worked as an Assistant Tech Support Engineer for four years at Kollas Technologies. He started (BCC) 14+ years as H/W, N/W Senior technical support engineer; he completed B.Com, M.Com, and MBA. He is pursuing PhD in entrepreneurship at (GSB), and Technopreneur.

Richa Banerjee (Ph.D., MBA, PGDM, B.B.A,) is working as Associate Professor at NMIMS . She has more than 16 years of experience in teaching and research and has qualified UGC-NET. She has published more than 40 research papers in reputed national and international journals. She has presented more than 50 research papers and articles in various national and international conferences.

Subeer Banerjee is Dean, Department of Management, Shri Ram Institute of Information Technology, Gwalior, M.P., India). He is in field of teaching for more than 12 years. He is having keen interest in psychology. He has published more than 45 research papers related to consumer behaviour, psychology etc.

Indukuri Bangar Raju is Assistant Professor at GITAM Deemed University. GITAM Deemed University. Visakhapatnam, Andhra Pradesh, India.

Raino Bhatia epitomizes the essence of an educator whose life is intricately woven with a profound dedication to the betterment of society through education. As the Principal cum Associate Professor of Akal College of Education, Eternal University, nestled in the serene landscapes of Baru Sahib, Himachal Pradesh, India, she orchestrates the symphony of learning with finesse and vision. She is M.Phil. and Ph.D. in Education, along with the accolade of UGC-NET, she stands as a paragon of scholarly excellence. Spanning over two decades, her journey in the realm of education has been marked by unwavering commitment and illustrious achievements. In 2009, she was bestowed with the prestigious National Award, a testament to her exemplary services in the field of education, a recognition that echoes her tireless efforts and unwavering passion. Dr. Bhatia's literary contributions resonate across academia, with her seminal work, "The Quest for True Happiness," serving as a guiding beacon for both educators and students alike. Complemented by a plethora of research papers published at both National and International levels, her intellectual footprint is profound and far-reaching.

Abhijeet Singh Chauhan is currently working as Assistant Professor in Department of Management, Prestige Institute of Management and Research, Gwalior. He is having around 4 years of academic and research experience.

Nupur Chauhan is a highly regarded academician and esteemed psychologist, currently heading the Department of Psychology at St. Xavier's College, Jaipur. Her academic journey is a testament to her dedication to the field of psychology, having completed a Bachelor of Arts (Hons) in Psychology, a Master's degree in Psychology, and an M.Phil. Furthermore, she has achieved the distinction of qualifying the National Eligibility Test (NET) with Junior Research Fellowship (JRF) and is presently pursuing her Ph.D., embodying a relentless pursuit of knowledge and excellence in research. Throughout her illustrious career, she has achieved significant recognition for her exceptional pedagogical techniques and innovative contributions to psychology education. Committed to advancing the understanding of psychology, her research interests encompass positive psychology, cognitive psychology research methodology and psychological statistics. She has published research impactful papers on Mobile Phone Dependence, Mental Health Care Act 2017, Job Satisfaction, Bhagavad Gita, and Emotional Intelligence in renowned national and international indexed journals. Her research enriches the fields of psychology and mental health, inspiring further exploration and understanding. She actively engages in academic forums, workshops, and public speaking engagements to foster greater mental health awareness and well-being in society. With a vision to drive pioneering research in psychology and bridge the gap between theory and practice, she remains an inspirational force, empowering the next generation of psychologists.

Francesca Di Virgilio (Ph.D in Organization, Technology and Development of Human Resources) is Full Professor (Tenured) of Organization Design and Human Resources Management, Department of Economics at University of Molise (Italy). She's Rector's delegate for Placement and Technology Transfer Activities. She is Coordinator of PhD courses in "Law and Economics" and "Organization, Technology and Development of Human Resources". She has successfully supervised and examined a number of Master and PhD theses (national and international) in the area of HRM. She has more than twenty years of teaching experience at undergraduate, graduate level and Master. She is board member of many international research excellence network. She has more than 50 publications in national and international academic journals, chapters to various edited books, and national and international books. She is reviewers of some academic international journals and editorial board member of national and international academic journals. She has presented more than 30 papers, at national and international conferences and including expert sessions as Keynote speaker. Her current research focuses on human resources management, organizational behaviour and knowledge management.

Chanda Gulati is Associate Professor of Human Resource Management working with Prestige Institute of Management and Research, Gwalior. She has more than 12 years of experience in academics and 2.5 years of corporate experience. She obtained her Ph.D. from Jiwaji University and MBA in HR Specialization from VIT University. She has published papers and case studies in ABDC, Scopus, Web of Sciences and Routledge. She has edited seven books. She is a MOOC content writer for E-pathshala platform of MHRD. She has chaired sessions in overseas conference. She is an active lifetime member of ISTD (Treasurer- Gwalior Chapter). She is member of review boards of many journals including SAJM, Sanchayan, GSSS of Jindal Global University, SAJM, etc. Her areas of interests are human resource management, industrial relations and organizational behaviour.

Umesh Holani retired from Jiwaji University after a successful 38-year tenure as Dean and Head of the Department of Commerce. He has supervised numerous Ph.D. and M.Phil. students and serves as a spiritual motivator for young faculty. Professor Holani held the position of President of the Indian Accounting Association and Secretary of the Gwalior branch of the I.A.A. He has chaired numerous technical sessions and delivered keynote speeches at various seminars and conferences.

Taran Kaur has +8 years of Research and Teaching experience as an academician in the field of Management currently working with IILM Institute for Higher Education and previously had worked for the renowned School of Real Estate, RICS SBE and Guru Gobind Singh Indraprastha University. She is an avid researcher with publications indexed in ABDC category (Category A and Category B) journals and top-tier journals of Scopus. She has won an Outstanding Researcher award in Emerald Literati Awards 2023 and an Outstanding Reviewer award by Scopus-indexed journals. She has submitted her Ph.D. in Management (Real Estate Management) at Amity Business School, Amity University Uttar Pradesh. She is a Commerce graduate, i.e., B.COM (Honours) from Delhi University and an M.B.A. in real estate from the RICS School of Built Environment, Amity University. She has presented papers at international conferences including IIM's and the University of Delhi. Her research credit has been donned with "Special Mention" at IIM, Nagpur and her publication was added to the global literature on Coronavirus disease at the World Health Organization database (covidwho-1462609). She is an ambitious researcher and her areas of interest include Facilities Management, Workspace Sustainability and Management of Corporate Real Estate.

Jagneet Kaur is a dedicated scholar in the field of Education. Drawing from her extensive academic background and research expertise, Kaur curates a collection of insightful contributions on educational research. Kaur emerges as a beacon of academic excellence. As the proud recipient of the prestigious gold medal in postgraduate studies from Eternal University, she stands at the pinnacle of her academic prowess. Kaur's achievements don't end there; she reigns as the all-round champion in her 2022 batch, leaving an indelible mark on her college's Master's in Education program. Jagneet Kaur is currently pursuing her Ph.D. in Education, having previously obtained degrees in B.Ed. and M.A. in Education. Her academic journey is marked by notable achievements, including qualifying for the UGC NET JRF on her first attempt and successfully clearing the CTET examinations. Her journey is one of continuous growth and achievement. With a passion for research, Kaur has demonstrated her proficiency by publishing numerous papers in esteemed journals such as those indexed in UGC CARE 1 and Scopus. Furthermore, her active involvement in both national and international conferences and workshops underscores her commitment to advancing knowledge in the field of education. Jagneet Kaur, editor of "Transforming Indian Education in the 21st Century," presents a manifesto for educational reform, offering strategies for modern learning. Her second edited book on the New Education 2020 is a comprehensive anthology reflecting her visionary outlook on India's educational future.

Rajinder Kaur is an Assistant Professor at the University School of Business, Chandigarh University, Mohali, Punjab. She has done PhD in Finance from the Department of Commerce, Punjabi University, Patiala. She holds an MCom and B.com degree. She is UGC NET-JRF qualified in the commerce field. Her industry and academic experience extends to 7 years. Her research interests include investment management, volatility in Financial Markets, Derivatives and Event Study. She is the author of numerous articles published in national and international journals.

Loke Kean Koay is a distinguished professional serving as the Academic Head of ViTrox Academy and ViTrox College, where he played a key role in developing several MQA-accredited programs. With expertise as a TRIZ International Expert and Consultant, he leads transformative initiatives in Part-ID standardization and project management at ViTrox's Center of Excellence. Recognized as a Professional Engineer by the Board of Engineers Malaysia, Ir. Dr. Koay has an exemplary academic background, earning first-class honors in Mechanical Engineering and receiving the Vice-Chancellor's Award for his Ph.D. studies. His diverse research interests include Bionic mechanism development, TRIZ-based engineering problem solving, and Green technology. He shares his knowledge through facilitation sessions, consultations, and academic mentorship, and actively contributes to grants focusing on various technological advancements. Outside of his professional pursuits, Ir. Dr. Koay enjoys photography and engages in charitable activities.

Sheue Hui Lim currently holds the position of Head of School (School of Engineering) and senior lecturer at ViTrox College, Malaysia. She earned an Ed.D. in Science Education and a master's degree in Electronic Systems Design Engineering from Universiti Sains Malaysia. Her expertise lies in science and engineering education, with a specific focus on curriculum development for higher education. With a rich 15 years of teaching experience in higher learning institutions, she actively engages in various projects with industries and other educational institutions. Additionally, she serves as a Certified Officer in Quality Assurance of Higher Education, overseeing the academic quality initiatives of the college and program accreditation. Dr. Lim is also recognized as the Associate Fellow of the Malaysian Scientific Association (MSA) and an Associate ASEAN Engineer.

Sridhar Manohar is currently working In Doctoral Research Center, Chitkara University, completed his doctorate in the area of Services Marketing from VIT Business School, VIT University. He has a Bachelor of Technology and Dual Masters in Business Administration and Organization Psychology. Dr. Sridhar further certified with FDP at IIM-A. He is expertise in Service Marketing, Innovation and Entrepreneurship, Scale Development Process and Multivariate Analytics and interests in teaching Business Analytics, Innovation and Entrepreneurship, Research Methodology and Marketing Management. He has published around 20 research papers that includes Scopus listed and ABDC ranked International Journals like – Society and Business Review, Benchmarking-An International Journal, Electronics Market, Corporate Reputation Review, International Journal of Services and Operations Management, International journal of Business Excellence and presented papers and ideas in numerous international conferences.

Joshy Mathew is working as a Lecturer at the University of Technology and Applied Sciences Al Musanna since 2014. Specialisation in Marketing, technology integration and management. Published papers (few are in progress) in Location-based marketing, Blockchain, and Marketing.

Garima Mathur is Professor in Management (HR). She is PhD, UGC-NET qualified, MA (Psych) and MBA. She is Head, HR Department & MBA Program with more than 19 years of research and academic experience. She has been engaged in corporate and academic trainings in a variety of industries such as manufacturing, services, education. She has chaired session/ delivered keynote speeches at various conferences including overseas conferences also. She is PhD guide and Six research scholars under her have already been awarded PhD degree. She is an active researcher and has in over ninety national and international refereed publications including Scopus, Web of Sciences ABDC etc due to her credit. She is an active Member of AIB, ISTD, IAA and GMA. She has also published five edited books. She is an editor of 'Prestige International Journal of IT & Management- Sanchayan' and a member of the editorial and review boards of many reputed journals including the Academy of Management- Annual Meeting, Inderscience Journals, Sage, etc.

Yash Mathur is an undergraduate student, pursuing BA Hons. Psychology Programme from St. Xavier's College, Jaipur. He is passionate about advancing the field of psychology. Actively pursuing workshops, courses, and academic opportunities, he continually seeks to expand his knowledge and expertise in psychology and mental health. This publication marks his debut in academic research, highlighting potential as a burgeoning scholar in psychology. As a research prodigy, he brings fresh perspectives and innovative approaches to his work. His first research paper is a testament of his commitment to contributing meaningful insights to the discipline.

Pooja Mehta is serving as Assistant Professor in Sri Aurobindo College of Commerce and Management, Ludhiana, India. Her research interests are in the areas of sustainability, socially responsible investments and work life quality. Pooja's research has been published in Psychology & Marketing, International Journal of Quality and Service Science, Qualitative Research in Financial Markets, Management of Environmental Quality, Society and Business Review, International Social Science Journal, and Review of Behavioral Finance and among others.

Akansha Mer is an Assistant Professor in the Department of Commerce and Management, Banasthali Vidyapith, Rajasthan, India. She has earned her doctorate on Work Engagement in NPOs from Banasthali Vidyapith. She has 2.5 years of corporate and 12 years of teaching experience. Her research interests include work engagement, adoption of technology by consumers, mindfulness, workplace spirituality, working pattern of non-profit organizations and Artificial Intelligence in HRM and marketing. She has published her research work with publishers such as Emerald, Springer, Wiley, Sage, Taylor and Francis, Inderscience, etc.

Jihene Mrabet is an accomplished assistant professor at Amity University Dubai with a PhD in Clinical Psychology and a deep interest in research and human psychology. She holds two master's degrees in professional research in Clinical Psychology and Psychopathology and has been practising since 2008. Dr. Mrabet is passionate about teaching and sharing her knowledge with students. Her research interests include Children and Adolescence Psychology, Addiction, Health Psychology, Psychopathology and remediation, Positive Psychology, and Trauma. Dr. Mrabet has also been actively publishing in reputable journals about different topics, including Borderline personality, the role of humour in sustainable education, the impact of the Covid pandemic on students' mental health, the perception of violence among children and teenagers in Dubai, plagiarism and family values.

Daisy Kee Mui Hung, an Associate Professor at Universiti Sains Malaysia, holds a Ph.D. in Business and Management from the University of South Australia. With a prolific academic career spanning over 17 years, she has authored 94 papers in ISI and Scopus-indexed journals. Dr. Kee serves as Country Director for the Association of International Business and Professional Management (AIBPM) in Indonesia and the STAR Scholars Network in the United States. She is recognized for her expertise in Organizational Psychology, Human Resource Management, and Leadership, while also holding esteemed editorial positions in prominent academic journals.

Navita Nathani is a professor and Ex deputy director of the Management Department at Prestige Institute of Management and Research Gwalior. She has been in teaching,training and administration for the last 20 years. She is the faculty in-charge of Incubation and Research Centre of the Institute. Her research interests fit in the domain of Core finance, Behavioural finance and Entrepreneurship. As an academic and an administrator, she held several key portfolios including the chairman and member on academic boards of many universities of repute. She is in the board of many national and international journals and published 82 research papers,case studies, book chapters and edited books. Furthermore she is mentoring, guiding and consulting projects of smart city incubation centre, Gwalior, MP Con and MSME .She has also excelled in culturally diverse, multidisciplinary, fast-paced environment and has studied the entrepreneurial growth in this area and conducted more than 20 MDPs for the budding and existing entrepreneurs. 5 students are pursuing and 12 students are awarded PhD under her guidance. In addition to this she has already worked on two projects sanctioned by AICTE and ICSSR and professionally associated with Academy of International business (AIB) USA, IAA, CII and ISTD. Dr. Nathani is an active social worker and has a passion to promote the well-being of society.

P. Manjushree is Professor at GITAM School of Business, GITAM University (Deemed), India.

Volha Rudkouskaya, Ph.D. in Economics, currently holds the position of Associate Professor and serves as the Head of Department at Belarus State Economic University, Belarus, Adjunct Professor at Lovely Professional University, India. With an impressive 17-year tenure as a seasoned professor, her academic focus revolves around Finance, Financial Management, and Strategic Development. Dr. Rudkouskaya has established herself as a leading expert in the fields of International Financial Reporting Standards (IFRS) and Financial Planning. Her dedication to academia is evident through her extensive contribution to research, having authored and published over 50 papers. In addition to her teaching and research roles, she assumes the role of the Annual Chair for the "Finance and Accounting" session at the International Economic Business Congress, showcasing her leadership and commitment to advancing knowledge in the realm of economics and finance.

Shilpa Sankpal currently works as Assistant Professor (General Management) with SVKM's Narsee Monjee Institute of Management Studies, Indore. She completed her PhD in Marketing from Jiwaji University Gwalior and her MBA from DAVV, Indore. She holds a Post Graduate Diploma in Travel and Tourism from University of Mumbai. Currently, she teaches courses in the domain of General Management and Marketing. In leisure time, she enjoys reading books, poetry and consuming genre-specific movie/series content. She has several research papers and cases to her credit.

Brahmmanand Sharma is an Associate Professor with a Ph.D. in Management and UGC NET qualification. Dr. Sharma has More than 12 years of academic experience as well as 2 years of corporate exposure from reputed institution of India. His job profile includes teaching subjects of marketing specialization and general management to MBA and BBA students. Additionally, he has been involved in various administrative and co-curricular activities such as coordinating committees, organizing conferences and webinars, and being a part of accreditation and admission committees. Prior to his current position. Dr. Sharma holds a Ph.D. in Management from Jiwaji University, Gwalior, and a Master's in Business Administration in Marketing from BLS Institute of Management New Delhi. Dr. Sharma has an impressive research background with several publications in renowned journals and conferences. His research interests include topics related to customer satisfaction, service quality, brand loyalty, green consumption behavior, and e-learning. He has presented research papers at various national and international conferences.

Kavita Sharma holds a Ph.D. in Management from Jiwaji University and is currently a faculty member at Maldives Business School. She has an MBA in HR and Marketing, an M.Com, and 1.5 years of corporate experience in Human Resources. Her teaching and research career spans 4.5 years, during which she served as an Assistant Professor at GLA University, Mathura, for 3.5 years, and at Bon Maharaj Engineering College, Vrindavan, Mathura, for 1 year. In the corporate sector, Dr. Sharma worked with Vodafone Essar as a Vodafone Store Executive and as a Research Associate in Recruitment at ALP Consulting Ltd. She has also various publication in reputed journal to her credit. Her diverse experience combines academic, research and corporate expertise, enhancing her contributions to the field of management and commerce.

Vandana Shukla is currently associated with the Tourism department, Jiwaji University, Gwalior. She has around 14 years of academic & research experience.

Tarika Singh Sikarwar is a Professor & Deputy Director at Prestige Institute of Management and Research Gwalior. She has more than seventeen years of rich experience in academics and Research. Eight students have been awarded Ph.D. under her guidance. She has published in reputed journals including Scopus, ABDC, and Web of Science Journals. She has been on the Panel of Reviewers of several journals being published in India and abroad. She is an energetic member of the Indian Accounting Association and Indian Commerce Association. She specializes in Corporate Finance, Sustainable Finance, Supply Chain Finance & Blockchain Technology, Data Science, Python, and Statistics for Financial Analysis. She has core competencies in Management Development Training, Curriculum Development, Research, Extra-Curricular Initiatives, Lesson Design & Development, Subject Knowledge, Leadership & Mentoring, and Technical Instruction.

Robert Studholme has a Masters in Applied Linguistics from the University of Southern Queensland and a Bachelor of Education from Leeds University. He has worked as an English teacher in Spain, Solomon Islands, Japan, Australia, Brunei Darussalam and the UAE.

Kok Ban Teoh currently serves as the Head of School and Senior Lecturer at ViTrox College in Malaysia, overseeing the School of Industrial Management. He holds a Bachelor's degree in Applied Statistics and a Master's degree in Statistics from the School of Mathematical Sciences at Universiti Sains Malaysia, and furthered his education with a doctorate in organizational behavior and development from the same university's School of Management, along with a second Master's degree in counseling from the School of Educational Studies. In 2020, Dr. Teoh received recognition for his contributions, including the Best Presenter award at the Industry 4.0 Regional Conference, the Editors' Pick at the International Postgraduate Symposium in Tourism and Hospitality, and the Best Poster award at the 6th ASIA International Conference. He is registered as a counselor with the Malaysian Board of Counselors (LKM), certified as a trainer by the Human Resources Development Fund (HRDF), serves as Deputy Country Director at the Association of International Business and Professional Management (AIBPM), and is recognized as a graduate technologist by the Malaysian Board of Technologists (MBOT). Actively involved in scholarly pursuits, Dr. Teoh holds editorial roles as the Editor-in-Chief for Annals of Human Resource Management Research, a Section Editor for SEISENSE Business Review, and a reviewer for Psychological Reports. Additionally, he is certified in various therapeutic modalities, including Neo-Cognitive Behavioral Therapy, Art Drawing-House Tree Person, Mindfulness Love Therapy, Mental Health Coaching, and Choice Theory Reality Therapy.

Notoya Thompson is lecturer at Fatima College of Health Science, UAE. She is avid researcher with interest area in health sciences.

Ivneet Walia is presently working as Associate Professor of Law at Rajiv Gandhi National University of Law, Punjab. She has completed her Doctorate and Post-Graduation from Rajiv Gandhi National University of Law, Punjab. She has completed her Law Graduation from Army Institute of Law, Mohali. She has completed approximately eight certificate courses and two post graduate diploma in different law subjects. She is also presently the Associate Dean (Academics) and Centre Coordinator for Criminology, Criminal Justice, and Victimology. She has worked as a Centre Coordinator for Centre for Advanced Studies in Criminal Law at the University. She is also the faculty for M.A. Criminology Course at B. R. Ambedkar University, New Delhi. She is also the recipient of prestigious Henry Dunant Fellowship. She was also awarded Scholarship by the Scholarship Committee of the International Institute of Human Rights, Strasbourg, France for participating in the 42nd Study Session in International and Comparative Law of Human Rights in Strasbourg, France. She is also the visiting faculty at Indian Institute of Management, Rohtak. She is a qualified (NCA) International Lawyer (Non-Practicing) in Canada. She has authored five books' latest being on Crime, Punishment and Sentencing in India published by Thomson Reuters. She has written several papers and attended conferences at national and international level. She has delivered guest lectures at Universities, Bar Associations and Police Academies.

Index

Symbols

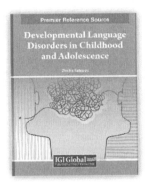

Ensure Quality Research is Introduced to the Academic Community

Become a Reviewer for IGI Global Authored Book Projects

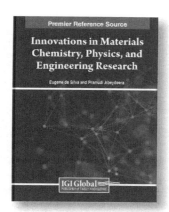
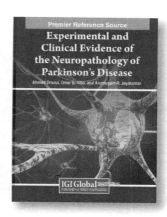
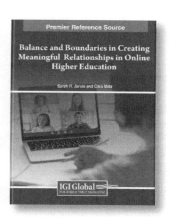

The overall success of an authored book project is dependent on quality and timely manuscript evaluations.

Applications and Inquiries may be sent to:
development@igi-global.com

Applicants must have a doctorate (or equivalent degree) as well as publishing, research, and reviewing experience. Authored Book Evaluators are appointed for one-year terms and are expected to complete at least three evaluations per term. Upon successful completion of this term, evaluators can be considered for an additional term.

If you have a colleague that may be interested in this opportunity, we encourage you to share this information with them.

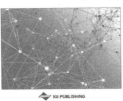

Printed in the United States
by Baker & Taylor Publisher Services